Imperial Benevolence

The publisher and the University of California Press Foundation gratefully acknowledge the generous support of the Ahmanson Foundation Endowment Fund in Humanities.

Imperial Benevolence

U.S. FOREIGN POLICY AND
AMERICAN POPULAR CULTURE SINCE 9/11

EDITED BY

Scott Laderman and Tim Gruenewald

UNIVERSITY OF CALIFORNIA PRESS

University of California Press, one of the most distinguished university presses in the United States, enriches lives around the world by advancing scholarship in the humanities, social sciences, and natural sciences. Its activities are supported by the UC Press Foundation and by philanthropic contributions from individuals and institutions. For more information, visit www.ucpress.edu.

University of California Press
Oakland, California

Library of Congress Cataloging-in-Publication Data

Names: Laderman, Scott, 1971- editor. | Gruenewald, Tim, editor.
Title: Imperial benevolence : U.S. foreign policy and American
    popular culture since 9/11 / edited by Scott Laderman and Tim
    Gruenewald.
Description: Oakland, California : University of California Press,
[2018] | Includes index. |
Identifiers: LCCN 2018004260 (print) | LCCN 2018007347 (ebook) |
    ISBN 9780520971028 (ebook) | ISBN 9780520299177 (cloth : alk. paper) |
    ISBN 9780520299184 (paperback : alk. paper)
Subjects: LCSH: United States—Foreign relations—21st century. |
    Popular culture—United States—History—21st century. |
    Imperialism—History—21st century.
Classification: LCC E895 (ebook) | LCC E895 .I47 2018 (print) |
    DDC 327.73009/05—dc23
LC record available at https://lccn.loc.gov/2018004260

Manufactured in the United States of America

27 26 25 24 23 22 21 20 19 18
10 9 8 7 6 5 4 3 2 1

For Marilyn B. Young, who taught us that culture matters in America's war without end.

CONTENTS

ACKNOWLEDGMENTS

This book began in May 2016 with the 7th American Studies Fulbright Conference at the University of Hong Kong (HKU). We would like to thank the Fulbright Program for supporting the Visiting Professor of American Studies position at HKU and for making this annual event possible. We would also like to thank all the workshop participants for their contributions and spirited discussions.

For its generous financial and logistical support of the conference and book, we are grateful to HKU's School of Modern Languages and Cultures (SMLC)—especially the school's head, Kendall Johnson. Lucilla Cheng, Evelyn Lo, C. K. Lee, Angel Wong, and other SMLC staff provided invaluable assistance, as did graduate students Ping Fan and Zhai Yue.

We thank the Consulate General of the United States, Hong Kong and Macau, which made a substantial monetary contribution to the workshop. It did so despite, as a diplomat working there told us, strongly disagreeing with the conference's premise. This says something, we think, about the refreshing open-mindedness and integrity of so many of the country's foreign service officers.

We are indebted, too, to the College of Liberal Arts at the University of Minnesota, Duluth, for its ongoing support.

At the University of California Press, we thank Niels Hooper for his support for this collection and, together with Bradley Depew, Francisco Reinking, Jolene Torr, and Nicholle Robertson, for shepherding it through production. We appreciate the excellent feedback provided by the two readers, H. Bruce Franklin and an anonymous referee.

And we of course thank our families. They continue to sustain us.

A BRIEF NOTE ON TERMINOLOGY

Language is hardly neutral. As the incessant debate over the term *radical Islamic terrorism* makes clear, the terminology employed in Washington's post-9/11 military campaigns is freighted with political meaning.[1] What is assumed or elided in referring to a *war on terror, global war on terrorism,* or *GWOT*? What is *terrorism,* and who is or is not a *terrorist*? Who gets to decide?

We have opted in this volume to allow each of the contributors to choose how they wish to label the overarching framework and constituent elements of Washington's confrontation with al-Qaeda, ISIS, and assorted other entities and individuals in recent decades. We recognize, as do our contributors, the problems inherent in most such terms. But because the expression of ideas requires the use of language, and because good writing often relies on linguistic compromises, choices must be made. We wish here to simply acknowledge this reality.

NOTE

1. On the politics of *radical Islamic terrorism,* see, for example, Peter Holley, "'Radical Islamic Terrorism': Three Words That Separate Trump from Most of Washington," *Washington Post,* March 1, 2017, accessed June 12, 2017, www.washingtonpost.com/news/the-fix/wp/2017/02/28/radical-islamic-terrorism-three-words-that-separate-trump-from-most-of-washington/?tid=a_inl&utm_term=.5594a4b5feof. On Trump's backpedaling from use of the term, see Kristine Phillips, "'Radical Islamic Terrorism,' Trump Said Over and Over. But Not in Saudi Arabia," *Washington Post,* May 22, 2017, accessed June 12, 2017, www.washingtonpost.com/news/the-fix/wp/2017/05/22/radical-islamic-terrorism-trump-said-over-and-over-but-not-in-saudi-arabia/?utm_term=.2a4f2794eddf.

INTRODUCTION

Camouflaging Empire

IMPERIAL BENEVOLENCE IN
AMERICAN POPULAR CULTURE

Scott Laderman

WHEN GREGOR JORDAN'S *BUFFALO SOLDIERS* (2001) premiered at the 2001 Toronto International Film Festival, audiences could not get enough.[1] The story of a corrupt U.S. Army clerk stationed in West Germany at the time of the Berlin Wall's collapse, the film offered a biting critique of the American armed forces and the troops serving on the frontlines of the European Cold War. Its protagonist, Specialist Ray Elwood (Joaquin Phoenix), is what the film's pressbook called "the ultimate risk-taker: a high-stakes arms dealer, a bureaucratic con artist, and a shrewd collector of other people's secrets," all of which he uses to "forge a lucrative career on the black market."[2] A devious but lovable grunt, Elwood's mischievous independence echoed that of other military figures who have graced the big screen in recent decades, from Hawkeye Pierce and Captain Yossarian to Joker Davis and Archie Gates.[3]

A bidding war began—the Hollywood trade paper *Variety* named *Buffalo Soldiers* the Toronto festival's "most-sought after" picture—and Miramax, the Disney subsidiary run by the power brokers Harvey and Bob Weinstein, ultimately scooped it up.[4] They agreed to open the British-German production in the United States within a year. That was on September 10. The following day, in a sequence of events seared into American memory, four hijacked planes flew into the World Trade Center towers in New York City, the Pentagon building outside Washington, DC, and a tree-lined field in rural Pennsylvania. The American mood changed overnight, and *Buffalo Soldiers* suddenly looked less like a potential source of profit than a political hot potato.

Acknowledging that the United States had any faults—or even wondering whether this might be possible—proved perilous in the attacks' aftermath. George W. Bush, who at the time had been in office less than a year, echoed much of the nation's mood in his assertion of a startlingly simple moral universe. "This will be a monumental struggle of good versus evil," he announced as the dust was still settling at the World Trade Center. "But," he assured the nation, "good will prevail."[5] The United States, in the president's uncomplicated formulation, was a positive force for humanity and a champion of all that was right and decent. The leadership of both major parties agreed. This was, after all, what they and millions of other Americans had been told by countless films and programs over the years, with good, in these narratives, almost invariably overcoming evil.

If Hollywood had been harboring any thoughts of challenging the conventional wisdom, the industry made it quite clear that it had received the president's message. "You needed to have your head examined if you thought this was a time for questioning America," the not-yet-disgraced Harvey Weinstein asserted.[6] Miramax, which had acquired not just *Buffalo Soldiers* but *The Quiet American* (2002), the second filmic iteration of Graham Greene's 1955 novel about the United States in Vietnam, quietly shelved both projects.[7] Uncomfortably for Miramax, *The Quiet American* showed not only the origins of America's bitter war in Vietnam; it also presented the United States as a sponsor of terrorism, with an undercover U.S. intelligence operative (Brendan Fraser) responsible for the detonation of two car bombs in Saigon that kill and maim numerous innocent civilians. In the wake of the 9/11 attacks, such a notion was simply verboten. Americans were terrorism's victims; they could not be its perpetrators. The film thus had to be buried. And so it was—at least for a while.

Had it not been for the persistence of the filmmakers and its leading man, Michael Caine, *The Quiet American* may never have seen the light of day. But slowly, nervously, and tepidly, Miramax did allow it to be resurrected— though only after first testing the political waters in Canada, where it was rapturously received.[8] Yet even with the positive attention the film garnered, Miramax remained nervous. When the movie did finally open, its release was initially limited to two American markets (New York and Los Angeles) and the United Kingdom. *Variety* summed up its marketing campaign this way: "Michael Caine is great in a movie that's about, well, don't ask what it's about. He's just great in it."[9] Indeed, the film garnered Caine an Oscar nomination (he lost to *The Pianist*'s [2002] Adrien Brody), and *The Quiet American* earned rave reviews.

Buffalo Soldiers, meanwhile, enjoyed considerably less success. Miramax promised to eventually release Jordan's romp about the U.S. military in Cold War Germany, but it delayed the release a remarkable five times.[10] When a

FIGURE I.I. Alden Pyle (Brendan Fraser) dresses down a Vietnamese police officer after a U.S.-sponsored terror attack. The implication that the United States was a perpetrator of terrorism, not just a victim of it, nearly killed *The Quiet American*. © Intermedia Films, IMF—Internationale Medien und Film GmbH & Co. 2 Produktions KG, and Miramax Films.

test screening was held in New York in January 2002, the reaction was decidedly cool. "I think this is a time when we need to be patriotic and I don't think the American people should see it," one audience member was said to have counseled.[11] Miramax and its parent corporation, Disney, meanwhile, fielded complaints from what *Variety* identified as "military representatives and right-wing consumers."[12] When *Buffalo Soldiers* was invited to the Sundance Film Festival in January 2003, a woman in the audience hurled a water bottle at Jordan—it missed him and, according to at least one account, hit actress Anna Paquin—reportedly screamed "bastard!" and accused the film of being anti-American and antiarmy "propaganda." She was escorted into the lobby but escaped before the police could be summoned.[13]

It would not be until July 2003, nearly two years after its original showing, that Miramax opened *Buffalo Soldiers* in American theaters. But by then, with major wars ongoing in Afghanistan and Iraq, its story of corrupt American soldiers "with nothing to kill except time," according to Elwood, seemed positively dated. "War is hell," Phoenix's character says at one point, "but peace? Peace is fucking boring." It's undoubtedly a catchy line. But in the context of thousands of Americans suffering death and injury in the Middle East and Central Asia, not to mention the far greater number of casualties suffered by Iraqis and Afghans, it must have seemed jarring. The film was a box-office disaster, grossing a measly $354,421 during its ten-week American run.[14]

That *Buffalo Soldiers* proved so controversial says more about the limits of the American political imagination than it does about serious political

FIGURE I.2. With its suggestion of military incompetence and criminality, *Buffalo Soldiers,* which starred Joaquin Phoenix, *shown,* proved controversial in the wake of the 9/11 attacks. © Film Four Limited, Grosvenor Park Productions UK, and Miramax Films.

dissent in American popular culture. To be sure, the film presented a scathing portrait of ignorance, corruption, and criminality within the ranks of the armed forces. But it did not really challenge the basic foundations of U.S. foreign policy. It may have mocked the cluelessness of Americans abroad, but it did not question the propriety—let alone even acknowledge the existence—of an American empire. Dennis Lim in the *Village Voice* called the picture "merely a softer-than-Wilder satire of bored peacetime mischief."[15] A. O. Scott, reviewing it for the *New York Times,* found *Buffalo Soldiers* to be "ultimately unsure of what it is mocking and in what spirit."[16] The closest the film came to challenging American global power was Elwood's pronouncement that "Vietnam was the thorn in everybody's side." But this was not because that war demonstrated American aggression. It was because the United States lost. "They stopped the draft and asked for volunteers," Elwood says, "except nobody volunteered. I mean, who wants to play for a losing team?"

So, according to *Buffalo Soldiers,* the Vietnam War was not wrong or immoral, as most Americans believed; it was simply a failure.[17] This is what passed for controversial in the wake of 9/11. In fairness, it should be noted that *Buffalo Soldiers* did not claim to challenge American power—or at least not *only* American power. "The film says that the American Army and armies around the world are full of psychopaths whose aim is to go out and kill people," director and coscreenwriter Jordan told the *New York Times.* "It's not antipatriotic. It asks the question, Why do people want to keep killing each other?"[18] Viewers might wonder just how *Buffalo Soldiers* represented the antiwar screed that Jordan suggested; like Sam Fuller and his anti-Communist, pro-French Vietnam War film *China Gate* (1957), which Fuller later remarkably claimed "didn't make any judgment about who was right or wrong in the Indochina conflict," Jordan apparently thought his film posed more of a political challenge than it did.[19] In fact, one of his cowriters, Eric Weiss, was adamant that precisely the opposite was true. *Buffalo Soldiers* was not, Weiss insisted, "unpatriotic. It doesn't really comment on what we are doing now [in Iraq]."[20] And Weiss was certainly correct. *Buffalo Soldiers* offered a narrowly focused critique of the bad behavior of some American troops in Germany in the closing moments of the Cold War. But even that proved too much.

The essays in this volume argue that, at a moment when much of the world has probably been more openly critical of U.S. foreign policy than at any time since the Vietnam War, American popular culture since September 11, 2001, has broadly presented the United States as a global force for good, a reluctant hegemon working to defend human rights and protect or expand democracy from the barbarians determined to destroy it. Even as senior officials in Washington boasted that the United States was an imperial power—"We're an empire now," one told journalist Ron Suskind—most cultural producers still could not come to terms with this reality.[21] It is undoubtedly true that some policy makers, such as the eminently quotable Donald Rumsfeld, did continue to disavow the imperial possibility. "We don't seek empires. We're not imperialistic. We never have been. I can't imagine why you'd even ask the question," the secretary of defense snapped at an Al Jazeera reporter who asked about "empire building" just weeks after the Bush administration commenced its 2003 invasion of Iraq.[22] But Rumsfeld was speaking defensively as a political bureaucrat charged with realizing an imperial vision; his stated view, it is safe to say, resides well outside the scholarly consensus.

Imperialism is, of course, a bad word in the American political lexicon— it's something they do, not us. Millions of Americans prefer to see their government's actions abroad as selfless, benevolent, even divinely inspired. This belief in American beneficence has deep roots, from the humanitarian objectives ascribed to eighteenth- and nineteenth-century continental expansion to the more recent characterizations of the United States as a global policeman tasked with upholding international norms and laws.[23] When cultural producers have attempted to challenge this sacred axiom, as did the acclaimed filmmaker Paul Greengrass in his Iraq War picture *Green Zone*

(2010), they have often faced attack. "I am getting sick of Hollywood leftists changing stories to make America look bad," complained film critic Tony Medley, speaking, perhaps, for what Richard Nixon called America's "silent majority," in the small but influential *Tolucan Times*.[24]

However much we may agree or disagree with Medley's views of Hollywood or *Green Zone,* he was undoubtedly correct in recognizing the power of popular culture in what Amy Kaplan, writing in her now classic essay supporting American Studies' transnational turn, called the "dominant imperial culture" of the United States. Imperialism, Kaplan noted, is "not only about foreign diplomacy or international relations"; it is "also about consolidating domestic cultures and negotiating intranational relations," the last of which are capable of either "abet[ting] the subjugation of others" or "foster[ing] . . . resistance."[25] Melani McAlister, writing later about U.S. foreign policy in the Middle East, pointed to the ways that popular culture, together with political discourse, the corporate media, and a number of social and religious movements, has "worked to construct a self-image for Americans of themselves as citizens of a benevolent world power" in defining and giving meaning to American interests in that region.[26]

Yet it is not just the Middle East—as McAlister would be the first to recognize. Popular culture's influence is global, persistent, and, at a time when relatively few Americans stay abreast of the news, perhaps more powerful than ever. Eric Johnston recognized as much more than half a century ago. As head of the Motion Picture Association of America from 1946 to 1963, Johnston occupied probably the most commanding perch in Hollywood during the crucial two decades following the Second World War. "There is not one of us who isn't aware that the motion picture industry is the most powerful medium for the influencing of people that man has ever built," he conceded.[27] Given that the Cold War, like the war on terror, was fundamentally an ideological conflict, his was an awesome responsibility.

Yet he and his colleagues, then and later, proved up to the task. John Wayne, for example, took it upon himself to battle the creeping belief by the mid- to late 1960s that Washington might be an imperial actor. He would have none of it. Writing to the White House in 1965, Wayne proposed to make a film—the box-office hit *The Green Berets* (1968)—that would convey to "not only the people of the United States but those all over the world" that "it is necessary for us to be in [Vietnam]." The "most effective way to accomplish this," he told President Lyndon Johnson, "is through the motion picture medium."[28] Unbeknownst to Wayne at the time, *The Green Berets* would be the only major American fictional film about the Indochina wars to appear between the insertion of official U.S. combat troops in 1965 and the reunification of Vietnam in 1976. In the decade that followed, Hollywood released a flurry of movies, most of which sought to recast U.S. intervention as either the "noble cause" posited by Ronald Reagan (think *Rambo: First Blood Part II* [1985]) or, like the Academy Award winners *The Deer Hunter* (1978) and *Platoon* (1986), an overwhelmingly American—as opposed to Vietnamese—tragedy.[29]

At the center of American imperial culture, during the Cold War and now, is the popular view of the United States as a uniquely endowed nation lacking the selfish global ambitions that have characterized other great powers. With roots in its eighteenth-century founding, this belief is at the core of the American political system, with one of the nation's two major parties exploiting every possible opportunity to attack the other for allegedly failing to recognize "American exceptionalism." Yet imperial fantasies are a bipartisan matter, with the leadership of the Democratic Party just as wont to assert the nation's special endowment as its Republican counterpart. "The United States of America is and will remain the greatest force for freedom the world has ever known," President Barack Obama characteristically pronounced in 2014.[30] Channeling former secretary of state Madeleine Albright, Democratic presidential candidate Hillary Clinton said two years later that the United States was not just "an exceptional nation" but "the indispensable nation." In fact, the country was "the"—not just *a*—"global force for freedom, justice, and human dignity," she insisted.[31]

Much like expressions of national sovereignty in the 1940s and 1950s reflected, as Mark Bradley put it, "persisting fears of sovereignty's precariousness rather than its hegemonic power and legitimacy," performative assertions of American exceptionalism took on an almost reflexive quality in the face of what seemed to many like twenty-first-century U.S. decline.[32] Did such declarations represent genuinely held beliefs? Or were they evidence of imperial anxiety? Regardless of their impetus, when political leaders have occasionally shown a willingness to stray from this seeming consensus on the righteousness of American power, as did President Donald Trump in February 2017 by questioning whether "our country" is "so innocent," their colleagues have immediately attempted to rein them in.[33] "I do think America is exceptional. America is different," Senate Majority Leader Mitch McConnell said in response to the president's sacrilege. The United States is "the greatest freedom-loving nation in the history of the world," Senator Ben Sasse likewise retorted.[34] The *New York Times,* representing the liberal wing of the establishment, lashed out at Trump's heterodoxy. While the paper allowed that the United States had "made terrible mistakes, like invading Iraq in 2003 and torturing terrorism suspects after Sept. 11," it was adamant that, "at least in recent decades, American presidents who took military action have been driven by the desire to promote freedom and democracy."[35]

Fifteen years after the 9/11 attacks, the future of U.S. foreign policy seemed uncertain, with President Trump unselfconsciously demonstrating his widespread ignorance, employing unprecedented levels of mendacity, and, even more than his fellow Republicans, generally opting for the comfort of a world unencumbered by empirical realities.[36] Concerns over what the president's inexperience, distaste for tradition, diplomatic boorishness, and "America first" rhetoric might mean for American global power grew during the first months of his administration. The neoconservatives, liberal internationalists, and others who populated the nation's foreign-policy establishment worried about the "ethnonationalist" tendencies suggested by "alt-right" spokesperson Stephen Bannon's appointment as a top White House advisor and about Trump's seeming rejection of long-standing imperial assumptions. From his criticism of "nation-building" and his openness to a recently assertive Russia—a country whose relationship with the Trump campaign became the subject of an FBI investigation—to his questioning of the North Atlantic Treaty Organization (NATO), the value of the Korean and Japanese alliances, a two-state solution for Israel and Palestine, and the "one China" policy for the People's Republic of China and Taiwan, this was not how American presidents were expected to behave. Beltway officials wondered whether Trump, like his predecessors, would continue to employ force as the most visible instrument of U.S. foreign policy or whether, worrisomely, he might reject the bipartisan consensus on American militarism in favor of a twenty-first-century neoisolationism.

The president appeared to offer an answer in April 2017, launching fifty-nine tomahawk missiles without United Nations sanction at a Syrian government airbase in response to an alleged chemical weapon attack. Not only had Trump employed unilateral military force but he had done so against a close ally of the Russian president, Vladimir Putin, who was seen by much of the establishment, but apparently not by the White House, as a figure of some concern. Washington and the corporate media—which, apart from Fox News and elements of the right-wing press, had on many issues been atypically adversarial in their coverage of the new administration—were

BREAKING NEWS
U.S. CRUISE MISSILES STRIKE SYRIAN AIR BASE | CNN
Fareed Zakaria | CNN Host, "Fareed Zakaria GPS"   5:51 AM PT
RIGHT NOW   BOSTON   46°   NEW YORK   46°   PHILADELPHIA   46°
                                                         NEW DAY

FIGURE 1.3. The media responded enthusiastically to Donald Trump's order to launch fifty-nine cruise missiles at Syria on April 6, 2017. Brian Williams of MSNBC gushed about the "beauty of our weapons," for example, while Fareed Zakaria of CNN, *shown,* said Trump "became president of the United States" that night. © CNN.

ecstatic. The top congressional Republicans, Senator McConnell and Speaker of the House Paul Ryan, both gave the attack their "enthusiastic support," reported the *New York Times.* The ranking Democrat on the Senate Foreign Relations Committee, Ben Cardin, praised Trump for his "clear signal that the United States will stand up for internationally accepted norms and rules against the use of chemical weapons."[37] The media were even more adulatory, equating the unilateral employment of state violence with exemplary leadership. "I think Donald Trump became president of the United States" that night, CNN host (and former *Foreign Affairs* editor) Fareed Zakaria gushed.[38] The missile strike was "very presidential" and "sets a moral compass for the United States," agreed Marty Schenker of Bloomberg News.[39] Like others, the *Washington Post* insisted that the attack was "right as a matter of morality" and yielded "a host of practical benefits." The paper's only concern was whether the strike represented merely "a one-off response" or whether it signaled a welcome change in Trump's "conception of U.S. foreign interests."[40]

For months afterward the answer remained unclear, with the administration continuing its antipathy to what it called "globalism" in favor of an increasingly global ethnonationalism marked by racism and Islamophobia, support for Brexit, opposition to immigrants and refugees, and a reactionary backlash to "free trade" and neoliberalism. Trump did occasionally employ hypermilitarist rhetoric, such as his widely derided threat to rain "fire and fury" on North Korea or to pursue a "military option" in Venezuela, but his statements were generally treated as impetuous and irresponsible excesses rather than the sober vows to employ military force that one had come to expect as the hallmark of American empire building.[41] Trying to make sense of Trumpian foreign policy proved a challenge, and how popular culture might treat it remained a mystery.

There can be little doubt, however, that the decade and a half following the 9/11 attacks witnessed the same sorts of discourses that marked the previous fifty years: exceptionalist narratives of American virtue, only this time with an Islamist, not Communist, enemy in the crosshairs. But it was not just Islamists. As working-class everyman Hank Deerfield (Tommy Lee Jones) says of the Iraq War in *In the Valley of Elah* (2007), "My son has spent the last eighteen months bringing democracy to a shithole." Deerfield's rather unrefined statement on the U.S. overthrow of the secular Iraqi regime echoed explanations found elsewhere. "Every American president since at least the 1970s has used his office to champion human rights and democratic values around the world," claimed the *Washington Post*'s White House bureau chief in 2017.[42] The United States apparently cannot help itself; it suffers from a "humanitarian impulse," Emile Simpson wrote in *Foreign Policy*.[43]

While there have been notable exceptions, most popular culture since 9/11 has assumed American benevolence.[44] At the same time, most popular culture dealing with the war on terror, as Andrew McKevitt has observed, "did not confront the GWOT [global war on terrorism] directly. Instead, it interpreted the military and political response to 9/11 through allegory and metaphor," with fantastical tales that presented U.S. foreign policy "not unlike how George W. Bush articulated it": as an "apocalyptic, universal struggle between good and evil."[45] In this struggle, whether portrayed metaphorically or not, the United States may appear ruthless, it may occasionally be a bungler, and there can be rogue elements that attempt to undermine the government's official policies, but the basic goodness that drives American foreign relations—its diplomacy, its military interventions, its people-to-people encounters—has rarely been challenged. This is not necessarily a matter of conscious intentionality. It is simply a reflection of the extent to which imperial ideology has been naturalized in American life.

For scholars, this should come as no surprise. One has only to remember the century that just passed. The ideological conflict that marked most of its second half ended triumphantly for the United States, with the culture industries, which consistently parroted the conventional wisdom about the Communist threat and American leadership of the "free world," providing essential service to the nation's foreign-policy objectives.[46] As one of the contributors to this volume noted elsewhere, the Cold War was marked by a collaboration of state and private actors that "sometimes openly, sometimes discreetly" sought to mobilize American and foreign opinion "in the pursuit and projection of 'freedom' and 'independence.'"[47] There were exceptions, of course, just as there have been more recently. But in looking at the post-9/11 era, for every *Buffalo Soldiers*—as tepid of a political statement as it was— there have been a dozen films like *Tears of the Sun* (2003), the Defense Department–endorsed picture starring Bruce Willis about steely but benevolent American troops attempting to save a group of Nigerians fleeing murderous rebels.[48] For every critical documentary that might make its way to public television, there has been a *24* or a *Homeland,* the far more popular fictional series about U.S. intelligence agents attempting to make the world right. And for every critical utterance by the Dixie Chicks, whose Natalie Maines told a London audience in March 2003 that "we're ashamed" that President Bush was from their home state of Texas, there have been enraptured, screaming crowds for Toby Keith belting out "Courtesy of the Red, White, and Blue (The Angry American)."[49]

The authors in this volume approach empire and popular culture from different disciplinary backgrounds and with different questions. What draws them together is a conviction that popular culture matters. Movies, television, video games—these are not just objects of mindless consumption.[50] On the contrary, people are heavily influenced by the cultural products with which they engage every day. Sometimes they educate, other times they challenge, and quite often they reinforce their audience's beliefs. At times popular culture can tell us something about how countless Americans view their nation's role in the world, and it can drive how countless people come to understand it. Of course, popular culture is complicated. It can be interpreted differently by different individuals. And much of popular culture does not engage issues of empire at all—an elision that is in fact critical to imperial preservation. But in those cases in which U.S. foreign policy is explicitly addressed, its politics, the contributors to *Imperial Benevolence* argue, are overwhelmingly apologetic.

Rebecca Adelman takes up the emotional elements of this apologia—including its gendered construction—in her chapter on women's lamentations over the lethal affective work they must perform in serving the imperial mission. Empire is a complex undertaking, and the humans charged with its preservation at times find themselves having to do emotionally difficult things. Take drone operators, who must make life-and-death decisions thousands of miles from the field of battle; with the press of a button in the Nevada desert, an entirely family can be obliterated in the Yemeni outback. Adelman, in exploring the intersections of gender, sadness, and imperial violence in several films and television shows, focuses on the crying female protagonists, including drone operators, who populate the media landscape of the war on terror. Whether it is Maya (Jessica Chastain) in the critical darling *Zero Dark Thirty* (2012) or Carrie Mathison (Claire Danes) in the popular Showtime series *Homeland,* the tears they shed, she writes, help "to lubricate the machinery of empire."

Yet not all popular-culture protagonists feel emotionally conflicted about their service. Edwin Martini, in chapter 2, addresses the case of *American Sniper,* the best-selling 2012 memoir by U.S. Navy SEAL Chris Kyle that was turned into a 2014 film by Clint Eastwood. *American Sniper* was a major cultural force. The book remained on the *New York Times* best-seller list for months, with the film proving even more popular; it earned more than $100 million in its opening weekend, received an Academy Award nomination for Best Picture, became the highest-grossing picture of 2014 at the American box office, and overtook *Saving Private Ryan* (1998) as the top domestic-grossing war movie of all time.[51] But, Martini shows us, Kyle was not one to shed tears. On the contrary, he stoically accepted his assignment as a "sheepdog" protecting the American people—the "sheep"—from the "wolves" out to get them. While this framework ascribed positive, self-defensive objectives to the American campaign in Iraq, the reception to the book and the film was divided. As Martini notes, it mirrored the larger political debates—though often within the same simplistic frames of reference—about race, religion, and foreign policy that have so riven the nation since 2001.

The fact that Kyle met his fate not in Iraq or Afghanistan but at the hands of a fellow veteran in Texas in 2013 suggests the psychological damage that the post-9/11 wars have inflicted upon thousands of men and women in the U.S. armed forces. These are men and women that most people will never meet. With the end of conscription in 1973, only a tiny minority of Americans—many of them with few promising choices in life—now join the military.[52] The emotional distance from U.S. foreign policy that this affords most of the public is only heightened by the fact that, as David Kieran argues, veterans of the nation's recent conflicts have not been encountered in popular culture anywhere near as often as their World War II and Vietnam War counterparts. When they have, moreover, it has often been as supporting characters. There has not been a *Best Years of Our Lives* (1946) to address the readjustment to civilian life, there has been no *Born on the Fourth of July* (1989) to reflect the military antiwar movement, and even the films that have addressed psychologically damaged veterans, such as the Hollywood drama *Brothers* (2009), have had a far more marginal influence on American society than earlier motion pictures, such as *Taxi Driver* (1976) or *The Deer Hunter* (1978). But where the most popular of popular culture has fallen short, documentary films have stepped in, offering stories of veterans' psychological rehabilitation through an immersion in outdoor pursuits. Such stories—which, Kieran notes, frame American veterans' injuries as largely inconsequential and their recovery as private—have obscured the costs of empire for those tasked with maintaining it, contributing to U.S. imperialism's discursive normalization.

What about those fighting men and women who are not actually members of the U.S. armed forces? This may have seemed an odd question in past decades. Mercenaries have always existed, but their numbers have typically been quite low. That changed in the post-9/11 era, however, with battlefield responsibilities increasingly farmed out to well-paid private contractors subject to only minimal levels of public accountability. Sometimes this has presented considerable problems. In 2007, for example, a group of Blackwater security contractors opened fire on dozens of Iraqi civilians in Baghdad's Nisour Square. Seventeen people were killed and another twenty injured. It was only after widespread Iraqi outrage that charges were brought against the Blackwater personnel, with four men ultimately convicted of murder or manslaughter. Yet despite their centrality to the American war effort, military contractors have been largely absent in the nation's news media. They have proved a helpful foil in American popular culture, however. As Stacy Takacs demonstrates, television programs since 9/11, in a departure from earlier series such as *Soldiers of Fortune* (syndication, 1955–1957) and *The A-Team* (NBC, 1983–1987), have presented these contractors as scapegoats for the negative outcomes generated by U.S. interventionism. The problems experienced by the United States have not been the fault of its official opera-tives (that is, its uniformed personnel), the more recent programs suggest, but rather of irresponsible mercenaries driven by a quest for profits. Such depic-tions, Takacs argues, have allowed the American public to retain its faith in the United States as a global force for good, innocently pursuing its noble cause abroad.

At the heart of the noble cause in the Barack Obama era was a belief that only "just war" is pursued by Washington. As Min Kyung (Mia) Yoo sug-gests, this belief was embodied in three of the more popular television series during the eight years following the change of presidential administrations in 2009. While the shows are not in fact about U.S. foreign policy—or at least not explicitly so—the three protagonists of *The Walking Dead* (AMC, 2010–), *Gotham* (Fox, 2014–), and *Fargo* (FX, 2014–) are all well-meaning, innocent men who only reluctantly resort to violence when confronted with a threat to the larger population for which they have assumed responsibility. In this they resemble former president Obama—or at least the conventional portrait of President Obama popular with American liberals. "We did not choose this war," he told American forces stationed in Afghanistan in 2012. "This war came to us on 9/11. . . . We don't go looking for a fight. But when we see our homeland violated, when we see our fellow citizens killed, then we understand what we have to do."[53] Like the United States, the protagonists discussed by Yoo are morally imperfect and flawed, but their use of force is understood by audiences as an essential response to the evil they face. They are not aggressors. They kill only because the protection of decency demands it. They are, in other words, driven by the purest of intentions.

In reality, of course, American forces have not been so reluctantly dis-patched nor have their missions gone especially well. Given the chaos unleashed by the nation's post-9/11 wars, what Washington may ultimately need to win its self-described "war on terror" is a handful of superheroes. At least, this is what is suggested by the recent outpouring of them on the big screen, where they have repeatedly taken on and defeated the dark forces besieging the United States. These superheroes not only win, but they do so as moral guardians of all that is right and just. Superheroes have long popu-lated the comic-book industry and have even occasionally appeared in film, with *Superman* (1978) and *Batman* (1989) probably the best, and certainly among the most lucrative, historical examples. But nothing prepared us for the wave of superhero films that flooded the United States after 9/11. Having been turned into what essentially amounts to one big self-referential franchise, such pictures now regularly cost in the hundreds of millions of dollars. There is no doubt that this has proved a good investment, however, with several having earned more than $1 billion each. The content of these films, Tim Gruenewald maintains, has been overwhelmingly supportive of U.S. military power. The superheroes—and this is especially true of Captain America, who, as his name suggests, serves as the symbolic embodiment of the United States—demonstrate a strong concern for the fate of civilians. Their protection drives the superheroes' actions, and the superheroes do everything possible to ensure that, in violently confronting the forces of evil, no harm befalls the world's legions of noncombatants.

Given just how violent these stories can be, that is a considerable challenge. But like the United States—or at least like how millions of Americans envision the United States—the superheroes see their raison d'être as the protection of the innocent. No effort is thus too great. This is abundantly clear in what, by the end of 2016, remained the most commercially successful superhero film in history: *The Avengers* (2012), whose worldwide gross topped $1.5 billion.[54] Yet it would be a mistake to think of *The Avengers* in strictly commercial terms. As Ross Griffin argues, it is freighted with cultural symbolism about the role of the United States in maintaining world order. The Avengers—from Iron Man to Captain America—must overcome myriad challenges, including a 9/11-mimicking attack on New York City, before collectively defeating the threat of evil attempting global domination. The film, Griffin suggests, offers a powerful legitimization of violence, though only when used—as it is with the superheroes and, by implication, Washington— as a reluctant response to an existential menace.

All the chapters up to this point have dealt largely with representations of U.S. foreign policy, whether directly or indirectly, since 9/11. But the post-9/11 era has also witnessed cultural products that have creatively revisited the American past. Among the most influential of these has been the Steven Spielberg picture *Bridge of Spies* (2015), perhaps, according to Tony Shaw, Hollywood's most important Cold War film since the fall of the Berlin Wall. The story of a fabled 1962 exchange of prisoners by the United States and the Soviet Union, *Bridge of Spies* is only one of several motion pictures Spielberg has made since 2001 that address either the Cold War, the threat of aggression, or the so-called war on terror. His *Indiana Jones and the Kingdom of the Crystal Skull* (2008) had an aging Harrison Ford battling Soviet agents, for example, while *War of the Worlds* (2005) featured Tom Cruise fighting alongside U.S. troops in defending against an alien invasion. Drawing a possibly clearer line to the post-9/11 moment, Spielberg's *Munich* (2005) recounted the pre-9/11 use of terror as an element of Middle East politics, in this case through the Black September murder of eleven Israeli athletes during the 1972 Olympic Games. But *Bridge of Spies,* which received six Academy Award nominations, including for Best Picture, is arguably the most significant of the recent films from this most prominent of American filmmakers. As numerous historians have documented, the Cold War—whatever else it may have involved—saw the United States repeatedly undermining democracy and sponsoring a number of dictators around the world.[55] But that is not the story Spielberg chose to tell. On the contrary, his *Bridge of Spies* presents Washington as a fierce defender of human rights, in the process offering what Shaw calls "a near-perfect advert for American exceptionalism in a period characterized by doubts about the U.S. war on terror."

Not all recollections of the past have been products of the big screen, however. The small screen, whether through television or video games, has also done substantial cultural work in redefining the world for the post-9/11 era. In probably no locale is this truer than for Latin America. As Patrick William Kelly writes, Latin America occupied a special place in the U.S. geopolitical imaginary during most of the Cold War. It was the site of the Cuban revolution and Missile Crisis, the Chilean coup of 1973 (the "other 9/11"), Operation Condor, the Sandinista revolution, and the Guatemalan genocide, among countless other phenomena. Yet since 2001, it has largely been recast in American popular culture through an imperialist discourse that, Kelly argues, justifies the past, present, and future of U.S. policy. Whether it is the "war on drugs" as seen through television's *Narcos* (Netflix, 2015–) or *Breaking Bad* (AMC, 2008–2013), the stereotyping of Latino immigrants in *Ugly Betty* (ABC, 2006–2010) and *Modern Family* (ABC, 2009–), or the refighting and reimaging of the Latin American cold war in the games *Grand Theft Auto* and *Call of Duty,* the small screen has perniciously transformed the region historian Stephen Rabe called "the killing zone" into a chaotic frontier where America endeavors to do good.[56] This is a shame, for Latin America has much to teach the United States. It is "empire's workshop," after all, the place where Washington sharpened the ideological justifications and practical methods that would prove instrumental to the U.S. imperium in the post-9/11 era.[57]

Kelly's discussion of two of the more popular video games on the market offers a powerful entrée into the focused analysis by Penny Von Eschen of video games and the "new Cold War" with Russia. Although receiving relatively scant scholarly attention, video games are hardly a marginal cultural issue. They are now big business. Indeed, with their 2015 sales eclipsing global cinema's total box office by greater than two to one, video games have come to represent a substantially larger commercial enterprise than the higher-profile film industry.[58] While they may not enjoy the cultural cachet of Hollywood's celebrity megawattage, they are catching up. Since 2001, in fact, there has emerged a growing bridge between the gaming and film industries, with an increasing number of movies based on their video-game counterparts, from *Prince of Persia: The Sands of Time* (2010), *Lara Croft: Tomb Raider* (2001), and *Lara Croft Tomb Raider: The Cradle of Life* (2003) to the *Resident Evil* series, *Warcraft* (2016), and even *The Angry Birds Movie* (2016). These have proven extremely popular; the last two films alone grossed nearly $800 million.[59] But video games are not just politically detached shoot-em-ups for speed-driven all-nighters. They also perform important memory work. Von Eschen explores the ways they have sought to reboot Cold War binaries, not only allowing players to refight that era's battles—one can assassinate Fidel Castro or take a machine gun through divided Berlin, for example—but presenting Russians as terrorist enemies bent on the destruction of innocence.

American popular culture in the post-9/11 era, these essays reveal, has behaved a lot like American popular culture during the Cold War. While only rarely a product of the state, it has nevertheless accepted the discursive assumptions of American exceptionalism and in doing so has consistently served the interests of the state and its elites. Twenty-first-century productions may be more polished, more diffuse, and even occasionally more nuanced than their twentieth-century predecessors, but they have, with relatively few exceptions, persisted in fundamentally presenting the United States as a global force for good. This may seem like an unsustainable notion in the context of America's post-9/11 record of war making, drone striking, and buttressing of despots but, it is now clear, the same blinders that rendered popular culture such an important force in shoring up the twentieth-century U.S. empire appear to be securely fastened in the twenty-first.

NOTES

I am grateful to Tim Gruenewald, Patrick William Kelly, Walter Hixson, and two referees—one anonymous and the other H. Bruce Franklin—for their thoughtful comments and suggestions on drafts of this introduction.

1. John Horn, "Soldiering On," *Los Angeles Times,* July 20, 2003.

2. Pressbook for *Buffalo Soldiers,* Clippings File: *Buffalo Soldiers* (2003), Margaret Herrick Library, Academy of Motion Picture Arts and Sciences, Beverly Hills, CA (hereafter cited as CF, MHL), 2.

3. Hawkeye Pierce (Donald Sutherland) was a character in *M*A*S*H* (1970), Captain Yossarian (Alan Arkin) was a character in *Catch-22* (1970), Joker Davis (Matthew Modine) was a character in *Full Metal Jacket* (1987), and Archie Gates (George Clooney) was a character in *Three Kings* (1999).

4. Charles Lyons, "Miramax Near Deal on 'Buffalo,'" *Daily Variety,* September 11, 2001, CF, MHL.

5. George W. Bush, "Remarks Following a Meeting with the National Security Team," September 12, 2001, *Public Papers of the Presidents of the United States: George W. Bush, 2001,* book II (Washington, DC: Government Printing Office, 2003), 1101.

6. Harvey Weinstein, quoted in David Hochman, "From Popcorn Movies to a Diet of Salty Politics," *New York Times,* November 24, 2002. In 2017, Weinstein's standing in Hollywood plummeted amid numerous allegations of sexual harassment and assault.

7. *The Quiet American* was first made into a film by the Academy Award–winning director and screenwriter Joseph Mankiewicz in 1958. For more on *The Quiet American* and 9/11, see H. Bruce Franklin, "Our Man in Saigon," *Nation,* February 3, 2003, 43–44; Scott Laderman, "Spotlight Essay/Film: *The Quiet American,*" in *September 11 in Popular Culture: A Guide,* ed. Sara E. Quay and Amy M. Damico (Santa Barbara, CA: Greenwood, 2010), 197–199; and Jon Wiener, "*Quiet* in Hollywood," *Nation,* December 16, 2002, 6–7.

8. On the film's eventual release, see Laderman, "*Quiet American,*" 198.

9. Bill Higgins, "'Quiet' Campaign Is Getting a Bit Louder," *Variety,* December 9, 2002.

10. John Horn, "Snake-Bitten 'Soldiers' Is Delayed Again," *Los Angeles Times,* April 21, 2003; Horn, "Soldiering On."

11. Horn, "Snake-Bitten 'Soldiers.'"

12. David Rooney, "Inside Move: 'Buffalo' Stirs Up Controversy," *Variety,* July 13, 2003, accessed August 17, 2016, http://variety.com/2003/film/markets-festivals/inside-move-buffalo-stirs-up-controversy-1117889250/; Susan King, "Battle Lines Drawn for 'Soldiers,'" *Los Angeles Times,* July 15, 2003.

13. Gregg Kilday, "'Buffalo' Helmer Soldiers On after Screening Fracas," *Hollywood Reporter,* January 23, 2003; Mike Goodridge, "Taking a Shot at Buffalo Soldiers," *Screen International,* January 24, 2003, CF, MHL.

14. "Buffalo Soldiers," Box Office Mojo, accessed January 10, 2017, www.boxofficemojo.com/movies/?page=main&id=buffalosoldiers.htm.

15. Dennis Lim, "Unnatural Selection," *Village Voice,* February 5–11, 2003, 106.

16. A. O. Scott, "A Portrait of the Army, But Few Heroes in Sight," *New York Times,* July 25, 2003.

17. On Americans' view of the Vietnam War as "fundamentally wrong and immoral," see John E. Rielly, "Americans and the World: A Survey at Century's End," *Foreign Policy* 114 (Spring 1999): 100.

18. Anne Thompson, "Films with War Themes Are Victims of Bad Timing," *New York Times*, October 17, 2002.

19. Samuel Fuller with Christa Lang Fuller and Jerome Henry Rudes, *A Third Face: My Tale of Writing, Fighting, and Filmmaking* (New York: Applause Theatre and Cinema, 2002), 347. On the politics of *China Gate*, see Scott Laderman, "Hollywood's Vietnam, 1929–1964: Scripting Intervention, Spotlighting Injustice," *Pacific Historical Review* 78 (November 2009): 589–593.

20. Horn, "Snake-Bitten 'Soldiers.'"

21. Ron Suskind, "Without a Doubt," *New York Times Magazine*, October 17, 2004, 51. Suskind did not identify the official, referring to him simply as "a senior adviser to [President] Bush," but he has been identified elsewhere as Karl Rove. Mark Danner, for example, wrote that it is "widely known" that Rove was the unnamed official; see Mark Danner, "Words in a Time of War: On Rhetoric, Truth, and Power," in *What Orwell Didn't Know: Propaganda and the New Face of American Politics*, ed. András Szántó (New York: Public Affairs, 2007), 23.

22. Eric Schmitt, "Rumsfeld Says U.S. Will Cut Forces in Gulf," *New York Times*, April 29, 2003.

23. For an earlier and still influential volume that explored some of these themes, see Amy Kaplan and Donald E. Pease, eds., *Cultures of United States Imperialism* (Durham, NC: Duke University Press, 1994).

24. Medley especially took issue with the movie's suggestion of U.S. duplicity—as opposed to ineptitude—in its claims about Iraqi weapons of mass destruction. Tony Medley, "At the Movies: *Green Zone*," *Tolucan Times*, March 31, 2010, Clippings File: *Green Zone*, Pacific Film Archive, University of California, Berkeley (hereafter cited as CF, PFA). Michael Moore, conversely, praised Greengrass's movie. "I can't believe this film got made," he tweeted. "It's been stupidly marketed as action film. It is the most HONEST film about Iraq War made by Hollywood." Michael Moore (@ MMFlint), Twitter, March 13, 2010, accessed December 21, 2016, https://twitter.com /MMFlint/status/10436619971. Greengrass was not the reflexive leftist suggested by Medley. He in fact supported (or, as he put it, "assent[ed]" to) the U.S. and British invasion, declining to join much of the Left in questioning the Bush and Blair administrations' problematical intelligence claims. It was only "later," Greengrass told Gavin Smith of *Film Comment*, when "they didn't find the WMD, when it became clear that this intelligence had been manipulated and contaminated, I felt angry, and that definitely drove this film. To me, the WMD issue was the moment of our original sin, if you like." "Chaos Theory," *Film Comment* 46 (March–April 2010): 30, CF, PFA.

25. Amy Kaplan, "'Left Alone with America': The Absence of Empire in the Study of American Culture," in Kaplan and Pease, *Cultures of United States Imperialism*, 14.

26. Melani McAlister, *Epic Encounters: Culture, Media, and U.S. Interests in the Middle East since 1945*, updated ed. (Berkeley: University of California Press, 2005),

xi. For McAlister's discussion of American "benevolent supremacy" at the dawn of what Henry Luce called "the American Century," see especially 43–83.

27. Johnston, quoted in Lary May, *The Big Tomorrow: Hollywood and the Politics of the American Way* (Chicago: University of Chicago Press, 2000), 176.

28. Lawrence H. Suid, *Guts and Glory: The Making of the American Military Image in Film*, rev. ed. (Lexington: University Press of Kentucky, 2002), 248. For more on *The Green Berets*, see Scott Laderman, "War and Film," in *At War: The Military and American Culture in the Twentieth Century and Beyond*, ed. Edwin Martini and David Kieran (New Brunswick, NJ: Rutgers University Press, 2018), 317–320; Tony Shaw, *Hollywood's Cold War* (Amherst: University of Massachusetts Press, 2007), 199–233; and Suid, *Guts and Glory*, 247–277.

29. Reagan first publicly used the term *noble cause* in a 1980 campaign speech at the Veterans of Foreign Wars convention in Chicago; see the transcript of the speech at https://reaganlibrary.archives.gov/archives/reference/8.18.80.html, accessed June 5, 2017. For more on postwar Hollywood and Vietnam, see Gilbert Adair, *Hollywood's Vietnam: From "The Green Berets" to "Full Metal Jacket"* (London: Heinemann, 1989); Michael Anderegg, ed., *Inventing Vietnam: The War in Film and Television* (Philadelphia: Temple University Press, 1991); Albert Auster and Leonard Quart, *How the War Was Remembered: Hollywood and Vietnam* (New York: Praeger, 1988); Jeremy M. Devine, *Vietnam at 24 Frames a Second: A Critical and Thematic Analysis of over 400 Films about the Vietnam War* (Austin: University of Texas Press, 1995); Linda Dittmar and Gene Michaud, eds., *From Hanoi to Hollywood: The Vietnam War in American Film* (New Brunswick, NJ: Rutgers University Press, 1990); Michael Lee Lanning, *Vietnam at the Movies* (New York: Ballantine, 1994); Eben J. Muse, *The Land of Nam: The Vietnam War in American Film* (Lanham, MD: Scarecrow Press, 1995); Julian Smith, *Looking Away: Hollywood and Vietnam* (New York: Scribners, 1975); and Mark P. Taylor, *The Vietnam War in History, Literature, and Film* (Tuscaloosa: University of Alabama Press, 2003). For more on films about the Vietnam War since 9/11, see Justin Hart, "The Vietnam War Film in the Age of Terror," in *The Vietnam War in Popular Culture: The Influence of America's Most Controversial War on Everyday Life*, vol. 2, ed. Ron Milam (Santa Barbara, CA: Praeger, 2017), 143–161.

30. "Remarks by President Obama at the 70th Anniversary of D-Day—Omaha Beach, Normandy," June 6, 2014, accessed March 1, 2018, https://obamawhitehouse. archives.gov/the-press-office/2014/06/06/remarks-president-obama-70th-anniver sary-d-day-omaha-beach-normandy.

31. Daniel White, "Read Hillary Clinton's Speech Touting 'American Exceptionalism,'" *Time*, September 1, 2016, accessed September 1, 2016, time. com/4474619/read-hillary-clinton-american-legion-speech/. On Albright's view of the United States as "the indispensable nation," see her interview with Matt Lauer on *The Today Show*, February 19, 1998, accessed January 10, 2017, https://1997-2001 .state.gov/www/statements/1998/980219a.html.

32. Mark Philip Bradley, "The Ambiguities of Sovereignty: The United States and the Global Human Rights Cases of the 1940s and 1950s," in *The State of*

Sovereignty: Territories, Laws, Populations, ed. Douglas Howland and Luise White (Bloomington: Indiana University Press, 2009), 126. I am indebted to Patrick William Kelly for drawing my attention to this connection.

33. Abby Phillip, "O'Reilly Told Trump That Putin Is a Killer. Trump's Reply: 'You Think Our Country Is So Innocent?,'" *Washington Post,* February 4, 2017, accessed June 5, 2017, www.washingtonpost.com/news/post-politics/wp/2017/02 /04/oreilly-told-trump-that-putin-is-a-killer-trumps-reply-you-think-our-countrys -so-innocent/?utm_term=.4febaede2402. Emblematic of Trump's tendency to contradict himself, he later tweeted that "America's men & women in uniform is the story of FREEDOM overcoming OPPRESSION, the STRONG protecting the WEAK, & GOOD defeating EVIL! USA." Donald J. Trump (@realDonald Trump), Twitter, July 2, 2017, 7:13 p.m., accessed July 13, 2017, https://twitter.com /realdonaldtrump/status/881697281233354753.

34. Mike DeBonis, "GOP Senators Blanch at Trump's Latest Defense of Putin," *Washington Post,* February 5, 2017, accessed February 6, 2017, www.washingtonpost .com/news/powerpost/wp/2017/02/05/gop-senators-blanch-at-trumps-latest -defense-of-putin/?utm_term=.6a731a7c6f84. Sasse is also a historian; he earned his PhD in history from Yale University in 2004. For an insightful analysis of Trump and American exceptionalism, see Stephen Wertheim, "Donald Trump versus American Exceptionalism: Toward the Sources of Trumpian Conduct," H-Diplo/ ISSF Policy Series, February 1, 2017, accessed February 17, 2017, https://issforum .org/ISSF/PDF/Policy-Roundtable-1-5K.pdf.

35. Editorial Board, "Blaming America First," *New York Times,* February 7, 2017. For an analysis of Trump and the *Times* editorial, see Adam Johnson, "NYT: Unlike Russian Wars, U.S. Wars 'Promote Freedom and Democracy,'" *Fairness and Accuracy in Reporting,* February 9, 2017, accessed February 22, 2017, http://fair.org/home /nyt-unlike-russian-wars-us-wars-promote-freedom-and-democracy.

36. On, for example, the Republican Party's persistent denialism about global warming, see Coral Davenport and Eric Lipton, "How G.O.P. Leaders Came to Reject Climate Science," *New York Times,* June 4, 2017. As the political scientists Thomas Mann and Norman Ornstein famously wrote in 2012, the modern Republican Party had become "unpersuaded by conventional understanding of facts, evidence, and science." Thomas E. Mann and Norman J. Ornstein, *It's Even Worse Than It Looks: How the American Constitutional System Collided with the New Politics of Extremism* (New York: Basic, 2012), xiv.

37. Jennifer Steinhauer, "G.O.P. Lawmakers, Once Skeptical of Obama Plan to Strike Syria, Back Trump," *New York Times,* April 8, 2017.

38. Mark Hensch, "CNN Host: 'Donald Trump Became President' Last Night," *Hill,* April 7, 2017, accessed June 1, 2017, http://thehill.com/homenews /administration/327779-cnn-host-donald-trump-became-president-last-night.

39. Schenker, quoted in Media Matters for America, "Media Fawns over Trump's Syria Strike," April 7, 2017, accessed June 1, 2017, www.youtube.com/watch?v =X42FqPIjkSU. I am indebted to Media Matters for America for its compilation of media commentary on this issue; in addition to the video in the above link, see Jared

Holt, "Media Praise Trump for Ordering Missile Attack on Syrian Airbase," Media Matters for America, April 7, 2017, accessed June 1, 2017, www.mediamatters.org/research/2017/04/07/media-praise-trump-ordering-missile-attack-syrian-airbase/215956.

40. Editorial Board, "Trump's Chance to Step into the Global Leadership Vacuum," *Washington Post,* April 7, 2017, accessed June 5, 2017, www.washington post.com/opinions/global-opinions/trumps-chance-to-step-into-the-global-leader ship-vacuum/2017/04/07/9c7f6f46-1ba7-11e7-855e-4824bbb5d748_story.html?utm _term=.84a658121514.

41. Peter Baker and Choe Sang-Hun, "In Chilling Nuclear Terms, Trump Warns North Korea," *New York Times,* August 9, 2017; "Trump Remark on Venezuela Stirs Dispute," *New York Times,* August 12, 2017.

42. Philip Rucker, "Trump Keeps Praising International Strongmen, Alarming Human Rights Advocates," *Washington Post,* May 2, 2017, accessed June 27, 2017, web.archive.org/web/20170501230210/washingtonpost.com/politics/trump-keeps -praising-international-strongmen-alarming-human-rights-advocates/2017/05/01/6 848d018-2e81-11e7-9dec-764dc781686f_story.html?utm_term=.5270aed3885d. The article was later revised to clarify that this was done "at least occasionally"; see www .washingtonpost.com/politics/trump-keeps-praising-international-strongmen -alarming-human-rights-advocates/2017/05/01/6848d018-2e81-11e7-9dec-764dc78 1686f_story.html?utm_term=.dc39ab33d007, accessed June 27, 2017. For bringing this piece to my attention, I am indebted to Adam Johnson, "Syria the Latest Case of U.S. 'Stumbling' into War," *Fairness and Accuracy in Reporting,* June 22, 2017, accessed June 27, 2017, http://fair.org/home/syria-the-latest-case-of-us-stumbling -into-war/.

43. Emile Simpson, "This Is How Great-Power Wars Get Started," *Foreign Policy,* June 21, 2017, accessed June 27, 2017, http://foreignpolicy.com/2017/06/21 /this-is-how-great-power-wars-get-started/. Simpson was referring to the Obama administration's interventions in Libya and Syria.

44. The exceptions have been most obvious in documentary films, from Michael Moore's *Fahrenheit 9/11* (2004) to *Why We Fight* (2005) and *Dirty Wars* (2013). Fictional productions have been more likely to level pragmatic objections to the perceived excesses of U.S. foreign policy (*Rendition* [2007]), to the criminal behavior of some American troops (*Redacted* [2007]), to the psychological damage suffered by the nation's warriors (*In the Valley of Elah* [2007]), or to the injustice of compulsory multiple tours (*Stop-Loss* [2008]) than to acknowledge and challenge the larger imperial enterprise. Washington's intentions have generally remained benevolent. We have yet to see a *Missing* (1982) for the post-9/11 epoch.

45. Andrew C. McKevitt, "'Watching War Made Us Immune': The Popular Culture of the Wars," in *Understanding the U.S. Wars in Iraq and Afghanistan,* ed. Beth Bailey and Richard H. Immerman (New York: New York University Press, 2015), 240–241. I thank Walter Hixson for bringing McKevitt's essay to my attention.

46. For more on Cold War triumphalism, see Ellen Schrecker, ed., *Cold War Triumphalism: The Misuse of History after the Fall of Communism* (New York: New

Press, 2004). The literature on Cold War popular culture is voluminous. For several examples, see Daniel J. Leab, *Orwell Subverted: The CIA and the Filming of "Animal Farm"* (University Park: Pennsylvania State University Press, 2007); Ronnie D. Lipschutz, *Cold War Fantasies: Film, Fiction, and Foreign Policy* (Lanham, MD: Rowman and Littlefield, 2001); J. Fred MacDonald, *Television and the Red Menace: The Video Road to Vietnam* (New York: Praeger, 1985); Nicholas Evan Sarantakes, "Cold War Pop Culture and the Image of U.S. Foreign Policy: The Perspective of the Original *Star Trek* Series," *Journal of Cold War Studies* 7 (Fall 2005): 74–103; and Shaw, *Hollywood's Cold War*.

47. Shaw, *Hollywood's Cold War*, 5–6.

48. *Tears of the Sun*, according to its production notes, was "the first movie about Navy SEALs to receive the full cooperation and endorsement of the United States Navy and Department of Defense." Its director, Antoine Fuqua, called it a tribute to the "men and women who protect us and go into places and do great things about which too little is said. I wanted to make a film that actually shows you that there are men and women out there in the military, who make it okay for us to sit and drink our morning coffee, while they are out there fighting and sometimes dying, and we never even know their names." *Tears of the Sun* Production Notes, 3, Press Kit Collection, Pacific Film Archive, University of California, Berkeley.

49. Betty Clarke, "The Dixie Chicks," *Guardian* (London), March 12, 2003, accessed August 31, 2016, www.theguardian.com/music/2003/mar/12/artsfeatures. popandrock. According to Reebee Garofalo, the popular music previously "associated with rebellion, defiance, protest, opposition, and resistance" instead became used, in the post-9/11 era, "in the service of mourning, healing, patriotism, and nation building. In this new order, the dissent—and in particular the antiwar protest music—that helped provide the basis for the national debate on Vietnam was nowhere to be found on mainstream media during the invasions of Afghanistan and Iraq. If anything, country anthems that pushed the envelope in support of government policy seemed more likely to capture the popular imagination." Reebee Garofalo, "Pop Goes to War, 2001–2004: U.S. Popular Music after 9/11," in *Music in the Post-9/11 World*, ed. Jonathan Ritter and J. Martin Daughtry (New York: Routledge, 2007), 4. For a good introduction to the politics of popular music in the first few years following 9/11, see Dorian Lynskey, *33 Revolutions Per Minute: A History of Protest Songs, from Billie Holliday to Green Day* (New York: Ecco, 2011), 506–533.

50. Among many other works, see John Clarke, "Pessimism versus Populism: The Problematic Politics of Popular Culture," in *For Fun and Profit: The Transformation of Leisure into Consumption*, ed. Richard Butsch (Philadelphia: Temple University Press, 1990), 28–44; Stuart Hall, "Notes on Deconstructing 'The Popular,'" in *People's History and Socialist Theory*, ed. Raphael Samuel (London: Routledge, 1981), 227–240; George Lipsitz, "'This Ain't No Sideshow': Historians and Media Studies," *Critical Studies in Mass Communication* 5 (June 1988): 147–161; Tim Nieguth, ed., *The Politics of Popular Culture: Negotiating Power, Identity, and Place* (Montreal: McGill-Queen's University Press, 2015); Michael Parenti, *Make-*

Believe Media: The Politics of Entertainment (New York: St. Martin's Press, 1992); and John Street, *Politics and Popular Culture* (Philadelphia: Temple University Press, 1997).

51. James Guerrasio, "How 'American Sniper' Became the Highest-Grossing U.S. Film of 2014," *Business Insider,* March 11, 2015, accessed January 5, 2017, www.businessinsider.com/american-sniper-highest-grossing-us-film-of-2014-2015-3; Linda Ge, "'American Sniper' Overtakes 'Saving Private Ryan' as No. 1 Domestic Grossing War Movie of All Time," *Wrap,* January 30, 2015, accessed January 5, 2017, www .thewrap.com/american-sniper-overtakes-saving-private-ryan-as-no-1-war-movie-of -all-time/.

52. Karl W. Eikenberry and David M. Kennedy wrote in 2013 that "less than 0.5 percent of the population serves in the armed forces, compared with more than 12 percent during World War II. Even fewer of the privileged and powerful shoulder arms." Karl W. Eikenberry and David M. Kennedy, "Americans and Their Military, Drifting Apart," *New York Times,* May 27, 2013.

53. "Remarks by President Obama to the Troops in Afghanistan," May 2, 2012, accessed January 9, 2017, www.whitehouse.gov/the-press-office/2012/05/01/remarks -president-obama-troops-afghanistan.

54. "Box Office/Business for *The Avengers* (2012)," IMDb, accessed January 6, 2017, www.imdb.com/title/tt0848228/business?ref_=tt_dt_bus.

55. See, for several examples, David F. Schmitz, *Thank God They're on Our Side: The United States and Right-Wing Dictatorships, 1921–1965* (Chapel Hill: University of North Carolina Press, 1999); Schmitz, *The United States and Right-Wing Dictatorships, 1965–1989* (Cambridge: Cambridge University Press, 2006); Steven Kinzer, *Overthrow: America's Century of Regime Change from Hawaii to Iraq* (New York: Times Books, 2006); and Stephen G. Rabe, *U.S. Intervention in British Guiana: A Cold War Story* (Chapel Hill: University of North Carolina Press, 2005).

56. Stephen G. Rabe, *The Killing Zone: The United States Wages Cold War in Latin America* (New York: Oxford University Press, 2012).

57. Greg Grandin, *Empire's Workshop: Latin America, the United States, and the Rise of the New Imperialism* (New York: Metropolitan, 2006).

58. Colin Campbell, "Worldwide Video Games Market Will Grow 9.4 Percent This Year, Says Report," *Polygon,* April 22, 2015, accessed January 9, 2017, www.poly gon.com/2015/4/22/8471789/worldwide-video-games-market-value-2015; Pamela McClintock, "Global 2015 Box Office: Revenue Hits Record $38 Billion-Plus," *Hollywood Reporter,* January 3, 2016, accessed January 9, 2017, www.holly woodreporter.com/news/global-2015-box-office-revenue-851749. I am grateful to Tim Gruenewald for bringing these sources to my attention.

59. "Warcraft," Box Office Mojo, accessed January 25, 2017, www.boxofficemojo .com/movies/?id=warcraft.htm; "The Angry Birds Movie," Box Office Mojo, accessed January 25, 2017, www.boxofficemojo.com/movies/?id=angrybirds.htm.

ONE

Imperial Cry Faces

WOMEN LAMENTING THE WAR ON TERROR

Rebecca A. Adelman

"IT'S OKAY," SHE SAYS THROUGH HER TEARS, patting the bald eagle on the head. She has shifted her torch and tablet to the crook of her left arm and has stretched out her right to console her feathered friend, who weeps with his talons wrapped around a flagpole extended over the waves. This crayon drawing of a crying Statue of Liberty—by an elementary school student named Eddie Hamilton from Knoxville, Tennessee—is part of the Library of Congress September 11, 2011, Documentary Project.[1] Young Eddie was far from the only person to imagine this kind of emotion from the copper-clad woman. One of his classmates imagined her similarly distraught and so did a number of political cartoonists, along with more than a few tattoo artists (as I discovered serendipitously during an Internet search). But if crying for the American victims of the September 11th attacks felt so necessary and so automatic that even a statue could do it, the appropriate emotional response to the wars that followed is much harder to discern. And as September 11th recedes further into the past, its emotional imperatives become murkier—a diffusion complicated by U.S. geopolitical aggressiveness and lethal efforts to consolidate American power abroad. So who cries for U.S. empire?

Perhaps the passage of time and the balms of revenge and preemption have offered Lady Liberty comfort like that she once extended to the eagle. But apparently, not everyone can survey the landscape of contemporary American militarism with so stiff an upper lip. Accordingly, this chapter maps the intersections of gender, sadness, and imperial violence as embodied by the crying female protagonists who populate the American media landscape of the global war on terrorism. The ruthless interrogator who weeps quietly at the end of *Zero Dark Thirty*, the drone operator whose eyes spill over during missile strikes in *Good Kill,* the one who dissolves into tears after a strike in *Eye in the Sky,* and the Central Intelligence Agency (CIA) agent who sobs theatrically all the time, over everything, in *Homeland:* these women do the lethal, affective work of empire. And it makes them feel bad: not necessarily bad *about* it but certainly bad *around* it.

My goal here is not simply to analyze these representations of emotionally frail female warriors; rather, I want to consider the political and emotional complexities of their crying in context. Presumably, the feminization of crying—and emotion more generally—explains why these phenomena are often deemed politically irrelevant.[2] Although the films and television show I consider represent crying as an act with no efficacy to change actual conditions, they also endow it with great political and moral significance. I argue that this investment is problematic, as it may perpetuate the very forms of violence the tears seem to condemn. My inquiry emerges from my abiding curiosity about the role of emotion in contemporary American militarism and more specifically, my skepticism about the capacity of sentiment to challenge it. Marita Sturken has argued that in the aftermath of September 11th, "the paradoxical effect of the nation under threat is that modes of sentiment that might have been perceived as weakening its stature become the terrain through which it is recuperated."[3] In this way, feeling bad for the victims of U.S. imperialism coexists easily with notions of American exceptionalism, on the logic that only so enlightened a nation would be sensitive enough to lament the casualties it causes. Judith Butler, in both *Antigone's Claim* and *Frames of War,* has argued for the radically transformative potential of grief to alter relationships between state and citizen and state and enemy, respectively.[4] According to Butler, the act of grieving in ways the state does not sanction, such as mourning the loss of lives the state does not recognize as valuable, undermines its authority to wage war. The grief of the characters I consider here, however, co-opts this potential, tightening the identification between citizen and state by uniting them in sympathy while edging the enemy further outside the sphere of the meaningfully lamentable.

My analysis here is bounded by specific parameters and conceptual ambitions. First, I am concerned only with fictionalized depictions of the war on terror and hence, media artifacts in which the characters cry intentionally and by design. Even, and perhaps especially, when the stories purport to be based on actual people and events, the performance of crying takes on additional symbolic significance. Second, I focus on crying women. While crying women appear in nearly all forms of popular entertainment, they typically cry for intensely personal (usually romantic) reasons rather than matters of state. By contrast, male tears, when they appear in cultural productions, are almost always assumed to be both justified and weighty. The female characters I consider here are actually involved in the prosecution of the war in roles that are more active than the stock figures of aggrieved military mother, wife, or widow. Deborah Cohler argues that the first phases of the war on terror, during the George W. Bush presidency, were "historically noteworthy for mainstreaming of media images of female U.S. combatants" as part of a larger, militaristic "nationalist feminism" that leveraged the apparent equality of American women as a sign of civilizational advancement.[5] These early representations cleared space for women to appear as agents of U.S. militarism and also, in the process, as persuasive ambassadors for its benevolent imperialism. Indeed, by gendering the imperial project as (sad) feminine, these films enhance its claim to benevolence. All the texts I consider also date from the latter part of the ongoing war on terror.[6] *Zero Dark Thirty* was released in 2012, *Good Kill* in 2014, and *Eye in the Sky* in 2015. *Homeland* began in 2011, airing its seventh season in early 2018. All originated, notably, during the Obama presidency.

A detailed consideration of the differences and continuities between the Bush and Obama administrations' approaches to the war on terror is beyond the scope of my analysis here, but the presidential connection matters because it changes the ideological and affective stakes of both prosecuting the war and critiquing it, particularly for liberals. From this vantage, it would have been relatively easy to cry bitter, oppositional tears over the policies of George W. Bush, a righteousness that mingled easily with the lingering grief over the civilian casualties of September 11th. Obama, on the other hand, explicitly distanced himself from his predecessor's approaches and tactics while presiding with varying degrees of reluctance over the intensification of drone warfare, military operations in places such as Libya, continued detention operations at Guantánamo, and renewed conflict in both Iraq and Afghanistan. Despite the hope that an Obama presidency might entail a reversal of aggressive militarism, the actual outcomes of this second phase of the war on terror were mixed, which stranded liberal supporters in a vexed ideological and affective position.[7] For those audiences, I argue that the crying female characters in question channel a combination of weariness, frustration, and resignation. In the process, these women tell a very particular story of U.S. imperialism and tearfully promise U.S. benevolence.

COLD COMFORTS: CRYING, GENDER, AND MILITARISM

Crying provides a comfort, cold and meager though it might be. But comfort, in the context of imperialism, is never uncomplicated. Sturken argues, for example, that during the global war on terrorism, the rhetoric and experience of comfort has been a "primary mode through which the U.S. practice of torture is mediated" and that torture became normalized as citizens grew more comfortable with the idea of it.[8] To the extent that popular cultural texts provide audiences with pleasurable experiences, then, we need to ask what kinds of comforts and pleasures are afforded by the sight of women crying through drone strikes or after participating in waterboarding. By crying, these women dramatize key elements of the purported benevolence of American empire: the compunction and expressions of regret that regularly accompany its violence. Whether the architects of U.S. imperialism deny their ambitions or the critics of U.S. imperialism demand that it not be undertaken "in our names," the affective landscape of the imperium is saturated with apology and denial. The act of crying acknowledges the militarized violence of contemporary American empire—drone strikes, torture, quasi-legal special operations—while disavowing the imperial ambitions that underpin it.

Two assumptions about the act of crying, in general, inform my analysis here. First, tears do not always lend themselves to interpretation. Anyone who has ever tried to soothe an inconsolable child or has found themselves crying without really knowing why understands this intuitively. Tom Lutz, in his singular volume on crying, identifies this inscrutability at the heart of the interpersonal dilemma that crying poses because crying appears to be such an insistently communicative behavior.[9] Second, tears, like any other emotional phenomenon, have both individual and structural origins. Ann Cvetkovich, in her work on depression, raises the possibility that systems such as neoliberal capitalism, along with war, states of exception, and intense securitization, might manifest in individual depressions.[10] Working from these premises, I focus here not so much on the narrative conditions in which these female protagonists cry but rather on how their crying might register the historical moment from which these texts emerged and what kinds of affective pleasures and pedagogies they might offer their audiences.

The act of crying, at least in contemporary Western cultures, is gendered feminine. This gendering begets ambiguous consequences. Crying men, for example, can elicit either ridicule or profound sympathy, depending on the context. The tears of a male crier could readily signify as authentic indices of the gravitas of a situation and the man's emotional depth and maturity; on the other hand, male tears might seem to suggest mental or emotional instability on the part of the crier. Female tears, however, are almost always trivialized or evaluated negatively. Lutz notes that in canonical depictions of crying, like those found in literature or epic poetry, men cry predominantly about matters of state, such as war, peace, and political ideals; women's tears are reserved for the personal.[11]

However, the films and television show I analyze here deviate from that pattern, at least partially, as all the female criers emote for reasons that cannot be reduced to individual woe. Elisabeth Anker's work on the ascendance of a melodramatic style in American politics since the mid-twentieth century suggests a pervasive emotionalism in U.S. policy, both domestic and foreign. The melodramatic style, as Anker describes it, "casts politics, policies, and practices of citizenship within a moral economy that identifies the nation-state as a virtuous and innocent victim of villainous action." She continues: "By evoking intense visceral responses to wrenching injustices imposed upon the nation-state, melodramatic discourse solicits affective states of astonishment, sorrow, and pathos through the scenes it shows of persecuted citizens."[12] Melodramatic political discourses, like melodrama itself, are animated by the (perceived) affliction of the innocent and the helpless; translated onto the nation-state, they "draw upon a moral economy that locates goodness in national suffering, and that locates heroism in unilateral state action against dominating forces."[13] Hence, the weeping Statue of Liberty. On the other hand, the crying ladies of *Zero Dark Thirty*, *Good Kill*, *Eye in the Sky*, and *Homeland* sob and snivel from positions of power; they are agents of the state, authorized to wield its force and its violence.

Their imperial tears fall in the context of a U.S. military reorientation, in both theory and practice, toward an "emotionally intelligent" mode of warfighting. Laleh Khalili describes this turn as a deliberate move away from the highly mechanized and technologized approach to warfare entailed in the Revolution in Military Affairs that predominated in the late twentieth century.[14] Emotionally intelligent warfare requires emotionally intelligent warfighters and depends on the weaponization of their emotional capacities, particularly in counterinsurgency operations, engineering them to be responsive to the emotional conditions of their enemies. Ultimately, a tactical discourse of emotions also provides a screen for the actual violence inherent in counterinsurgency and, relatedly, imperialism. Indeed, Derek Gregory describes how the U.S. military has cast its new approach to warfighting as "intrinsically therapeutic" for the "host nations" of its occupying counterinsurgencies.[15] The female protagonists in the stories I analyze here cry both during and after their exercises of state violence: while piloting a drone strike that will harm civilians or after a strike that did, after authorizing or participating in the torture of enemy combatants, or while overseeing quasi-legal special operations. Doubtless, these tears would signify differently at other historical moments or for audiences in other countries; my focus here, however, is on how they fall at the current juncture of those imperial ambitions and tacit certainty about their benevolence.

Lutz observes that women's crying has often been both denigrated and valorized as the opposite of state systems of war-making and oppression.[16] Given their marginalized status, the question of women's agency in imperial enterprises is layered and complex; colonizing women are, in Anne McClintock's terms, "ambiguously complicit" with the arrangements in which they operate.[17] The gendered politics of contemporary American imperialism in the global war on terrorism is further complicated by both the reliance on "feminist" rhetoric to justify the war (to liberate Middle Eastern women) and the increased visibility and inclusion of women in the U.S. military.

When the female protagonists I analyze here preside over a situation that unfolds badly, they appear in intertextual reference with those actual women involved in military debacles. Of course, in practice when combat operations go awry and women are involved, they readily become both hypervisible and scapegoated. The revelations of torture at Abu Ghraib are a clear example of this.[18] For example, Colonel Janis Karpinski was widely portrayed as losing control of her personnel there, while female participants in prisoner abuse, such as Lynndie England, became the objects of intense criticism and speculation. Errol Morris's *Standard Operating Procedure* (2008), the definitive filmic treatment of Abu Ghraib, focuses heavily on the stories of the women involved. When she appears on camera, Karpinski is intense, clear-eyed, and direct, her voice wobbling only when she narrates her experience of being relieved of command after the scandal (Karpinski has maintained that top Department of Defense officials knew about—and authorized—the abuse of prisoners at Abu Ghraib). Megan Ambuhl Graner, the wife of Charles Graner, who is also the father of Lynndie England's child and spent six and a half years imprisoned in Leavenworth for his role in the abuse, speaks steadily and a little defensively. Of all the women, Lynndie England's persona is the hardest to describe—at times hesitant, other times more assertive, and occasionally even mirthful; at one moment in the film, as she describes detainees being forced to masturbate, she seems to start to laugh and then stops herself. By contrast, Sabrina Harman appears tentative, her voice small and almost childlike. Morris seems to give her the most narrative leeway in the film, in which she reads letters she wrote to her wife, Kelly, that describe her misgivings about all she witnessed and participated in. She ultimately concedes that had she known what was going to happen, she would never have joined the army at all. Throughout her interviews, she asserts that she photographed the abuse for documentary purposes, knowing it was wrong but sensing that no one would believe it, and the structure of the film lends her claim some credibility. But none of the women confess or apologize. Or truly cry. By their lack of visible remorse and their simultaneous inability to justify their actions, these women twice refuse audiences the consolations of American exceptionalism.

Minimally, tears are a signal and an acknowledgment that something significant has happened, at least from the perspective of the person crying. Tears falling on screen cue spectators to emotional curiosity and attunement. Owing to the simultaneous symbolic richness and indeterminacy of tears in general, those shed by the female protagonists I analyze here are polyvalent and semiotically capacious. They can mean a number of different, seemingly contradictory things at once. If we desire an antiwar message in our media, the tears might seem to acknowledge the wrongness of militarism or profess an apology for state-sponsored wrongdoing. When the crying state operatives stand in for the United States as a whole, they can serve a misogynist representational function by appearing to embody a hysterical nation-state gone rogue in its fight against terror. On the other hand, if viewers are skeptical of women's fitness for combat, the sight of them crying might resonate with familiar narratives about female weakness or sensitivity and read as tears of frustration, a sign of expressly feminine emotional delicacy and a related inability to carry out a mission. For audiences who wish the United States would exercise more geopolitical dominance, these tears might be yet another sign of American weakness and global irrelevance. As commercially produced texts designed to appeal to wide swaths of the American public, the films and television show I analyze here could potentially accommodate any of those interpretations. But I argue that the primary narrative function of these women's tears is to enact a story of American exceptionalism and reluctant imperialism. The tears communicate a national willingness to do what is necessary for the greater (global) good, coupled with a moral sensitivity keen enough to regret the costs of such actions.[19]

LAMENTING THE "GREATEST MANHUNT IN HISTORY": TEARS OUT OF CONTEXT IN *ZERO DARK THIRTY*

Promotional materials for *Zero Dark Thirty* (2012) characterized the film as the story of "the greatest manhunt in history": the ten-year search for Osama bin Laden. Directed by Kathryn Bigelow, following her historic directorial Oscar for *The Hurt Locker* (2008), the film is noteworthy in part for its focus on a female protagonist, a CIA wunderkind named Maya.[20] A fictionalized representation of an actual CIA agent, Maya is brash, tenacious, and single-minded in her pursuit.[21] Maya, as Timothy Melley writes, is "ruthless and abstemious, she eschews sex and other pleasures" to focus doggedly on her pursuit.[22] Maya has a rather narrow emotional spectrum, ranging from faint disgust to indignation, but she nevertheless provides an affective pedagogy for spectators. Tracking her evolving responses to the torture she witnesses, from an inability to look to a willingness to authorize, David Bromwich characterizes Maya as a "'reflector' for the audience."[23] Jane Mayer suggests that her discomfort with torture at the outset provides the impression of a "baseline of moral awareness" for the film that gets eroded as the chase intensifies.[24]

As the film successively validates her instincts and her methods, it echoes the claim, made by an actual female CIA agent, that women simply "make fantastic analysts." Those "fantastic" analysts are the protagonists of a 2013 HBO documentary, *Manhunt: The Search for Osama bin Laden*. A central theme in *Manhunt* is that of an embattled "sisterhood" of analysts who have dedicated themselves to tracking bin Laden, often in the face of (male) administrative skepticism and derision. Crying runs as a leitmotif throughout. Interviewees mention crying in their descriptions of CIA norms for expressing frustration ("men throw chairs, women cry") and repressing emotion ("cry at home" and come back the next day ready to work); in their accounts of the long years during which they were unable to locate bin Laden; and in their reflections on President Obama's speech announcing that he had been killed. These are consistently righteous tears, even when bitter or remorseful, shed by criers who finally receive recognition for decades of invisible work and sacrifice.

Manhunt portrays the CIA bureaucracy as obstructionist, almost to the point of compromising the search for bin Laden, but all accounts indicate that the CIA later cooperated readily with the production of *Zero Dark Thirty*. Bigelow and her team enjoyed a level of access to operational details about the search for bin Laden that some commentators described as surprising, even unprecedented.[25] Even as the Department of Defense reprimanded some members of the Navy SEAL team involved in the raid on bin Laden's compound, it too assisted the producers.[26] A voluminous, if often rather dull, e-mail correspondence between the CIA, the Department of Defense, and the filmmakers captures all of this mutual goodwill. Many of their exchanges are logistical or bureaucratic, arranging meeting times or clarifying protocol, and there are few traces of governmental hesitation about working with Bigelow and screenwriter Mark Boal in this capacity. In fact, the e-mails document a quick consensus that this partnership represents the state's best option for telling, or controlling, the story of the hunt.[27]

This collaboration between the filmmakers and the government had fairly predictable consequences, including what many critics characterized as a vindication of torture as a practice that begets, albeit circuitously, the intelligence that leads the team to bin Laden's compound.[28] Reviewing the film for the *Huffington Post,* David Bromwich critiques its overall "mood of acceptance" for coercive interrogation tactics.[29] Similarly, in the *Guardian,* Glenn Greenwald contends that the film renders "torture exactly as its supporters like to see it: as an ugly though necessary tactic used by brave and patriotic CIA agents in stopping hateful, violent terrorists," which neatly encapsulates the film's tendency toward both justification and disavowal.[30]

The tension between these two impulses manifests in the inscrutability of the film's final scene. With bin Laden dispatched and the mission complete, Maya boards an empty cargo plane; when the pilot asks her where she'd like to go, she does not, and apparently cannot, answer. Instead, she cries, at first haltingly and then with (relative) abandon—a few quiet hiccups and a sniffle or two before her affect flattens, her mouth gapes, and the screen cuts to black. The film marks this display of emotion as significant, framing it in tight close-up for a better look at Maya's uncharacteristic self-indulgence.

Yet Maya's tears do not fall without controversy. Some CIA women have objected, for example, to the cinematic and televisual trope of the female spy as hypersexual or unstable, as in *Homeland.*[31] On the other hand, in an interview with *Esquire,* the "man who shot bin Laden" recalls that the "agency woman" overseeing the raid on his compound was crying when he brought her over to identify bin Laden's body.[32] In the film itself, however, Maya does not cry at the sight of bin Laden's corpse; in that scene, she appears stunned, a little swoony, but her eyes are dry. Her crying at the end is decontextualized (she is alone, in transit to an unspecified destination, her mission accomplished), wordless, and without explanation or resolution. She could be crying, equally plausibly, for her now-rudderless existence, for the victims of terrorism, or for the things she has seen and done. While the crying CIA agents in *Manhunt* tear up for obvious and explicable reasons, Maya cries inarticulately and so invites viewers to project their own interpretations onto her sadness. In the film, the clearest predecessor for her concluding tears is a quick, hyperventilating breakdown in a bathroom after participating in a waterboarding, but that cry is represented as more exhaustion than guilt. Because the ends in *Zero Dark Thirty* clearly justify the means, Maya's last tears are superfluous to the plot but central to the film's affective pedagogy. Falling without a referent, they suggest that there is no specific reason to cry over American militarism, that it suffices, ethically and politically, to feel bad in retrospect, after the victory is secured and the dirty work is done.

FANTASIES OF EXCEPTIONALIST PLENITUDE: TEARS OF REMORSE IN *GOOD KILL*

Crying in *Good Kill,* on the other hand, is far less equivocal, as the film relies on the weeping woman to serve as the moral barometer of the film and by extension, drone warfare more generally. Vaguely promising to be "based on actual events," *Good Kill* tells the story of Tommy Egan, an air force drone pilot with a troubled conscience, frustrated ambitions, and a disintegrating marriage. These problems become more acute when the CIA takes command of the drone operation and orders increasingly questionable strikes. His copilot is a younger Latina woman, Vera Suarez, who is clear-eyed and competent from the outset. However, as their missions become more indiscriminate— killing women, children, and mourners and frequently "double-tapping" by firing on bystanders who come to inspect the damage after a strike—she monitors her screens and instruments through watery eyes that spill over even as she guides the missile to its target. Egan sublimates his angst into drunk driving and domestic violence against his wife, Molly. Molly, for her part, is beautiful, dim, and apparently unconflicted about her husband's job, only shedding a single tear during a brief moment of closeness when Egan tells her about piloting a strike on a funeral for a man he had killed twenty-four hours prior.[33]

Released in 2014, *Good Kill* appeared as the U.S. military was deliberating about whether to open all combat jobs to women. The Department of Defense formally took this step in late 2015, although the wars in Iraq and Afghanistan had changed the boundaries of "combat" so dramatically that many women had already been serving, largely without official recognition, in such capacities for over a decade.[34] The film treads ambivalently into this ongoing and contentious debate and even gestures to it a few times as Suarez defends herself to skeptical male colleagues. She ultimately concedes at the end of the film that she is not cut out for "battlefields and blackjack," as shorthand for masculine military cultures. And so her character is situated within a vexed genealogy of (in)famous American military women. On the one hand, her moral sensibilities distance her from women like Lynndie England. On the other, her apparent—and relative—fragility aligns her more with the figure of Jessica Lynch, whose broadcast rescue from an Iraqi hospital in 2003 and subsequent representations simultaneously affirmed and undermined women's positions on the frontlines.[35] By lamenting the casualties as she does, Suarez enacts conservative and liberal positions at once, intimating that women are too sensitive for warfare while also demonstrating that they have the necessary skills for this new type of combat and may be even better at it, at least morally and philosophically, than their male counterparts.

Orders come through a speakerphone in the form of a male voice who identifies himself only as Langley—a signal that he represents the CIA. In this way, *Good Kill* dramatizes what Peter Asaro theorizes as "bureaucratized killing," which combines, in the person of the drone operator, the bureaucracy of the military with immediate authority over life and death.[36] Egan and Suarez represent the burgeoning ranks of drone operators and support personnel that Joseph Beller names "melancholic functionaries."[37] Egan follows orders reluctantly, generally registering his discomfort with small grimaces and furrowed brows that escalate into insubordination when he deliberately botches a mission that Langley ordered. Egan's character is imparted this moderate level of complexity, but Suarez's crying is uncomplicated: a simple expression of grief at the carnage she is inflicting, contrasted to Langley's cold rationality as he justifies the orders by invoking a pseudo-ethics of just war and proportionality. In one scene, Suarez cries as she obeys Langley's order to "follow up" on a strike with another in quick succession, which will surely kill the civilians who have rushed to rescue the casualties of the first. After the damage assessment—twelve dead—is complete and Langley has signed off, Suarez asks her commanding officer, "Was that a war crime, sir?" To which he replies, "Shut the fuck up, Suarez," which both validates her assessment of the situation and renders it inconsequential.

Suarez's crying serves as a denial not of the violence itself but of responsibility for it. Crying always marks a distance between the crier and the object of her tears, whether in the case of mournful tears (the distance between the crier and something precious that is lost) or remorseful tears (the distance between the crier and what she wishes she had done differently). Crying indicates an irreparable breach: something lost that cannot be regained or an act that cannot be undone. Crying also expresses a wish that things could be otherwise, though this wish is nearly always futile (and unlikely to be fulfilled, except in fairy tales, by the act of crying itself). Even if the act of crying itself almost never alters the conditions that precipitated the tears, public performances of sadness serve a purpose nonetheless; they make visible the crier's wish for things to be different and so demonstrate that the crier is morally, politically, and affectively astute enough to recognize—and regret—that something is awry. They are a form of conditional remorse. Tears typically signal that the crier is powerless to change her circumstances; American imperial tears intimate that geopolitical conditions could not be otherwise, and the United States could not reasonably have pursued a different course of action. Simultaneously, the act of crying indicates an awareness that such a hypothetical but clearly impossible different arrangement would be preferable. The tears mark the preceding action as a necessary evil, remorsefully but stoically undertaken by a nation-state that has now become a martyr to its own conscience.

Ultimately, the film situates Suarez's embodiment of American goodness and clarity of conscience as incommensurable with drone warfare. Accordingly, Suarez turns in her wings in an act of protest and an acknowledgment of personal defeat, though the film undermines the significance of this act by hinting that it was expedited by her interest in a previously prohibited and presumably sexual fraternization with Egan. But her surety and confident smile as she informs Egan of her resignation prove that goodness to be redeemable. Of course, the drone war continues offscreen and uninterrupted. Thus, the film achieves a fantasy of exceptionalist plenitude, wherein American military personnel (and by extension, the American people as a whole) heed their consciences even as the state persists in its morally dubious warmaking.

MORAL VICTORIES AND TACTICAL WINS:
NATIONALIZED TEARS IN *EYE IN THE SKY*

The critical consensus around *Eye in the Sky,* a film about drone warfare released less than a year after *Good Kill,* suggests that it is, overall, a better movie than its predecessor in both concept and execution.[38] Promotional materials for the film emphasize the moral dilemma at its core,[39] and this complexity figures heavily in the positive reviews of the film.[40] In *Good Kill,* the disembodied voice of Langley orders indiscriminate killing with scanty justification, irrespective of the consequences, while all the credible characters object. By contrast, *Eye in the Sky* begins from a more complicated premise. The film tells the story of a joint operation by British, American, and Kenyan forces against a small cell of al-Shabab militants. Teams from all three nations deliberate what to do as their surveillance reveals the militants are preparing a large-scale suicide attack. However, their plans for a targeted strike are complicated by the presence of a young girl, Alia, who is selling bread outside their compound and who will almost certainly be killed or seriously injured by the missile.

The British officer in charge of the operation, Colonel Powell (played by Helen Mirren), urges government officials to authorize the strike regardless of the girl's presence, while those officials dither about legality and politics. Meanwhile, the American team of air force drone operators—a male pilot, Steve Watts, and a female sensor operator, Carrie Gershon—become the voices of ethical warfare. Notably, this is the same gendered division of drone labor as in *Good Kill;* as sensor operators, the women are actively involved in the kill chain but neither give orders nor finally carry them out. Instead, they do the more feminized work of operating the sensors that track targets. This ambiguous position of involvement but indirect responsibility is a perfect vantage from which to cry and is similar to the emotional position of anti-drone civilians who object to strikes carried out "in their names" but who are only tangentially (or imaginatively) affected by those operations. Indeed, Carrie's name telegraphs the emotional investment, the *care,* that she brings to her role. Throughout, *Eye in the Sky* explicitly nationalizes her tears, drawing a contrast with the steely Colonel Powell through frequent cuts between the two women.

Eye in the Sky is unique among the representations I consider here because the film does not suggest that women are, by nature, unstable or unfit for this work. Indeed, women of various nationalities are involved in all aspects of the mission, and they are all represented as competent and reasonable. The only exception is the character of Angela Northman, an officious and dowdy parliamentary advisor who is new to the job and intransigent in her opposition to the mission, in part because one of the targets is a British national. At the end of the film, Northman, who has watched everything unfold from a briefing room, gives a teary-eyed reprimand to the general (played by Alan Rickman) who oversaw Powell's strike. "In my opinion," she sniffs, "that was disgraceful. And all done from the safety of your chair." Reflecting that he has directly attended the casualties from five suicide bombings, he intones, "What you witnessed today, with your coffee and biscuits, is terrible. What these men would've done would have been even more terrible. Never tell a soldier that he does not know the cost of war." In response, she crumples into an ugly cry face, looking ashamed. With his dressing-down, Benson invalidates her assessment of the situation and hence her tears; this diminishment serves to intensify the impact of Carrie's when they fall.

Carrie plays the ingénue, who often looks, literally, to her male counterpart for guidance. We learn early on that she's originally from Ohio (the Heartland) and that she only qualified for her position a month ago. She is a foil to Powell's years of experience and perfunctory regard for male authority. The first time Carrie sees Alia on one of the screens she is monitoring, the girl is Hula-Hooping; she zooms in and smiles. Carrie and Steve work in a darkened room, and the glare of the monitor on her dark eyes makes them look perpetually wet. Steve actually tears up before she does, when he finally executes the strike. Prior to launching the Hellfire, however, Steve interrupted the mission by demanding that Powell run a new estimate of collateral damage; Carries responded to this strategy with whispered praise. Like Egan in *Good Kill*, who makes a deliberate error to undermine Langley and protect innocents, Steve has—and exercises—greater agency than his female counterpart. We often see Steve fighting back tears, but he always prevails, as they never spill over. After the strike, once Alia's fate becomes clear, the camera cuts back to Carrie, whose cheeks are already tracked with tears. She disgustedly removes her headset and begins to sob gracefully, unlike Northman. Though she is perhaps expressing what Steve cannot, he demands composure, instructing her to zoom back in so they can confirm that the severed head in the rubble belongs to their intended target, and so she does.

Powell's direct control over and unflinching commitment to the mission at all costs is an icy counterpoint, and her failure to conform to gendered expectations about emotion and judgment only heightens the effect of

Carrie's softness. In turn, Carrie's normative emotional performance further endorses the rightness of American sensibilities. The sequence in which we first meet Powell establishes her as a woman with a typical homelife (snoring husband, lazing dog) but also a garage "situation room" that features a collage of the terrorist network she's been tracking for years. Her reactions are generally muted: a hand that flutters briefly over the mouth, a furrowed brow, a frown, a shake of the head, or an exasperated sigh. While she seems momentarily discomfited by the sight of the girl in the strike area, she quickly composes herself and advises everyone to proceed. She is, for the most part, neutrally watchful, getting most exercised at the possibility that the mission could be compromised, rather than at the notion that it might engender collateral damage. She makes a utilitarian argument about the necessity of the strike, saying that Alia is "just one girl" and that many more civilians will be endangered if the militants are not prevented from carrying out their suicide bombing. In her zeal to prosecute the mission as planned, Powell repeatedly tries to juke the collateral damage estimate for the strike, and in the end goes so far as to order a subordinate to alter his report. In short, Powell is not meant to be likable.[41] But even her questionable ethics are largely exonerated in the film as dedication to the mission.[42]

Neither *Eye in the Sky* nor *Good Kill* offers a substantive diegetic explanation for the women's tears, as if they are doubly self-evident: obvious indices of feminine sensitivity and American conscientiousness. In both films, the women's tears fall too late to make a difference; they cry under orders they must obey, or as missiles drop toward their targets, or once civilians are already dead. In this way, they afford the United States a combination of moral victories and tactical wins that would otherwise be irreconcilable: the expiating pleasure of remorse coupled with the tactical victory of an eliminated threat. This arrangement is reinforced by the structure of command in the film, which ensures that all the Americans are only ever following orders from the British.

Good Kill offers the comfort of a narrative resolution to the Americans' ethical dilemma: Suarez's decisive resignation. In the final scene of that movie, we see Egan driving toward the new home of his estranged wife, presumably with the intent to reconcile, but the film does not address his future as a pilot, drone or otherwise. *Eye in the Sky,* however, ends much more ambivalently, with a commanding officer congratulating the operators and instructing them to go home and rest before returning for another shift. Steve's eyes by now are dry and clear; Carrie tears up again. Presumably, this scene is meant to be a haunting commentary on the entrenchment of drone warfare. But it also places lamentation outside the sphere of political relevance or efficacy. This renders crying (and criers) impotent and simultaneously insulates them from accountability for any consequences. For her part, Colonel Powell—who seems willing, even eager, to assume most of the responsibility for the collateral damage in the strike—does not shed a tear. By contrast, the American operators are clearly troubled by what they have done. In this way, *Eye in the Sky* provides a much more layered account of the psychological consequences of drone warfare for the people who actually carry it out. At the same time, it vindicates them as both capable warriors and compassionate humans.

"SUPERPOWER DISORDER": CRYING OVER EVERYTHING IN *HOMELAND*

By comparison, the crying in *Homeland* is much harder to parse, largely because there is so much of it. The premium cable series has consistently garnered critical acclaim; Obama himself pronounced it a favorite. Its main character, Carrie—another Carrie—Mathison, is a talented CIA analyst (played by Claire Danes) who becomes fixated on the possibility that an American prisoner of war named Nicholas Brody has been turned in captivity and has returned to the United States intending to carry out a terrorist attack. Like most "quality television," *Homeland*'s plot is too complex to summarize concisely, but the story is also largely extraneous to my interest in Carrie's emoting, which does not correspond predictably to developments in the narrative. Lots of things make Carrie cry. And while crying in the films goes largely unremarked, in *Homeland* it, along with Carrie's emotionalism more generally, draws a great deal of attention, both inside and outside the diegetic world of the series.

Homeland is an American adaptation of an Israeli series called *Prisoners of War*, but the character of Carrie is a specifically American addition, as the preceding series had no equivalent.[43] A *New York Times* comparison of the shows summarizes their difference as follows: "*Prisoners of War* is about soldiers, while *Homeland* is about Claire Danes."[44] Of course, the addition of Carrie is only one of many alterations to the adapted series, but she is central to both the narrative of the show and its reception. Something in her character is widely and profoundly resonant. In every year from 2012 to 2016, Danes was nominated for the Outstanding Lead Actress in a Drama Series Emmy, and she won the award in 2012 and 2013.[45]

This suggests that there is some margin of public approval for crying women. For example, when Hillary Clinton's eyes famously went misty in response to a "personal" question from a New Hampshire voter in 2008, many observers suggested that this humanizing moment delivered her surprise primary victory over Obama there.[46] Even if a definitive answer about when and where women's public tears are acceptable remains elusive, it is nonetheless significant that over the course of the series and seemingly in every episode, sometimes multiple times, Carrie cries. Dramatically. When she is vindicated; when she is wrong; when she is in danger; when she is safe; in manic episodes and depressive ones; out of love for Brody, both sadly and happily; when she is institutionalized and when is not; and so on, Carrie cries.

Superficially, Carrie's illness plays on a long history of associating women with mental infirmity. Anat Zanger argues that "Carrie's bipolar disorder enables the series' creators to use 'clinical discourse' . . . in order to repeatedly neutralize her authority and her moral and intellectual superiority."[47] Reading her character metaphorically, Alex Bevan identifies Carrie as the personification of the global war on terrorism, writing that "Carrie's mind and body territorialize geopolitical struggles that elude representability because of their very lack of national, spatial, and material boundaries."[48] Stephen Shapiro theorizes that Carrie's recurrent mental illness undermines a linear and progressive model of history, dramatizing instead the cyclical nature of crisis.[49] In many ways, Carrie conforms to what Lindsay Steenberg and Yvonne Tasker describe as the "familiar construction of a professional woman whose personal trauma underpins her role as a truth seeker and law enforcer," which leaves her "damaged and overinvested in her work," as opposed to focusing on more appropriate pursuits like marriage and motherhood.[50]

The main wrinkle in Carrie's character, besides an apparently uncontrollable sexuality that leads her into a liaison with Brody, is that she has bipolar disorder. In interviews, both Danes and the show's producers have described this condition as a "superpower disorder" that enables her "to gather, interpret, and intuit intelligence in ways that her rational male superiors cannot."[51] More generally, commenting on the popular fascination with women involved in the prosecution of the global war on terrorism, Kelly Oliver observes that all such figures "share, perhaps more subliminally, the problematic notion of women as both offensive and defensive weapons of war, a notion that is symptomatic of age-old fears of the 'mysterious' powers of women, maternity, and female sexuality."[52] Superficially, the nomenclature of a superpower disorder compares Carrie to a superhero, but it also begets a double entendre, alluding to the United States itself as a global superpower and hence attributing to it a special sensitivity. In this way, Carrie's crying suggests that the United States is always on the verge of coming undone under the emotional strain of sustaining a benevolent empire but insists on soldiering on because it is compelled by necessity to do so.

EMPIRE AND THE "UGLY CRY FACE"

Maya, Suarez, Carrie, and Carrie are represented as at least passably good at their jobs and loyal to their countries, if not always to their command structures. To the extent that they are the heroes of their stories, then, they also operate pedagogically to their audiences. But what are they teaching? Many scholars have enumerated the sundry functions that popular culture serves in the global war on terrorism. For example, Stacy Takacs has argued that the resurgence of spy shows after September 11th "helped normalize the state of emergency and promote acceptance of policies of surveillance, detention, interrogation, and interdiction."[53] Mark Andrejevic traces the development of what he calls "securitainment" programming, which acts as an "injunction for the public to take on some of the duties of law enforcement and intelligence organizations."[54] *Zero Dark Thirty, Good Kill, Eye in the Sky,* and *Homeland* bear traces of both these agendas, but their female protagonists also provide a different, related pedagogy on the affective landscape of the war, modeling a solipsistic form of lamentation that smooths over the contradictions inherent in the very notion of "imperial benevolence." However, the most exaggerated forms of this kind of mourning also, if inadvertently, open up an alternative affective possibility.

While tears are typically but not entirely gendered feminine, the "ugly cry face" is almost exclusively the purview of women. Lexically, we owe the phrase to Oprah.[55] Historically and culturally, as Rachel Vorona Cote argues, the phenomenon of "ugly crying" traces its lineage to nineteenth-century discourses of hysteria, as a pathologizing response to seemingly "excessive" female emotiveness. She writes: "Acceptable as either verb or noun, to 'ugly cry' means to weep so fervidly that one's face contorts in ostensibly unattractive ways. An ugly cry summons expressions that render us strange to ourselves and to others, largely because we've relinquished our bodies to wild, emotive energy. We cease to assimilate, to self-curate, and our face mutates into social illegibility."[56] Women's tears are already suspect; tears cried ugly, in their exaggeration and apparent disregard for propriety and aesthetics, elicit far more scorn than sympathy.

And so it is that Carrie's crying has taken on another dimension extrinsic to the plot of the show: Claire Danes's cry face (apparently common to almost all her roles but showcased most vividly and prolongedly in *Homeland*) has become a meme and an object of fixation and mockery. Predictably, the snark directed at Carrie's behavior often veers problematically into criticisms of Danes's "ugliness" when she cries. Danes herself avers that she is untroubled by these comments and indeed, variations on them have followed Danes since the beginning of her career. Such commentaries are obviously sexist. But if we can sift the criticism of Danes's appearance out and develop a critique of her lachrymal hyperbole instead, we might be able to find a new critical, intellectual, and affective vantage on U.S. imperialism. When we roll our eyes at Carrie's crying, turn it into a drinking game, or reproduce her cry face as a Halloween costume, such deliberate affective desynchronization troubles the primacy of the emotion in post-9/11 American culture and politics. However snidely, these strategies engender the potential to refuse the affective imperatives that followed the attacks of September 11th and then helped to license subsequent militarization. At the same time, they belie the speciousness of imperial guilt.

Despite the moral weight that tears carry in the texts I consider here, they are essentially futile and, in both practical and psychic terms, noncathartic. They resolve nothing for the woman who cries them or the nation-state for which she works. Maya cries after the torture is over (and even as it presumably continues offscreen). Suarez guides missiles with tears practically dripping onto the controls. Carrie Gershon weeps on her way home to rest before going back to the same job the next day.[57] And Carrie Mathison's inconsolability suggests that wartime sadness is an abiding condition rather than a transient feeling. Moreover, their tears are unlikely to provoke catharsis in spectators as their crying is rarely framed as pitiable, a disconnect dramatized vividly in the Carrie cry-face memes.

Surely, these women's tears reflect their own helplessness before the forces of history, as well as the perceived victimization and vulnerability of the United States. Indeed, Anker has argued that prevailing discourses about the war on terror conform to the generic pattern of the "women's weepie" orbiting around a lack of agency.[58] Yet rather than valorizing the helplessness of the United States or reshaping it into a justification for military aggression, these noncathartic tears could slide and puddle in the direction of a different kind of critique. In *Ugly Feelings*, Sianne Ngai explores the political potential of "ugly feelings" to index abiding structural problems.[59] Such feelings are "explicitly *amoral* and *non*cathartic, offering no satisfaction of virtue, however oblique, nor any therapeutic or purifying release."[60] The noncathartic tears these dewy-eyed heroines shed can be read, then, as imperial confessions and as signals of the pointlessness of crying over imperialism and by extension the meaninglessness of imperial remorse.

To make an imperial cry face is to lament the besmirching of American exceptionalism. On the other hand, to read those cry faces askance is to take a critical distance from the sentimentality that accompanies contemporary U.S. militarism, which is in turn deployed to mask its imperial ambition. And to detect an ugliness in the imperial cry face is to refuse a flimsy ethic in which contrition offsets bodily, even lethal, harm to others. The tears these women cry point to both the inevitability and the solipsistic pointlessness of being saddened by war. They also reveal the ease with which such hyperbolic emoting deflects attention off the targets of their violence.

Ultimately, even as these sentimental dramas unfold in unlikely places— unmanned aerial vehicle control rooms, the hold of a military cargo plane, secure CIA locations—they also suggest a need to reconsider the affective dimensions of anti-imperialist critique so often saturated in remorse and framed as a national apology. Obviously, I am not advocating for an unapologetic imperialism but rather suggesting that apology is beside the point. These tears, operating as a metonym for a larger national hand-wringing, illuminate the limits of imperial grief. After all, none of these women seem to be manipulative or disingenuous criers; even the excess of Carrie's emotional life appears sincere. But this kind of sincerity is scarcely consequential. Instead, these crying state operatives have the potential to pose a troubling challenge to the power of grieving even as their tears ostensibly serve to lubricate the machinery of empire.

NOTES

1. Eddie Hamilton, "It's OK," 2001, Library of Congress American Folklife Center, AFC 2001/015: gr015d, www.loc.gov/item/afc911000239/.

2. For a consideration of the political power of affect, see Deborah Gould, "On Affect and Protest," in *Political Emotions,* ed. Janet Staiger and Ann Reynolds (New

York: Routledge, 2010), 18–44. For a more theoretical account, see John Protevi, *Political Affect: Connecting the Social and the Somatic* (Minneapolis: University of Minnesota Press, 2009).

3. Marita Sturken, "Feeling the Nation, Mining the Archive," *Communication and Critical/Cultural Studies* 9 (December 2012): 353–364, quot. 357.

4. Judith Butler, *Antigone's Claim: Kinship between Life and Death* (New York: Columbia University Press, 2002); and Butler, *Frames of War: When Is Life Grievable?* (London: Verso, 2010).

5. Deborah Cohler, "Keeping the Homefront Burning: Renegotiating Gender and Sexuality in US Mass Media after September 11," *Feminist Media Studies* 6, no. 3 (2006): 245–261, quot. 245.

6. Thanks to Dave Kieran for helping me think through possible periodizations of the war on terror.

7. On the vexed politics of hope, see Susan McManus, "Hope, Fear, and the Politics of Affective Agency," *Theory and Event* 14, no. 4 (2011), https://muse.jhu.edu/article/459120.

8. Sturken, *Feeling the Nation*, 424.

9. Tom Lutz, *Crying: The Natural and Cultural History of Tears* (New York: W. W. Norton, 1999), 19.

10. Ann Cvetkovich, *Depression: A Public Feeling* (Durham, NC: Duke University Press, 2012), 11–12. She also contends that most theorizations of these systems are too abstract to capture their emotional consequences for individuals. Alternatively, Sara Ahmed charts the ways that happiness functions as an affective endorsement of various forms of subjugation in *The Promise of Happiness* (Durham, NC: Duke University Press, 2010). See also Lauren Berlant, *Cruel Optimism* (Durham, NC: Duke University Press, 2011).

11. Lutz, *Crying: The Natural History*, 64. Of course, when women don't cry in situations where they apparently should, they are regarded as unfeeling at best, suspect at worst. For example, many people have noted with curiosity that Mariane Pearl (the widow of Daniel Pearl, a journalist who was beheaded by Pakistani militants in early 2002) does not cry in public. The filmic adaptation of her story, *A Mighty Heart,* reflects this.

12. Elisabeth R. Anker, *Orgies of Feeling: Melodrama and the Politics of Freedom* (Durham, NC: Duke University Press, 2014), 3.

13. Ibid., 31.

14. Laleh Khalili, *Time in the Shadows: Confinement in Counterinsurgencies* (Stanford, CA: Stanford University Press, 2013), 45.

15. Derek Gregory, "'The Rush to the Intimate: Counterinsurgency and the Cultural Turn in Late Modern War," *Geographical Imaginations,* 2012, https://geographicalimaginations.files.wordpress.com/2012/07/gregory-rush-to-the-intimate-full.pdf, 40.

16. Lutz, *Crying,* 185.

17. Anne McClintock, *Imperial Leather: Race, Gender, and Sexuality in the Colonial Contest* (New York: Routledge, 1995), 6.

18. Bruce Tucker and Sia Triantafyllos, "Lynndie England, Abu Ghraib, and the New Imperialism," *Canadian Review of American Studies* 38, no. 1 (2008): 83–100, 91.

19. Donald Pease describes American exceptionalism as a "fantasy that permitted U.S. citizens to achieve their national identity through the disavowal of U.S. imperialism." Pease, *The New American Exceptionalism* (Minneapolis: University of Minnesota Press, 2009), 20.

20. It is significant, of course, that Bigelow was the first—and so far only—woman to win an Academy Award for Best Director, for *The Hurt Locker* in 2010, widely regarded as the definitive filmic representation of combat in the global war on terrorism.

21. For a character-by-character comparison between the film and the actual personnel involved, see David Haglund, Aisha Harris, and Forrest Wickman, "Who Are the People in *Zero Dark Thirty*?," *Slate,* January 14, 2013, www.slate.com/blogs/browbeat/2013/01/14/zero_dark_thirty_fact_vs_fiction_who_are_the_real_life_inspirations_for.html.

22. Timothy Melley, "Covert Spectacles and the Contradictions of the Democratic Security State," *Storyworlds: A Journal of Narrative Studies* 6 (Summer 2014): 61–82, quot. 71.

23. David Bromwich, "Torture and Zero Dark Thirty," *Huffington Post,* January 19, 2013, www.huffingtonpost.com/david-bromwich/torture-zero-dark-thirty_b_2512767.html.

24. Jane Mayer, "Zero Conscience in 'Zero Dark Thirty,'" *New Yorker Blog,* December 14, 2012, www.newyorker.com/online/blogs/newsdesk/2012/12/torture-in-kathryn-bigelowszero-dark-thirty.html.

25. Amy Zegart, "Langley Goes Hollywood," *Foreign Policy,* September 11, 2012, www.foreignpolicy.com/articles/2012/09/11/langley_goes_hollywood.

26. Melley, *Covert Spectacles,* 65.

27. Judicial Watch, "Judicial Watch Obtains Stack of 'Overlooked' CIA Records Detailing Meetings with bin Laden Filmmakers," *Judicial Watch,* August 28, 2012, www.judicialwatch.org/press-room/press-releases/judicial-watch-obtains-4-to-5-inch-stack-of-overlooked-cia-records-detailing-meetings-with-bin-laden-film makers/.

28. Peter J. Hutchings explores the correspondence between a legal willingness to entertain torture and widespread acceptance of media depictions of torture as entertainment. Peter J. Hutchings, "Entertaining Torture, Embodying Law," *Cultural Studies* 27 (January 2013): 49–71.

29. Bromwich, "Torture and Zero Dark Thirty."

30. Glenn Greenwald, "Zero Dark Thirty: CIA Hagiography, Pernicious Propaganda," *Guardian,* December 14, 2012, www.guardian.co.uk/commentis-free/2012/dec/14/zero-dark-thirty-cia-propaganda. On this point, see also Michael Richardson, *Gestures of Testimony: Torture, Trauma, and Affect in Literature* (London: Bloomsbury Academic, 2017), chap. 3.

31. As quoted in Maureen Dowd, "A Tale of Two Women," *New York Times,* December 11, 2012, www.nytimes.com/2012/12/12/opinion/dowd-a-tale-of-two-women.html.

32. Phil Bronstein, "The Man Who Killed Osama Bin Laden . . . Is Screwed," *Esquire,* February 11, 2013, www.esquire.com/news-politics/a26351/man-who-shot -osama-bin-laden-0313/.

33. In my assessment, this is a confused and spectacularized effort to visualize the combat stress of drone operators and so to humanize them, an ethically and ideologically vexed recuperation that I hope to explore in more detail.

34. Matthew Rosenberg and Dave Phillips, "All Combat Roles Now Open to Women, Defense Secretary Says," *New York Times,* December 3, 2015, www.nytimes. com/2015/12/04/us/politics/combat-military-women-ash-carter.html.

35. With her seemingly unassailable virtue and courage, Lynch embodies the ideal American soldier. Simultaneously, however, by her incapacity and need for rescue, she reinvigorates doubts about women's fitness for combat. By contrast, much of the discourse about the first two, and far less famous, women to finish Army Ranger School in August 2015 emphasized their refusal to differentiate themselves from their male counterparts. See, for example, Mary Jordan and Dan Lamothe, "How Did These Two Women Become the First to Complete Army Ranger School?" *Washington Post,* August 19, 2015, www.washingtonpost.com /world/national-security/how-did-these-two-women-become-the-first-to-complete -army-rangers-school/2015/08/19/a745c962-46af-11e5-8ab4-c73967a143d3_story .html.

36. Peter M. Asaro, "The Labor of Surveillance and Bureaucratized Killing: New Subjectivities of Military Drone Operators," *Social Semiotics* 23, no. 2 (2013): 196–224, quot. 198.

37. Jonathan Beller, "Pathologistics of Attention," *Discourse* 35 (Winter 2013): 46–71, quot. 63. He enumerates them as follows: "asymmetrically incorporated pilots (who will go home to kiss their kids after pulling the trigger on someone else's family half a universe away), along with their entire staff of statisticians, researchers, and commanders who serve both machine and country."

38. The film's festival premier occurred in late 2015, and it was widely released in the United States in the spring of 2016.

39. Bleecker Street, "Eye in the Sky," 2015, www.bleeckerstreetmedia.com /eyeinthesky, accessed June 17, 2017.

40. See, for example, Ann Hornaday, "'Eye in the Sky' Is a 'Fail Safe' for the Drone Generation," *Washington Post,* March 17, 2016, www.washingtonpost.com /goingoutguide/movies/eye-in-the-sky-is-a-fail-safe-for-the-drone-generation/2016 /03/17/16257aa6-ead1-11e5-a6f3-21ccdbc5f74e_story.html; Peter Travers, review of *Eye in the Sky,* directed by Gavin Hood, *Rolling Stone,* March 9, 2016, www.rolling stone.com/movies/reviews/eye-in-the-sky-20160309.

41. Stephen Holden, "'Eye in the Sky': Drone Precision vs. Human Failings," review of *Eye in the Sky,* directed by Gavin Hood, *New York Times,* March 10, 2016, www.nytimes.com/2016/03/11/movies/review-eye-in-the-sky-drone-precision-vs -human-failings.html.

42. Her single-mindedness would signify differently—and perhaps more positively—if her character were male.

43. Anat Zanger, "Between *Homeland* and *Prisoners of War:* Remaking Terror," *Continuum: Journal of Media and Cultural Studies* 29, no. 5 (2015): 731–742. Zanger suggests, however, that both shows evince similar gender politics, situating their female characters as sites of instability and sexualized danger.

44. Mike Hale, "A 'Homeland' in Its Original Packaging, Subtitles, Too," *New York Times,* July 24, 2012, www.nytimes.com/2012/07/25/arts/television/prisoners -of-war-the-israeli-original-of-homeland.html.

45. Television Academy, "Homeland," 2016, www.emmys.com/shows/home land, accessed October 22, 2016.

46. Michael Kruse, "The Woman Who Made Hillary Cry," *Politico,* April 20, 2015, www.politico.com/story/2015/04/the-woman-who-made-hillary-clinton -cry-117171; Suzanne Goldenberg and Richard Adams, "The Tears over Coffee That Turned round the Poll," *Guardian,* January 10, 2008, www.theguardian.com /world/2008/jan/10/hillaryclinton.uselections20082.

47. Zanger, *Between Homeland,* 736.

48. Alex Bevan, "The National Body, Women, and Mental Health in *Homeland,*" *Cinema Journal* 54 (Summer 2015): 145–151, quot. 145.

49. Stephen Shapiro, "*Homeland*'s Crisis of Middle-Class Transformation," *Cinema Journal* 54 (Summer 2015): 152–158, quot. 154. Shapiro argues that this nonlinear model is visualized in the board that Carrie constructs on a wall of her house during a severe manic episode, mapping out the networked relationships between various actors and terrorist attacks.

50. Lindsay Steenberg and Yvonne Tasker, "'Pledge Allegiance': Gendered Surveillance, Crime Television, and *Homeland,*" *Cinema Journal* 54 (Summer 2015): 132–138, quot. 132–133.

51. James Castonguay, "Fictions of Terror: Complexity, Complicity, and Insecurity in *Homeland,*" *Cinema Journal* 54 (Summer 2015): 139–145, quot. 140–141.

52. Kelly Oliver, "Women: The Secret Weapon of Modern Warfare?," *Hypatia* 23 (Spring 2008): 1–16, quot. 1.

53. Stacy Takacs, *Terrorism TV: Popular Entertainment in Post-9/11 America* (Lawrence: University of Kansas Press, 2012), 64.

54. Mark Andrejevic, "'Securitainment' in the Post-9/11 Era," *Continuum: Journal of Media and Cultural Studies* 25 (April 2011): 165–175, quot. 165–166.

55. Merriam-Webster Online, "The Origin of the 'Ugly Cry,'" *Words We're Watching,* 2016, www.merriam-webster.com/words-at-play/ugly-cry-origin -meaning.

56. Rachel Vorona Cote, "The Agony and the Ecstasy of the Ugly Cry," *New Republic,* April 1, 2016, https://newrepublic.com/article/132289/agony-ecstasy-ugly -cry.

57. Asaro argues that this powerlessness is built into the role of the drone operator. He writes, "While a soldier on the ground can use his or her hands to administer medical aid, or push a stalled car, as easily as they can hold a weapon, the drone operator can only observe and choose to kill or not kill. Within this limited range

of action, meaningful social interaction is fundamentally reduced to sorting the world into friends, enemies, and potential enemies." Asaro, *Labor of Surveillance,* 221.

58. Anker, *Orgies of Feeling,* 242ff.

59. Sianne Ngai, *Ugly Feelings* (Cambridge, MA: Harvard University Press, 2005), 3.

60. Ibid., 6.

TWO

"Prowarrior, But Not Necessarily Prowar"

AMERICAN SNIPER, SHEEP, AND SHEEPDOGS

Edwin A. Martini

DURING AN EARLY SCENE IN THE 2014 film *American Sniper*, a father tells his two young sons:

> There are three types of people in this world: sheep, wolves, and sheepdogs. Some people prefer to believe that evil doesn't exist in the world, and if it ever darkened their doorstep, they wouldn't know how to protect themselves. Those are the sheep. Then you've got predators who use violence to prey on the weak. They're the wolves. And then there are those blessed with the gift of aggression, an overpowering need to protect the flock. These men are the rare breed who live to confront the wolf. They are the sheepdog.[1]

The oldest of those two sons goes on to become famed U.S. Navy SEAL Chris Kyle, arguably the most famous sniper in U.S. military history. The film portrays Kyle's evolution as a sheepdog as he enlisted in the military after the attacks on overseas U.S. embassies in 1998 and headed to Iraq in 2003 to protect other soldiers and ostensibly the United States itself from the threat of so many wolves.

Seeking to contextualize and to justify the 160 confirmed "kills" Kyle registered during four tours of duty in Iraq, the film also aims to justify and rationalize the American imperial project in the post-9/11 world. In doing so, it captures the very essence of U.S. imperial benevolence, portraying soldiers, marines, SEALs, and the United States itself as the sheepdogs: a global force for good, protecting itself and humanity as a whole from savage barbarians determined to destroy it. It also shows, to a limited degree, the costs of U.S. wars to the soldiers who fight them—and their families. Grossing over $500 million at the worldwide box office and garnering critical acclaim and multiple Oscar nominations, the film has taken its place among the most important popular culture representations of the U.S. global war on terrorism

(GWOT). The film, based on Kyle's memoir of the same name and cowritten with Jim DeFelice, was controversial from the outset, in large part because of its representation of Iraqi and other Middle Eastern figures, who are framed solely in relation to the crosshairs of Kyle's rifle and reduced simply to "evil" and "savages."[2] As the debate over the film played out during 2015, it often served as a proxy for political and ideological arguments about the U.S. war in Iraq and the effects of the war on U.S. soldiers.

This chapter explores the reception of the film and the book on which it is based to examine how American empire—and the inevitable violence it shapes and is shaped by—permeates American culture. In a steadily growing public discourse over Kyle's story, the terms of debate quickly came to mirror those of the larger debate about the American war in Iraq. Generally, critics of the book and the film focused on the texts' potentially offensive representations of race, religion, and ethnicity, while defenders of Kyle and his story praised the "honesty" of the book and the film's ability to be "prowarrior" but not necessarily "prowar." Still, despite claims of being prowarrior, neither the book nor the film nor any significant voices in the public debates about the film followed through on the possibility of exploring ways in which both the wolves (Iraqi/Muslim/fanatic/terrorist/the Other) and the sheepdogs/soldiers are mutually constitutive subject positions created and maintained through long, complicated, racialized, and gendered imperial histories, simply reframed more recently through contemporary wars and cultures. The reception of the film—and what it reflects about Kyle and, by proxy, so many other soldiers and veterans—thus raises questions about the possibility of creating spaces and representations by which these subjectivities can be dissected and explored together, rather than in isolation, with the hopes of dismantling the more simplistic, Manichaean worldview that supports and reinforces the contemporary American empire. The inability to move beyond simplistic terms of debate, I argue, results in the status quo for the majority of mainstream American popular culture since 9/11: uncritical and shallow rhetorical support for the sheepdog/warriors protecting the outposts of American empire without challenging the effects of the war on those most directly affected by it on all sides.

AMERICAN BOOK

The story of *American Sniper* really begins with the release of Kyle's memoir in 2012. Having made a name for himself as a sniper in Iraq, Kyle had already begun to garner some fame prior to leaving the navy. As his wife,

Taya Kyle, stated in her own memoir, *American Wife* (also cowritten with Jim DeFelice and also published by HarperCollins), Kyle "had heard that people were interested in writing about him" but had been "adamantly opposed" to the idea.[3] However, after a senior editor at HarperCollins reached out to him in the summer of 2010 and introduced him to DeFelice, Kyle agreed. Throughout the remainder of 2010 and into 2011, Kyle "told" his story to DeFelice over multiple conversations. DeFelice transposed those stories into a personable narrative that sought to maintain Kyle's voice and the conversational style in which he had told it, including the raw, frank, and arguably racist statements about the nature of the enemy he encountered in Iraq.

The book traces Kyle's upbringing in Texas, his dreams of being a cowboy, and his actual work as a rancher and as a rodeo bull rider. It details his romance and up-and-down marriage with Taya. It describes in detail his indoctrination and training as a SEAL and a sniper, his disappointment at not being called into combat after the attacks of September 11, and his exhilaration at finally being able to go to war in Iraq. The vast majority of the book, however, like the film, focuses on Kyle's four tours in Iraq: the role of a SEAL sniper; the difficult battles of Nasiriya, Fallujah, and Ramadi; and the challenges of urban counterinsurgency combat operations. Some of the most powerful passages in the book provide vivid, harrowing accounts of Kyle accompanying marine and army units as they clear houses in Iraqi cities.

Central to his identity as a Texan, a SEAL, and a sniper, he also writes at length about weaponry. Having been raised in a culture that embraced guns, Kyle had long been interested in firearms. Throughout the book, Kyle offers in-depth descriptions of the different weapons he used and, more jarringly, of the joy he took in firing and killing with them. Early in the book, he describes the "fun" of shooting "the big machine gun."[4] Later, learning about a marine operation he would be supporting, Kyle writes, "Man, this is going to be good, I thought. We are going to kill massive amounts of bad guys. And I'm going to be in the middle of it."[5] Encountering a group of insurgents using beach balls to keep themselves afloat while traversing a river, Kyle called to his buddies, telling them, "Y'all gotta see this," as he began shooting the beach balls, one by one. The majority drowned while the rest were put "out of their misery" by the marines. "It was kind of fun," he writes. "Hell, it was a *lot* of fun."[6] On a particularly productive day for his kill count, outside the insurgent stronghold of Sadr City, Kyle describes the spoils of this "target rich environment" in a manner more befitting a video game or a carnival shooting arcade: "It got to the point where I had so many kills that I stepped back to let the other guys have a few." After killing a final three insurgents, he "rolled over and said to one of the officers who'd come over, 'You want a turn?'"[7]

So closely was Kyle's identity tied to guns that after his final tour he came to embrace firearms as a form of rehabilitation. Similar to the types of hunting and shooting experiences described in David Kieran's essay in this volume, Kyle's belief in the redemptive power of guns led him to work with fellow veterans, some of whom were dealing with significant posttraumatic stress disorder (PTSD). In these insulated—and isolated—experiences, Kyle became part of a recovery narrative that focused largely on individual experiences not to be shared with larger communities. In the end, the guns he so valorized did not save Kyle. In fact, they helped lead to his demise, when a troubled fellow Iraq veteran named Eddie Ray Routh killed Kyle and his friend Chad Littlefield at a Texas gun range.[8]

Along with the accounts of the enjoyment he derived from shooting at and killing insurgents or, as he more often calls them, "bad guys," the most troubling aspects of the book are the descriptions he offers of the "bad guys" themselves. Kyle makes it clear from the outset that his motivation in serving in the military and fighting in Iraq was first to protect and defend his country and second, once engaged overseas, to protect his comrades in arms. To the extent that he gives any consideration to the identities, backgrounds, or motivations of those at whom he was shooting, Kyle repeatedly seeks to reduce them morally and racially to "evil" and "savages," respectively. Consistently, "they" are the wolves, and he is the sheepdog. In these constructions, Kyle's memoir echoes a range of benevolent, imperial U.S. cultural narratives, from Vietnam War combat stories to Cold War rationalizations for fighting communism in the developing world to Bush-era foreign policy justifications.

In the spirit of other combat narratives, Kyle's tale of brotherhood begins with basic training and continues through his SEAL training as he arrived in Iraq with a very tight-knit group of SEALs. Between bar fights, sexualized homosocial hazing, and his buddies' presence at his wedding ceremony shortly before deployment, Kyle constructs a band-of-brothers narrative that carries easily into combat sequences, as well as into his postwar period, during which he dedicated himself to working with other veterans, particularly those injured and traumatized by their service.

Kyle clearly saw this as an extension of his service, his commitment to his brother SEALs, and his sheepdog mentality—he wanted to protect at home as he had abroad.

Taya would later echo these same sentiments in her memoir. She writes that Kyle's tactical shift from rooftop sniping to ground-level house clearing with the marines was driven, even against orders from his superior officers, by his belief that it was the best way to protect them: "That was pure Chris. Part of the reason was that he wanted to be where the action was. And another part was that he was a naturally-born protector. Just as he'd stood up for kids in the high school cafeteria, he was sticking up for Marines and Iraqis now—though with higher stakes. He felt he could do more to protect them if he was going into the houses with them."[9]

Taya's memoir, far more than Kyle's, focuses on the home front challenges the war posed and the effects that repeated tours had on Kyle and his family. That story line, however, would become much more central in the film and would be picked up by some reviewers as a point of praise for the movie. Kyle as the sheepdog clearly saw the protection of his family, his nation, and his brothers-in-arms as inextricably linked, reinforcing a particularly gendered form of nation and empire that relies on an external threat to justify violence. The idea that he was "sticking up" for Iraqis, however, is another matter.

Despite Taya's assertions, there is no evidence in Kyle's memoir that he gave much thought to his role in protecting Iraqi civilians and quite a bit of evidence to the contrary. Perhaps she was rationalizing his actions or attempting to distract or distance herself from some of his coarser language, but in fact Kyle's emphasis on fighting for his own becomes particularly clear when he juxtaposes his motivations with the alternative of fighting to protect Iraq or Iraqis. Reflecting on the failures of political reconciliation in Iraq, Kyle writes that he "never really believed the Iraqis would turn the country into a truly functioning democracy," noting that he "didn't risk his life to bring democracy to Iraq. I risked my life for my buddies, to protect my friends and fellow countrymen. I went to war for *my* country, not Iraq. My country sent me out there so that bullshit wouldn't make its way back to our shores. I never once fought for the Iraqis. I could give a flying fuck about them."[10]

This sentiment becomes clear to the reader when Kyle turns his attention to the enemies he faced—and killed—in Iraq. Under the chapter subheading of "Evil," he writes:

I had never known that much about Islam. Raised as a Christian, obviously I knew there had been religious conflicts for centuries. I knew about the Crusades, and I knew that there had been fighting and atrocities forever. But I also knew that Christianity had evolved from the Middle Ages. We don't kill people because they're a different religion.

The people we were fighting in Iraq, after Saddam's army fled or was defeated, were fanatics. They hated us because we weren't Muslim. They wanted to kill us, even though we'd just booted out their dictator, because we practiced a different religion than they did.

Isn't religion supposed to teach tolerance?[11]

Later in that same section, Kyle continues to describe the "fanatical" enemy. "The fanatics we fought valued nothing but their twisted interpretation of religion," he writes. "And half the time they just *claimed* they valued their religion—most didn't even pray. Quite a number were drugged up so they could fight us. Most of the insurgents were cowards."[12]

At one point, Kyle was briefly investigated for one of his kills after, in his telling, the deceased's weapon was removed from the scene after Kyle killed him. The wife of the dead soldier told the army investigator that her husband "was on his way to the mosque carrying a Koran."[13] This version of the story would certainly support Kyle's theory about insurgents hiding behind the cloak of religion, but his frustrated response to investigators contradicts his own stated belief in "tolerance" and his assertion that U.S. forces "don't kill people because they're another religion." "I don't shoot people with Korans," he told them. "I'd like to, but I don't. I guess I was a little hot."[14] That moment of potential reckoning by Kyle, however, is short-lived; his embrace of his Christian crusader identity only strengthens throughout his story.

On a trip home between tours, Kyle added a new set of tattoos, the explanation for which further belies the absence of a religious or racialized construction of his "kills." "One was a trident," he states, the symbol of the SEALs. The other was a crusader cross, directly appropriating the imagery from the very Crusades Kyle had previously wished to banish as a relic of Christianity's past. Now, however: "I wanted everyone to know I was a Christian. I had it put in red, for blood. I hated the damn savages I'd been fighting. I always will. They've taken so much from me."[15] Kyle makes no effort to explain or contextualize this transformation, leaving it to stand alone as a major contradiction.

Taya herself would later defend her husband against accusations of hatred toward Muslims or Iraqis: "Every one of those kills represented one, two, three, twelve—countless lives that were protected. And given that more Iraqi citizens were killed by terrorists than by American soldiers during the conflict, most of the people who owe him their lives are Iraqi, and Muslim. So when he's called a racist or anti-Islam, I just shake my head."[16]

Certainly, Chris hated the terrorists and insurgents he was fighting, she adds, citing the story of an interpreter he later helped immigrate to the United States. "But that hatred didn't translate into blind rage against all Muslims."[17] As she had earlier, Taya seeks to rationalize Chris's actions, adding a degree of nuance that simply does not exist in his writing while ignoring evidence that would call her conclusions into question.

In yet another echo of Vietnam War memoirs, Kyle's descriptions even of his ostensible allies in the Iraqi armed forces, often referred to as *jundis,* tend toward the essentialized—just as U.S. combat veterans in Vietnam would mock and ridicule the Army of the Republic of Vietnam forces as unwilling or unable to fight. "A lot of jundis were just lazy," he claims. "You'd tell them to do something, and they'd reply *'Inshallah.'* Some people translate that as 'God Willing.' What it really means is 'ain't gonna happen.'" The jundis, Kyle writes, were only serving "for a paycheck" or, in some cases, "for their tribe." "They were so backward in terms of their education and technology that for Americans it often felt like being in the Stone Age."[18] As is shown so often throughout the book, Kyle is more than comfortable describing Iraqis as an essentialized Other whose actions can be explained solely by their racial, ethnic, or religious background.

Even the families of his victims are not spared from this type of superior judgment from the crusading American warrior. Kyle describes the response to a series of killings in Ramadi: "I'd see the families of insurgents display their grief, tear off clothes, then rub the blood on themselves. *If you loved them, I thought, you should have kept them away from the war. You should have kept them from joining the insurgency. You let them try to kill us—what did you think would happen to them?"*[19]

The passage is eerily reminiscent of the My Lai Massacre-inspired scene in Oliver Stone's Vietnam film *Platoon* (1986), in which the main character, Chris, played by Charlie Sheen, narrates just prior to a horrific attack on civilians that "if the village had known we were coming that day, they would have ran." This begs the question of where villagers would have run in order to escape the war that had completely engulfed their country. The same could certainly be said for the families of Ramadi. After this passage, almost as if sensing the limits of this argument—how could they possibly keep anyone from the war—Kyle makes a rare attempt at empathy. "It's cruel, maybe," he mused, "but it's hard to sympathize with grief when it's over someone who just tried to kill you. Maybe they'd have felt the same way about us."[20]

Perhaps. But considering the larger construction of all Iraqis in the story as "lazy," "backwards," and above all "savage," Kyle's short-lived attempt at empathy rings hollow. More to the point, his reliance upon a racialized, savage Other, the proverbial wolves, remains critical to his own construction as the sheepdog and to justify the violence he and others committed in defense of the flock. While Taya's book makes a concerted effort to portray Kyle as a defender of noncombatant Iraqis, Kyle for the most part ignores them altogether. Like the Manichaean logic of the Bush administration's policies, Kyle's justifications consistently revolve around the assumption that "the bad guys" are always trying to kill "us," eliding the imperial ambitions of the invader and occupier and the gendered and racialized assumptions on which those ambitions were being built.

At the time of its release, the book was an immediate success. Kyle was besieged at bookstores on a nationwide tour, with twelve hundred people reportedly showing up at his first signing.[21] *American Sniper* debuted at number two and quickly rose to number one on the *New York Times* bestseller list. It stayed on the *Times* list for twenty-two weeks as a hardcover before entering the paperback charts at number three upon its release in February 2013, just days before fellow veteran Routh killed Kyle at the gun range.[22]

Reviewers of various stripes noted the raw descriptions of Kyle's kills and his coarse language regarding those whom he killed, and the book was widely praised for its "honesty" and "straightforwardness" across the political spectrum. The conservative *Washington Times* described Kyle's portrayals of the insurgents as "especially revealing" but did not quote the more troubling or offensive terms, focusing more on his "valor" in battle and the critical tactical role played by snipers.[23] The *Los Angeles Times* called Kyle's view "blunt, and simplistic" and "unpossessed by political correctness," noting that "for those who like their American military personnel to be diffident and dutifully respectful of their enemies, this book is not for them." It suggested that the most powerful aspect of the book was the questions it raised about the effects of war on soldiers, spouses, and families.[24] Similarly, the *Huffington Post* wrote, "At times politically incorrect or even crude, Kyle's writing seems relentlessly honest. Kyle is not an intellectual, although the book will make readers think—about the enormous costs of war and what Iraq has meant for American soldiers and their families."[25] If the book, despite its provocative content, largely avoided debates over race, religion, and "political correctness," the film would immediately catapult those issues into the center of the debate over *American Sniper.*

AMERICAN FILM

There was no real public debate about *American Sniper,* the book. As Kyle became a celebrity, appearing regularly on television, radio, and various social media outlets, and as that celebrity continued to fuel book sales, there was little debate about Kyle, about his descriptions of enemies, or about anything potentially controversial. Even a minor public tiff and a libel suit from former SEAL, former governor of Minnesota, and critic of the Iraq War Jesse Ventura about whether or not Kyle had knocked out Ventura in a bar fight was relatively minor news and did little if anything to detract from Kyle or his book. The film, starring Bradley Cooper and directed and produced by Clint Eastwood, changed all that.

I propose that the debate about the film stemmed from several sources. First, quite simply by nature of the medium, films in U.S. culture tend to generate far more public discussion and media coverage than most books, so controversies that may have arisen from the book were simply given a wider audience. Second, Eastwood's film reframes Kyle's story in multiple ways, interjecting a degree of nuance and subtlety that actually makes the film more difficult to categorize and label than the book. As multiple publics attempted to respond to and negotiate the meaning of the film, it thus operated much more as a blank screen onto which various constituencies could project their own histories and politics. Finally, the film was released nationwide in early 2015, into a U.S. cultural space noticeably transformed from 2012, particularly by the politics of race and religion. From major protests over police shootings in Ferguson, Missouri; Cleveland, Ohio; and elsewhere to campus-based protests at colleges and universities throughout the country, including those over "trigger warnings" and the desire of some students to be shielded from potentially offensive and traumatic material, the film *American Sniper* emerged in a notably different context that clearly shaped its reception. In the final analysis, however, the debate failed to move beyond predictable ideological lines and went without any significant discussion of American empire or American innocence. In that, it reflects a particular cultural logic of empire, one that rejects nuance and subtlety and instead relies on binary constructions of heroes and enemies, of insiders and outsiders, and ultimately, of sheep and wolves.

Released in December 2014, just in time to qualify for the following year's Academy Awards, *American Sniper* proved to be a remarkable box office success. It earned over $100 million in its nationwide opening weekend, breaking multiple records. The film garnered several Oscar nominations, including Best Picture and Best Actor, although it won only the award for Best Achievement in Sound Editing. Reports at the time suggested that a major part of the film's initial box office success was driven by its appeal to audiences not normally attracted to standard Hollywood fare. The studio behind the project, Warner Bros., made a point of advertising the film widely on politically conservative outlets, including Fox News, military blogs, and *Soldier of Fortune* magazine. The studio also offered multiple special screenings for veterans' groups and active military personnel, including at twenty military bases around the world. During its opening weekend, the film far outperformed expectations and averages in areas across the South and Southwest United States, which skew more conservative and have higher proportions of active military personnel and veterans. Most of these top-performing markets were located near military installations, in cities such as San Antonio, Houston, and Richmond, Texas; Moore and Oklahoma City, Oklahoma; and Albuquerque, New Mexico. Conversely, the film dramatically underperformed in areas that are normally strong for traditional Hollywood blockbusters, including Northern California, the Pacific Northwest, and the Northeast.[26] The fact that Eastwood is a well-known Republican, having made a prime-time appearance (albeit an odd one, speaking to an empty chair while "conversing" with an imaginary President Obama) at the 2012 Republican National Convention, likely did not hurt with many of these constituencies.

Warner Bros. also made efforts to reach the female audience not normally seen as a target market for combat films. It framed trailers for the film without loud, action-filled sequences, focusing instead on moral dilemmas, children, and family and reaching out to military spouses and their families as part of its base-screening program. "To talk about this film as just a war film really would have been to sell it short," said Sue Kroll, president of worldwide marketing and international distribution for Warner Bros. "This is a portrayal of a man who's torn between his family and his sense of duty. This is a relationship movie with a backdrop to war."[27] In the initial response to *American Sniper,* many critics used this as a jumping-off point, but the overall reception of the film among critics was decidedly mixed—far more so than the book.

At one end of the continuum was journalist and war correspondent Chris Hedges, writing for the website *TruthDig* in a piece provocatively titled "Killing Ragheads for Jesus": "*American Sniper* lionizes the most despicable aspects of U.S. society—the gun culture, the blind adoration of the military, the belief that we have an innate right as a 'Christian' nation to exterminate the 'lesser breeds' of the earth, a grotesque hypermasculinity that banishes compassion and pity, a denial of inconvenient facts and historical truth, and a belittling of critical thinking and artistic expression."[28]

And that was just the first sentence. Along the same lines, David Edelstein, writing in *New York* magazine, specifically called out Eastwood's Republican credentials, noting that "the people Kyle shoots always represent a 'savage, despicable evil,' and the physical and mental cost to other Americans just comes with the territory. It's a Republican platform movie."[29] Conservative publications did indeed fairly uniformly praise the movie, singling out Eastwood and Cooper in particular for their work. However, they were careful in parsing out the tensions in the film, tending to label it "prowarrior" but not necessarily "prowar." Conservative commentator Sean Hannity, who regularly featured discussions of the film and Kyle on his television show, called it the best film of the year.[30] *National Review* argued that the film was "very pro-soldier, but it's not pro-war, or at least not unambiguously pro-war."[31] The *Wall Street Journal* celebrated the film's "celebration of courage and patriotism" but also its eye for "tragedy, and the toll the war takes on the warrior."[32] The *Washington Times* went so far as to note that "the film's narrow perspective, centered on Kyle, is both the best and worst thing about it. 'American Sniper' may be a much-needed tribute to the sacrifice of American soldiers, but it's lacking context. Few Iraqis here are seen as anything but the enemy." The piece ended by calling for "a companion" film to show "the other side" of the war, as Eastwood had done with *Flags of our Fathers* and *Letters from Iwo Jima*.[33] Eastwood himself said that the film is "at its heart 'anti-war,' because it shows 'the fact of what [war] does to the family and the people who have to go back into civilian life like Chris Kyle did.'"[34]

Others, however, focused more directly on the ambivalence of the film, particularly in its departures from the book. *Christian Century* mentioned the movie's "unabashed patriotism" but noted that the film raises a number of questions about the war, its effects on soldiers, and the role of America as sheepdog, even if Kyle himself does not.[35] *Commonweal* was less generous, arguing that these "antiwar moments," the same described by *Christian Century* and others, "are allowed into the film the way a liberal is allowed onto Fox News: state a mildly dissenting case before being overwhelmed by the other panelists."[36] Some, such as National Public Radio's Terri Gross, saw the film's nuance as its strength, praising *American Sniper* as "full of complexity and ambivalence" on *Fresh Air*.[37] Others saw the ambivalence as a shortcoming; A. O. Scott in the *New York Times* also noted the essential ambivalence of much of the film, calling it "less a war film than a western" and arguing that it should be seen "as upholding the Hollywood western tradition of turning complicated historical events and characters into fables and heroes. In other words, it's only a movie."[38] Perhaps. But given its subject matter and the context of its reception, it became much, much more. Alexander Nazaryan, writing in *Newsweek,* seemed to get it right, stating that the film version of Kyle "is far more likeable than the one in the book, even if the latter is more faithful to life" and correctly predicting that "invariably, both the right and left will use *American Sniper,* though the movie is far less susceptible to political manipulations than the book on which it is based."[39]

After its record-breaking opening, *American Sniper* continued to be a monster success at the box office. By March, it had eclipsed $500 million in global box office sales, including $163 million in overseas tickets, bypassing Steven Spielberg's *Saving Private Ryan* (1998) as the highest grossing U.S. combat film of all time.[40] Much of the domestic box office was likely driven by a growing public debate over the film, which focused on the politics of Kyle and his story and played out largely in social and mainstream media. When celebrities such as Seth Rogen and Michael Moore tweeted potential disapproval of the film, they were quickly pounced on, first by other celebrities, such as musician Kid Rock, actor Dean Cain, and former vice presidential candidate Sarah Palin. Mainstream papers soon covered these back-and-forths as part of the story, thrusting *American Sniper* into the middle of what the *Washington Post* described as another "culture war."[41]

Shortly after these debates escalated, the American-Arab Anti-Discrimination Committee went public with news that its members had reported a sharp uptick in threats directed at Arab Americans and called on Eastwood and Cooper to address the violence being carried out by supporters of the film. "I think a lot of this has to do with the language that's used in the film," said the group's president, Samer Khalaf, referring specifically to the film's descriptions of Iraqis as "ragheads" and "savages."[42] And indeed, supporters of the film, including anti-Muslim activist Pamela Gellar, pointed specifically to this language as one of the film's merits, calling it one of the "best films in decades"—a film that "tells the truth about the war we are in and the savages we are fighting."[43] In other words, it took just a matter of weeks for debate over the film to play out over predictable political and ideological lines.

What makes this all the more remarkable is that the film is indeed far more subtle and nuanced than the book, providing at least the opportunity for a thoughtful, engaged debate about the ways in which the cultural construction of U.S. soldiers relies on the gendered and racialized construction of the Other and the effects of contemporary wars on both. In Eastwood and Cooper's hands, Kyle's sheepdog remains a prototypical, masculinized white American male, building on long-standing myths of the individual frontiersman, the gunslinger, and the cowboy. But the film's version of Kyle resides more often in the gray fog of war and its fallout than in the black-and-white, Manichaean world of good and evil that Kyle himself narrates and reinforces in the book. As in the book, Cooper's Kyle continues to note the presence of "evil," but in the film, these scenes are regularly and repeatedly framed against a backdrop of children, both American and Iraqi—many instances of which are not in Kyle's memoir. For the infamous opening scene, in which, it is implied, Kyle cautiously but coldly kills an Iraqi child carrying a live grenade toward an American convoy, Eastwood added the child, whereas in the book it was solely an Iraqi woman. The film also invents a local radical nicknamed "the butcher" who terrorizes local families and brutalizes a young child. While these scenes do not follow the letter of Kyle's own account, they are consistent with its angry recitations of the evil, fanatic "bad guys." They also serve as clear juxtapositions, followed by abrupt cuts to scenes of Kyle's own children being born or playing. The imagery of innocence in need of protection is clearly on display, but the film complicates these representations by asking audiences to consider the roles of children and families caught on all sides of the war. In adding these moments of complexity to scenes of terrible and ostensible "evil," Eastwood conferred a degree of fictitious nuance to Kyle's tale, similar to those Taya offered in her memoir.

In two other significant departures, the film progressively complicates the more simplistic worldview of the book. First, the film creates small spaces for critiques of the war, suggesting it was perhaps not so clearly a noble effort to protect the United States from supposed evils abroad. At the start of his second tour in Iraq, Kyle sees his brother, now a marine, on the tarmac. Kyle attempts to comfort his brother, who is clearly shaken, by telling him that he and their father are proud of him. "Fuck this place," his brother replies, repeating the phrase before walking away and heading back into combat. Shortly thereafter, Kyle is putting together a direct-action squad to track "the butcher" when one of his team members begins to question Kyle and the mission. "I just want to believe in what we're doing here," he tells Kyle. "There's evil here. We've seen it," Kyle replies. "There's evil everywhere," the man tells him dismissively before walking out of the tent and into the night.

Second, the film openly embraces the voice and story of Taya Kyle, helping to drive home the effects of war on both the soldiers and their loved ones. Some of these scenes are in the book, mostly in the form of direct asides from Taya, but they become an integral part of the film's narrative, helping to highlight the ways in which the war has changed Kyle. At the midpoint of the film, Kyle's transitions to and from home between his first and second tours and the birth of his first child are given prolonged attention, probing the symptoms of PTSD that Kyle exhibits and how they are affecting his marriage and family. "They're savages. They're fucking savages," he tells Taya, who replies, "It's not about them. It's about us." Later she flatly tells him, "If you don't think this war is changing you, you're wrong."

This line of inquiry still has its limits. Ultimately, the film, like the book, still refuses to focus attention on the work that Kyle did in coming home. We are not allowed to read or to see his struggles or how he dealt with pain and trauma. We are not allowed to read or to see much about his work with fellow veterans, which is barely an epilogue in either work. Again, as David Kieran reminds us in his essay, rehabilitation can help make empire more palatable to the American public—but only when it's done in a way that reinforces private processing and individual resilience, rather than communal or public rites of passage back into civilian life. To a certain degree, this lack of attention is also consistent with Kyle's wishes. "What wounded veterans don't need is sympathy," he writes in the book. "They need to be treated like the men they are: equals, heroes, and people who still have tremendous value for society."[44] In reducing these moments to an afterthought, the film maintains the invisibility of the trauma and the healing for American veterans that are so very much a part of the discourse of the effects of the contemporary wars in the United States. It is particularly striking that Eastwood did not take the opportunity to explore this part of the story, given that he knew that Kyle ultimately died at the hands of a troubled veteran and that he otherwise consistently sought to complicate Kyle's own straightforward narrative.

These textual nuances notwithstanding, there was little ambivalence and subtlety to the debate over *American Sniper* in early 2015. Moderate and left-leaning sources decried the racism and jingoism of the film, while conservative outlets defended Kyle, Eastwood, and the warriors for whom they ostensibly crafted their stories. But the fact that in a hyperpolarized U.S. culture, driven by echo chamber media outlets, things played out along somewhat predictable lines should not be surprising. What is perhaps more telling about American society—and the limits of debate over war, empire, and militarism more than fifteen years removed from the attacks of 9/11—is what happened when *American Sniper* came to U.S. college campuses in the spring of 2015.

AMERICAN CAMPUS

American Sniper was screened and protested at a range of U.S. colleges and universities in the spring of 2015. The events at and around two public flagship campuses suffice to demonstrate the responses and counterresponses to the film and what those suggest about the politics of this film, the politics of American empire, and the politics of free speech in higher education at this historical moment. While the film is certainly more nuanced than the book, its representations of Iraqis, and of Arabs and Muslims in general, is not. In building off the public, cultural debate over representations of Middle Eastern subjects in the film, campus activists seized on the racism of *American Sniper,* seeking to cancel screenings of the film in the name of "safe spaces." Lost in the moment was any acknowledgement of the loss of teachable moments, particularly regarding the effects of U.S. wars on those who fight them.

During the first week of April, the Center for Campus Involvement at the University of Michigan scheduled a Friday night screening of the film. Almost immediately, students across campus, including many who identified as Arab American or Muslim American, began circulating a petition to cancel the screening. "As a student who identifies as an Arab and Middle Eastern student, I feel that *American Sniper* condones a lot of anti-Middle Eastern and North African propaganda," said Lamees Mekkaoui, a member of Students Allied for Freedom and Equality and the Middle East and Arab Network. "It was released at a time when these anti-Arab, anti-Muslim and anti-Middle-Eastern [and] North African hate crimes were already skyrocketing, and this movie only contributed to that."[45] The petition read in part, "The movie *American Sniper* not only tolerates but promotes anti-Muslim and anti-MENA rhetoric and sympathizes with a mass killer."[46] The connection between the film and a rise in threats against Middle Eastern and Arab groups is already well established, but it is worth noting here the reductionist rhetoric of campus activists, which does not even attempt to locate the nuances of the distinctions between "mass killer" and combat soldier.[47]

In response to the outcry, the group canceled the screening, replacing it with *Paddington,* an animated film about a talking bear, and posted a note on its Facebook page that read:

> Student reactions have clearly articulated that this is neither the venue nor the time to show this movie. . . . We deeply regret causing harm to members of our community, and appreciate the thoughtful feedback provided to us by students and staff alike. We in the Center for Campus Involvement and the UMix Late Night program did not intend to exclude any students or communities on campus through showing this film. Nevertheless, as we know, intent and impact can be very different things. While our intent was to show a film, the impact of the content was harmful, and made students feel unsafe and unwelcome at our program. . . . We will take time to deeper understand and screen for content that can negatively stereotype a group.[48]

In response to this, a countermovement immediately mobilized, starting its own petition that called Kyle a "war hero," "not a racist mass murderer or a criminal," and arguing that "as adults at a public university, we should have the option to view this movie if we so choose and have the opportunity to engage on the topics it presents to come to our own conclusions on the subjects."[49] Michigan football coach Jim Harbaugh even joined the fray, tweeting, "Michigan Football will watch 'American Sniper'! Proud of Chris Kyle & Proud to be an American & if that offends anybody then so be it!"[50] The university administration apparently agreed with at least the free-speech claims of the petition, releasing a statement that read, "The initial decision to cancel the movie was not consistent with the high value the University of Michigan places on freedom of expression and our respect for the right of students to make their own choices in such matters."[51] Throughout the week, several groups and individuals reported a rise in anti-Arab and anti-Muslim rhetoric on campus and across social media. Both *Paddington* and *American Sniper* were eventually screened, the latter with the inclusion of a postfilm discussion.[52]

The next major protest around the film to garner national attention was at the University of Maryland, College Park, just days later. Similar to events at Michigan, after the screening was announced, a petition was circulated, this time led by the Muslim Student Association (MSA) at Maryland, which argued that the film "dehumanizes Muslim individuals, promotes the idea of senseless mass murder, and portrays negative and inaccurate stereotypes." It labeled the film "war propaganda guised as art, which reveals a not-so-discreet Islamophobic, violent, and racist nationalist ideology."[53] As at Michigan, the initial response of the student group was to cancel the screening, which it did, only to find an even more hostile backlash in which invectives and threats were directed at the MSA, and the Beltway media chimed in.[54] In response to the counteroutcry, the campus chapters of the College Democrats and the College Republicans came together to support and sponsor a rescheduled screening of the film, followed by a panel discussion—a decision publicly praised by the president, who used the example to highlight the language of inclusiveness: "Working together, despite differences in philosophy and doctrine, is a laudable example for us all."[55]

In the hours leading up to the screening, the MSA handed out flowers in the student center with small pieces of paper attached inscribed with words such as *Raghead* and other verbatim threats the students had received throughout the past week. Allied protesters along the same hall held signs that read, "If you like American Sniper you may also like:—Racism—Murder—KKK—Holocaust—Fox News," and "MLK was also killed by an American Sniper." The screening went off without incident, as did the panel discussion, which was described by several attendees as "uncomfortable," but students spoke out and argued, and some discussions, according to the *Chronicle of Higher Education,* "spilled out into the evening afterwards."[56]

CONCLUSION: AMERICAN SHEEP(DOGS)

In many ways, then, the debate on college campuses over *American Sniper* mirrored and reinforced the larger public debate over the film, retreating into familiar and predictable ideological lines along which questions of diversity, inclusion, race, religion, and potential critiques of the American imperial project could be effectively marginalized and silenced with little more than the equivalent of "Support the Troops." And yet, as with conservative supporters of the film, who argued that it was prowarrior without necessarily being prowar, these terms of debate speak volumes about their own silence regarding those who fight U.S. wars and how those wars affect these soldiers and their families.

Arguably, the "honest" and "straightforward" language of Kyle is indicative of a wide range of U.S. military personnel who serve in Iraq and Afghanistan and of the military machine that trains them, in part, by dehumanizing "the enemy." This is in fact central to the maintenance of an imperial worldview that justifies violence against countries and communities halfway around the world from Kyle's West Texas. Part of what the film attempts to show, however, as well as part of what was quickly lost in public debates about the film, are the ways in which the dehumanization of the enemy—and the violence engendered by that process—dehumanizes the supposed sheepdogs as much as the alleged wolves. While the film itself also refuses to follow this narrative too far, the larger story of *American Sniper,* taken to its eventual conclusion, includes only more pain, more trauma, and more senseless violence as Kyle and his friend are murdered by a psychologically disturbed veteran Kyle is attempting to help.[57] But almost nowhere in the public debate over the film and certainly nowhere in the campus debates do we see any attempt to forge this connection or to move beyond the reductionist lines of argument that essentially mirrored the celebrity Twitter spats and Fox News talking points from months prior.

So much of contemporary political debate, particularly on college campuses, seems to mistake comfort for safety, and comfort, in many ways, is as much an enemy of inquiry, hindering honest debates about the forces of racism, sexism, and imperialism that should be ripe for campus discussion. One strategy that could help move this and similar debates forward is the explicit inclusion of the voices of veterans from recent U.S. conflicts. As veterans continue to make up an increasingly large percentage of students on U.S. campuses, they often remain an invisible group, with particular needs that continue to go largely unaddressed. Surely there is room in these debates, as well as in larger debates over American militarism and American warfare, for the voices of veterans from our contemporary conflict, particularly with the recognition that veterans are far from a homogeneous group. While they may have shared experiences, they also have widely varying histories, backgrounds, and politics. One can imagine those veterans complicating the dualistic thinking about sheep and wolves and humanizing their own experiences while deconstructing the racialized and gendered basis of those constructions. But what U.S. culture needs at the end of the day are not "aggressive" sheepdogs like Kyle, sent into battle to protect the nation from evil. What is needed instead are new analogies, new texts, and new discourses that can liberate us from reductive debates and comfort-seeking instincts and provide us with the tools to engage and represent the foundations of empire wherever they are being built and reinforced.

NOTES

1. *American Sniper,* produced and directed by Clint Eastwood (Burbank, CA: Village Roadshow and Warner Bros., 2014).

2. Chris Kyle, with Scott McEwen and Jim DeFelice, *American Sniper: The Autobiography of the Most Lethal Sniper in U.S. Military History* (New York: HarperCollins, 2012).

3. Tara Kyle, with Jim DeFelice, *American Wife: Love, War, Faith, and Renewal* (New York: HarperCollins, 2015), 111.

4. Kyle, *American Sniper,* 70. Based on the success and notoriety of *American Sniper,* Kyle went on to coauthor, with William Doyle, a book focused on guns, *American Gun: A History of the U.S. in Ten Firearms* (New York: William Morrow, 2013).

5. Kyle, *American Sniper,* 131.

6. Ibid., 178.

7. Ibid., 341.

8. Gregory Cowles, "Inside the List," Sunday Book Review, *New York Times,* February 8, 2013. For more on the killing of Kyle, see Nicholas Schmidle, "In the Crosshairs," *New Yorker,* June 3, 2013.

9. Kyle, *American Wife,* 53.

10. Kyle, *American Sniper,* 194.

11. Ibid., 86.

12. Ibid.

13. Ibid., 198.

14. Ibid., 199.

15. Ibid., 219.

16. Kyle, *American Wife,* 117–118.

17. Ibid.

18. Kyle, *American Sniper,* 253.

19. Ibid., 273 (emphasis in original).

20. Ibid.

21. "Military Memoirs Find an Audience," *New York Times,* March 19, 2012.

22. Schmidle, "In the Crosshairs."

23. Joshua Sinai, review of *American Sniper: The Autobiography of the Most Lethal Sniper in U.S. Military History,* by Chris Kyle, with Scott McEwen and Jim DeFelice, *Washington Times,* January 13, 2012.

24. Tony Perry, review of *American Sniper: The Autobiography of the Most Lethal Sniper in U.S. Military History,* by Chris Kyle, with Scott McEwen and Jim DeFelice, *Los Angeles Times,* March 5, 2012.

25. Review of *American Sniper: The Autobiography of the Most Lethal Sniper in U.S. Military History,* by Chris Kyle, with Scott McEwen and Jim DeFelice, *Huffington Post,* www.huffingtonpost.com/taylor-dibbert/book-review-american-snip_b_6753216.html.

26. "*American Sniper* Gets a Hero's Welcome," *Wall Street Journal,* January 20, 2015, B1; "*American Sniper:* The Strategy behind Warner Bros.' $107m Opening," *Hollywood Reporter,* January 30, 2015, www.hollywoodreporter.com/news/american-sniper-strategy-behind-warner-765462.

27. "In Marketing *American Sniper,* Warner Bros. Treads Carefully with Gender and Politics," *Los Angeles Times,* January 18, 2015, www.latimes.com/entertainment/movies/moviesnow/la-et-mn-in-marketing-american-sniper-warner-bros-treads-carefully-with-gender-and-politics-20150108-story.html.

28. Chris Hedges, "Killing Ragheads for Jesus," *TruthDig,* January 25, 2015, www.truthdig.com/report/item/killing_ragheads_for_jesus_20150125.

29. David Edelstein, "Movie Review: *American Sniper:* It's a Crackerjack Piece of Filmmaking, but the Moral Stakes Are Almost Nonexistent," review of *American Sniper,* directed by Clint Eastwood, *New York,* December 29, 2014.

30. "Exclusive: Screenwriter on Significance of *American Sniper,*" January 15, 2015, www.foxnews.com/transcript/2015/01/16/exclusive-screenwriter-significance-american-sniper/.

31. "*American Sniper:* Indisputably Pro-Soldier, but Hardly Pro-War," *National Review* Online, www.nationalreview.com/campaign-spot/397694/american-sniper-indisputably-pro-soldier-hardly-pro-war-jim-geraghty?target=topic&tid=3335.

32. "*American Sniper:* The Good, The Terse, and the Tragic," review of *American Sniper,* directed by Clint Eastwood, *Wall Street Journal,* December 24, 2014, www.wsj.com/articles/american-sniper-review-the-good-the-terse-and-the-tragic-1419443121.

33. "Review: *Sniper* is Quintessential Eastwood," review of *American Sniper,* directed by Clint Eastwood, *Washington Times,* January 7, 2015, www.washingtontimes.com/news/2015/jan/7/review-american-sniper-is-quintessential-eastwood/.

34. "Civil Rights Group: Eastwood and Cooper Need to Help Stop Anti-Arab Speech Inspired by *American Sniper,*" *Washington Post,* January 28, 2015.

35. "On Media: Sheepdog or Sheep?," *Christian Century,* March 4, 2015.

36. Rand Richards Cooper, "Mawkish and Hawkish: 'American Sniper,'" *Commonweal* 142 (March 2015), 24.

37. "Full of Complexity and Ambivalence, 'American Sniper' Shows the Cost of War," *Fresh Air,* January 28, 2015.

38. A. O. Scott, "A Sniper Does His Deeds but the Battle Never Ends," *New York Times,* December 24, 2014, C12.

39. Alexander Nazaryan, "'American Sniper' and the Soul of War," *Newsweek,* January 30, 2015.

40. "Box Office: *American Sniper* Shatters Records with $90.2 Million Weekend," *Variety,* January 18, 2015, http://variety.com/2015/film/news/box-office-american-sniper-shatters-records-with-90-2-million-weekend-1201408252/; "Box Office Milestone: 'American Sniper' Hits $500M Globally, Becomes Top 2014 Title in U.S.," *Hollywood Reporter* Online, March 8, 2015, www.hollywoodreporter.com/news/box-office-milestone-american-sniper-779977.

41. "Everything You Need to Know about the *American Sniper* Culture Wars Controversy," *Washington Post,* January 20, 2015.

42. "Civil Rights Group: Eastwood and Cooper Need to Help Stop Anti-Arab Speech Inspired by *American Sniper,*" *Washington Post,* January 28, 2015.

43. Ibid.

44. Kyle, *American Sniper,* 373.

45. "University of Michigan Will Show *American Sniper* after Protests," *Time,* April 9, 2015.

46. "University of Michigan Backtracks after Canceling *American Sniper* Screening," *Newsweek,* April 9, 2015, www.newsweek.com/university-michigan-backtracks-after-canceling-american-sniper-screening-321230.

47. On the link between the film and violence against Arab and Muslim groups, see "Civil Rights Group," *Washington Post.*

48. "University of Michigan Backtracks," *Newsweek.*

49. "University of Michigan Will Show *American Sniper* after Protests," *Time.*

50. "University of Michigan Backtracks," *Newsweek.*

51. University of Michigan Will Show *American Sniper* after Protests," *Time.*

52. "Amid 'American Sniper' controversy, students cite incidents of racist remarks, threats," *Michigan Daily,* April 10, 2015, www.michigandaily.com/news/amid-american-sniper-controversy-students-cite-incidents-racist-remarks-threats.

53. Andy Thomason, "Coming Soon to a Campus Near You," *Chronicle of Higher Education,* May 6, 2015.

54. "'American Sniper' Will Be Screened at U of Maryland," *Inside Higher Ed,* April 29, 2015, www.insidehighered.com/quicktakes/2015/04/29/american-sniper-will-be-screened-u-maryland.

55. "Coming Soon to a Campus Near You," *Chronicle of Higher Education.*

56. Ibid.

57. Schmidle, "In the Crosshairs."

THREE

"The First Step toward Curing the Postwar Blues Is a Return to Nature"

VETERANS' OUTDOOR REHABILITATION PROGRAMS AND THE NORMALIZATION OF EMPIRE

David Kieran

IN MARCH OF 2016, SENATOR RON WYDEN (D) of Oregon introduced the Recreation Not Red-Tape Act, a bill designed to ease public access to federal lands. Among its otherwise mundane provisions was one that encouraged the "Interior and USDA [to] work with the Department of Defense and the Department of Veterans Affairs to ensure veterans have access to outdoor programs."[1] This was not the first time Congress had made this suggestion. In nearly every session since 2006, a version of the Veterans Eagle Pass Parks Act, which would guarantee honorably discharged veterans discounted lifetime admission to the United States' national parks, has been introduced in the House.[2] In 2014, Representative Raul Ruiz (D-CA) introduced the Wounded Veterans Recreation Act, which would have made admission permanently free to veterans with service-connected disabilities.[3] Central to each of these bills is the assumption that outdoor recreation promises veterans an opportunity to heal from the physical and psychological wounds of war. Discussing his bill at a hearing in 2014, Ruiz told his fellow legislators, "National Parks give our veterans an opportunity to connect with nature and to exercise, which leads to better spiritual, mental, and physical health. . . . There is a strong want for connect[ion], for living their life the way they had before they were injured or wounded, it is not only medicine for the body, but also medicine to the mind and medicine to the soul to be able to go visit those same national parks that they have . . . defended with their service."[4] There is a lot to unpack in Ruiz's statement, starting with the dubious claim that anyone who served in Fallujah or the Shahi-Kot Valley was thinking about Grand Teton or the Cascades or the implicit assumption that the wounds incurred in the United States' most recent imperial venture might be healed on land taken in an earlier one.[5] However, what is most significant is the question of what is at stake, culturally, in positioning outdoor recreation as a crucial avenue for veterans healing from the psychological trauma of combat.

These bills, despite seeming innocuous and being focused on a constituency that hardly struggles to receive congressional support, have yet to become law. Nonetheless, they are indicative of a larger trend in twenty-first-century U.S. culture. There are programs that teach veterans how to fish and how to hunt, to climb mountains or whitewater raft, to ride horses or take outdoor photography, and more. These programs remain widely popular and have been the subject of considerable coverage in local news, national outdoor magazines, and documentary film. Their effectiveness has also been hotly debated. While a growing body of scientific literature suggests their effectiveness, a significant number of those invested in veterans' mental health remain skeptical of whether they offer any meaningful, long-term relief to veterans' mental health issues.[6]

This chapter examines the proliferation of rehabilitative outdoor programs for veterans during the United States' wars in Iraq and Afghanistan and asks how their cultural representation contributes to a discourse that links rehabilitation, militarism, and empire. Moving beyond questions about these programs' health benefits and recognizing that many veterans enjoy them, I illuminate how popular representations of these programs help perpetuate U.S. empire by promising veterans' uncomplicated recuperation from the wounds of war, asserting that civilians bear no responsibility for facilitating that rehabilitation or engaging with the realities of the event that caused it, and normalizing military culture as an indelible component of American culture.

I develop this argument through the close reading of media coverage about and promotional materials for a range of veterans' programs and particularly through an analysis of Michael Brown's 2012 documentary *High Ground,* which follows eleven veterans wounded in Iraq and Afghanistan as they attempt to scale Mount Lobuche, a twenty-thousand-foot Himalayan peak. Together, these sites of cultural production mobilize ideas about nature, rehabilitation, and masculinity that have animated U.S. culture since at least the nineteenth century to construct a narrative that supports the endurance of American empire and the wars that enable it. This narrative is one in which the consequences for U.S. veterans of the United States' imperial wars are easily addressed through private charity and individual initiative, veterans require no public engagement, and military skills have value in the domestic realm.

MILITARISM, EMPIRE, NATURE, AND THE WOUNDED SOLDIER BODY

American empire is produced and legitimated in a variety of cultural locations, but the global presence of the U.S. military and the interventions that it undertakes retain primacy of place among them. In the twenty-first century, the United States has mounted invasions and subsequently, lengthy occupations of both Iraq and Afghanistan, and over the course of the fifteen years since the September 11, 2001, terrorist attacks, U.S. military power has been deployed in Pakistan, Yemen, Somalia, and elsewhere. According to journalist Nick Turse, the United States has deployed troops to well over one hundred countries in the years following the 2011 killing of Osama bin Laden.[7] And yet, all this activity has been carried out by a relatively small number of Americans; fewer than 1 percent of the population serves in the military.

The military thus perpetuates U.S. empire at a distance from most Americans, whom legal scholar Mary Dudziak points out have been asked for little more than their uncritical support for the troops and acquiescence to wars that are at once persistent and invisible. As the Iraq War putatively ended but troops remained in combat, she explains, "Military engagement no longer seemed to require the support of the American people, but instead their inattention."[8] Andrew Bacevich agrees with Dudziak, writing that "except as spectators, Americans abrogated any further responsibility for war in all of its aspects."[9] Despite being the United States' longest wars, the conflicts in Iraq and Afghanistan epitomize the phenomenon that Amy Kaplan diagnosed in her now-classic essay "Left Alone with America: The Absence of Empire in the Study of American Culture": the reality of American empire remains obscure—and continues to be denied—in many corners of American culture.[10]

One of the primary exceptions to empire's invisibility in twenty-first-century American public life has been the attention that service members wounded in Iraq and Afghanistan have received. Advances in medical technology mean that many more soldiers survive battlefield injuries, and that in turn means that more veterans are returning home with visible injuries.[11] As of 2014, 1,186 U.S. troops had lost a limb in Iraq or Afghanistan, and the loss of multiple limbs has not been uncommon.[12] Eye injuries have also been common, totaling 138,636 by 2013 and, the army reports, "About 2,000 service members were left with low vision and about 200 were blinded."[13] There have been other injuries as well. Posttraumatic stress disorder (PTSD) and traumatic brain injury have profoundly affected many troops. There have been nearly 300,000 mild traumatic brain injury (mTBI) diagnoses since the war began, and the U.S. Department of Veterans Affairs (VA) estimates that "about 11–20 out of every 100 Veterans (or between 11–20%) who served in OIF [Operation Iraqi Freedom] or OEF [Operation Enduring Freedom] have PTSD in a given year."[14]

Despite these figures, Americans have infrequently encountered the wounded or psychologically struggling Iraq veteran in popular culture. If such veterans were a staple of post–World War II and post-Vietnam popular culture—consider, for example, *The Best Years of Our Lives* (1948), *Taxi Driver* (1976), and *Born on the Fourth of July* (1989)—they have been largely absent during the twenty-first century. Partly, this is because they only infrequently appear, usually as supporting characters: Colonel Joan Burton in the Lifetime series *Army Wives*, Colton Rhodes in FX's *Justified*, and Damian Lewis in Showtime's *Homeland*. But it is also because popular culture about the wars in Iraq and Afghanistan has been almost universally unpopular with American audiences. Although there has been no shortage of cinematic treatment of these conflicts, the historian Andrew C. McKevitt is bluntly accurate in his assessment that, with few exceptions, "films about the Iraq War tanked at the box office."[15] As Edwin Martini shows in the essay preceding this one, *American Sniper* and the relatively few other films that have done well are those that do not demand a complicated reckoning with veterans' postwar needs. As a result, Americans' thinking about returning veterans' struggles has often occurred in other venues. One of the most significant cultural spaces in which Americans have been asked to reckon with those costs has been in descriptions of the work of nonprofit organizations such as the Wounded Warrior Project (and the controversies that sometimes surround them) and cultural phenomena such as the #22PushUpChallenge, in which individuals perform twenty-two push-ups a day, for twenty-two days, to raise awareness of veteran suicide.[16]

That the wounded or troubled veteran has been largely absent from U.S. popular culture, however, has not meant that she or he has not been the subject of intense attention and anxiety in the media and among the war's critics in Congress and elsewhere. PTSD and mTBI have been termed the "invisible wounds of war," but the difficulty of noticing their presence in a particular soldier body contrasts sharply with the significant attention they have received in the press, before Congress, and in popular culture.[17] In this, they join other wounds as a profound subject of discussion and dissent during these wars. As the historian John Kinder explains, "The disabled soldier remains a popular symbol among critics of American militarism and government indifference."[18] Certainly, in the twenty-first century, veterans' physical wounds and psychological struggles emerged as a powerful club that critics used to attack the wars. Critiquing President Bush's 2007 troop surge and demanding withdrawal from Iraq, for example, Representative Hilda Solis (D-CA) railed that "more than 23,400 service men and women have been wounded in action, and nearly half of those wounded will not be able to lead a normal life because of severe injuries, permanent disabilities, and post-traumatic stress syndrome. . . . The president's proposal to escalate ignores the real needs of our troops and the grave reality of this situation."[19] A few months later, her colleague Jim McDermott (D-WA) argued that "the truth about September [when the Bush administration promised an update on the surge's effectiveness] will be that the President is still losing the Iraq War" and complained that "the President [will not] tell the American people that he has no plan to treat the gravely wounded soldiers returning from Iraq."[20] For the war's opponents, the injured soldier body was a disturbing product of the Bush administration's folly and evidence that the war needed to end.

This is, Kinder explains, hardly unique to the country's twenty-first-century wars. Yet the wounded soldier body functions in other ways as well. Diagnosing what he terms "The Problem of the Disabled Veteran," Kinder illuminates the two ways in which Americans have responded to the reality that wars create injured bodies. If wounded soldiers were "portents of a terrible new age of unparalleled violence," the potential to recuperate a body suggested "the United States' ability to enter the global arena and return home functionally, if not aesthetically, unscathed" and "an even more tantalizing promise: future generations of political leaders could remove the social consequences of veterans' disabilities from the calculus of American war-making."[21]

Discourses on rehabilitation promise that bodies can be made whole again, or at least returned to normative public and private lives, and in that sense, rehabilitation offers the promise that the reality of the "centrality of injuring in war" that Elaine Scarry illuminates in *The Body in Pain* can be mitigated.[22] As Zoe H. Wool explains, "Work on the body of the injured soldier—rehabilitative and imaginative alike—is thus also work to smooth over public visions of war and post-war life in contemporary America, to obscure the violence and pain of war in gestures of hope and gratitude that are nonetheless based on their presence."[23] The possibility of rehabilitation and the return to normative able-bodiedness thus challenges the antiwar sentiment determinedly linked to the spectacle of the wounded body. It suggests instead that the war might not be deserving of protest or at least that the current terms of protest are illegitimate. Moreover, if soldier bodies are one of the primary means through which American empire is achieved and maintained, the rehabilitated soldier body promises that empire's costs can be attenuated; in this way, rehabilitation makes empire palatable for American audiences.

"THE RECOVERY THAT I PERSONALLY EXPERIENCED OUTDOORS IS INCREDIBLE": VETERAN RECUPERATION AND DISENGAGED CITIZENSHIP

Veterans' outdoor recreation programs respond to the anxiety provoked by injured bodies and the cost of waging imperial wars, which they make visible in two ways. First, they promise that the wounded body can be rehabilitated and once again made exceptional. Outdoor programs and *High Ground* present soldier bodies capable not simply of managing the quotidian tasks of everyday life but also of participating in exceptional activities like trekking in the Himalayas. Second, they assert that this rehabilitation will occur at a distance. In these programs, the veteran is quite literally removed from a society posited as failing to understand or appreciate him or her to a natural space to be repaired and rejuvenated in preparation for a successful reintegration.

In thus framing recuperation, accounts of veterans' outdoor rehabilitation resolve the two questions that Kinder asserts are central to America's concerns about wounded veterans—"What are the nation's obligations to those who fight in its name? Who is ultimately responsible for veterans' disabilities[?]"—by offering a narrative of individualism in which neither government programs nor broader social concern are required to address the impact that war has on soldier bodies and minds.[24] In framing the veterans' rehabilitative journey in these ways, these texts promise that recuperation can occur without a public reckoning with the war's realities, a narrative that helps facilitate the unfettered continuation of militarism and empire.

Central to the cultural construction of these programs is the assurance that veterans will in fact heal through their participation and will return capable not only of participating in everyday life but also, in many cases, of performing extraordinary acts. When the House of Representatives held a hearing on the Wounded Veterans Recreation Act, for example, Iraq veteran Garret Reppenhagen told the panel:

> To say the least, I had come home with post-traumatic stress disorder. I suffered from intrusive thoughts, hyper-vigilance, anxiety, troubled sleep, aversion to crowded areas, depression, relationship issues. If it wasn't for my ability and my knowledge to go out into our public lands and enjoy nature, I probably wouldn't be sitting here today. The recovery that I personally experienced in our outdoors was incredible. It allowed me to transition back on a time of my choosing, and I was able to find peace of mind in the serenity of our outdoors.[25]

Elsewhere, Reppenhagen has been more explicit in crediting being outdoors with preventing his suicide. In an interview with the Pew Charitable Trust, he remarked that Pike National Forest in Colorado was "the retreat that saved my life when I came home from war and learned to transition to my civilian life."[26]

Each of these accounts identify outdoor activities as avenues for healing, if not, in Reppenhagen's case, salvation. This is, of course, hardly a new claim. The notion that the wilderness holds the potential for rehabilitation—and particularly the recuperation of masculinity—is a familiar trope in U.S. culture. As Richard Slotkin writes in his masterwork *Gunfighter Nation: The Myth of the Frontier in Twentieth-Century America,* "The Myth of the Frontier is our oldest and most characteristic myth," one in which "the American must cross the border into 'Indian country' and experience a 'regression' to a more primitive and natural condition of life so that the false values of the 'metropolis' can be purged and a new, purified social contract enacted. Although the Indian and Wilderness are the settler's enemy, they also provide him with the new consciousness through which he will transform the world."[27]

Claims like Reppenhagen's thus join a long history of cultural claims about the rejuvenating potential of nature.[28] Emerson famously promised that "in the woods, we return to reason and faith. There I feel nothing that can befall me in life—no disgrace, no calamity ... which nature cannot repair."[29] At the end of the nineteenth century, the historian Karen R. Jones writes, the notion of mastering the wilderness became an antidote to the class-based and gendered anxieties brought about by modernity. "Configured as a crucible of personal renewal," she writes, "the West allowed emasculation anxieties, middle-class ambition, and imperial muscles to be flexed with abandon and romantic flourish."[30]

Perhaps most famously, she notes, it was Theodore Roosevelt who "engaged in a process of regeneration on the frontier."[31] The future president "head[ed] west to forget about the past" after his wife's death, as his biographer Edmund Morris put it, landing in the Dakotas, where "all [the] activity left Roosevelt little time to brood."[32] Another Roosevelt biographer, Roger L. DiSilvestro, explains that "Bereft in his home life and bewildered by the downward drift of his career, [Roosevelt] sought to escape in one of the most remote and rugged places in the United States" and that "within two years he would find physical strength and emotional stability, salvaging the wreckage of his life and forging himself into the historical figure who would gaze down in stone from Mount Rushmore."[33] If DiSilvestro's language is a bit bombastic, it nonetheless illustrates how deeply intertwined nature, masculinity, and recuperation have been in American culture; both the nineteenth-century figure and his twenty-first-century biographer believed that wilderness was recuperative. And, as Jones and others have shown, Roosevelt became an evangelist for wilderness as the site at which American masculinity would be recuperated.[34]

These sentiments echo throughout the rhetoric of other outdoor programs. On Wilderness.org's website, for example, retired chaplain Scott Roney expounds that "I see firsthand the soul-redeeming power of the outdoors.... Many veterans, in fact, do need a place to decompress, and nature is the best pressure release valve.... It is amazing how a hunting trip, a fishing outing, or even a walk in the woods can help heal the physical and mental scars of war"; elsewhere, the website promises that "often haunted by the horrors of war and the loss of unit camaraderie, many combat veterans find that extended time in the great outdoors allows a space for healing."[35] An essay by Joshua Brandon, an army veteran, on the Sierra Club's website explains in nearly Emersonian terms that "many of my fellow soldiers and I have always had difficulty in processing these experiences.... I feel at home in the mountains, seemingly balanced halfway between my old life and my new one, and for a brief moment, I am able to transcend my daily life into a state of clarity, able to see and understand who I have become, where I have been, and where I am headed."[36]

These ideas have also permeated popular culture about veterans' outdoor activities. The web-based television series *Veteran Outdoors,* for example, declares that its mission is "to demonstrate the therapeutic effects that being in the outdoors actually has on the mental and physical disabilities of our country's wounded men and women."[37] The descriptions accompanying several of the episodes likewise assert that recuperation occurs simply through participation in these activities. "They say some service men and women return from war with a thousand-yard stare. But perhaps the first step toward curing the post-war blues comes with a hunt, a return to nature and perhaps even that quintessential trophy deer, fish or even bear," the description of an episode devoted to a fishing trip in Texas declares.[38]

This sentiment is also central to *High Ground*. The film premiered in the fall of 2012 to positive reviews in U.S. newspapers and on National Public Radio, was profiled on National Geographic's adventure blog, and subsequently won awards at the Vail Film Festival, the Boulder Film Festival, the Newport Beach Film Festival, and the Seattle International Film Festival.[39] Following the film's release, the director and cast attended screenings around the country, some of which particularly engaged veterans diagnosed with PTSD.[40]

The film opens with a prologue that reminds viewers that in the Iraq and Afghanistan wars, "fifty thousand [U.S. troops] have suffered physical injuries. Hundreds of thousands more have returned home with post-traumatic stress and traumatic brain injuries" and that "with minds and bodies changed by war, many still struggle to overcome their wounds."[41] However, the film's primary message is the degree to which veterans can overcome their disabilities. Central to this claim is that veterans' injuries are not the barriers to recovery and achievement that newspapers around the country have often portrayed them as being and that many civilians might assume they are.[42]

This point is made through the veterans' repeated rejections of the expectations that health-care providers set for them. These assertions exist alongside claims that the military and VA do not adequately provide for veterans. Matt Nyman, whose leg was amputated after a helicopter crash, complains that "the care at Walter Reed was beyond inadequate"; former marine Katherine Ragazzino became homeless after the VA lost her benefits paperwork; and national guardsman Ashley Crandall sought counseling for suicidal thoughts only to be evacuated from Iraq to Walter Reed, where "things have gotten progressively worse." Beyond this incompetence, the veterans' health system is portrayed as discouraging veterans' complete recuperation. Chad Butrick, who had been an avid mountaineer prior to losing his leg in Iraq, reflects that "when I got injured and lost my leg, there were many aspects of life that I thought were over. And the mountains were one of them. When I was going through my therapy, I had a nurse case manager who told me that I should get new hobbies." Likewise, Nyman recalls that "I was told I'd never stand again, let alone walk."

Against this portrayal of a veterans' health-care system that discourages veterans and treats their injuries as permanent, veterans present themselves as not only able to withstand the demands of mountaineering but able to recuperate through the process. Butrick's response is emblematic: "I'm a little bit hard headed and that just motivated me all the more." And indeed, throughout the film other veterans suggest that their participation in outdoor activities has illustrated their potential to overcome their injuries. The opening scene presents veterans eagerly assembling climbing gear in an outdoor store and introduces Steve Baskis, an army veteran blinded in an improvised explosive device (IED) attack in Iraq who presents that injury as hardly inhibiting him. "When they first told me that I was blind," he explains, he "just tried to stay busy and pursue the dreams that I've always had. One of them is to see the world." Other veterans echo Baskis, and the possibility of overcoming adversity through adventure is central to the film. Lona Parten, who joins the veterans in her own effort to recover from her son's death in Afghanistan, reflects that "one thing I've learned from these soldiers, to be here with these soldiers and to watch them overcome what's happened to them and push up this mountain [is] that's life, that's grief, that's pain. But you still take that step and keep going."

Butrick's prosthesis figures prominently in these moments of success. The first dialogue of the film appears as the camera shows Butrick's prosthetic leg alongside his other foot, clad in a hiking boot as the team selects gear in a Colorado REI store. "Well, I told them that I wanted to get one," he explains, as the film cuts to Butrick holding a single sandal, "and they scratched their heads for a minute, and they gave me one." Later, as the team trudges along a snow-packed ridge on Lobuche, the camera returns to Butrick's specialized artificial leg, in which the foot has been replaced with a special crampon. Here, the prosthesis sinks into the snowpack, an example of what climbers term *post-holing*. Crucially, though, his other foot sinks in as well. The message is clear: if the notion that an amputee might desire outdoor equipment initially seems strange, the climber's attitude and his specialized prosthesis allow him to be as successful as any other climber.

And ultimately, the film suggests that most of the veterans on the trip do experience some measure of recuperation. Ashley Crandall begins the film by reflecting that "I'm never going to be the person I was. And it literally almost killed me to come to that realization." By the end, however, her attitude is cautiously positive: "I won't say that this place is going to heal me. That's going to be a long road, a long process. But this country speaks to me.... It's something that I found that I didn't have before." For her, it is the outdoor experience, rather than clinical mental health treatment, that offers fulfillment and the potential for recovery.

Moreover, the film's concluding montage shows the majority of the veterans not only reintegrating but rather living exceptional lives that deny that their injuries have any continuing impact. Steve Baskis, viewers learn, "recently reached the summit of Kilimanjaro and completed the Chicago Marathon." Parten "trekked to another mountain peak on this expedition." Two other veterans became mountaineering guides in their own right. Another, we discover, "has returned to active duty in Afghanistan." Through these portrayals, *High Ground* thus asserts that physically and psychologically injured soldiers can not only recover but retain or develop the capacity to engage in exceptional and challenging activities simply through their participation in outdoor recreation.

In doing so, the film contributes to a broader discourse that minimizes injury and denies the need for public programs that address the physical costs of the United States' imperial endeavors. Although numerous accounts of the VA's faulty scheduling system attest to its frequent failures to deliver quality care promptly, the VA's struggles and staff shortages—in September 2015, for example, the VA had only about 80 percent of the psychologists required to meet veterans' needs—are best understood as part of a nationwide shortage of mental health professionals.[43] In casting recovery as a matter of individual initiative and private charity, however, *High Ground* and other portrayals of veterans' rehabilitative recreation contribute to what Kinder critiques as "the ideology of individualism" in which "many Americans continue to view *social* problems as *individual* problems" and cast recuperation as something that can be achieved privately, without reforming the VA or addressing the larger question of the accessibility of quality mental and physical health care in the United States.[44]

Most important is the argument that the film makes about *how* recovery occurs. *High Ground* and the promotional material for veterans' outdoor programs determinedly present veteran recovery as occurring away from a civilian society that fails to understand their experiences or needs and only among other veterans who have shared their struggles. These representations thus invert a narrative that has been critical of how little attention U.S. culture has paid to returning veterans by normalizing veteran exceptionalism and insisting that recovery occurs when veterans are isolated from the wider community. In doing so, these texts enable further public disengagement from the wars and the violence endemic to them.

This affirmation of veterans' social isolation and public disengagement is evident throughout promotional materials for these programs. Wilderness.org's website argues that "one way to help veterans process their emotions, is to give them time for introspection as well as the opportunity to bond with others who have had similar experiences."[45] The website goes on to argue that "veterans who have served in warzones often experience a profound sense of isolation after returning home" but that "specialized outdoor programs can help veterans deal with these losses by bringing vets together to bond with others who share similar experiences."[46] Likewise, America's Heroes Enjoying Recreation Outdoors, an Alabama fishing program "operated by Iraq and Afghanistan Marine Corps and Army veterans who understand the challenges war veterans face today in re-engaging the civilian world," makes a similar promise. In a magazine profile of the organization, one outing is described as veterans "enjoy[ing] the quiet fellowship of telling stories and jokes around a blazing campfire with the only people who truly understand what they experienced—other veterans" and quotes Afghanistan veteran Daniel Meisenholder, who insists that "it's a lot easier talking to someone who was deployed and who shared the same experiences than someone who has no idea what we're talking about."[47]

Here again are echoes of long-held assumptions about wilderness culture, homosocial masculinity, and American identity. Karen R. Jones explains that as anxieties over industrialization and an enervated society troubled many Americans in the late nineteenth century, "Hunting, in particular, stirred the attentions of many as an activity that . . . promised healthy physical exertion and manly camaraderie."[48] She further explains that the experience of hunting was not simply about stalking and killing but also about the production of a community defined by shared experience: "The camp, and particularly the campfire, emerged as a geographic center for the construction of an *experience* with the wild and, most importantly, for the retelling of the quest. The fireside, in particular, served as staging post and center of the mobile community. . . . The camp represented a space of masculine corroboration, conviviality, and memorialization. Hunters mustered at the end of the day to ritualistically ruminate and commit the chase to the spiritual wood smoke, collectively choreographing their encounters with wild things."[49]

Although what is being memorialized in twenty-first-century veterans' programs is not the outdoor activity itself but rather the larger experience of veteran identity, Jones's notion of the production of a "mobile community" rings true here as well. Veterans who have gone hunting with the Wounded Warriors in Action Foundation have posted reviews that share this sentiment. "I don't fit in much but this trip lets me know that there is a lot of family out there and I'm glad I got to do this," wrote an army veteran who went alligator hunting. Another wrote, "What an amazing group of guys. . . . Just being able to be around other folks that have been through and have faced the same uphill battles was phenomenal." And yet another, this one a marine who went fishing, wrote, "The thing I liked most of all is having someone that I can talk to and being able to relate about the same issues."[50] Likewise, in a *Veteran Outdoors* episode dedicated to elk hunting in Wyoming, retired army sergeant first class Jason Burr explains that "you don't know the other soldiers' limitations. They might not know theirs. But as you come together and talk, there's an overcoming of the events that have happened to them. . . . It's the old motto, you may be hurt but you're not dead yet. You keep on going."[51]

This claim is also central to *High Ground*. Repeatedly, the veterans stress that they no longer feel comfortable in civilian society. Dan Sidles, a marine veteran struggling with PTSD, explains that "coming home is rough. . . . In my opinion, that's when the war's fought, when you get back here. You just see people living life, happy to be alive, and you wonder, 'why don't I feel that'? . . . It's really hard to try to reestablish yourself in society because it's just so different. It's just so boring."

That civilians are incapable of understanding veterans' experiences and that veterans must turn inward to a community based on their shared experiences is also central to the experience of Katherine Ragazzino, a marine veteran who is suffering from mTBI. For her the solution is to bond with other veterans. "It's so hard for me to be out here in this world, because it doesn't seem like I fit," she explains. "The only time I feel comfortable is around other military personnel. Because anyone out there can say you're a little off, you're loopy. . . . It's sad because people still don't get it that not all pain is physical." In Ragazzino's experience, the civilian world refuses to even recognize the veterans' struggles, and it is only the community of veterans that can appreciate them.

Ultimately, it is only within the community of veterans offered by the expedition that Sidles can find any solidarity, or even affection. "The camaraderie and being around the vets, I feel that a lot," he reflects late in the film. "Kind of like how I felt it in the Marine Corps. And since I got out, that's been gone. And now I feel that again. I feel that love and it feels good. I think that's human nature to want to be loved." This is true for Ragazzino as well. Central to the film is her friendship with a fellow marine and TBI patient, Cody Miranda. "Sometimes you feel so lost. Well, maybe this person will understand me more because they've been through it." Miranda agrees, asserting that "we just relate so much to each other. It's kind of hard to pick one of your friends from high school. You talk to them, they don't know what you're talking about half the time."

Each of these excerpts advances the same argument: veterans will heal in a community, but that community must be isolated from a larger culture that inherently cannot understand them and in which they are marginalized. This emphasis on veterans' outdoor rehabilitation programs as spaces separate from an ignorant, unappreciative civilian society in which veterans can heal by making connections with others who have shared their deployment experiences further inhibits the development of a narrative of shared social responsibility in two ways.

First, the insistent assertion that veterans can heal simply through conversations with other veterans dismisses the importance of evidence-based therapies in the treatment of mental health issues. Research conducted during the wars in Iraq and Afghanistan has provided increasing indications that three therapies—eye-movement desensitization and reprocessing, cognitive processing therapy, and prolonged exposure therapy—offer significant promise in treating PTSD. Concurrent with this, however, has been a growing skepticism of the older methods of group therapy and talk therapy first used to treat Vietnam veterans as part of the "rap sessions" instigated by psychologists such as Robert Jay Lifton and Chaim Shatan. As Paula P. Schnurr, a researcher at the VA's National Center for PTSD, explained in 2008, "Although group therapy is widely used in VA, military, and civilian settings, there have been few [randomized controlled trials] of group therapy and the existing evidence is weak."[52]

Second, none of these programs purport to help veterans' ability to share their stories with nonveterans, and even those programs that promise to help veterans "'move on' with their lives" seem premised on the assumption that veterans' stories have to be processed but not shared. Thus, in establishing endeavors like this as the primary avenue through which healing will take place, media coverage of and advertising for outdoor recreation programs reinforce the civilian/military divide and prevent veterans' accounts of their experiences, as well as a more complete understanding of the physical and psychological costs of war, from being part of the public debate over American militarism. And as Martini points out with regard to the absence of veteran voices in the debate over *American Sniper,* the greater inclusion of those who have fought these wars in conversations about their history and significance should be a priority as the nation grapples with these conflicts' legacies.

Providing better access to care and better treatment for veterans depends upon a cultural understanding of veterans' issues as a shared social responsibility—one that requires increased awareness of veterans' struggles and of the research and treatment they require and greater political advocacy to ensure the financial commitments necessary to hire the staff, fund the research, and build the facilities necessary to develop and implement the treatments that show the most promise for helping veterans recover. The discourse that *High Ground* and other portrayals of veterans' outdoor programs create, however, inhibits the development of the consciousness that is a necessary prelude to those commitments. In presenting veterans' recuperation as happening through casual conversations, they undermine the need for fully funded, publicly provided research and treatment. In casting that recovery as happening only among other veterans, and in spite of the public's disengagement, they undermine the need for a greater public awareness of and a commitment to veterans' issues. Together, these two outcomes help perpetuate American empire. In casting the wars' physical and psychological consequences as easily managed and recuperation as occurring privately and requiring no public commitment, these texts implicitly deny the significant costs of the expeditionary conflicts in Iraq and Afghanistan that have been central to the maintenance of American empire. In doing so, they contribute to empire's enduring invisibility and, thus, to its perpetuation.

"I JUST HAD IN THE MILITARY WHAT I'M MISSING IN THE OUTSIDE WORLD, AND THIS IS KIND OF A REFLECTION OF THAT": NORMALIZING MILITARISM IN AMERICAN CULTURE

Beyond suggesting that veteran rehabilitation can happen easily and without public attention and thus that the public is absolved from meaningfully attending to the costs of the U.S. imperial wars, there is one additional way in which cultural products about veterans' outdoor programs contribute to the endurance of U.S. empire. They normalize its trappings. That is, the film and advertising for veterans' rehabilitation programs do not present veterans' recuperation as dependent on shedding their military identities as they return to civilian society. Rather, representations of these programs consistently suggest that they are appropriate for veterans because they allow them to make continued use of their military skills in a civilian environment. In doing so, they suggest that recovery and healing can take place without disowning the trappings of militarism and, in fact, that those trappings play an important role in American culture as a whole.

These portrayals are not the only place in American culture where this discourse has emerged; the concluding minutes of *American Sniper,* for example, portray Chris Kyle's work with wounded veterans as—quite literally—an effort to recuperate lost masculinity through the continued application of military skill. When a wounded veteran whom Kyle takes shooting hits the target, he remarks, "Damn, if that don't feel like I got my balls back."[53] The veteran recreation programs that I have discussed throughout this chapter likewise contribute to the maintenance of American empire by normalizing the militarism required to maintain it. The domestication of the tools of empire has been a subject of increasing interest for scholars concerned, for example, with the militarization of domestic law enforcement and the deployment of military techniques and technologies on marginalized communities within the United States. As Ariana E. Vigil writes, for example, "the use of militarized violence within particular communities speaks to the extent to which armies do not only use force 'over there.'"[54] Rather, she points out, the boundary between the manifestations of U.S. empire abroad and the subjugation of communities inside the United States is quite porous.[55] As she points out, "violent practices associated with war occur with increasing frequency in supposedly nonmilitarized spaces."[56] For Vigil, the United States' southern border is such a space due to the immigration and antinarcotics policies that are enforced around it.[57] But there are, of course, other ways in which the militarized technologies of U.S. empire pervade American culture, including in urban policing practices and the prison-industrial complex.[58]

The acceptability of such practices, Alicia C. Decker, Summer Forrester, and Elliot Blackburn explain, relies upon what they term "normalizing the militarization of everyday life," including a cultural acquiescence to militarism's manifestations—one in which military technologies and capabilities initially designed to wage war and maintain empire come to be viewed as normal in domestic spaces.[59] As the historian Michael Sherry has shown, the principles and values of what he terms "militarization" permeate American culture and have for decades "provided the memories, models, and metaphors that shaped broad areas of national life."[60] More bluntly, Decker and her colleagues draw on Cynthia Enloe's formulation that militarism is evident when an object "becomes *controlled by, dependent on, or derives its value from* the military as an institution or militaristic criteria" to argue that "militarism is all around us" and that "the roots of militarism run deep and can be found in some of the most unexpected places."[61] The normalization of U.S. empire and the militarism that sustains it, that is, depend upon narratives that establish the principles and practices of that militarism as innocuous, if not essential, aspects of everyday life.

The presentation of veterans repurposing their military training as part of rehabilitative recreational pursuits is, I suggest, one of these "unexpected places." Throughout the advertisements and media coverage of these programs, and particularly in *High Ground,* outdoor recreation is posited as an activity that allows veterans to maintain their military identity and continue making use of the skills central to their military careers. The implication of these claims is twofold. First, these accounts cast capacities that facilitate war making not as technologies of violence but rather as innocuous parts of everyday life. Second, they suggest that a veteran can recuperate from the physical or psychological ravages of war without disowning the vestiges of militarism. Rather, the capacities become essential to that recovery. These portrayals thus help normalize U.S. militarism and facilitate its further deployment in the service of U.S. imperialism.

This idea informs much of the rhetoric that surrounds these programs. In accounts of veterans going hunting, stalking a wild animal is described in language specifically intended to evoke combat operations in Iraq and Afghanistan. Once again, the presentation of these programs profoundly echoes the arguments made for big game hunting and other outdoor activities by those late-nineteenth-century Americans who worried that modernity had sapped something crucial from American manhood and believed that "time spent in pursuit of game offered welcome retreat into a past age of action, instinct, and survivalism."[62] Veterans can "[become] a makeshift platoon" or be "as good a solder in this field as he was in others," and the hunt can be explicitly described as "a way of using your combat skills."[63] Wilderness. org explains that while for veterans "the sense of camaraderie, adventure, intense team work, and commitment to a cause larger than oneself is often replaced by mundane tasks. . . . Outdoor settings can help replicate teamwork opportunities or the sense of physical accomplishment in outdoor survival situations that is so inherent in military service."[64] For Joshua Brandon, writing on the Sierra Club's website, "Mountaineering has always replicated the good things that come from combat. Camaraderie, putting your life in the hands of your team in pursuit of a dangerous objective, the inherent risk and thrill, operations and logistics, an adversary, and a sense of self worth and extraordinary accomplishment. The mountains have been a place for me to move on with my life and heal after ten years in the Army."[65]

Though Brandon posits mountaineering as a way of "moving on," he offers, in fact, a celebration of combat. As a result, the healing that he discovers does not require him to disown that earlier identity but rather to more fully embrace it. In a similar vein, though perhaps even more explicit, is Outward Bound's description of its veterans programming: "These expeditions purposefully scaffold wartime experiences (carrying heavy packs, sore shoulders, rubbery legs, sleeping out, strange noises, sweat, dirt, frustration, and anger) with authentic achievements to create positive emotional and mental outcomes. . . . Many veterans experienced courage, brotherhood, and a real sense of power while in combat. Outward Bound gives Veterans and service members an opportunity to re-experience these strengths in themselves in a different context, thus helping them transition back to civilian life."[66]

In these stories, the skills that service members learn in their training and deploy in combat are explicitly, and uncritically, redefined as beneficial in the civilian world, and here as well the transition to civilian life does not require a disowning of the previous military identity but merely its adaptation to a new set of demands. These narratives thus contribute to the United States' enduring embrace of militarism and its increasing presence in domestic life.

This sentiment is also central to *High Ground,* which repeatedly casts the expedition as one in which veterans make use of skills they first honed in the military. Early in the film, journalist Brian Mockehaupt, who was embedded with U.S. troops in Iraq, explains, "I've really been amazed at the parallels between the military and mountaineering. There's this sense of, one, camaraderie, and the personalities can be quite similar. You know you're getting all this gear together, you're preparing, you're training, you're going out, there's these, you know, mission briefings, the same thing as when you're getting ready for patrol."

Beyond the similarities, however, is the insistent notion that former service members will recapture the "sense of camaraderie," purpose, and accomplishment they had felt while deployed. "I can't explain why," one member of the expedition explains, "but those are some of the best moments of my life. And here I think there's a way you can replicate that." When former marine Cody Miranda decides not to attempt the summit of Lobuche in order to stay with Ragazzino, who is suffering from altitude sickness, he tells the other veterans in the expedition that "I just had in the military what I'm missing in the outside world, and this is kind of a reflection of that. It's a good thing to hold on to. It's not always about what's out there. It's about the guy next to you." Dan Sidles, meanwhile, offers an even more explicit account of how outdoor adventure replicates the combat experience:

> When you get out of combat you're kind of lost because you don't have that threat, you know what I'm saying. And it's like your mind almost needs that. Not necessarily from another human being, but that challenge, that adrenaline, and that's kind of why I'm here, and I hope I can kind of get that back. Climbing a mountain in the Himalayas, there's that chance you might not come back. And going to war, there's definitely a chance you might not come back. But I guess that makes you keep your guard up, pay attention, make you not want to let down the guy to your left or right, or the woman to your left of right.

Sidles's comment is important because it identifies outdoor adventure not as an opportunity to recuperate or escape from the tribulations brought on by combat but rather as an opportunity to maintain the psychological posture that combat demands. Significantly, these are behaviors that the army has explicitly endeavored to reduce in returning troops through the Battlemind program, which casts them as useful behaviors in a combat zone that can prove problematic at home. "The battle mindset that sustained your survival in the *combat-zone*," a brochure by the Walter Reed Army Institute for Research's Land Combat Study Team, which developed the Battlemind program given to returning soldiers, explains, "may be hazardous to your social and behavioral health in the *home-zone*."[67] For example, "tactical awareness" in the combat zone becomes "hypervigilance" at home, while "emotional control" becomes "detachment."[68] Much of the army's efforts, then, have been around helping soldiers expect that behaviors learned during deployment will persist upon return but that a successful adjustment to civilian life requires that they dissipate.[69] "It is CRITICAL," the brochure explains, "that you not let your combat behaviors and reactions determine how you will respond at home."[70] Indeed, central to the army's efforts to reduce suicide and other negative outcomes for returned soldiers has been reducing their participation in what are termed "high-risk behaviors," which include those that seek to recreate the emotional rush of combat.[71]

In *High Ground,* however, the desire to replicate the adrenaline rush of combat is embraced, not cautioned against, and the potential for an outdoor adventure to replicate it is celebrated. In making this assertion, the film suggests that the attitudes and behaviors that service members cultivate in the military are not problematic in civilian life and should in fact be encouraged. If this sentiment is troubling, given the high incidence of suicides and accidental deaths that the army attributes to high-risk behavior, it also works to normalize those attitudes and behaviors within American culture more generally. Militarized behavior, the film posits, is something to embrace and celebrate, not something that veterans must abandon in order to heal.

CONCLUSION: "WOUNDS SALVES CAN'T TOUCH"

In much of the United States, late September means that deer season is a few weeks away. And that means, in turn, that local newspapers are again publishing articles about organizations that will take veterans hunting. Such articles, unsurprisingly, are replete with the discourses that I have analyzed throughout this essay. Georgia's *Augusta Chronicle,* for example, explained in a September 21, 2016, article that "the combination of reflective time spent alone in the dappled light of the deep woods and the focus of the hunt followed by camaraderie around a campfire can heal wounds salves can't touch."[72]

Certainly, many veterans enjoy these activities, just as nonveterans do, even if the psychological benefits of the hunt and the camaraderie that attends it are unproven. Moreover, it is certainly the case that veterans who return from war with physical injuries or behavioral health conditions can and should be able to participate in a range of outdoor activities and that making those activities accessible has inherent benefits. Quite apart from these questions, however, is the question of how the popular representation of these programs enables Americans to think about the realities of the United States' twenty-first-century wars and the militarism that enables American empire. The concept of "imperial benevolence" that animates this volume contends that the United States' global interventions in the twenty-first century have relied upon narratives rooted in American innocence and the benign nature of its global actions. Although these discourses have been constructed in a variety of cultural locations, the high visibility of wounded U.S. troops returning from increasingly unpopular wars in Iraq and Afghanistan has troubled assertions that the wars have been worthwhile or that they have not had a devastating impact on a generation of American service members. Indeed, the visibility of the wounded has consistently served as evidence for antiwar sentiment.

Against these representations, however, the growing popularity of outdoor recreation programs for veterans helps reassert the imperial benevolence at the heart of contemporary U.S. foreign policy. *High Ground* and other portrayals of veteran rehabilitation contribute to the construction of American benevolence by offering a facile narrative of rehabilitation, promising that Americans can and should be absolved from engaging with, and paying for, the physical costs of the wars that help perpetuate American empire and normalizing militarism as a beneficial component of American culture. In doing so, they offer a problematic narrative that distances Americans from the realities of U.S. war making while minimizing the personal and collective consequences of that violence and denying public responsibility for it. In framing veterans' injuries as largely inconsequential and their recovery as private, that is, these programs contribute to the persistence of narratives that normalize American empire while obscuring its costs.

NOTES

1. S.2706, www.congress.gov/bill/114th-congress/senate-bill/2706.

2. H.R. 5452, 109th Cong., 2d Sess. (2006), https://www.congress.gov /bill/110th-congress/house-bill/652.

3. H.R. 3976, 113th Cong., 2d Sess. (2014), www.congress.gov/bill/113th -congress/house-bill/3976/text.

4. House Committee on Natural Resources, Subcommittee on Public Lands and Environmental Regulation, H.R. _____, *"Federal Lands Recreation Enhancement Act; H.E. 2743, "Veterans Eagle Parks Pass Act"; and H.R. 3976, "Wounded Veterans Recreation Act,"* 113th Cong., 2d Sess. (2014), 6–7.

5. On the domestic histories of empire that are central to the National Park system, see Mark David Spence, *Dispossessing the Wilderness: Indian Removal and the Making of the National Parks* (New York: Oxford University Press, 1999). On the relationship between westward expansion, racism, and imperialism, see also

Richard Slotkin, *Gunfighter Nation: The Myth of the Frontier in Twentieth-Century America* (Norman: University of Oklahoma Press, 1998), 10.

6. For articles suggesting the benefits of these programs, see among others Jason Duvall and Rachel Kaplan, "Enhancing the Well-Being of Veterans Using Extended Group-Based Nature Recreation Exercises," *Journal of Rehabilitation Research and Development* 51, no. 5 (2014): 685–696; Elizabeth Jane Vella, Brianna Milligan, and Jesse Lynn Bennett, "Participation in Outdoor Recreation Program Predicts Improved Psychosocial Well-Being among Veterans with Post-Traumatic Stress Disorder: A Pilot Study," *Military Medicine* 178, no. 3 (2013): 254–260; Stephanie Westlund, "'Becoming Human Again': Exploring Connections between Nature and Recovery from Stress and Post-Traumatic Distress," *Work* 50, no. 1 (2015): 161–174; Nick Caddick, Brett Smith, and Cassandra Phoenix, "The Effects of Surfing and the Natural Environment on the Well-Being of Combat Veterans," *Qualitative Health Research* 25, no. 1 (2015): 76–86.

7. Nick Turse, "Tomgram: Nick Turse, A Secret War in 135 Countries," *TomDispatch,* September 24, 2015, www.tomdispatch.com/post/176048 /tomgram%3A_nick_turse,_a_secret_war_in_135_countries.

8. Mary Dudziak, *War Time: An Idea, Its History, and Its Consequences* (New York: Oxford University Press, 2012), 132.

9. Andrew Bacevich, *Breach of Trust: How Americans Failed Their Soldiers and Their Country* (New York: Metropolitan, 2013), 13.

10. Amy Kaplan, "'Left Alone with America:' The Absence of Empire in The Study of American Culture," in *Cultures of United States Imperialism,* ed. Amy Kaplan and Donald E. Pease (Durham, NC: Duke University Press, 1993), 11.

11. Jacqueline Klimas, "More Than 1,000 Troops Have Lost Limbs in Iraq, Afghanistan: Report," *Washington Times,* December 17, 2014.

12. Ibid.; Matthew S. Goldberg, "Updated Death and Injury Rates of U.S. Military Personnel During Conflicts in Iraq and Afghanistan," Congressional Budget Office Working Paper 2014-08, December 2014, 10, www.cbo.gov/sites /default/files/113th-congress-2013-2014/workingpaper/49837-Casualties_Working Paper-2014-08_1.pdf.

13. Elizabeth M. Collins, "The Day the World Went Black: Soldiers Blinded in the Line of Duty," *Soldiers: The Official U.S Army Magazine,* n.d., http://soldiers. dodlive.mil/2014/03/the-day-the-world-went-black-soldiers-blinded-in-the-line -of-duty/.

14. David Kieran, "Veterans' Readjustment after the Iraq and Afghanistan Wars," in *Understanding the U.S. Wars in Iraq and Afghanistan,* ed. Beth Bailey and Richard H. Immerman (New York: New York University Press, 2015), 387; "How Common is PTSD?," National Center for PTSD, Department of Veterans Affairs, August 13, 2015, www.ptsd.va.gov/public/PTSD-overview/basics/how-common-is -ptsd.asp.

15. Andrew C. McKevitt, "'Watching the War Made Us Immune:' The Popular Culture of the Wars," in Bailey and Immerman, *Understanding the U.S. Wars,* 244.

16. See, for example, Stefany Bornman, "62-Year-Old Completes 22 Push Up Challenge to Raise Awareness for Veteran Suicide," WJBF, November 25, 2016, http://wjbf.com/2016/11/25/62-year-old-completes-22-day-push-up-challenge -to-raise-awareness-for-veteran-suicide/; "Wounded Warrior Project's Top Execs Fired amid Lavish Spending Scandal," Fox News, March 10, 2016, www.foxnews .com/us/2016/03/10/wounded-warrior-project-reportedly-fires-top-executives -amid-spending-controversy.html.

17. Terri Tanielian and Lisa H. Jaycox, eds. *Invisible Wounds of War: Psychological and Cognitive Injuries, Their Consequences, and Services to Assist Recovery* (Santa Monica: RAND, 2008).

18. John M. Kinder, *Paying with Their Bodies: American War and the Problem of the Disabled Veteran* (Chicago: University of Chicago Press, 2015), 292.

19. Cong. Rec. H1524 (February 13, 2007) (Representative Solis of California).

20. Cong. Rec. H7056 (June 25, 2007) (Representative McDermott of Washington, speaking on "Bring the Soldiers Home").

21. Kinder, *Paying with Their Bodies*, 4.

22. Ibid., 122; Elaine Scarry, *The Body in Pain: The Making and Unmaking of the World* (Oxford: Oxford University Press, 1985), 80.

23. Zoe H. Wool, *After War: The Weight of Life at Walter Reed* (Durham, NC: Duke University Press, 2015), 12–13.

24. Kinder, *Paying with Their Bodies*, 3. Kinder addresses the role that individualist discourses play in shaping attitudes toward war-related injury (295).

25. House Committee on Natural Resources, Subcommittee on Public Lands and Environmental Regulation, H.R. _____, *"Federal Lands Recreation Enhancement Act; H.E. 2743, "Veterans Eagle Parks Pass Act"; and H.R. 3976, "Wounded Veterans Recreation Act,"* 113th Cong., 2d Sess. (2014), 6–7.

26. Mike Matz, "Why Veterans Fight for Conservation of U.S. Public Lands," Pew Charitable Trusts, November 11, 2015, www.pewtrusts.org/en/research-and- analysis/analysis/2015/11/10/why-veterans-fight-for-conservation-of-us-public -lands.

27. Slotkin, *Gunfighter Nation*, 10, 14.

28. For an analysis of one critique of this rhetoric, see Caren J. Town, "'The Most Blatant of All Our American Myths': Masculinity, Male Bonding, and the Wilderness in Sinclair Lewis' *Mantrap*," *Journal of Men's Studies* 12, no. 3 (2004): 193–205.

29. Ralph Waldo Emerson, "Nature," American Transcendentalism Web, n.d., http://archive.vcu.edu/english/engweb/transcendentalism/authors/emerson /nature.html

30. Karen R. Jones, *Epiphany in the Wilderness: Hunting, Nature, and Performance in the Nineteenth Century American West* (Boulder: University of Colorado Press, 2015), 39.

31. Ibid., 56.

32. Edmund Morris, *The Rise of Theodore Roosevelt* (New York: Random House, 1979), 259, 280. See also Roger L. DiSilvestro, *Theodore Roosevelt in the Badlands: A*

Young Politician's Quest for Recovery in the American West (New York: Walker, 2011), 67.

33. Ibid., 2–3.

34. Jones, *Epiphany in the Wilderness,* 39.

35. "Veterans Find Healing in the Wilderness," The Wilderness Society (blog), November 8, 2013, http://wilderness.org/blog/veterans-find-healing-wilderness; Ibid.

36. Joshua Brandon, "Warriors and Film in the North Cascades," *Sierra Club Outdoors,* Sierra Club, August 11, 2014, www.sierraclub.org/outdoors/2014/08 /warriors-and-film-north-cascades.

37. Tony Maples, *Veteran Outdoors,* 2016, http://veteran-outdoors.com.

38. Matthew McGowan, "Episode 8: Matagorda Bay Texas," *Veteran Outdoors,* December 3, 2015, https://veteran-outdoors.com/episode-8-matagorda-bay-texas/.

39. Jeannette Catsoulis, "Therapy from a Mountaintop," *New York Times,* November 1, 2002; Kenneth Turan, "Movie Review: Summit is One of Many Challenges in 'High Ground,'" review of *High Ground,* directed by Michael Brown, *Los Angeles Times,* November 1, 2012; Ian Buckwalter, "Battered but Not Broken, Vets Seek 'High Ground,'" National Public Radio, November 1, 2012, www.npr. org/2012/11/01/163010120/battered-but-not-broken-vets-seek-high-ground; Avery Stonich, "Can Outdoor Adventure Heal the Wounds of War?" *Beyond the Edge: National Geographic Adventure* (blog), November 9, 2012, http://adventureblog. nationalgeographic.com/tag/high-ground/; Amy Bounds, "'Chasing Ice' Wraps Up Boulder International Film Festival," *Boulder Daily Camera,* February 19, 2012; *High Ground,* n.d., http://highgroundmovie.com.

40. "Ohio: Blind Veteran and Adventurer Steve Baskis to Give Presidential Lecture at Wright State," *Plus Media Solutions,* March 31, 2015; "Willow Glen Shorts: Library Screens 'High Ground,'" *San Jose Mercury News,* November 5, 2014; "Filmmaker, Climber to Answer Questions at Screening," *Feather River Bulletin,* October 9, 2013.

41. *High Ground,* directed by Michael Brown, Khumbu Pictures, 2012, DVD.

42. For accounts of veterans claiming that their injuries have been barriers to success, see among many others David Bruce, "Erie Veteran Lives with Traumatic Brain Injury," *Erie Times-News,* April 9, 2010; Malcolm Garcia, "The Fog of War: Vet Struggles with Brain Injury," *Monterey County Herald,* October 16, 2008; Thomas Himes, "California Home to More Wounded and Killed Veterans of Iraq and Afghanistan Than Any Other State," *Whitier Daily News,* May 29, 2011; Paul Thissen, "Returning Veterans Now Battling at Home," *Contra Costa Times,* July 14, 2009; "A Trying Transition," *Daily News of Newburyport,* September 9, 2010; and "Brain-Injured Veterans Face Lifelong Struggles," *Chico Enterprise-Record,* March 31, 2008. See also Kieran, "Veterans Readjustment," 401–402.

43. Megan Hoyer, "Half of Critical Positions Open at Some VA Hospitals," *USA Today,* September 4, 2015; Jeanette Steele, "Not Enough Psychiatrists for Veterans," *San Diego Tribune,* September 16, 2015.

44. Kinder, *Paying with Their Bodies,* 295.

45. "Veterans in Wilderness," Wilderness Society.

46. Ibid.

47. John N. Felsher, "Helping Veterans Heal Through Hunting, Fishing," *Alabama Living*, n.d., http://alabamaliving.coop/article/helping-veterans-heal -through-hunting-fishing/.

48. Jones, *Epiphany in the Wilderness*, 37.

49. Ibid., 63–64.

50. "Wounded Warrior Testimonials," Wounded Warriors in Action Foundation, n.d., www.wwiaf.org/testimonials.php.

51. "Episode 4: Sheridan Wyoming Part I," *Veteran Outdoors*, November 30, 2015, http://veteran-outdoors.com/episode-4-sheridan-wyoming-part-1/.

52. Paula P. Schnurr, "Pharmacotherapy," *PTSD Research Quarterly* 19, no. 8 (2003): 2.

53. *American Sniper*, directed by Clint Eastwood (Los Angeles, CA: Warner Bros., 2014), Amazon video.

54. Ariana E. Vigil, *War Echoes: Gender and Militarization in U.S. Latina/o Cultural Production* (New Brunswick, NJ: Rutgers University Press, 2014), 4.

55. Ibid., 3–4.

56. Ibid., 9.

57. Ibid., 191.

58. Daryl Meeks, "Police Militarization in Urban Areas: The Obscure War against the Underclass," *Black Scholar* 35, no. 4 (2006): 36. See also Abigail R. Hall and Christopher H. Coyne, "The Militarization of U.S. Domestic Policing," *Independent Review* 17, no. 4 (2013): 486; Nancy Scheper-Hughes, "The Militarization and Madness of Everyday Life," *South Atlantic Quarterly* 113, no. 3 (2014): 642. This militarization of the everyday is also reflected in the popularity among veterans of first-person shooter games, which have been used in both training and as therapy. See Steve Wilson, "Video Games Show Promise as Therapy," Military.com, April 9, 2014, www.military.com/benefits/2014/04/09/video-games-show-promise-as-therapy.html; Colin Campbell, "How Games Are Helping Veterans Recover from Injury," *Polygon*, April 29, 2016, www.polygon.com/features /2016/4/29/11530306/operation-supply-drop. On the use of video simulation throughout service members' careers, see John Pettegrew, *Light It Up: The Marine Eye for Battle in Iraq* (Baltimore: Johns Hopkins University Press, 2015), 65–95; and Robertson Allen, "Software and Soldier Lifecycles of Recruitment, Training, and Rehabilitation in the Post-9/11 Era," in *The War of My Generation: Youth Culture and the War on Terror*, ed. David Kieran (New Brunswick, NJ: Rutgers University Press, 2015), 144–170.

59. Alicia C. Decker et al., "Rethinking Everyday Militarism on Campus: Feminist Reflections of the Fatal Shooting at Purdue University," *Feminist Studies* 42, no. 1 (2016): 203.

60. Michael S. Sherry, *In the Shadow of War: The United States since the 1930s* (New Haven, CT: Yale University Press, 1995), xi.

61. Decker et al., "Rethinking Everyday Militarism on Campus," 194–195.

62. Jones, *Epiphany in the Wilderness,* 39–40.

63. Katy Steinmetz, "Patriot Game," *Time,* June 22, 2013, http://swampland
.time.com/2013/06/22/patriot-game-groups-promote-hunting-as-therapy-for-veter
ans/; Jonathan Miles, "The Silencer: An Iraq War Veteran Finds Healing through
Hunting," *Field and Stream,* n.d., www.fieldandstream.com/articles/hunting
/2016/04/the-silencer-an-iraq-war-veteran-finds-healing-through-hunting.

64. "Veterans in Wilderness," Wilderness Society.

65. Brandon, "Warriors and Film in the North Cascades."

66. "About Outward Bound for Veterans," Outward Bound, 2018, www.out
wardbound.org/veteran-adventures/about/.

67. WRAIR Land Combat Study Team, "Battlemind Training I: Transitioning
from Combat to Home," February 15, 2006, www.ptsd.ne.gov/pdfs/WRAIR
-battlemind-training-Brochure.pdf.

68. Ibid.

69. On the clinical success of the Battlemind training program, see Amy B.
Adler, et al., "Battlemind Debriefing and Battlemind Training as Early Interventions
with Soldiers Returning from Iraq: Randomization by Platoon," *Journal of
Consulting and Clinical Psychology* 77, no. 5 (2009): 928–940.

70. WRAIR Land Combat Study Team, "Battlemind Training I."

71. See, for example, Elisabeth Bumiller, "Army Studies Thrill-Seeking
Behavior," *New York Times,* October 30, 2010.

72. Parish Howard, "Avid Hunter Provides Free Hunting Opportunities for
Veterans," *Augusta Chronicle,* September 21, 2016, http://chronicle.augusta.com/news
/metro/2016-09-21/avid-hunter-provides-free-hunting-opportunities-veterans#.

FOUR

Exceptional Soldiers

IMAGINING THE PRIVATIZED
MILITARY ON U.S. TELEVISION

Stacy Takacs

All the world thinks of the United States as an empire, except the people of the United States. . . . Foreigners pay little attention to what we say. They observe what we do. We on the other hand think of what we *feel*. And the result is that we go on creating what mankind calls an empire while we continue to believe quite sincerely that it is not an empire *because it does not feel to us the way we imagine an empire ought to feel*.

WALTER LIPPMANN,
"Empire: The Days of Our Nonage Are Over," 1927[1]

THOUGH HE WAS DISCUSSING THE VARIOUS U.S. interventions in Latin America and the Caribbean in the early twentieth century, political commentator Walter Lippmann's suggestion that "feeling," or emotion, plays an important role in the disavowal of American imperialism seems as apt today as it was then. Feminist scholars like Elizabeth Anker, Lauren Berlant, Linda Williams, and Tanine Allison link this feeling of innocence specifically to the propensity for melodrama in U.S. popular and political cultures.[2] "As an emotionally heightened narrative form that works to establish moral virtues in a secular world," melodrama foregrounds the role of love and hate, pathos and fear, in the constitution of national identity.[3] Yet melodrama does not just use emotion to reinforce attachments to the nation; it also works, narratologically, to convert national shame into national virtue. As Anker puts it: "Melodramatic political discourse casts [the] politics, policies, and practices of citizenship within a moral economy that identifies the nation-state as a virtuous and innocent victim of villainous action. It locates goodness in the suffering of the nation, evil in its antagonists, and heroism in sovereign acts of war and global control coded as expressions of virtue. . . . [As such, it] provides the tableaux and the legitimacy for the late-modern expansion of state power."[4] This chapter examines the role American television programs have played in the production and reproduction of such feelings of imperial innocence. It maintains that the U.S. television industry's parochialism, coupled with its preference for melodramatic tales of redemption through violence, reinforces the national preference for perception over reality when it comes to assessing American foreign policy ventures. We Americans do not reckon with our actions, at least in part, because we do not represent them honestly to ourselves. Instead, we see them as heroic acts of redemption necessitated by some injury to ourselves and our nation.

One way to create a feeling of American innocence is through projection, a mode of disavowal whereby unpleasant facts are acknowledged, but responsibility for them is laid at the feet of others. This essay examines an increasingly important locus of such projection—the privatized military and security corporation, or PMSC. Since the end of the Cold War and the downsizing of state militaries that followed, the market for militarized security and support services has exploded, altering the calculus by which we understand geopolitics. In the United States, for example, private firms now provide the bulk of the logistics, training, security, and support services required to stage a war. They have become such an indispensable part of the U.S. war machine that the military literally could not deploy without them.[5] Moreover, because private military firms are not subject to the same forms of regulation and oversight, their existence undermines international conventions for the use of force and alters the political calculations associated with waging war. PMSCs offer an expedient way for elites to bypass legal and political restrictions on the use of force to achieve policy goals, making war easier to conduct and manage. Meanwhile, PMSCs stand to make a lot of money by providing such military services with few questions asked. Under such conditions, critics contend, there is little incentive to pursue diplomatic means to resolve security crises, and war becomes a self-perpetuating profit machine on a scale President Dwight D. Eisenhower could hardly have imagined when he delivered his well-known indictment of the "military-industrial complex" in 1961.[6]

Of course, mercenary forces have a long and storied history. Mercenary armies were central to the defense of European strongholds during the Middle Ages; flourished in Switzerland, France, and most importantly, Italy, during the early modern period, and figured prominently in conflicts such as the American Revolution, the Latin American revolts of the 1800s, the American Civil War, the post–World War I uprisings in China and Spain, and the various colonial/anticolonial struggles of the late twentieth century.[7] The U.S. Department of Defense has relied on contractors to provide maintenance and support services since the Vietnam War, and the practice grew in scale and scope—with contractors taking on additional logistics, training, and even combat duties—as the United States moved toward an all-volunteer force in the early 1970s.[8] Nevertheless, most Americans think military contracting is a recent phenomenon, developed after 9/11 as a manifestation of the Bush administration's faith in neoliberal economics.[9] They only heard about private military firms after a series of scandals involving inflated contracts and excessive civilian casualties exposed the lack of checks and balances on PMSCs working in Iraq and Afghanistan.[10] Particularly damaging was the trial and conviction of a group of Blackwater security contractors for the murder of seventeen civilians in Nisour Square in Baghdad in September 2007.[11] Part of the reason for this ignorance has to do with neglect by the U.S. media. In 2007, the Pew Research Center conducted a content analysis of over four hundred mainstream media outlets in the United States and found that "fewer than one-quarter of those outlets—only 93 of them—ever mentioned private military contractors beyond a brief account of a death or injury. Moreover, 61 of those 93 outlets ran only a single story on the subject. In other words, only 32 news outlets, or 7% of the outlets examined, have delved into the issue of [privatized security] forces more than once, beyond a brief mention in a story about casualties or incidents." In total, less than 1 percent of the news stories about the U.S. war in Iraq addressed PMSCs, and most of those stories centered on the Blackwater trial.[12]

Content analysis of this sort provides the barest overview of public knowledge on the subject, however. Pew's researchers provided no in-depth evaluation of individual representations, no measurement of audience reaction, and, perhaps most egregiously, no information on the portrayal of private contractors in entertainment television, though representations of such parties steadily increased as the wars in Iraq and Afghanistan dragged on. This seems a serious omission given that Americans still spend, on average, thirty-five hours per week watching television, and they are not really watching the news (only half of Americans get their news from television).[13] This essay seeks to redress the omission by examining the portrayal of privatized military firms on U.S. television since 9/11. Again, my argument is that such depictions work to disavow responsibility for an aggressive foreign policy by displacing the bad outcomes onto irresponsible private operators, whose symbolic sacrifice may redeem the mission and its "official" operatives (that is, soldiers, sailors, and marines). To understand this pattern as unique to the contemporary political landscape, however, we will have to take a brief detour through television history. How have mercenaries been portrayed on television more broadly? When, where, and why have they shown up on the tube in previous ages, and how do such representations compare to contemporary ones?

GODS OF WAR—MERCENARIES ON TELEVISION, 1950–2001

The term *mercenary* has often carried negative connotations due to the suspicion that private soldiers are motivated by greed, rather than ideology, loyalty, or moral sensibility. So, it is somewhat surprising that early television depictions of "hired guns" were largely supportive of mercenaries and their activities. During the high network era (roughly 1948–1987), when ABC, CBS, and NBC enjoyed a monopoly on audience attention and television was able to exert a centrifugal influence on the public—binding citizens together in an "imagined community" of shared experience—adventure programs such as *Soldiers of Fortune* (syndication, 1955–1957), *Have Gun—Will Travel* (CBS, 1957–1963), and *The A-Team* (NBC, 1983–1987) offered heroic images of for-profit fighters, all of whom were said to be motivated by a desire to "protect the innocent" and "right injustice."[14] The question is: Why is there such a coherence around images of mercenaries as forces for good during these periods? One thing to note is that the series run for each of these programs coincided with a moment of relative restraint in U.S. foreign policy, at least in terms of the use of military force to advance American objectives. The Cold War with the Soviet Union led the United States to adopt a policy of nuclear deterrence, which significantly raised the stakes of military confrontation. It also spurred a debate in foreign policy circles about the best way to counter Soviet expansionism—through ideological or military means? The U.S. government was not passive during these periods, of course, but it did use "softer," less obvious, and less obviously coercive means of expanding its influence in the world.[15] These older adventure shows seem designed (whether consciously or unconsciously) with such strategy debates in mind and, in some cases, may have served as ideological weapons in the struggle itself.

It seems clear, for instance, that 1950s series like *Soldiers of Fortune* and *Have Gun—Will Travel* expressed common frustrations with the seemingly "tepid" foreign policy of the Eisenhower administration. Rather than deploy the military, Eisenhower utilized a combination of economic incentives and covert operations, backed by the threat of "massive retaliation," to counter Soviet expansionism. Because people could not *see* such operations unfold, however, they did not recognize how active Eisenhower's administration actually was.[16] A series of Soviet gains in the late 1950s—the establishment of a leftist dictatorship in Cuba, the renewal of hostilities in Vietnam, the launch of *Sputnik,* and more—further exacerbated public anxiety and led his political opponents (namely, John F. Kennedy) to call for a more "robust" and "vigorous" response to communism.[17] This is the background against which *Soldiers of Fortune* and *Have Gun—Will Travel* debuted and the context within which they thrived.

Whereas Eisenhower lamented the U.S. involvement in Korea, was reluctant to deploy U.S. troops abroad, and criticized the idea of a permanently mobilized military, Tim Kelly (John Russell) and Toubo Smith (Chick Chandler) of *Soldiers of Fortune* traipsed the globe in search of adventure, openly confronting Communists, criminals, and authoritarian rulers and trouncing them on a weekly basis (see figure 4.1). Though mercenaries, Kelly and Smith were often commissioned by U.S. diplomats and business leaders to undertake benevolent interventions on behalf of local populations threatened by authoritarian leaders (if American political or economic interests were also served by such endeavors, well, that was just a secondary benefit). In "Jungle Rebel" (March 23, 1955), for example, Kelly and Smith arrive in French colonial Vietnam and are enlisted by a Colonel Le Clerc (Sydney Mason) to convince their old World War II ally, Min Hue Chi (Michael Ansara), to negotiate for peace. The episode opens with the unwarranted bombing of a police lorry ("Why'd he do that?" Kelly asks), which frames the Viet Minh as terrorists and the French as innocent victims of rebel aggression. The occupiers only want peace, we are told, and have "agreed to leave" the country but have been prevented from doing so by the rebels and their "civil war" (there is no mention of the French defeat at Dien Bien Phu or the foot-dragging that followed). The rebels, meanwhile, have turned farmers into thugs and are said to be "responsible for the murder of hundreds of [their] countrymen." Though Kelly and Smith claim to be neutral (indeed, apolitical), they are forced off their middle-of-the road position when Min's fighters assault them, and Min himself betrays their trust by setting up an ambush for Le Clerc. In the end, Kelly and Smith dispatch the rebels and save Le Clerc, thereby symbolically legitimating the call for greater U.S. involvement in Vietnam. If the United

FIGURE 4.1. In *Soldiers of Fortune* (1955–1957), Tim Kelly (John Russell) and Toubo Smith (Chick Chandler) demonstrate how the command of guns translates into command of the globe. © Timeless Media Group and Revue Studios.

States were more directly involved in Vietnam, the episode seems to say, the Vietnamese and their French rulers would all be better off.

Have Gun—Will Travel was originally designed to be a globe-trotting adventure series along the lines of *Soldiers,* but the popularity of television Westerns led CBS executives to pressure the producers for changes. It remained a mercenary-themed adventure series but confined itself to exploring colonial politics on the post–Civil War Western frontier.[18] *Have Gun—Will Travel* featured a dashing hero, known only as Paladin (Richard Boone), whose gallant deeds provided a weekly argument for strength over diplomacy. Though the show predates John F. Kennedy's presidency by four years, Paladin can only be described as Kennedyesque. He is erudite, dapper, charming, and strong-willed, and his mercenary instincts are always tempered by the desire to do good. Yet he is an expert swordsman, gunslinger, and martial artist who is well schooled in military strategy and tactics, having served as an officer in the Union Army. Paladin is thus a war hero turned political mediator, like Kennedy, who, also like Kennedy, is willing to "pay any price, bear any burden, meet any hardship, support any friend, oppose any foe to assure the survival and the success of liberty" and justice on a frontier where might makes right, and racism, xenophobia, and greed are everyday affairs.[19] Though Paladin always *tries* to settle disputes using diplomacy, the program usually ends with Paladin shooting, knifing, strangling, or otherwise maiming someone. In fact, as film historian Gaylyn Studlar notes, "Because violence on *Have Gun—Will Travel* was not only frequent but also often fatal, the series became a magnet for criticism in an intensifying cultural debate about the impact of television on viewers."[20] Yet the show was one of the most popular of its age and inspired a legion of fans with its complex depictions of the "opportunities and . . . perils . . . hopes and . . . threats" to be found on the (New) Frontier.[21] Its activist orientation was arguably one of its most compelling elements for mid-century Americans, who were routinely told to view the world as a dangerous place and themselves as the best hope for securing the peace.

These reassuring images of mercenary activity faded away as U.S. overseas "entanglements" became increasingly contentious. The Vietnam War in particular seems to have temporarily cured the television industry of its fascination with militarist adventurism. There were almost no depictions of mercenaries on television from 1967 to 1983, and the military dramas and sitcoms that had saturated the schedule in the 1960s had also virtually disappeared by 1972. The only exception to this "no-adventurism" rule was the sitcom *M*A*S*H* (CBS, 1972–1983), whose antimilitarist perspective seemed to embody the political mood of the day. However, with the ascendancy of President Ronald Reagan, the phenomenon of heroic mercenarism roared back to life in the form of the fantastic adventure series *The A-Team* (NBC, 1983–1987). The wildly popular series featured a motley group of Vietnam vets, unjustly court-martialed for a crime they did not commit, who escape to the Los Angeles underground and survive by selling their martial expertise to the downtrodden and oppressed. Although the outlandish do-gooding hyperviolence caused consternation among social commentators, audiences loved it for the same reason they loved President "Peace through Strength" Reagan and macho melodramas like *Rambo: First Blood Part II* (1985) and *Missing in Action* (1984): the series worked to recuperate the Vietnam War as a "good war" lost through political and bureaucratic malfeasance.[22] In the process it also redeemed war as a potential diplomatic tool. By fetishizing military hardware and training and presenting military violence, liberated from the fetters of administrative control, as the last, best hope of a weakened state, *The A-Team* helped make war palatable again. Each episode offered a litany of fistfights, car chases, and helicopter rides, punctuated by more than occasional gunfire and explosions, always undertaken in the defense of liberty, equality, and justice. This was righteous violence, unleashed by "good" men in the pursuit of "just" causes. The violence was so righteous, in fact, that it never resulted in harm or injury. Bad guys were stabbed, shot, and blown up by the scores in each episode, but they always walked or were carted away alive and repentant.

In sum, *The A-Team*—however goofy and postmodern in its depiction of fantasy violence—was perfectly in sync with the more aggressive foreign policy posture adopted by the Reagan administration. For Reagan and his aides, America's reluctance to use force abroad post-Vietnam had increased global insecurity; the remedy was to uncrate the guns and bombs and put them back in service, or at least be *perceived* as doing so. For the most part, Reagan's foreign policy was, like the hyperviolence on *The A-Team,* more spectacle than substance. Though he joked about dropping bombs on the Soviet Union (on a live National Public Radio feed, no less), he preferred oblique and covert military activities to direct confrontation. Thus, he launched proxy wars in Angola, Cambodia, Indonesia, and Nicaragua and mobilized the military only in spaces where he could guarantee swift victory, like the tiny island of Grenada, which he invaded in 1983 to "rescue" American medical students caught in a leftist coup.[23] Though Reagan did send U.S. troops into Beirut, Lebanon, in 1983, he also swiftly removed them when a terrorist bomb blew up a barracks there, killing some 241 marines. When terrorists associated with Muammar Gaddafi bombed a Berlin discotheque in 1986, killing one U.S. service member and injuring sixty-three, Reagan chose to bomb Libya, rather than put boots on the ground. These incidents show how sensitive U.S. leaders remained to the "optics" of military casualties post-Vietnam. Reagan talked a good game, but even he was reluctant to mobilize the military to achieve his policy goals. It is during such times that television mercenaries emerge as potent fantasy figures—proxy fighters in a symbolic war to make military adventurism viable again.

Together, these series constructed a heroic image of for-profit violence as a form of salvation, a pattern I will label the "Gods of War" motif. In such series, mercenaries are not contemptuous or corruptible warmongers who place the pursuit of profit over all other motives; rather, they are patriots and civilizing agents, dispatched to savage lands to bring order and security. Though they rarely use diplomacy to resolve conflicts, they place their martial skills in the service of the downtrodden and innocent and serve as the ultimate guarantors of liberty and justice. They are good guys who must occasionally do bad things but always for the right reasons. In other words, they are perfect melodramatic heroes. This Gods of War motif seems strongest during transitional periods in American politics, when U.S. leaders are advocating for—but have not yet been able to implement—a more aggressive and expansive foreign policy. During the Cold War in particular, when the threat of nuclear annihilation and a series of disastrous proxy wars made large-scale military deployments politically untenable, the televisual celebration of mercenary activity offered a way to keep hawkish hopes and traditions alive.

For further confirmation of this theory, we might look to the failure of the post–Cold War Don Simpson/Jerry Bruckheimer series *Soldier of Fortune, Inc.* (syndication, 1997–1999). With the cessation of hostilities between the United States and the Soviet Union, the United States was finally able to "kick the Vietnam Syndrome" via full-scale military engagements in the Persian Gulf (1991) and Bosnia (1992–1995).[24] Yet, as the *Inc.* in the title of the series indicates, this was also the period when PMSCs became significant players in the international market for security.[25] The mercenaries of *Soldier of Fortune, Inc.* are thus positioned as "gray hats" willing to "[go] where the government cannot and will not openly venture, to protect national and international interests and to maintain the balance of power."[26] They are "an elite fighting unit" led by "former Army Special Forces Major Matt Shepherd," so they straddle the line between official military agents and unofficial shadow warriors. The program seemingly featured all the ingredients for a hit: attractive leads, spectacular militarized action, political cache, and a powerhouse production team with an established track record of success in the action genres.[27] Nevertheless, it failed to find either a network distributor or an audience, even after a season 2 reboot that brought beloved "bad boy" Dennis Rodman into the story. Part of the problem lay in the poor quality of the storytelling, no doubt, but much of it seems to reflect the altered historical context. For one thing, it was no longer necessary for martial warriors to act outside the system to achieve American security, a fact the producers tacitly acknowledged when they changed the name to *SOF: Special Ops Force* for season 2 (see figure 4.2).[28] For another, by the mid-1990s, the United States had become the world's uncontested superpower. It seems wish-fulfillment fantasies have little purchase when one actually *has* all the power. This exception to the Gods of War motif thus proves the rule: Positive representations of the mercenary trades succeed best when security talk is tough, but action remains impractical. Once action becomes possible again, Americans seem to prefer different sorts of stories with different types of heroes.

FIGURE 4.2. The Jerry Bruckheimer–produced *Soldier of Fortune, Inc.* (1997–1999) failed to find an audience in an age of American global supremacy. © Don Simpson/Jerry Bruckheimer Films and Rysher Entertainment.

DOGS OF WAR—MERCENARIES ON TELEVISION, 2001–PRESENT

After the terrorist attacks of September 11, 2001, the United States predictably turned to military force to redress the assault and its psychic aftermath (feelings of violation, weakness, desire for revenge, and more). The wars in Afghanistan and especially Iraq were not designed merely to salve the American soul, however. They were also calculated attempts to secure valuable land and resources for capitalist exploitation. It is no coincidence that the first act of the Coalition Provisional Authority in Iraq (CPA) was to privatize social services and open a variety of Iraqi industries, from oil production to telecom provision, to foreign bidders.[29] The CPA's tout court dismissal of all Ba'athist party members from government and security service, coupled with the rise of vengeful Shiite ideologues in the government, virtually ensured the peace would be lost. Sunni insurgents and Shiite troublemakers flooded into the newly "liberated" state, and U.S. troops became favored targets of both. The military's heavily armored response to such attacks ensured that civilian casualties would mount, thereby alienating even sympathetic locals. Meanwhile, Iraq became a testing ground for new fighters, weapons, and tactics, which were then exported to Afghanistan, Syria, and elsewhere in the Middle East and North Africa. While Barack Obama won the presidency by promising to end both wars, his administration merely shifted tactics. True, the number of U.S. troops deployed overseas declined after 2009, but the use of remote drone warfare increased, and thousands of advisory units and private contractors remained in both countries to equip, train, house, feed, and generally assist the Iraqi and Afghan security forces. By spring 2016, these policies had failed, and Obama ordered four thousand soldiers to return to Iraq to assist in combat against the Islamic State of Iraq and the Levant (ISIL, better known as the Islamic State in Syria, or ISIS, in the U.S. press); the presence of private contractors in theater grew almost tenfold to accommodate this surge.[30] Meanwhile, in Afghanistan, over thirty thousand private contractors remained in the country (as of September 2016) to provide base support, security, training, and logistics for fewer than ten thousand U.S. troops.[31] Clearly, American political leaders had decided to turn to private contractors and "shadow warriors" to solve the publicity problems associated with the continuation of these occupations.[32]

The material increase in the number of contractors fighting in the name of the United States has been matched by a symbolic increase in representations of contractors on U.S. television. As in real life, however, the work of these mercenary forces has been largely misrepresented. The military contractor has emerged in American popular culture as a bogeyman and scapegoat for the failures of U.S. foreign policy. No longer imagined as Gods of War who fight the good fight when (and because) we cannot, mercenary forces are now imagined to be "Dogs of War" whose hyperviolent shenanigans are responsible for screwing up the "good wars" in Iraq and Afghanistan. This trend was most pronounced during the height of the Sunni insurgency in Iraq, from 2004–2006. The terrorist thriller 24 (Fox, 2001–2010, 2014), for example, featured evil private military firms in both season 4 (2004–2005) and season 7 (2007–2008). The main villain in season 4 is a Middle Eastern terrorist named Habib Marwan (Arnold Vosloo), whose position as a defense contractor allows him to procure an "override" key with the power to melt down all the nuclear power plants in the United States. Marwan's company, McLennan-Forrester, is more interested in covering up its responsibility in the matter than in preserving national security, so it sets off an electromagnetic pulse in downtown

Los Angeles to wipe the company computers and sends a paramilitary unit to kill the hero, Jack Bauer (Kiefer Sutherland). In season 7, a PMSC called Starkwood (an obvious homage to Blackwater) helps an African terrorist storm the White House and later smuggle a bioweapon into the country. In both cases, the program implies that private military firms are a threat to security, rather than an aid to it. Perhaps most tellingly, given *24*'s frequent plot reversals, no member of a PMSC is ever redeemed in any of the seasons; private contractors are all greedy mercenaries whose lust for money, power, and resources makes them irredeemable. Like the other villains in the show, the misdeeds of these contractors provide the excuse needed to recuperate Jack Bauer's frequent violations of human and civil rights. Bauer can play the "good guy" because, in classic melodramatic style, his enemies are so exceedingly "bad."

The generally promilitary program *JAG* (NBC 1995–1996; CBS 1997–2005), likewise, used security contractors as alibis for military excess. In "Camp Delta" (Nov. 19, 2004), for example, the program offered a ripped-from-the-headlines story about the beating of a prisoner by military police stationed at Guantánamo Bay.[33] The episode opens with the savage beating, which leaves the prisoner hospitalized and causes viewers to momentarily question the benevolence of the U.S. military. The thrust of the program is to redeem the soldiers (and implicitly, the ethos of militarism) by assigning blame for the incident to a private security contractor. The soldiers claim the contractor asked them to soften up the prisoners prior to interrogation, and they were simply following orders. A videotape showing the contractor at the scene of the beat down seems to corroborate their claims, and they are eventually exonerated. While the episode momentarily entertains a debate about the morality and legality of torture and indefinite detention, it deflects all blame for such "repugnant" practices onto politicians and the private firms they have contracted to do the nation's dirty work. The U.S. military emerges from the scandal with its integrity, and presumptive benevolence, intact.

The postapocalyptic science fiction series *Jericho* (CBS, 2006–2008) likewise staged a return to American innocence via the damnation of PMSCs. In the first episode, the major population centers of the United States are wiped out by nuclear strikes, and the survivors must figure out how to govern themselves in the absence of a federal bureaucracy. Nicknamed "Little Panic on the Prairie" by *New York Times* critic Ginia Bellafante, *Jericho* represented "a biting rebuke of [the policies of] excessive militarism, executive privilege, and preemption" embraced by the Bush administration and justified via a rhetoric of exceptionalism.[34] Yet the program also managed to redeem American innocence by displacing extreme violence onto politicians and their privatized security forces. At the end of season 1, an occupation force arrives to resettle the prairie; it is spearheaded by a for-profit logistics and security firm called Jennings and Rall (J&R), whose ties to the ruling political regime are so close as to be "one and the same" (shades of Vice President Dick Cheney's ties to Halliburton and its subsidiary Kellogg Brown and Root, which held the lucrative Logistics and Civil Augmentation Program contract in Iraq). J&R controls the town's access to electricity, food, water, and medical supplies, and it maintains a private security force, called Ravenswood (again, a takeoff on Blackwater), that competes with the military for control of the population. We are primed to be suspicious of Ravenswood even before relations start to decline because hometown hero Jake Green (Skeet Ulrich) worked for them in Iraq and tells us about a massacre he witnessed while deployed: "When it was done," he tells Major Edward Beck (Esai Morales), "there were six gunmen dead, four bystanders, one of them was a 12 year old girl. . . . there were no repercussions. None. The army had no authority over us, the police didn't . . . the company wanted it kept quiet, so it was. Do you understand? Do you understand who we're dealing with? These guys, they don't answer to anybody" ("Jennings & Rall," February 26, 2008).

Back in Jericho, the Ravenswood detail is led by a guy named Goetz (D. B. Sweeney), who uses his authority to choke off the town's flow of supplies, embezzles from the government, and then raids a local farmhouse to cover up his misdeeds ("Oversight," March 4, 2008). The raid leaves one of the more beloved characters—the deaf sister of farm-boy hero Stanley Richmond (Brad Beyer)—dead, and when the military refuses to act because Goetz claims he was fired upon first, Stanley shoots Goetz in the head and allows a group of insurgents to string his dead body up from a tree at the edge of town ("Termination for Cause," March 11, 2008). The staging of the scene (see figure 4.3) clearly references the lynching of four Blackwater security contractors in Fallujah in 2004, but it directs sympathy *away* from the contractors and *toward* the vigilantes, whose violence is depicted as a regrettable but necessary evil under the circumstances. The series ends on a redemptive note, with a military-civilian alliance beating back both the vigilante threat and the fascistic politico-corporate conspiracy responsible for the nuclear attacks. Thus, *Jericho* uses its critique of for-profit warriors—and the unpredictable security regime they foster—to preserve faith in the U.S. military and recuperate a sense of American innocence.

FIGURE 4.3. In "Termination for Cause," the political thriller *Jericho* (2006–2008) references the lynching of four Blackwater contractors in Fallujah, Iraq, in 2004, but it directs sympathy toward the rebels, rather than the contractors. © CBS Paramount Network Television, Junction Entertainment, and Fixed Mark Productions.

Since 2010 and the revelations of various scandals involving PMSCs, the redemption of the U.S. military has become an even more explicit theme. Private contractors in programs like *American Odyssey* (NBC, 2015) and *Blindspot* (NBC, 2015–) have become completely delinked from the military and are less rogue operatives than open adversaries of U.S. service personnel. *American Odyssey* follows the misadventures of U.S. Army Sergeant Odelle Ballard (Anna Friel), who, while on a special operations mission in North Africa, uncovers evidence that a U.S. corporation called Societel, or SOC, is secretly funding terrorist organizations. SOC calls in a Blackwater-type security agency (called OSELA) to confiscate the evidence and eliminate the witnesses, including both the special ops unit and the drone pilot who unwittingly carries out the order to kill them. Ballard survives the attack, and her attempts to return home and expose the corporation's traitorous malfeasance constitute the "odyssey" of the title.

The villains of the piece are large corporations whose desire to protect their overseas interests leads them to hire private militias with no allegiance to the state. As part of their "duty of protection," OSELA agents repeatedly attack and terrorize U.S. soldiers, rendering them innocent victims of aggression, rather than enforcers of U.S. imperial policy. A recent episode of *Blindspot* ("Scientists Follow Fortune," March 7, 2016) goes even further, suggesting that PMSCs would parasitically prey on U.S. soldiers for their own profit. In the episode, a private military contractor named Northlake kidnaps and fakes the deaths of five decorated soldiers so that its scientists can run experiments on them. The experiments are designed to create a breed of "super soldiers" and "change the face of modern warfare." In the dialogue, the (female) doctor in charge of the experiments is associated directly with "the face of the devil," and U.S. soldiers appear innocent, weak, and in need of rescue by contrast. This is the quintessential stuff of melodrama, and as with most melodramas, it works to redeem the idea of war by disassociating it from the powerful United States and its equally powerful military. America is once again constructed as a "space of innocence" where good men and women may be asked to do terrible things but only in the name of conquering evil.[35] We, the audience, can "feel good" about the exploits of our men and women in uniform because they are clearly *not* like those evil mercenaries who fight only for selfish reasons. The suffering and endurance of soldiers, especially at the hands of greedy profiteers, redeems the U.S. mission by recoding it as something other than economically and politically exploitative.

In sum, there has been a shift in presentations of mercenaries on U.S. television from the 1950s to the present (circa 2017). Private operators acting on behalf of the U.S. government appear as Gods of War during periods when actual military engagement is either impossible or impractical. They act with a freedom and potency denied to official government agents and thus assuage popular anxieties about American weakness and vulnerability. When the government acts boldly to assert its global authority, however, tales of mercenary fervor tend to take on a negative cast, for they appear to undermine the purity of the national mission. As Dogs of War, mercenaries become scapegoats onto whom the worst excesses of American militarism might be projected and disavowed. Although the Dogs of War motif represents an improvement over the mindless celebration of violence in the earlier programs, it remains unclear whether this change makes us *feel* any differently about American empire. For one thing, it belies the reality of the growing convergence between state violence and privatized military violence. It is not easy to draw a bright line between contractors and soldiers, those who fight for a buck and those who fight for patriotic ideals, when soldiering in the United States is treated as a job, and contracting pools are staffed by ex-military personnel, many of whom are as idealistic as the most devoted soldier.

For another, the process of scapegoating contractors works to redeem state violence as an effective diplomatic instrument. We learn through these tales that there are good and bad ways to use force, and we are invited to identify with the soldiers and sailors who show us the "right" (or righteous) way. That there might be a third way—the way of diplomacy, compromise, and peace—is anathema to such melodramatic tales.

Thus, it hardly matters which of these motifs predominates in any given period, for they both work through processes of projection and scapegoating to recuperate a sense of American innocence. The difference lies in where the two motifs point the finger—at a weakened state or at a strengthened corporate mercenary sector. When faith in the state's capacity or willingness to act is low, mercenary forces emerge as saviors—manly men and roguish vigilantes who will defend liberty and protect the "people" in the absence of a national will to power. When the state's exercise of power produces uncomfortable consequences, mercenary forces become devils, whose symbolic excoriation allows the public to retain its faith in the official military (and state-sponsored violence) as a force for good in the world. Either way, these presentations support the myth of American exceptionalism and allow us to go on *feeling* innocent and noble. And, as Lippmann, Ankar, and their colleagues contend, these feelings are really the crux of the matter.

By providing an agreeable, ego-reinforcing tableaux of American benevolence, melodramatic representations of military adventurism help to legitimize policies that might more accurately be characterized as imperialist, even dictatorial ("it's Washington's way or the highway"). They also direct our attention to the wrong things—to the nature of the tactics used by PMSCs rather than to the strategy of privatizing and outsourcing national security in the first place. Since the latter incentivizes war, even as it undermines the formal and informal mechanisms for policing it, these fantasies have dangerous implications. War, once a contingent (albeit often prolonged) endeavor, could become a perpetual motion machine, spewing chaos out in all directions without regard for the distinctions of morality, justice, or proportionality. That is an outcome we should all feel uncomfortable with and work to oppose . . . starting now.

NOTES

1. Walter Lippmann, "Empire: The Days of Our Nonage Are Over," in *Men of Destiny* (New Brunswick, NJ: Transaction Publishers, 1927), 216.

2. Elisabeth R. Anker, *Orgies of Feeling: Melodrama and the Politics of Freedom* (Durham, NC: Duke University Press, 2014), Kindle edition; Lauren Berlant, *The Female Complaint: The Unfinished Business of Sentimentality in American Culture* (Durham, NC: Duke University Press, 2008); Linda Williams, "Melodrama Revised," in *Refiguring American Film Genres: History and Theory*, ed. Nick Browne (Berkeley, CA: University of California Press, 1998); Tanine Allison, "Destructive Sublime: World War II in American Film and Media," (unpublished manuscript, 2017).

3. Allison, "Destructive Sublime," 227.

4. Anker, "Orgies of Feeling," Kindle location 284 of 8491.

5. For perspective, the ratio of U.S. military personnel to private contractors in Vietnam was five to one; in Iraq (in 2009) it was one to one; in Afghanistan (also in 2009) it was one to two. See Thomas C. Bruneau, *Patriots for Profit: Contractors and the Military in U.S. National Security* (Palo Alto, CA: Stanford University Press, 2011), 115; and "Workforce Reports and Publications," U.S. Department of Defense, Washington, DC, 2009. In 2011, as U.S. troops pulled out of the two active war zones, contract labor surged once again with the result, as Anne Hagedorn reports, of "contractors outnumbering traditional troops [by] a ratio of 10-to-1, outnumbering State Department personnel 18-to-1 and USAID workers 100-to-1." Hagedorn, *The Invisible Soldiers: How America Outsourced Our Security* (New York: Simon and Schuster, 2014), 10, Kindle edition.

6. President Dwight D. Eisenhower articulated his concerns in his "Farewell Address" of January 17, 1961. However, he was speaking of investments in the military proper; he warned against the dangers of a permanently mobilized military and calculated the social costs of increased financial investments in militarization. Today, the military-industrial complex has grown to include myriad private corporations who operate relatively independently of state affiliations and need "market growth" to generate profits. That is, they need to perpetuate war to meet shareholder expectations and the legal requirements of incorporation. Such a development is not conducive to the pursuit of global peace and security. For a comparison of conditions then and now, see Andrew Bacevich, "The Tyranny of Defense, Inc.," *Atlantic*, January/February 2011; and Jonathan Turley, "Big Money behind War: The Military-Industrial Complex," Al-Jezeera News, www.aljazeera.com/indepth/opinion/2014/01/big-money-behind-war-military-industrial-complex-20141473026736533.html.

7. On early modern mercenaries, see Janice Thomson, *Mercenaries, Pirates, and Sovereigns: State Building and Extraterritorial Violence in Early Modern Europe* (Princeton, NJ: Princeton University Press, 1994). Singer extends the analysis in chapter 2 of *Corporate Warriors: The Rise of the Privatized Military Industry* (Ithaca, NY: Cornell University Press, 2007), 19–39.

8. The increase in contract labor for maintenance and logistics during this period was about freeing soldiers from the "chickenshit" details and "make work" that alienated young recruits. As one booklet on the transition explained: "In the new Army, the primary job of soldiers will be soldiering." Beth Bailey, *America's Army: Making the All-Volunteer Force* (Cambridge, MA: Harvard University Press, 2009), 56.

9. See, for example, John Helyar, "Fortunes of War," *Fortune,* July 26, 2004; and Allison Stanger, *One Nation under Contract: The Outsourcing of American Power and the Future of Foreign Policy* (New Haven, CT: Yale University Press, 2011). For a fuller indictment of the Bush administration's faith in neoliberalism, see Rajiv Chandrasekaran, *Imperial Life in the Emerald City: Inside Iraq's Green Zone* (New York: Vintage, 2007).

10. See Leo Shane III, "Report: U.S. Wasted $60 Billion in Contracting Fraud, Abuse," *Stars and Stripes,* August 31, 2011; Bruce Falconer and Daniel Schulman, "Blackwater's World of Warcraft," *Mother Jones,* March 20, 2008. The richest account of these scandals remains Hagedorn, *Invisible Soldiers,* 97–98.

11. Matt Apuzzo, "Former Blackwater Guards Convicted in Iraq Shooting," *New York Times,* October 22, 2014.

12. "A Media Mystery," Pew Research Center, www.journalism.org/2007 /06/21/a-media-mystery/.

13. The first statistic is from a 2013 Nielsen Media Research study, reported in Felix Richter, "Americans Consume 60 Hours of Electronic Media Per Week," *Statista.com,* www.statista.com/chart/1695/electronic-media-use-in-the-us/. The second is from Amy Mitchell, "State of the News Media 2015," Pew Research Center, www.journalism.org/2015/04/29/state-of-the-news-media-2015/.

14. On the high network era, see Amanda Lotz, *The Television Will Be Revolutionized* (New York: New York University Press, 2007). On the nation as "imagined community," see Benedict Anderson, *Imagined Communities: Reflections on the Origin and Spread of Nationalism* (London: Verso, 1992). On the role of television in the production of national community, see Jane Feuer, "The Concept of Live Television: Ontology as Ideology," in *Regarding Television: Critical Approaches,* ed. E. Ann Kaplan (Frederick, MD: University Publications of America and the University Film Institute, 1983); J. Fred MacDonald, *One Nation under Television: The Rise and Decline of Network TV* (New York: Wadsworth, 1993); and Alan Nadel, *Television in Black-and-White America: Race and National Identity* (Lawrence, KS: University of Kansas Press, 2005).

15. Political scientist Joseph Nye defines "soft power" as the ability to get others to do what you want through persuasion and appeal (diplomacy and cultural influence), rather than bribery or coercion (economic "carrots" and military "sticks"). Joseph S. Nye, *Soft Power: The Means to Success in World Politics* (New York: Public Affairs, 2004), 5.

16. Eisenhower established a puppet regime in Vietnam, funded the French colonial government there, overthrew the democratically elected governments of Iran, Guatemala, and Indonesia, and massively expanded espionage operations against the Soviet Union, culminating in the downing of a U-2 spy plane over the Soviet union in 1960. My thanks to reviewer H. Bruce Franklin for helping me clarify this part of the argument.

17. See for example, Kennedy's acceptance speech at the 1960 Democratic National Convention, in which he blamed Eisenhower for a "shifting" balance of power abroad: "Meanwhile, Communist influence has penetrated further into Asia, stood astride the Middle East and now festers some ninety miles off the coast of

Florida. Friends have slipped into neutrality—and neutrals into hostility. As our keynoter reminded us, the President who began his career by going to Korea ends it by staying away from Japan." John Fitzgerald Kennedy, "Democratic National Convention Nomination Acceptance Address, July 15, 1960," *American Rhetoric,* www.americanrhetoric.com/speeches/jfk1960dnc.htm.

18. As film historian Gaylyn Studlar notes, however, *Have Gun—Will Travel* remained unusually transnational in its depictions of the West, featuring stories about U.S. relations with Hawaii (an unincorporated territory at the time), Japan, Canada, and Ireland, to name just a few. Studlar, *Have Gun—Will Travel* (Detroit, MI: Wayne State University Press, 2015), Kindle edition.

19. John Fitzgerald Kennedy, "Inaugural Address of President John F. Kennedy," January 20, 1961, John F. Kennedy Presidential Library and Museum, www.jfklib rary.org/Research/Research-Aids/Ready-Reference/JFK-Quotations/Inaugural -Address.aspx.

20. Studlar, *Have Gun—Will Travel,* Kindle location 188 of 3669.

21. The quotes are from Kennedy, "Democratic National Convention Nomination Acceptance Address."

22. "Peace through strength" was a prominent campaign slogan of Reagan's during the 1980 race against incumbent Jimmy Carter. You can view one of his campaign commercials at: Seewald, "Reagan—Peace through Strength (1980)," YouTube video, https://youtu.be/DWYrcnehito.

23. Reagan positioned Grenada's new government as a threat to the United States by claiming an extra-long runway on the island was part of a "Soviet-Cuban" plot to "militarize" the Caribbean. Phil Gailey and Warren Weaver Jr., "Touching Down in Grenada," *New York Times,* March 26, 1983.

24. It was President George H. W. Bush who declared, "By God, we've kicked the Vietnam Syndrome once and for all" after the invasion of Iraq in 1991. Maureen Dowd, "After the War: White House Memo," *New York Times,* March 2, 1991.

25. Plan Colombia represents the first full-scale use of U.S. public funding to outsource war to private firms. The plan was basically written by Military Professional Resources, Inc. (MPRI), a logistics and training firm, and DynCorp was hired to direct the drug crop eradication efforts of the National Police. Firms specializing in combat operations, including Armour Group and Silver Shadow, were also tasked with aiding the Colombian military in kinetic operations (that is, combat). Official military commitments were minimized, enabling the president, Bill Clinton, to wage war without public input, debate, or monitoring. It was a perfect example of the dangers of escalation associated with the emergence of the corporate security firms. For details, see *Singer, Corporate Warriors,* 206–208.

26. According to *TV.com*'s summary, at any rate. "Special Ops Force," *TV.com,* www.tv.com/shows/special-ops-force/news/.

27. Simpson and Bruckheimer had teamed up to create some of the most iconic film hits of the 1980s and 1990s, including *Flashdance* (1983), *Beverly Hills Cop* (1984), *Top Gun* (1986), *Bad Boys* (1995), and *The Rock* (1996). *SOF,* as fans called the series, was their first foray into television production.

28. Wikipedia.com and TV.com both note that "the series was renamed *SoF: Special Ops Force*" in season 2, and the change is confirmed by Tim Brooks and Earle F. Marsh, eds., *The Complete Directory to Prime Time Network and Cable TV Shows, 1946-Present*, 9th ed. (New York: Ballantine, 2007), 1185.

29. Neoconservatives had been arguing for an increase in military spending to sustain a "global security order that is uniquely friendly to American principles and prosperity" since the end of the first Persian Gulf War. Their principle arguments can be found in *Rebuilding America's Defenses: Strategy, Forces and Resources for a New Century*, The Project for the New American Century, September 2000, www .informationclearinghouse.info/pdf/RebuildingAmericasDefenses.pdf. On the dominance of neoliberal economic ideology among the CPA, see Chandrasekaran, *Imperial Life in the Emerald City*.

30. From 250 contractors in January 2015 to 2,028 in January 2016. "Contractor Support of U.S. Operations in the U.S. Centcom Area of Responsibility," Program Support, Assistant Secretary of Defense, U.S. Department of Defense, Washington, DC, 2016.

31. Ibid. See also Marcus Weisgerber, "Back to Iraq: US Military Contractors Return in Droves," *DefenseOne.com*, www.defenseone.com/threats/2016/02 /back-iraq-us-military-contractors-return-droves/126095/.

32. Andrew Bacevich, "America's Rising Shadow Wars," *Mother Jones*, May 29, 2012.

33. In both the real and fake incidents, the man beaten was a soldier planted to test the military police's conduct and ensure that prisoners were receiving humane treatment. In real life, the soldier, Specialist Sean Baker, suffered permanently debilitating injuries and sued the Pentagon for misconduct; in the episode, the soldier refuses to identify his attackers, claiming they were justified in using force because the men held at Guantánamo were "hardened killers." For a full comparison, see Stacy Takacs, *Terrorism TV: Popular Entertainment in Post-9/11 America* (Lawrence, KS: University Press of Kansas, 2012), 129–131.

34. Ginia Bellafante, "Little Panic on the Prairie: The Odd World of 'Jericho,'" *New York Times*, www.nytimes.com/2008/02/19/arts/television/19bell.html? _r=1&scp=1&sq=little%20panic%20on%20the%20prairie&st=cse.

35. Williams, "Melodrama Revised," 64.

FIVE

Obama's *"Just War"*

THE AMERICAN HERO AND JUST VIOLENCE IN
POPULAR TELEVISION SERIES

Min Kyung (Mia) Yoo

Detective Dix: Gotham's golden rule, Harvey.
Harvey: No heroes.

S. 1, ep. 6 in Gotham

UPON ACCEPTING THE NOBEL PEACE PRIZE for his rather symbolic "extraordinary efforts to strengthen international diplomacy and coopera-tion between people,"[1] President Barack Obama avowed, "I face the world as it is, and cannot stand idle in the face of threats to the American people. For make no mistake: Evil does exist in the world. . . . And it will require us to think in new ways about the notions of *just war* and the imperatives of a *just peace*."[2] As he approached the end of his two terms, Obama believed that "very little is accomplished in international affairs without U.S. leadership,"[3] echoing former president George W. Bush's discourse on the crusade of "good versus evil"[4] with regard to his wars in the Middle East. "For all of our warts, the United States has *clearly* been a force for good in the world," Obama said in an interview.[5] He defended his foreign policy and the military decisions of his administration with confidence, saying, "If you compare us to previous superpowers, we act less on the basis of naked self-interest, and have been interested in establishing norms that benefit everyone. If it is pos-sible to do good at a bearable cost, to save lives, we will do it."[6] How did the U.S. government with its presidents as commander in chief justify its post-9/11 use of violence against the "Other" in the new "American norm," and how did its "just war" philosophy manifest in the popular culture? This chap-ter observes how the image and rhetoric of Obama as world leader differed from that of George W. Bush, regardless of Obama's much-criticized and contradictory foreign policy implementations. I connect the making of

Obama's hero image and the new hero trope mirrored in popular culture—one that is reluctant and ideal yet nonetheless violent.

Obama's Nobel Peace Prize owed much to the hero narrative of his 2008 presidential campaign,[7] which won the hearts and minds of the American people and even those outside the United States[8] with the slogans "Change we can believe in" and "Yes, we can." Obama emerged as the poster child for the American Dream, hybridity,[9] global democracy, and multilateralism as his messages rang with a strong sense of idealism, contrasting with Bush and his administration's rather candid claim to a realist perspective.[10] He criticized Bush's "stupid" wars,[11] calling them an abuse of executive power,[12] as Obama's recognition of "America's past failures overseas as a means of checking American self-righteousness"[13] promised a significant change. His just war[14] philosophy would differ from what one writer called President Bush's "Ugly American culture and cowboy diplomacy."[15] Yet the paradox of Obama's Niebuhrian ideals[16] and his just war philosophy was criticized for its moral impossibility[17] within the sites of global politics and wars, for he could not escape the accusations of continuing the war on terror under a different guise.[18] In "Obama and the Image," Susan Buck-Morss alludes to W. J. T. Mitchell's theory of the power of the image to argue that "as much as defenders of reason would like to think that issues of policy are determining, it is as image that politics appears on the global stage. . . . An image empowers; but it can also deceive."[19] Mitchell wrote that images are "animated and desiring subjects," which, in the case of Obama, inspire "by making visible the self-proclaimed ideal that what binds this nation of immigrants . . . [are] principles of democratic rule, equal opportunity, and universal inclusion."[20] The just war philosophy, which limits and controls the destructive potential of war, supports the U.S. government as the global sovereign power that decides what is just, ethical, moral, and necessary violence, transcending those exact codes of law and defying such values of democracy and a sense of inclusion. Hence, Obama's image as an ideal national and world leader becomes problematic and paradoxical, yet it was somehow globally well received, for he embodied the hero image that many sought. Michael Walzer explained that the just war theory projects *images* of leaders and technologies concerned with collateral damage and minimizing violence in which "strategies are evaluated morally as well as militaristically."[21] No doubt, Obama's position on just war first and foremost supported his image as a moral world leader while claiming sovereignty and exposing the exceptional status of the United States as the global superpower. The distinction between the wars under the Bush and Obama administrations can be detected in how they are justified and imagined in the global public through either aggressive or remorseful images of violent leadership. The post-9/11 American hero, specifically in popular culture, has been depicted as holding similar idealism or innocence before resorting to violence in protecting the greater population.

This chapter explores how nationally and internationally acclaimed American television series present a world in a state of emergency and the American hero image constructed within the violent acts of just war. The three white male policemen in *The Walking Dead* (2010), *Gotham* (2014), and *Fargo* (2014) attempt to achieve peace and order through their reluctant use of violence when confronting their fears and maintaining their positions of power. Obama's just war rhetoric, his image as an ideal hero presented in the media, and the narrative of these characters play out under similar sets of themes, motifs, and narrative logic to establish "just peace" under a new norm of American just war. Rick Grimes from *The Walking Dead,* "Jim" Gordon from *Gotham,* and Gus Grimly from *Fargo* unwillingly take up their role as executioners, eliciting sympathy from their viewers as they prioritize protecting those who depend on their exceptional use of power. Resorting to gun violence to stop the Other as "serious evil"[22] in times of crisis, each of these policemen transforms from an average man to a messianic—yet morally imperfect and flawed—hero.

The moral defense of their violence echoes the American government's declaration of the war on terror post-9/11 and its exceptional use of force within the state of emergency. To fight against al-Qaeda in this "new kind of war," Jason Ralph argued, "the U.S. response to 9/11 was understood as being exceptional to the extent it was seen as 'exempting' itself from the normative regimes of the existing liberal order—institutions it had done so much to create."[23] Giorgio Agamben, who elaborated the term *state of exception*[24] upon observing the U.S. government's domestic and international global war on terrorism, stated that the exceptional use of force is normalized within the emergency state, as "emergency becomes the rule, and the very distinction between peace and war (and between foreign and civil war) becomes impossible."[25] He used the term state of exception to describe the post-9/11 sociopolitical condition of the United States under President Bush's state of emergency, in which the state has the power to override any human rights during a national crisis.

The two types of annihilated Other in the three series are both foreign and familiar and always present among us unnoticed until they threaten our heroes' position of power: the faceless masses that threaten our protagonists' lives (such as the army of zombies or *Gotham*'s mythic warrior-monks, the Order of Saint Dumas) and the individuals (Shane in *The Walking Dead,* Theo Galavan in *Gotham,* and Lorne Malvo in *Fargo*) who challenge the protagonists' strength and moral values. These antagonists are killed in order for the heroes to overcome their fears and emerge as leaders who can protect their community and achieve just peace under their own terms. Although these series differ vastly in their genres, their target audience, and their narrative styles, their portrayals in the rhetoric of fear and logic of violence are consistent—us versus them. Law enforcement officers with a strong sense of optimism, these protagonists abide by judicial systems in the beginning, and the audiences feel great sympathy for these good-hearted men as their world descends into chaos.

In these images of a hero in the making, violence is grudgingly used but indispensable in a world where idealism and naïveté lead everyone to danger. Unlike other power-hungry leaders, they half-heartedly ascend to their leadership positions, for they are *made* heroes, as their sense of responsibility pressures them into leading the people living in fear and desperate for an authority figure with a license to kill. This further echoes Buck-Morss's reading of Mitchell and Obama's image during his presidential campaign, in which she ties Mitchell's theory to the "liveliness" of images that "emanate from the viewer; the active ingredient is perception itself."[26] Similarly, the protagonists are rather made heroes in the eyes of the audience the moment they pull the trigger, as powerful and reliable leaders are commonly believed to take responsibility for their violent actions rather than cower behind their idealism.

Government agents or law enforcement officials portrayed in the first decade of the post-9/11 era, most notably Jack Bauer in *24*, present "supercop" characters who, as well-trained agents, readily accept their fate and meet life-threatening challenges head-on. The three male protagonists of *The Walking Dead, Gotham,* and *Fargo* develop rather gradually, bringing about a cathartic experience for the audience at the moments of their violent acts. Their acts of violence are depicted dramatically as moments of moral and personal growth for the characters, and it takes several episodes, or even seasons, for these characters to finally pull the trigger leading up to that point. The guilt, trauma, and sense of disbelief expressed by these characters after their acts of murder draw sympathy from the audience. These heroes are even seen as martyrs. The dilemmas and moral ambiguity presented in these moments of manslaughter and in the events building up to their decisions present a hero narrative of just peace that is obtained through the reluctant use of violence. The justification for their violence resonates with Obama's unwilling but "realist" view in his use of violence,[27] along with his Niebuhrian[28] realism. Fans quickly forgive and forget the crimes of these "heroes," as these characters have to become stronger in order to continue the narrative of survival that pleases the general audience—or, in the case of Obama, that appeases the American public.

POST-9/11 FEARS AND AMERICAN HEROES

To communicate or sell the post-9/11 American violence under "just war/just peace" nationally and abroad, media entertainment has proved to be an effective tool.[29] American entertainment industries, especially Hollywood films, have dominated the world mass culture industry and have been criticized for their cultural hegemonic or cultural imperialistic influence across the globe, notably during the Cold War.[30] Following 9/11, America became the victim, survivor, and "the supernaturally endowed hero who was judge, jury and executioner, the crime fighting god disguised, omnipotent, triumphant."[31] During Bush's two terms, U.S. military aggression, represented through war coverage and Bush's speeches in the news media, created fear, anger, and anxiety in the eyes of the world. America as a global police force fighting against the evil Other was Bush's continuing theme of "good versus evil," and there were continuing traces of this philosophy in Obama's foreign policy. The three protagonists discussed in this chapter and their "evil" antagonists—either as a specific figure or unspecified mass—embody the good (us) versus evil (Other) debate, with America as symbolic police and executioner against a backdrop of emerging crises. This Other, annihilated without trial at the hands of our hero, is seen and defined as the "serious evil," and regardless of their undemocratic methods, these men can only rise up as true leaders and saviors after they get blood on their hands. The logic in this narrative of crisis and its heroes echoes Niebuhr's philosophy that "use of force is considered an inevitable option to attain the lesser evil"[32] when our everyday lives are threatened by the "known unknown." Narratives of these series build up to create a cathartic experience for their audiences at the fatal moment, selling violence to their domestic and international viewers.

The fans of these series in the post-9/11 world are no strangers to the crisis and fear experienced by these protagonists, since these series have their basis in the familiar scenario of the zombie apocalypse, crime-filled world of Gotham before the arrival of Batman, and in the original film version of

Fargo (1996). The zombie apocalypse narrative of *The Walking Dead* is one of the many portrayals of a zombie-filled-world survival story that experienced a sudden renaissance around 9/11.[33] These narratives were widely argued to represent twenty-first-century fears during the era of the global war on terrorism.[34] *The Walking Dead* television series focuses on how Rick and his group of survivors respond to new rules and values in a postcivilization world. *Gotham* is a prequel to the well-known *Batman* series, which follows the early years of Commissioner Jim Gordon's career at the Gotham City Police Department (GCPD), set during an uncertain age in which Bruce Wayne's parents and the old mob bosses of organized crime, who function as anchors of Gotham society, are murdered. As the balance of power is disrupted by the lurking evil, there is a looming sense of crisis and fear. Detective Jim Gordon, who is not a multimillionaire superhero like Bruce Wayne but an average cop with an extraordinary sense of responsibility and courage, holds the city together amid various life-threatening attacks by the villains. The crisis portrayed in *Fargo* takes place at a local level, yet the "evil" that threatens this small Minnesota town—as in the original film version—is as diabolical as any omnipotent villain. In this ten-part television series, Lorne Malvo, the highly intelligent, dark-humored sociopathic contract killer, enters a peaceful town to turn it upside down in order to test its strength and moral ground, just like the devil himself.[35] Cunning, attractive, cool, and vicious, Malvo's pure drive is to bring out evil within the weak by first awakening their suppressed anger, vengeance, and violence, as he does with Lester Nygaard, a pushover "nice guy," in the first episode.

These television series, broadcast alongside news reports, amplify the rhetoric of fear[36] and reiterate the experience of trauma,[37] loss, and shock following 9/11 and the normalized "war on terror" across the globe. Many media theorists and cultural scholars have investigated the circulation of these apocalyptic themes in the changed world.[38] Fascination with the spectacles of destruction, the end of humanity and civilization as we know it, and the use of "just" violence to reestablish security creates a cathartic experience for the audience, reaffirming an essentialist view of the world and social crises and encouraging a realist rhetoric. As these series are exported and popularized abroad, they play a significant role in creating global consent with regard to just peace,[39] prompting international viewers to form a similar binary worldview of good/evil, civilization/barbarism, order/chaos, us/Other, and law/lawlessness, according to the George W. Bush's "axis of evil" doctrine.[40] Presenting such allegories of the 9/11 attacks and America's philosophy of the war on terror, these television series exported abroad reiterate the American worldview on just peace according to these narratives. *The Walking Dead* aired almost simultaneously in over one hundred countries,[41] as did *Gotham,* which has been consistently renewed for new seasons. The active discussions circulating among global fans[42] reflect their shared sympathies with the characters and their experiences of shock, terror, and victory, proving the solidarity enabled through the ritualistic experiences of these shows; these American heroes have become global heroes.

There are different kinds of government agents and law enforcement characters in post-9/11 entertainment media. For example, *24*'s Jack Bauer is the nation's best-trained agent. He quickly moves from one mission to the next, bringing "nationalistic revenge fantasy"[43] to life. The comparably inexperienced and sympathetic Rick, James, and Gus gradually lose their innocence throughout the weeks or years of airtime. Unlike Bauer, who makes difficult decisions within the twenty-four-hour time frame—which heightens the suspense and thrill of his mission—these unlikely heroes take their time, hesitating to confront the Other with violence out of a sense of ethical conflict or fear. These Others will bring their fears and their "evil" within to surface. In those moments, they struggle with the failing principles of democracy. Rick realizes that he is as selfish and dangerous as Shane and that he, like everyone else in America, carries the zombie virus; Jim accepts that he has to commit small acts of crime to protect the greater good; and Gus learns from Malvo that humanity is merely a thin disguise for our survivalist nature. These characters suffer from the trauma of their own violence, falling into denial and separating themselves from their violent acts as they desire to see themselves as innocent and "ordinary" men.

"I didn't ask for this!" Rick howls in the season two finale at his team of survivors. In this scene, when everyone is still in shock from the zombie stampede and the death of their friends, Rick breaks the news to everyone that he killed his friend Shane in self-defense and that he is the only person who can single-handedly protect and lead the group. Shane was dangerous, as he was blinded by jealousy and could not cope with the fact that Rick had recovered from his coma and was resuming his relationship with Lori (Rick's wife and Shane's new lover) and taking control of their group. "I killed my best friend for you people, for Christ's sake! You saw how [violent] he was like. How he pushed me, how he compromised us, how he threatened us." Rick rambles on in excitement, shock, anger, and fear: "He gave me no choice! He was my friend, but he came after me. My hands are clean. Maybe you people are better off without me. Go ahead. Why don't—why don't you go out and find yourself. Send me a postcard! Go on, there's the door. You can do better. Let's see how far you get. No takers? Fine. But get one thing straight ... you're staying. This isn't a democracy anymore."[44]

Rick defends himself as though he is on trial, under the judgment of his peers who question him. This is the crucial moment in which the survivors are driven into a corner, and the "Ricktatorship"[45] is born, as Rick gives them an ultimatum. They accept and follow his leadership by giving up their rights, choosing safety over freedom, as the camera moves away from the group and shows a large prison in the distance under a stormy sky. Here, we see that Rick cannot hold his position as a democratic leader because a democratic system proves to be weak in a zombie apocalypse world. He denies that there is blood on his hands, as Shane was killed for the greater good. Perhaps Rick is right, as Shane, egocentric and radical, was even more unstable than Rick, and his self-destructive personality was jeopardizing everyone, including himself. In this sense, Rick is the hero that the group desperately needs at the moment, just as Jim and Gus from the other two series will prove to be.

RICK'S JOURNEY AS THE AMERICAN COWBOY TRADITION

Justifications for violence, control, and criminal acts carried out by these heroes in the name of protecting their people mirror the post-9/11 rhetoric on just peace and validations of a just war. These heroes are regular policemen[46] without any superpowers or special training, and the television series narratives suggest they initially reject their calling as a hero until they come to accept that they must take matters into their own hands. Rick, Gus, and Jim are protectors of democratic government and its basis in human rights until they realize how fragile and flawed is the state of emergency that does not abide by the same rules of war and peace. These protagonists must choose to adapt to the new threats outside the boundaries of judicial systems by making exceptional decisions to play both judge and executioner at the moment of confrontation. The new reality in the world of *The Walking Dead* is shown in Rick's key speeches throughout the seasons and its promotional posters. Rick undergoes constant character growth, not only as a man but as a father and a law enforcement officer. Before the crisis, Rick is a kindhearted father and husband who tries to keep his family safe and *feeling* safe, oblivious to the violence outside their home. It takes few episodes for Rick to grow from a man who is shocked at the face of death—"Son of a bitch shot me, you believe that?!"[47] he screams to his partner and best friend Shane with fear in his eyes—to a man who rises as a strong leader in a world where one has to kill or be killed.

Perhaps it is Rick's naiveté and pacifism as seen in the pre–zombie apocalypse world that dupes Shane when Rick stabs him to death after tricking him into thinking he was unarmed. And to the audience's surprise, it is Shane who hesitates to pull the trigger, whereas Rick quickly acts in the face of deadly confrontation. The series takes off as Rick wakes up in the hospital from his coma, abandoned and alone, months after he is shot. He then miraculously reunites with his wife, Lori, and their son, Carl, who were kept safe under the protection of Shane. The conflict between the two best friends increases as Rick joins their party, and Shane is threatened by Rick's presence. Although Shane was not an ideal leader, when Rick kills his best friend, he breaks down from the weight of the responsibility and the horror of his act. Under the moonlight, the two friends discuss who is right and wrong until Rick tricks Shane into lowering his gun and fatally stabs him. Afterward, Rick justifies his action to the group of survivors and to himself by claiming that he is the group's only line of hope. Offering protection and leadership in exchange for democratic rights, Rick first asks his group whether they have the courage and belief to remain democratic in times of crisis and seeks validation for his own actions by excusing himself. As Rick's group finds a safe haven in an abandoned prison, locking themselves up in cells every night, the group, led by a strong, authoritative, and emotionally detached leader, reflects post-9/11 American society in a state of emergency.

Sporting a cowboy hat, Rick also echoes the "cowboy myth" hero of the American frontier. Media representations of cowboys in the past have been associated with "American-style success—survival ... honesty, hard-work ethic, rugged individualism, cleverness, Protestant virtue, mental dexterity, physical toughness."[48] These American cowboys were often used as a symbol by presidents Reagan and George W. Bush, and Rick can also be seen as the quintessential American cowboy, "stripped down" and rebuilt, as "American man *cum* Adam."[49] The desperate search for a haven or surviving civilization in *The Walking Dead* resembles a frontier narrative, where people struggle to survive and maintain their humanity. But what does it mean to stay human in a world of the dead? In season two, by silently complying when Rick gives his speech about the end of democracy, Rick's group is forced to follow the new rules. His authoritative orders, however, offer a sense of relief, as his decisiveness promises a peaceful night's sleep for his people, and the audience can trust Rick's judgment in keeping his people safe. Slowly, Rick's philosophy convinces his people and the audience that a "realist" attitude is necessary in this new world. When they finally reach Alexandria Safe-Zone in season 5, the group members refuse to let their guard down because of their past experience with Other evil survivors. When the citizens of Alexandria prove clueless and unprepared for the terror beyond the walls, Rick's frustration builds up and reaches a breaking point. Alexandrians watch in horror as Rick waves his gun at the crowd after a bloody fistfight with one of the them: "You still don't get it. None of you do. We know what needs to be done and we do it. We're the ones who lived . . . You pretend like you know but you don't . . . Well if you want to live . . . Starting right now, we have to live in the REAL world . . . Your way's going to destroy this place. It's going to get people killed."[50]

In this scene, Rick is highly emotional and loses control. Covered in blood and with wild eyes, Rick is the most dangerous person in Alexandria until Michonne (his friend and lover in later episodes) steps in. Here, once again wearing the uniform of a police officer, Rick plays a law enforcement role. Rick proves himself right soon after when a zombie manages to enter the walled city of Alexandria, and the town's natives are powerless at the moment of confrontation. Stunned, people watch Rick kill the zombie, followed this time by a speech that is more composed and sincere:

> I didn't bring it in; it got inside on its own. They always will, the dead and the living because we're in here . . . and the ones out there, they'll hunt us, they'll find us, they'll try to use us and they'll try to kill us. But we'll kill them. We'll survive. I'll show you how. You know I was thinking . . . I was thinking how many of you do I have to kill to save your lives, but I'm not gonna do that . . . You're gonna change. I'm not sorry for what I said last night. I'm sorry for not saying it sooner. You're not ready, but you have to be, right now, you have to be. Luck runs out.[51]

Rick demonstrates the paradox of his form of justice and protection as he describes how he would have to see Alexandrians killed in order to save them from the zombies and the ignorance. He trusts his method of survival and tells others that they must also change, just as he had to in the past.

Rick's growth is also clearly visualized in the series' posters, as the poster for season 1 shows his back, with Rick riding his horse to the burning city, and the season 2 poster shows him running to Hershel's farm. He is turned toward the audience in seasons 3 and 4, with a gun in his hand. The changing angle of Rick's image and his readiness to pull the trigger reflects how he is growing increasingly confrontational in response to the danger and violence ahead. The season 5 poster shows him looking straight at the audience, with a piece of paper on the ground that reads, "The New World's Gonna Need Rick Grimes," making a strong claim for Rick's identity as the hero of the series and echoing George H. W. Bush's speech on the "new world order" founded by the United States and its allies. These posters sum up Rick's growing acceptance of and decisiveness in his leadership position by showing his readiness to use his gun and his firm belief in annihilating all threats to his people. Further, the audience also comes to accept Rick as a rightful hero who has kept his people alive throughout the seasons; in this new world, Rick's "just violence" keeps people safe under realistic values and moral expectations.

Law enforcement officers or commanders in chief like Rick as the saviors of society is a classic counterterrorism metaphor that responds to the discourse of fear.[52] Since 9/11, the media has portrayed police officers and firefighters as local heroes who must cope with sudden catastrophe at the frontline, witnessing the horror firsthand. President Bush and President Obama also prioritized their roles as commander in chief in the United States' states of emergency. With this new hero status ascribed to police officers and the nation's leaders in post-9/11 media representations, people began to lean toward the "safety rhetoric," "which often required them to permit police searches, condone 'overaggressive' police action, as well as join in a myriad of crime-prevention efforts."[53] Furthermore, the growth of these heroes revolves around the eradication of the antagonistic Other through the judgment of good versus evil, which echoes the imperialistic American philosophy of a just war.[54] These Others in opposition to our protagonists are justified as the axis of evil and are annihilated through the use of violence. In other politicized television series, such as *Homeland* (2011–), such a dichotomous identification and connection to our political situation is even more evident, as the Muslim world is mediated as the evil Other.

"JUST" VIOLENCE IN *GOTHAM*

Gotham city in danger and Batman as the Dark Knight have been regarded as a popular allegory[55] of America under threat from nationless terrorists and are what Donald Rumsfeld might have called the "known unknown"[56] Other. President Obama even referenced the 2008 Batman movie to "explain not only how he understood the role of ISIS, but how he understood the larger ecosystem in which it grew"[57] through the film's metaphor: "There's a scene in the beginning in which the gang leaders of Gotham are meeting... These are men who had the city divided up. They were thugs, but there was a kind of order... then the Joker comes in and lights the whole city on fire. ISIL is the Joker. It has the capacity to set the whole region on fire. That's why we have to fight it."[58]

It is into such a state of unknown terror that the world of *Gotham* is falling when Jim Gordon joins the GCPD. As a man of honor and idealism, he tries to follow the rules he was trained for, with a romanticized view of his hometown and its justice system.[59] With the help of his partner, Harvey, who sees through the flawed system and works with the bosses of the underworld, Jim slowly adapts to the rules of Gotham. His turning point comes when he blames himself for the death of his protégé, Officer Katherine Parks,[60] and for trusting the justice system to protect its people instead of killing the villains himself upon arrest.

Jim Gordon is a familiar character to us, as he has been depicted in various Batman comics and films prior to this television series, but this is the first time the audience is able to follow his growth into his role as commissioner from the beginning of his career. Jim is a brave, idealistic, and principled man, and when he is confronted with deep corruption and purely "evil" criminals, his values are shaken, for he doubts the ability of the justice system. The first time his values are jeopardized is when he is forced to kill a dangerous schemer, Penguin (Oswald Cobblepot, an umbrella boy of Falcone's gang member Fish Mooney), in order to gain the trust of Carmine Falcone, a *Godfather*-like Don Vito Corleone character and the most powerful boss of Gotham's underworld. Jim fakes Penguin's death, as he cannot bring himself to kill an innocent man,[61] but he realizes that in order to continue his police work in Gotham, he has to cooperate with the villains of the organized-crime world. Although Jim seems to concede to the rules of Gotham, he sticks to his belief that criminals should be placed on trial and sentenced accordingly in order to pay for their crimes. His faith in the justice system fails him throughout the seasons, as the corruption and incompetence of Gotham's police department leads to the deaths of innocent and brave officers, including his captain, Sarah Essen.[62]

Yet when Jim executes Galavan, who was responsible for Officer Park's death, it is not clear whether it is a selfish act following an emotional judgment or is being carried out for the protection of the population at large. Rather, the lasting safety of Gotham proves the justification for Jim's violence. In season 2, episode 16 ("Prisoners"), Jim breaks out of prison to prove his innocence and find the man who framed him for murder while also realizing that the penal system in Gotham is deeply flawed, arresting innocent men and punishing them for their blind loyalty to the "law." Ironically, the criminals, such as Carmine and Penguin, who acknowledge the justice system and believe in maintaining the old order in Gotham, become his biggest allies. Penguin is an evil mirror image of Jim, who assures the "good" in Jim even when Jim doubts himself: "I should put a bullet in your head right now," says Jim when Penguin returns to Gotham. Penguin challenges him—or saves himself—by replying, "And you have every right to do so. But you won't, Jim Gordon, because you're a good man. You may very well be the last good man in Gotham, and that's why I want to help you."[63]

Although at times, Penguin seems to be the only one who truly appreciates Jim's efforts to remain the "last good man in Gotham," he is the one who triggers him to kill Galavan. When Jim arrests Galavan for the second time, Galavan sighs with relief: "You scared me. I thought you were going to shoot me. Thank goodness for a simple man of principles who believes in the system." "This time you'll get the chair," says Jim. "You want to make a bet? Haha," replies Galavan, shrugging, as he is handcuffed and heading out the door. Jim's face freezes, and he quickly turns to Galavan and says, "Maybe you're right." It is at this moment that Captain Barnes enters to stop Jim and arrests both him and Galavan. But Penguin attacks Barnes from behind, to once again play the evil voice in Jim's head: "Forget that he nearly killed the mother of your child. Forget revenge. Think of the *greater good*. Think of Gotham. He has the courts in his pockets and billions of dollars at his command. Are you 100 percent sure that he won't beat this and walk free again? Are you sure, Jim?"[64] Fearing that Galavan will escape justice again, as he is a well-connected billionaire, Jim and Penguin team up to murder him. Jim has to confront the judicial system and lie in court. Later, as Galavan is revived from the dead—another reference to zombies—with supernatural strength, Jim is constantly haunted by his crime. When Jim is later framed for murder and jailed at the notorious World's End,[65] he meets Peter "Puck," who calls him a hero, recognizing him from the time Jim saved his sister from being kidnapped. Puck later dies from the attacks and the abuse from the wardens who bully Jim, and his death reminds Jim that he is the only hero who can save Gotham. This gives him the courage to break out of prison.

The television adaptation of *Fargo* retells a gruesome crime story through a mythological framework, with a new character of Gus Grimly and a more evolved supervillain, Malvo, to depict the "representation of American culture, and by extension, the human condition."[66] Lorne Malvo, a professional assassin and a sociopath, overpowers and outwits the simple-minded citizens of Bemidji, Minnesota. He is an identity-shifting, shapeless Other who disrupts the peace in the quiet town, sometimes disguised as one of the many strangers traveling through town or as a charming dentist, a minister, or a bodyguard who works for Milos, the Supermarket King. He is the fascinating yet frightening Other—the devil—murdering and reenacting the biblical plague for his amusement. Malvo's character continues the film version's portrayal of strangers as villains, which "taps into a specific set of contemporary American anxieties related to pathologies of xenophobia."[67]

The first real murder in town occurs at the home of Lester Nygaard, a Bemidji native and the butt of everyone's jokes as the pushover "nice" guy. Molly, Bemidji's detective, persistently investigates Lester, but because of Lester's reputation as the nice guy, her allegation against him is ignored. Malvo plants the idea of violent revenge in Lester's mind to test Lester's values and morality. When Lester gives in to the evil provocation, the peace and order in Bemidji are forever broken with the death of Vern Thurman, the police chief. Although many deaths in the series are portrayed with a touch of black comedy, Vern's death is portrayed with a sense of tragedy and drama, as he is a symbolic figure who secures order and peace in the community. Molly develops into a strong policewoman after Vern's death, but the kind of peace felt in Bemidji during Vern's time is never recovered in the series, as if he were the mighty bulwark that kept all terror at bay.

The sacrifice and heroism of the New York police officers and firefighters in the events of 9/11 were utilized to support similar mythic strength and ideas of manhood.[68] These local-but-national authorities represented the "best of America in their stalwart, masculine, and self-sacrificing response to that attack."[69] Gus also symbolizes such local heroism, as someone who is brought to the frontline without the same kind of training and emotional preparation, and at first he cowers in the face of evil and fear. When Gus confronts Malvo, *Fargo* tells a different story than the film by following the arc of Gus's heroism and the reassertion of American masculine heroism through the use of violence.

Gus is a complex and more "human" character who both follows and defies the commonly mediated representation of U.S. police officers and their use of violence following 9/11. Starting out as a peripheral character, he is an unlikely local hero who shoots the dying and unarmed Malvo to put an end to his killing spree. The scene in which Gus confronts Malvo at gunpoint is the climax of the series, as the two exchange a short dialogue quietly in the dark, and the audience waits for Gus to pull the trigger. Though this should be a moment of victory, violent gunshots breaking the rather intimate moment between the two and Malvo's bloody smile as he stares back at Gus make the audience question whether true justice has been done. The show's creator, Noah Hawley, explained to *TV Guide* that "at the beginning of every episode, it says, 'This is a true story,' which means that the story has to unfold like real life and not like the Joseph Campbell hero's journey . . . I think that there's something that is really complicated about what Gus does, that he shoots Malvo, an unarmed man, without giving him any opportunity to talk his way out of it or make a move. Is that an act of bravery or another act of cowardice?"[70] Here Hawley mentions Campbell to explain how instead of offering a nice closure, he likes to leave the unsettling mysteries hanging for greater realism in his tale of good versus evil in modern America.

In our violent and absurd world, there are no real heroes, while deaths and tragedies, specifically gun homicides, are a fundamental part of the American narrative. Now a mailman and a retired police officer, Gus, who cannot even seem to convince himself or his own daughter that he is a hero, is praised as one by the community for murdering Malvo. After 9/11, the American police became a symbol of "totalitarian ideals of planning and control,"[71] as police brutality and the excessive use of force have been consistently criticized, by groups such as Black Lives Matter, as the extreme measures taken in the war on terror. Constantly watched through government surveillance and in fear of being arrested, tortured, and even killed without a fair trial, democracy in America now entails taking away the individual rights and freedoms of the suspected few for the greater goal of safety.

Gus's annihilation of Malvo reaches a climax in the television series, though the central character in the original film is Marge, who brings in Malvo's character (Gaear Grimsrud in the film) in the back of her police car instead of murdering him on-site. The film *Fargo* ends with Marge sadly but assertively lecturing a deadly criminal like a mother to her son: "And for what [was the murder]? There's more to life than a little money, you know. Don't cha know that? And here ya are, and it's a beautiful day. Well I just don't understand it."[72] Marge's attempt to comprehend the violence and evil she witnesses from this strange Other seems impossible. In the film, Marge is "not a phallicized female"[73] or helplessly naïve, as she keeps calm, walking around with her pregnant belly, with sharp intelligence. Her confrontation at the end of the film with the atrocious killer contrasts with Gus's final interaction with Malvo, where Gus admits that he fully understands Malvo's actions and shoots him multiple times while Malvo looks him in the eyes and almost displays satisfaction before his death.

Instead of following the film version's heroic journey of a gentle yet brave policewoman, the television series portrays Gus's heroic transformation. In Gus and Malvo's first encounter, Gus stops Malvo for speeding while he is on the run after the murder of Chief Thurman. Gus's instincts tell him that he is in danger when Malvo threatens him, and in fear, Gus lets him go. Malvo continues to create chaos by going on a killing spree and taking pleasure in pushing the rather bland and spineless characters to their limit and bringing out their residual evil. The next time the two meet, Gus succeeds in arresting Malvo, but he walks free, as he presents himself as a minister with a false alibi. Shaken with anger and fright, Gus condemns Malvo's remorseless and sinister acts: "How do you do that, just lie like that?"[74] Composed, Malvo answers with a riddle: "Do you know why the human eye can see more shades of green than any other color? Once you can answer that, you'll have your answer."

Molly later explains to Gus that since human beings evolved from monkeys, we still carry our animalistic instincts in order to spot our predators, according to Darwinian theory. Gus is disturbed because the progress of civilization and humanity has been portrayed differently, beyond such survivalist logic. However, our justice system has failed to recognize, and hold accountable, true evil within society, and we are physically and morally unreliable beings. In other words, Malvo lives in a world where no laws or moral values of Western civilization apply—he is the Other from a foreign land and stands for the absolute, pure "evil" that undermines the power of law. Unlike Molly, who accepts that good and evil coexist and that she must maintain her role as "good," Gus is transformed by fear, rather than the logic of justice. Gus is an average man whose fear comes before his sense of justice: he confides to Molly that he "never wanted to be a cop, you know? I mean . . . Some kids grow up thinking about it, but not me. . . . You're gonna think it's funny, but I always wanted to work for the Post Office. And be a mailman . . . You know, be part of the community."[75]

Before Gus empties his rounds to kill the already half-dead Malvo in the final episode, he says, "I solved your riddle," though it was Molly who did. Gus's killing of Malvo does not feel like a clean victory since Malvo looks back at Gus as if to say: "Nice job, Gus. I taught you well. I guess this is it. My job is done." And "Isn't life funny?," according to Billy Bob Thornton, who played Malvo in the series.[76] Gus gasps for air in horror after he makes sure that Malvo is finally dead. Later, he tells Molly that he will receive a citation for bravery, and Molly is promoted to the position of chief. Here again is the portrayal of the average man embracing the status of hero after "just violence" is used to achieve "just peace."

In light of Obama's declaration of "just peace" and these white male police characters using violence to achieve it, America's reinforcement of its position as the central axis of goodness and justice after 9/11 can be traced, condemning all that goes against the United States as "pure evil." Gus's shortcomings, portrayed in his fear and inexperience, reveal such a transformation of the American policeman rising from ordinary man to hero in the wake of 9/11. The firefighters, who were sacrificed and considered national heroes along with the policemen, were praised by the mayor of New York at the time, Rudy Giuliani. "These men," he said, "are fighting the first battle," faced with a sudden supernatural catastrophe.[77] Gus, as the average man and domestic hero, is the underdog admired and sought out in times of unknown terror and states of emergency. Although he is just a mailman, Gus's act is labeled heroic, and he goes unquestioned for his execution-style murder since it was treated as a "just act" in exceptional circumstances.

The "evil Other" presented in these series threatens the values of humanity, justice, and democracy by revealing how feeble our justice system is and how our everyday lives are endangered by arbitrary acts of terror and violence lurking around every corner. As Obama criticized the "freeriders" who "push us [United States] to act but then [show] an unwillingness to put any skin in the games,"[78] he "[expected] others to carry their weight," hoping they recognized and willingly followed the heroic leadership of the United States and approved his courage to implement violence against "serious evil." In a zombie apocalypse *(The Walking Dead)*, a city under ceaseless attack from dangerous criminals *(Gotham)*, and a small town in Minnesota where a cold-blooded killer is on the loose *(Fargo)*, a strong leader who can annihilate evil is favored over the naïve and confused. When a state of emergency is called, the commander in chief must be able to think militaristically and prioritize survival and the protection of sovereign power through the use of exceptional force.

These narratives do not leave much room for peaceful options for these three heroes, mirroring the way that Obama's military decisions were excused as he ended his term under a rather positive light compared to President Bush.[79] Obama established a new rhetoric in continuing a U.S.-centric worldview,[80] whereby military dominance by the United States continued with a supposedly stronger sense of innocence through the guise of a "just war." The analysis of these fictional police officers' use of gun violence outside the judicial system is observed in order to present a different kind of hero within Obama's America; they follow Obama's Niebuhrian rhetoric of how a man should not be too cynical in thinking there is no moral end to any political action while simultaneously not being so naïve as to think that peace can be achieved through nonviolence. Bush's American hero would judge and punish through the language of "good versus evil,"[81] with vengeance and a strong affirmation of his crusade, whereas Obama's American hero, hesitant to fall into such violent fundamentalism, nevertheless searches for the "judicious"[82] aspect of violence. The new hero image is more complex, with various layers and dilemmas factoring into his decision-making process, in which his heroism is constructed not upon his readiness to become a "supercop" or "superspy";[83] rather, these characters—whether onscreen or on the stage of global politics—are afforded their hero status according to their extreme circumstances and by reluctantly accepting society's call for a hero in times of loss, trauma, and terror.

NOTES

1. Nobelprize.org, "The Nobel Peace Prize for 2009," press release, 2009, www .nobelprize.org/nobel_prizes/peace/laureates/2009/press.html.

2. Nobelprize.org, "Barack H. Obama—Nobel Lecture: A Just and Lasting Peace," 2009, www.nobelprize.org/nobel_prizes/peace/laureates/2009/obama -lecture.html (my emphasis).

3. Jeffrey Goldberg, "The Obama Doctrine," *Atlantic,* April 2016, www.theatl antic.com/magazine/archive/2016/04/the-obama-doctrine/471525/.

4. Mark Juergensmeyer and Wade Clark Roof, *Encyclopedia of Global Religion* (Thousand Oaks, CA: Sage Reference, 2012), 1371.

5. Goldberg, "Obama Doctrine."

6. Ibid.

7. Maureen Dowd points to Joseph Campbell's mythical adventure of a hero in tracing the arc of the political campaigns of 1992 and how the American myth, and Western civilization at large, is rooted in the hero narrative, as seen in popular Hollywood films. Obama successfully tapped into the voters' longing for a new American hero in his campaign in 2008. Dowd, "The 1992 Campaign: Political Memo; Of Knights and Presidents: Race of Mythic Proportions," *New York Times,* October 10, 1992, www.nytimes.com/1992/10/10/us/1992-campaign-political-memo-knights-presidents-race-mythic-proportions.html?pagewanted=all.

8. Richard Wike, "Obamamania Abroad," Pew Research Center's Global Attitudes Project, 2008, www.pewglobal.org/2008/07/16/obamamania-abroad/.

9. *Hybridity* was used to describe Obama's biracial identity and "American" identity that emerged through American higher education, a multiracial family, and multicultural experiences with relatives all over the world. Nicholas A. Yanes and Derrais Carter, *The Iconic Obama, 2007–2009* (Jefferson, NC: McFarland, 2012), 35.

10. "In the defense of our nation, a president must be a clear-eyed realist," claimed Bush in one of his early speeches on foreign policy. Blatantly naming the "axis of evil" in his 2002 "State of the Union Address," Bush was clear in drawing lines between the enemies and allies of the United States, taking an aggressive and matter-of-fact approach. George Bush, "A Distinctly American Internationalism," speech, 1999, Ronald Reagan Presidential Library, Simi Valley, CA.

11. Calling Bush's war in Iraq a "stupid war," Obama said in 2002, "I am not opposed to all wars. I am opposed to dumb wars." Richard Jackson, *Routledge Handbook of Critical Terrorism Studies* (New York: Routledge, 2016), 368.

12. Obama was highly critical of President Bush and his administration's abuse of "inherent power." See "The President's 'Inherent' Power," *University of Chicago Law School Faculty Blog,* 2005, http://uchicagolaw.typepad.com/faculty/2005/12/the_presidents_.html; Frederick A. O. Schwarz and Aziz Z. Huq, *Unchecked and Unbalanced* (New York: New Press, 2007).

13. Goldberg, "Obama Doctrine."

14. Unlike Obama, Bush was not too concerned with the moral and ethical aspect of a "just war," as his administration believed—or was portrayed to believe—that the United States' reaction to terrorism was justified by the violence and deaths experienced on 9/11. William Felice, "President Obama's Nobel Peace Prize Speech: Embracing the Ethics of Reinhold Niebuhr," *Social Justice* 37, no. 2/3 (2010): 48. Michael Walzer saw that Bush tended to use "just war" language in terms of religious crusades, "as if a war can be just only when the forces of good are arrayed against the forces of evil." Michael Walzer, "The Triumph of Just War Theory (and the Dangers of Success)," *Social Research* 69, no. 4 (2002): 931.

15. Michael Grunwald, "Obama's Nobel: Another Slap at George W. Bush," *Time,* October 9, 2009, http://content.time.com/time/nation/article/0,8599,1929433,00.html.

16. Critique of Obama's Niebuhrian philosophy, reflected in his views on foreign policy and in his Nobel Peace Prize speech, has been discussed widely to point

out the ethical precariousness in the justification of the war on terror. Obama is not the first American politician to borrow Niebuhr's concepts to defend the use of American force, but he stands out among the many for cleverly utilizing the theologian's words to balance his liberalism and Christian realism. See Felice, "President Obama's Nobel Peace Prize Speech"; Liam Julian, "Niebuhr and Obama," *Policy Review*, April 1, 2009, www.hoover.org/research/niebuhr -and-obama; Joseph Rhodes and Mark Hlavacik, "Imagining Moral Presidential Speech: Barack Obama's Niebuhrian Nobel," *Rhetoric and Public Affairs* 18, no. 3 (2015): 471.

17. Neta C. Crawford, "Just War Theory and the U.S. Counterterror War," *Perspectives on Politics* 1, no. 1 (2003): 5–25.

18. The Obama administration changed the name from *war on terror* to *overseas contingency operation,* a linguistic shift noted by the *Washington Post,* and *countering violent extremism* (CVE). Scott Wilson and Al Kamen, "'Global War on Terror' Is Given New Name," *Washington Post,* March 25, 2009, www.washingtonpost.com /wp-dyn/content/article/2009/03/24/AR2009032402818.html.

19. Susan Buck-Morss, "Obama and the Image," *Culture, Theory and Critique* 50, no. 2–3 (2009): 147.

20. Ibid., 151.

21. Michael Walzer, *Just and Unjust Wars* (New York: Basic, 2006), 933.

22. Judis noted that "as Obama put it, 'serious evil' will always exist in this world and thus injustice must be confronted but cannot be eliminated." John Judis, "Obama, Niebuhr, and U.S. Politics," *New Republic,* December 12, 2009, https:// newrepublic.com/article/71872/obama-niebuhr-and-us-politics.

23. Jason Ralph, *America's War on Terror* (Oxford: Oxford University Press, 2013), 3.

24. See Giorgio Agamben, *State of Exception* (Chicago: University of Chicago Press, 2005).

25. Ibid., 22.

26. Buck-Morss, "Obama and the Image," 153.

27. See Michelle Bentley and Jack Holland, eds., *The Obama Doctrine* (London: Routledge, 2016), 48–50.

28. Peter Josephson and R. Ward Holder, *The Irony of Barack Obama: Barack Obama, Reinhold Niebuhr, and the Problem of Christian Statecraft* (Burlington, VT: Ashgate, 2012); Judis, "Obama, Niebuhr, and U.S. Politics"; Eric Paul, "What Does Reinhold Niebuhr Have to Do with Drones?," *Other Journal,* September 26, 2012, http://theotherjournal.com/2012/09/26/what-does-reinhold-niebuhr-have-to-do -with-drones/.

29. See Bruce Baum, *The Post-liberal Imagination* (New York: Palgrave Macmillan, 2016).

30. See Klaus Dodds, *Geopolitics* (Oxford: Oxford University Press, 2014), 35–36, 150.

31. Superman has been widely compared to the United States and its military dominance. David Schmid, *Violence in American Popular Culture* (Santa Barbara,

CA: ABC-CLIO, 2015), 613; Jason Dittmer, *Captain America and the Nationalist Superhero* (Philadelphia: Temple University Press, 2013).

32. In discussing Christian realism found in Anglo-American political views, Pak Nung Wong connects Western Christian political ethics and foreign policies, building up to Bush's "axis of evil," Obama's policies, and Niebuhr. Pak Nung Wong, *Discerning the Powers in Post-colonial Africa and Asia: A Treatise on Christian Statecraft* (Singapore: Springer, 2015), 6–10.

33. There was a zombie renaissance around Bush's first term and a constant increase in global popular cultural productions. Gerry Canavan, "'We Are the Walking Dead': Race, Time, and Survival in Zombie Narrative," *Extrapolation* 51, no. 3 (2010): 431–453.

34. See Kyle William Bishop, *American Zombie Gothic* (Jefferson, NC: McFarland, 2010); Canavan, "'We Are the Walking Dead'"; Darren Reed and Ruth Penfold-Mounce, "Zombies and the Sociological Imagination: *The Walking Dead* as Social-Science Fiction," in *The Zombie Renaissance in Popular Culture,* ed. Laura Hubner, Marcus Leaning, and Paul Manning (New York: Palgrave Macmillan, 2015), 124–138.

35. Overmind, "Literally the Devil: Why Lorne Malvo Was the Real Winner in *Fargo*'s Finale," *Overmental,* June 8, 2014, http://overmental.com/content/literally -the-devil-why-lorne-malvo-was-the-real-winner-in-fargos-finale-408.

36. See Jeff Birkenstein, Anna Froula, and Karen Randell, "Introduction," in *Reframing 9/11: Film, Popular Culture, and the "War on Terror,"* ed. Jeff Birkenstein, Anna Froula, and Karen Randell (New York: Continuum), 1–10.

37. E. Ann Kaplan, *Trauma Culture: The Politics of Terror and Loss in Media and Literature* (New Brunswick, NJ: Rutgers University Press, 2005), 20.

38. Alexander Dunst, "After Trauma: Time and Affect in American Culture beyond 9/11," *Parallax* 18, no. 2 (2012): 56–71.

39. These popular television series produced in the United States and presented to global audiences suggest that "international order and conduct [consistent] with the domestic definition of a 'terrorism world' ... claim that the 'new world' was governed by evil terrorists rather than political gamesmanship." Many analyses have been written on Hollywood films and post-9/11 themes—most notably in superhero blockbusters. See Birkenstein, Froula, and Randell, *Reframing 9/11*, 16.

40. President George Bush declared a "War on Terror" not only on al-Qaeda but also on Iraq, North Korea, Iran, and its "terrorist allies," identified as the "evil of international terror." Juergensmeyer and Roof, *Encyclopedia of Global Religion,* 1371.

41. The series is shown worldwide through Fox International Channels and has been in high demand, continuing, as of 2017, for eight seasons. See Claire Suddath, "China's Love Affair with *The Walking Dead,*" *Bloomberg.com,* November 5, 2013, www.bloomberg.com/news/articles/2013-11-05/chinas-love-affair-with-the-walking -dead; "Fox Networks Group Reorganizes International Television Business," 21st Century Fox, January 11, 2016, www.21cf.com/news/business/2016/fox-networks -group-reorganizes-international-television-business.

42. Darryl Woodard, "*The Walking Dead:* Its Domestic and Foreign Fan Reach," *Huffington Post,* December 14, 2014, www.huffingtonpost.com/darryl -woodard/the-walking-dead-its-dome_b_5987038.html; Ji-eun Nam writes that after Glenn's death in season 7's first episode, "global fans need a group therapy" and that Fox Korea received many angry calls from Glenn's fans after it aired. See Ji-eun Nam, "'Walking Dead 7' Begins with a Shock," *Huffington Post,* October 27, 2016, www.huffingtonpost.kr/2016/10/27/story_n_12668742.html.

43. Mareike Jenner, *American TV Detective Dramas* (Basingstoke, UK: Palgrave Macmillan, 2016), 170.

44. "Beside the Dying Fire," *The Walking Dead,* directed by Ernest R. Dickerson, aired on AMC, March 18, 2012.

45. For "Ricktatorship," see Laura Bradley, "End the 'Ricktatorship': *The Walking Dead* Needs a Different Protagonist," *Slate Magazine,* November 9, 2015, www.slate.com/blogs/browbeat/2015/11/09/the_walking_dead_rick_grimes_rick tatorship_should_end.html; Jamie Sharpe, "What *The Walking Dead*'s Cast Thinks of the Ricktatorship," *Vulture,* October 12, 2015, www.vulture.com/2015/10/the -walking-dead-cast-on-the-ricktatorship.html.

46. Jim from *Gotham* joins the GCPD after retiring from the U.S. Army, but his experience in the military has not yet been discussed.

47. "Days Gone Bye," *The Walking Dead,* directed by Frank Darabont, aired on AMC, October 31, 2010.

48. Mark Cronlund Anderson, *Cowboy Imperialism and Hollywood Film* (New York: Peter Lang, 2007), 20–21.

49. Ibid., 21.

50. "Try," *The Walking Dead,* directed by Michael Satrazemis, aired on AMC, March 22, 2015.

51. "Conquer," *The Walking Dead,* directed by Greg Nicotero, aired on AMC, March 29, 2015.

52. Birkenstein, Froula, and Randell, *Reframing 9/11,* 19.

53. Ibid.

54. The U.S. media, especially entertainment, works along American imperialist impulses as "imperialism on media at home" through the television screen. Maximilian C. Forte and Kyle McLoughlin, *Emergency as Security: Liberal Empire at Home and Abroad* (Montreal: Alert Press, 2014), 115. Especially during Bush's presidential terms, U.S. corporate media's deliberate use of the representations of wars were described as "weapons of mass deception." See Douglas Kellner, *Media Spectacle* (London: Routledge, 2003), 63.

55. Birkenstein, Froula, and Randell, *Reframing 9/11,* 7.

56. "Defense.Gov Transcript: DOD News Briefing—Secretary Rumsfeld and Gen. Myers," February 12, 2002, U.S. Department of Defense, Washington, DC, http://archive.defense.gov/Transcripts/Transcript.aspx?TranscriptID=2636.

57. Uri Friedman, "Why Obama Thinks ISIS Is Like the Joker in Batman," *Atlantic,* March 10, 2016, www.theatlantic.com/notes/2016/03/obama-isis-joker -batman/473193/.

58. Ibid.

59. "Jim Gordon—Gotham Wiki—Wikia," *Gotham.Wikia.Com,* n.d., http://gotham.wikia.com/wiki/Jim_Gordon.

60. Barnes, whose instinct tells him that Jim killed Galavan, tries to trust Jim and understands that Jim changed after the death of Katherine Parks, a young rookie female police officer who was his protégé. In one of the most gruesome scenes in the series, Flamingo, a notorious hitman, murders Parks as he is on his way to the cell—he bites her in the neck, and Parks is killed almost immediately. On hearing this news, Jim is shattered from the shock and his sense of regret and guilt, as he had a chance to kill Flamingo (who was hired by Galavan) and save Parks.

61. "Pilot," *Gotham,* directed by Danny Cannon, written by Bruno Heller, aired on Fox, January 29, 2015.

62. Sarah Essen, who came to replace the corrupt Commissioner Loeb, dies in Jim's arms in season 2, episode 3, "Rise of the Villains: The Last Laugh," after the massacre in the GCPD led by the Joker-like villain, Jerome.

63. "Arkham," *Gotham,* directed by T.J. Scott, written by Bruno Heller, aired on Fox, February 24, 2015.

64. "Rise of the Villains: Worse Than a Crime," *Gotham,* directed by Jeffery Hunt, written by Bruno Heller, aired on Fox, November 30, 2015 (my emphasis).

65. This is where the general population of prisoners is held, some of whom are Gotham's worst criminals. "Wrath of the Villains: Prisoners," *Gotham,* directed by Scott White, written by Danny Cannon, aired on Fox, March 28, 2016.

66. R. Barton Palmer, *Joel and Ethan Coen* (Urbana: University of Illinois Press, 2004), 95.

67. William Luhr, *The Coen Brothers' Fargo* (Cambridge: Cambridge University Press, 2004), 28.

68. June Deery, *Consuming Reality* (New York: Palgrave Macmillan, 2012), 85.

69. Ibid.

70. Hanh Nguyen, "*Fargo* Finale Postmortem: The Predator Becomes the Prey," *TVguide.com,* June 18, 2014, www.tvguide.com/news/fargo-finale-noah-hawley-1083116/.

71. Birkenstein, Froula, and Randell, *Reframing 9/11,* 58.

72. *Fargo,* directed by Joel Coen and Ethan Coen (Universal City, CA: PolyGram Filmed Entertainment, 1996).

73. Luhr, *Coen Brothers' Fargo,* 70.

74. "Eating the Blame," *Fargo,* directed by Randall Einhorn, written by Noah Hawley, aired on FX, May 6, 2014.

75. Ibid.

76. Glenn Whipp, "Billy Bob Thornton on Shocking 'Fargo' Finale: 'Isn't Life Funny?'" *Los Angeles Times,* June 18, 2014, www.latimes.com/entertainment/envelope/goldstandard/la-et-st-billy-bob-thornton-fargo-finale-20140617-story.html.

77. Sally Jenkins, "Company of Heroes," *Washington Post,* September 20, 2001, www.washingtonpost.com/archive/lifestyle/2001/09/20/company-of-heroes/2201a80a-8bc3-4a96-b085-f65491970b3d/.

78. Goldberg, "Obama Doctrine."

79. See Richard Wike, Jacob Poushter, and Hani Zainulbhai, "As Obama Years Draw to Close, President and U.S. Seen Favorably in Europe and Asia," Pew Research Center's Global Attitudes Project, 2016, www.pewglobal.org/2016/06/29/as-obama -years-draw-to-close-president-and-u-s-seen-favorably-in-europe-and-asia/.

80. Josephson and Holder, *Irony of Barack Obama*, 685.

81. Juergensmeyer and Roof, *Encyclopedia of Global Religion*, 1371.

82. Christi Parsons, "Obama Defends 'Judicious' Use of Drone Strikes during Online Q&A," *Los Angeles Times*, January 30, 2012, http://articles.latimes .com/2012/jan/30/news/la-pn-obama-drones-google-interview-20120130.

83. Steven Peacock, *Reading "24": TV against the Clock* (London: I. B. Tauris, 2007), 89.

SIX

Superhero Films After 9/11

MITIGATING "COLLATERAL DAMAGE" IN THE MARVEL CINEMATIC UNIVERSE

Tim Gruenewald

I believe the perception caused by civilian casualties is one of the most dangerous enemies we face.

U.S. General Stanley A. McChrystal, ISAF Commander, June 2009[1]

ON NOVEMBER 11, 2001, an unlikely meeting took place in the Peninsula Hotel in Beverly Hills. One year after many of them had campaigned for Al Gore during the presidential election campaign, about fifty top Hollywood executives met with Karl Rove, then senior advisor and assistant to President George W. Bush. Among the participants were the heads of Paramount, Viacom, Disney, MGM, Fox, and Warner Bros. Jack Valenti, then chairman of the Motion Picture Association of America (MPAA), gave a sense of how unusual the meeting was: "I've never seen this kind of gathering. . . . There was a seamless web of unity."[2] The *Los Angeles Times* summarized the purpose of the meeting as "an attempt to enlist Hollywood in persuading the world that Americans are the good guys in the war on terrorism."[3] In the wake of the September 11 terrorist attacks, the executives were eager to contribute; as Paramount president Sherry Lansing put it, "All of us in the industry have had this incredible need, this incredible urge to do something."[4] One result of the meeting was that each participating studio would designate one executive as a liaison to a group that would be coordinated by the MPAA.[5]

Judging from the media reports of the meeting, all participants were eager to preempt any notion of government-steered propaganda, stressing that "content was off the table."[6] Yet, Rove did present a few specific ideas: "The entertainment industry could help make clear, for instance, that the war is against terrorism, not Islam, he said . . . It could help the administration clarify that this is a global conflict requiring a global response, and that it is a fight against evil rather than a disagreement between nations."[7] Three months later, a *Washington Post* follow-up article concluded that "concrete projects have failed to materialize, the zeal seems to have faded" and that the "White House seems to have bowed out of any further participation in the project."[8] Bryce Zabel, president of the Television Academy of Arts and Sciences, saw the reason for the failed initiative in the refusal to talk about content: "Everyone was bending over backwards to make sure that content was off the table. That was because everyone is very interested in protecting the First Amendment and free speech. But that strikes me as wrong. Content is always on the table. It's what the entertainment industry is about. The issue is how can we properly discuss it?"[9] As far as we know, this question was not resolved, and a systematic coordination among Hollywood studios to support the war on terror never occurred despite the excitement evident in the initial meeting of November 2001.

As this gathering suggested and as television producer Craig Haffner noted, it was not due to a "lack of desire"[10] on the part of Hollywood executives that this collaboration did not ultimately materialize. In this chapter, I trace, through the treatment of collateral damage in superhero films, how Hollywood has, in fact, contributed to the perception of the war on terror very much in the spirit of what Mr. Rove suggested. Focusing on the Marvel Cinematic Universe (MCU) from *Iron Man* (2008) and *Avengers: Age of Ultron* (2015) to *Captain America: Civil War* (2016), I demonstrate how the superheroes—and the main characters Captain America and Iron Man in particular—have increasingly shown concern for civilian casualties during battle. Thus, to the extent that these characters symbolize the United States, these films have supported the war effort by emphasizing the benevolent intentions behind the use of force against the nation's enemies at home and abroad. One significant way that these films have achieved this aim is by manipulating the discourse about collateral damage.

SUPERHERO FILMS AFTER SEPTEMBER 11

No other Hollywood genre was as much affected by September 11 as the superhero genre. The first Hollywood superhero blockbuster was *Superman* in 1978. Throughout the 1980s the genre languished until it was revived with Tim Burton's *Batman* in 1989. The 1990s again saw little to no growth until

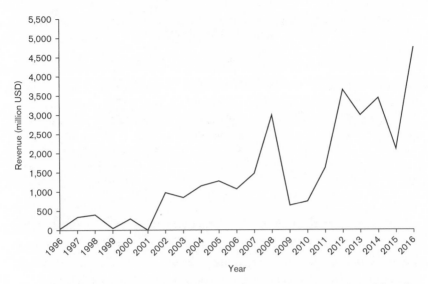

FIGURE 6.1. Approximate revenue for all superhero movies per year, not adjusted for inflation. Data from Box Office Mojo, www.boxofficemojo.com, accessed March 24, 2018.

the low point of 2001, when no significant superhero film was released. None of the sequels for *Superman* and *Batman* prior to September 11 were able to equal the commercial success of the first film.

The genre's box office exploded in 2002, when two films alone came close to generating $1 billion in revenue, nearly doubling the previous annual box office record for superhero films from 1994.[11] The years after 9/11 brought steady growth until revenue again doubled in the record-setting year of 2008 with close to $3 billion in box office, which included *The Dark Knight* (2008), the first superhero film to break the $1 billion mark. After a sharp pullback in 2009 and 2010, the upward trend resumed in 2011, reaching yet another box office record for the genre in 2012 with the arrival of the Avengers franchise on the big screen (see figure 6.1). *The Avengers* (2012), the sixth film in the MCU, set a new commercial record for a single film with a combined domestic and international box office of more than $1.5 billion. Since then three more films have exceeded the $1 billion mark, with the sequel *Avengers: Age of Ultron* taking the all-time second place with $1.4 billion. The year 2016 turned out to be the most successful for the genre ever. *Captain America: Civil War* achieved an all-time fifth best opening weekend of $180 million[12] and ended the year as the world's most successful film with a global box office of $1.153 billion.[13] The dominance of the superhero genre is set to

TABLE 6.1. Top four superhero films domestic vs. international box office.
All figures in U.S. dollars.

	Domestic	International	Worldwide
The Avengers (2012)	623,357,910	896,455,078	1,518,812,708
Iron Man 3 (2013)	409,013,994	805,797,258	1,214,811,252
The Avengers: Age of Ultron (2015)	459,005,868	946,397,826	1,405,403,694
Captain America: Civil War (2016)	408,084,349	745,220,146	1,153,304,495
Total	1,899,462,121	3,393,870,308	5,292,332,149

SOURCE: Data from Box Office Mojo, www.boxofficemojo.com, accessed March 24, 2018.

continue as more than twenty-five superhero films are scheduled to be released during 2018–2020, including several Marvel Studios films and two ultra-high-budget films from the Avengers series: *Infinity War I* and *II*, which are rumored to have a combined production budget of up to $1 billion.[14]

Finally, it is important to note that most of the superhero films generate over half their box office revenue in international markets. For example, the four films with the largest box office intake, all of which are Marvel Studios films, have generated approximately 64 percent of their total revenue in international markets (see table 6.1). The popular appeal and commercial success of those films is global, spanning Europe; the Asia Pacific; North, Central, and South America; and Africa. For example, the top ten international markets for *The Avengers* were, in descending order, China, the European Union, South Korea, Mexico, Brazil, Russia, Australia, Japan, Venezuela, and Taiwan.[15]

The popular appeal of superhero movies is hardly surprising in a post-9/11 world. Like the September 11 attacks, the climactic assaults in superhero movies often target real or fictional U.S. cities. Since 2001, New York City, or Gotham, alone has been the target of widespread destruction at least eight times (*Spider-Man* [2002], *Fantastic Four* [2005], *The Dark Knight, The Incredible Hulk* [2008], *Watchmen* [2009], *The Avengers, The Dark Knight Rises* [2012], *Man of Steel* [2013], and *Deadpool* [2016]). Superhero narratives provide an opportunity to experience fantasies in which heroes with superhuman abilities interfere with, prevent, mitigate, or avenge massive attacks by supervillains. Critics have explained the prevalence of such attacks in superhero narratives after 9/11 by referring to treatment approaches for trauma patients in clinical psychology. The rewriting and reenactment of the traumatic experience can help familiarize the unfathomable and thus contribute to healing, as Philip Smith and Michael Goodrum have argued:

By telling a story with a different location, happening to different people and with different outcomes (essentially, by telling a different story) an event can be stripped of its immediacy and horror whilst maintaining a certain kernel of truth which could not otherwise be told. In the case of mainstream superhero comic books, the re-enactment of the unspeakable is transformed in a manner which recognizes not only the events of the attacks, but the emotional impact of trauma that followed. Re-enactment as a healing process is visible in mainstream superhero comics. Not only are the events retold and rendered into a familiar framework but they are changed in a manner which radically redefines the event.[16]

In addition to fictionalizing the traumatic events of September 11, reintroducing a sense of control is a second important element. Witnesses to the terrorist attacks and the audience for their continuous media coverage felt a loss of control over their lifeworlds. Superhero narratives offer an antidote: "Superheroes can confront their enemies and exercise powers unavailable to normal people. By reliving the attacks through superheroes, a new narrative of the attacks becomes available, one with the crucial element of control inserted."[17] Reinserting a level of control in narrative fiction that was absent in the experience of the terrorist attacks also occurred with regard to the unintended consequences of the violence that followed in response to the attacks.

"COLLATERAL DAMAGE" AND CIVILIAN CASUALTIES SINCE THE GULF WAR

The term *collateral damage* is a euphemism with a long history of use by the U.S. military. Originally, the term appeared during the Cold War in the context of advocating in favor of the hydrogen bomb, which would leave the built environment intact while killing a maximum number of people through radiation. Ironically, collateral damage originally did not refer to civilian casualties but to buildings and infrastructure.[18]

During the first Gulf War, the meaning of the term collateral damage shifted to designate civilian casualties. The U.S. military employed an unprecedented media strategy to control the information presented in mass media around the world. One important tool in the military's media arsenal was video feeds from laser-guided missiles that would be used as evidence in support of the claim that revolutionary military technology during the massive aerial bombardment of Baghdad minimized the number of civilian casualties.[19] The abundance of such images in the war's coverage eventually resulted in the application of the nickname "video-game war."[20] The media were complicit in the military's strategy not only by disseminating the images but also by spreading the desired interpretation—as is evident, for example, in the *Newsweek* cover of January 18, 1991, which read, "The New Science of War/High-Tech Hardware: How Many Lives Can It Save?" Foregrounding advanced military technology was part of a larger rhetorical strategy that sought to "distance [the public] from death and encourage the denial of death in war" and to reject the "responsibility for war-related deaths."[21] Of course, as subsequent studies have shown, the notion that a massive aerial bombardment could be carried out on populated areas without incurring significant numbers of civilian casualties was a complete fiction.[22] Regardless, as Peter McLaren and Rhonda Hammer concluded in their study of the Gulf War's media coverage, "The construction of patriotism through the production of media unreality works—has meaning—as long as the viewer does not know his or her desire is being mobilized and structured through the advertisement mode of information."[23] Similarly, superhero narratives may affect a viewer or reader subconsciously despite their "unreality." Just as the U.S. military staged a visual spectacle of targeted bombings in the service of preventing civilian deaths, superhero films present "technologies" of superpowers, which could be read as allegories for U.S. military technology.

"You know, we don't do body counts," said General Tommy Franks at a press conference at Bagram Air Base in response to questions about the number of casualties resulting from Operation Anaconda in Afghanistan.[24] This statement by the commanding officer of the 2001 invasion of Afghanistan and the 2003 invasion of Iraq was perhaps the single worst public relations blunder of the military since September 11. In December of 2002, the Iraq Body Count project (IBC) was founded by academics and activists from the United Kingdom and the United States partly in response to General Frank's statement.[25] The IBC effort is ongoing and, as of August 2017, had counted between 178,792 and 200,267 civilian deaths in Iraq since the beginning of the U.S.-led invasion in 2003.[26]

Once the withdrawal of U.S. troops from Iraq was completed in December of 2011, the focus shifted toward civilian casualties from U.S. drone attacks, which increased during the Obama administration. Data on the number and the scale of drone attacks, let alone on civilian casualties, are difficult to obtain with certainty since it is a covert program. Various organizations have compiled data from media reports in an attempt to provide estimates. For example, the Bureau of Investigative Journalism estimates that in Pakistan alone between 424 and 969 civilians were killed from the inception of the program in 2004 through August 2017.[27] Following the leak of the Drone Papers in October of 2015, media coverage of the program and of civilian casualties resulting from it spiked. The leaked documents led to an extensive report on the program by the online platform *The Intercept*,[28] in which Ryan Devereaux concluded that during a five-month stretch of the drone program in the border region between Afghanistan and Pakistan, "nearly nine out of 10 people who died in airstrikes were not the Americans' direct targets."[29] This led to widespread, misleading reports that 90 percent of the people killed by drone strikes in Pakistan are civilians.

In summary, the number of civilian and military casualties resulting from the war on terror is staggering. Estimates diverge widely. A metastudy from 2015 by Physicians for Social Responsibility concluded that the war on terror had resulted in at least an additional 1.3 million deaths in Afghanistan, Iraq, and Pakistan.[30] The number of Iraqis killed since 2003 alone is estimated at up to one million, or 5 percent of the population.[31] The vast majority of these additional deaths were civilians.

SAVING CIVILIANS WHILE KILLING TERRORISTS: *IRON MAN*

While the films' narratives discussed in this chapter take place in the fantastic diegetic world of the MCU, I assume that they reflect sometimes explicitly but mostly implicitly the historical context of their production and reception. Let me begin by pointing out the Iron Man films' explicit connection to the post-9/11 world. Few if any superhero films have referenced the war on terror more directly.

The first installment, *Iron Man,* begins in Afghanistan, where Tony Stark is promoting a new Stark Industries cluster bomb, the Jericho, which is able to attack a very large area simultaneously, to the U.S. military. After the demonstration, Stark's convoy is ambushed, and he is taken hostage by Arabic-speaking terrorists who brandish a flag with crossed sabers reminiscent of the flags of the mujahideen in Chechnya or of al-Shabab in Somalia. As this unfolds, Stark realizes that the terrorists are using Stark Industries' weapons. He recalls that the United States, through the Central Intelligence Agency

(CIA), had funded and armed the mujahideen in Afghanistan, who in turn developed into al-Qaeda after the Soviet Union's withdrawal in 1989.[32]

While *Iron Man 2* (2010) takes a pause from referencing Islamic terrorism directly, *Iron Man 3* (2013) features the same terrorist group as in the initial installment, with the addition of a leader, the Mandarin, whose appearance and message seems to be modeled after Osama bin Laden. Reminiscent of tactics from terrorist groups such as al-Qaeda and ISIL, the terrorist organization Ten Rings uses video messages, which show statements from the Mandarin taking credit for and threatening further attacks against the United States, as well as a video of a hostage execution. Later in the film, it is revealed that the Mandarin is an actor from the United Kingdom, who only *performs* the role of a fundamentalist Muslim and who is used as a puppet by the real Mandarin (Iron Man's archenemy). This plot twist recalls the phenomenon of foreign fighters from Europe who have joined ISIL as well as the insistence by leaders in the West that Islamic terrorists do not represent Islam and are not "true" Muslims.[33]

The ideal of preventing collateral damage—that is, civilian deaths—in the fight against terrorists is central to the Iron Man trilogy. Consider the arrival of Iron Man on the big screen. Midway through the first installment of the trilogy, Stark is tinkering with an improved version of the Iron Man suit as he listens to a television report about civilian hostages in Afghanistan: "Simple farmers and herders from peaceful villages have been driven from their homes, displaced from their lands by warlords emboldened by a newfound power. . . . With no political will or international pressure, there's very little hope for these refugees." While the reporter is speaking, footage of streams of destitute refugees is shown on television, which prompts Stark to leave the safety of his tower in New York City and intervene on behalf of the civilian victims. Having just finished creating the iconic red-and-gold armored suit, he uses it to fly to Afghanistan, which is the very first appearance of Stark as Iron Man in the MCU. There he encounters a battle scene in which bombs, presumably from his own company's Jericho missile, are raining indiscriminately on villages from the sky. He immediately starts fighting the terrorists who are in the process of taking civilian hostages.

At the climax, the battle is interrupted as five terrorists simultaneously aim their guns at a half dozen women and children (see figure 6.2). The terrorists look confident and determined, as they believe they are safe behind the human shields. But they did not reckon with the superpowers of Iron Man. The film cuts to a point-of-view shot that depicts Stark's digitally

FIGURE 6.2. Terrorists threaten to kill hostages in *Iron Man*. © Marvel Studios.

FIGURE 6.3. Iron Man locks his aim onto the terrorists and identifies the civilians. © Marvel Studios.

augmented perspective of the hostage situation. We see crosshairs locking on one terrorist after another while the hostages are literally marked "civilian" (see figure 6.3).

In the next shot, several miniguns protrude from the suit and clinically execute all the terrorists at the exact same moment, freeing all the hostages completely unharmed. Thus, Iron Man turns out to embody the ultimate fantasy of targeted assassinations at the moment of his introduction.

Since Stark has just gone through the transformation from unscrupulous military-industrial-complex magnate to superhero on a mission to save mankind, the ideological subtext of the scene becomes supercharged. The implication of U.S. benevolence becomes more convincing, particularly to an international audience, since the film acknowledges the role of the United States in creating and arming the terrorist menace. Thereafter, the presentation of the reformed American hero, whose new mission is to save and protect civilians from terrorists, is all the more powerful. Stark commands superhuman technical and tactical abilities that allow him to assassinate terrorists without killing any civilians, even if the terrorists employ them as human shields. Presumably aided by an artificial intelligence (AI), he is able to pick out the terrorists from the crowd and eliminate all of them in one instant without fail. In a mere Hollywood fantasy, such a feat would hardly deserve any mention. This is what superheroes do; they accomplish the impossible. However, Iron Man mixes the fantastic with visual and narrative elements from mediated representations of the war on terror. For example, crosshairs locking onto human targets are a familiar image in the U.S. military's presentation of drone strikes. Regularly, terrorists and insurgent fighters from Afghanistan to Syria are accused of misusing civilians as human shields. Stark's ability to surgically kill the terrorists and liberate the hostages without incurring any civilian casualties is a fantasy the U.S. military would like the public to believe it can accomplish. By blurring the line between fiction and reality, *Iron Man* suggests the United States' intent and ability to avoid civilian casualties. Many more examples from *Iron Man 2* and *3* could be added here. Suffice it to say that preventing civilian casualties becomes one of the main concerns for Iron Man during his battle with the various terrorist antagonists of the franchise.

SAVING A CITY OR HUMANITY? SOLVING THE DILEMMA IN THE *AVENGERS* FILMS

The Avengers (2012) was preceded by five MCU films, all of which effectively served as elaborate commercials for the first MCU crossover movie.[34] Given that *The Avengers* and *Avengers: Age of Ultron* feature a starring role for four superheroes—Iron Man, Captain America, Hulk, and Thor—each of whom had already enjoyed his own successful franchise, it is hardly surprising that the two films were by far the highest-grossing superhero films so far.[35] In the following, we will see that the significance of avoiding civilian casualties was raised to a new level as it moved from an important but secondary plot element in the Iron Man films to increasing narrative prominence in the crossover films that culminated in the more recent *Captain America: Civil War* (2016).

FIGURE 6.4. People looking to the sky in horror and disbelief in *The Avengers*. © Marvel Studios.

The allusions in *The Avengers* to September 11 are obvious. The film features the struggle of the Avengers to prevent supervillain Loki from subjugating Earth. In the climactic battle, Loki opens up a wormhole over Stark Tower in Manhattan that allows an alien force to invade and attack New York City from the sky. The World Trade Center (WTC) of 9/11 becomes Stark Tower, and the terrorists are transformed into the alien fighting force attacking the city from blue skies. This narrative frame provides the opportunity to show several visual parallels to the real-world terrorist attacks. For example, we see the alien force flying literally into skyscrapers, people falling from the sky, massive debris plunging from the towers, people looking up in horror (see figure 6.4), mass panic in the streets of Manhattan, and images of a destroyed cityscape covered in dust and debris.

However, the script of September 11 is rewritten when it comes to the prevention of civilian death and to preventing the collapse of the tower. In an echo of the video footage and photos of victims leaping to their deaths from the WTC, Loki throws Tony Stark through the window of his penthouse. In a futuristic reimagination of Baron Munchausen's fantastic feat of pulling himself out of a swamp, Stark employs his technology to save himself. As he is falling toward the ground, he directs his Iron Man suit to catch up to him, stop his descent in midfall, and save his life and that of the people on the street who Stark would have hit. Ultimately, the Avengers win the battle, defeat Loki, and are able to close the wormhole and thus expel the

FIGURE 6.5. Tony Stark falling from the tower in *The Avengers*. © Marvel Studios.

FIGURE 6.6. The Iron Man suit saves Tony Stark. © Marvel Studios.

attacking force from New York and the United States. Thus, *The Avengers* provides the audience with a reassuring correction to the visual imagery from September 11. Technology saves the falling body (see figures 6.5 and 6.6), and the tower itself remains standing after the attack is repelled in contrast to the memories of the collapsing WTC.

The film's climactic twenty-five-minute battle between the Avengers and Loki's alien army is interrupted only twice, both times featuring Captain America as the leader of the Avengers. The first time concerns the evacuation and rescue of civilians as Captain America commands police officers: "You need men in these buildings. There are people inside that are going to be running right into the line of fire. You take them to the basement or to the subway." The second time shows Captain America as he devises the battle plan and directs the other members. Thus, the superhero most directly tied to the American national imagination is presented as being most concerned with preventing civilian casualties during the most heated and chaotic battle. At the same time, he is leading the coalition to defeat the alien enemy.

Finally, the question of collateral damage becomes the central plot element at the decisive moment of the battle. Unnamed government officials plan to detonate a nuclear bomb over Manhattan in order to destroy the attacking alien force, accepting massive numbers of civilian deaths in the process. Nick Fury, the commander of S.H.I.E.L.D., who is coordinating the Avengers from a helicarrier near New York, ignores the command and tries to prevent the detonation: "That is the island of Manhattan, councilman. Until I am certain that my men cannot hold it, I will not order a nuclear strike against the civilian population of Manhattan!" Subsequently, Fury is relieved of his command, and a nuclear missile is fired toward Manhattan. Having been warned by Fury, Iron Man attaches himself to the missile and redirects it into the wormhole, where the nuclear detonation far above the city closes it and thus saves Manhattan from catastrophe. This time, Iron Man becomes the force to prevent the mass murder of civilians through self-sacrifice. Notably, his choice to save Manhattan does result in a loss or even disadvantage in the battle as he is using ultimate force and U.S. military technology (the nuclear bomb) to defeat the enemy. Knocked unconscious from the detonation, Iron Man falls from the sky in a repetition of the scene from the beginning of the battle. Again, he is magically saved in midair as he is falling past the skyscrapers just before impact, this time by Hulk.

In *Avengers: The Age of Ultron,* the narrative takes place in the fictional Eastern European country Sokovia and pits the Avengers against a global artificial intelligence network called Ultron. Once again, preventing the death of civilians plays a central role in the film's narrative. While *Avengers* displayed the concern for American civilians, *Age of Ultron* showcases the

FIGURE 6.7. City being lifted and buildings crumbling in *Avengers: The Age of Ultron.*
© Marvel Studios.

rescue of foreign civilians. In an attempt to purge humanity from Earth,
Ultron lifts Sokovia's entire capital city into the sky in order to let it crash
back down and thus cause human extinction through an impact akin to that
of a giant meteorite. If it were ever acceptable to tolerate a limited number of
civilian casualties, saving the entire human race surely would be it. What
could possibly be the point of such a contrived narrative setup other than to
show that the Avengers—no matter the circumstance—would never allow
such a tradeoff? Unsurprisingly, the film goes over the top to make that case.
As the city is hovering above ground and entire apartment blocks are tum-
bling off the cliff (see figure 6.7), Iron Man hears his personal AI assistant:
"This building is not cleared, 10th floor!" He flies into the building to find a
family of three and saves them just in time before the entire building tumbles
off the edge. The script seems to be aware of its own absurdity and exploits
the scene for comic effect as Iron Man orders the family into the bathtub and
flies away with it just before the building collapses. At the same time, the
scene has a tragic allusion; the viewer cannot help but imagine the fate of
those trapped in the WTC towers at the moment of collapse, waiting in
vain for the miracle as it is imagined here. Once again, the script of 9/11 is
rewritten as American superheroes come to the rescue. The protection that
was granted to Americans in *The Avengers* is now extended to foreigners in
Age of Ultron.

After a few more spectacular rescues of individuals, the battle comes down
to the choice between exploding the city and vaporizing its residents or risking the extinction of humanity. Once again, Captain America leads the way,
arguing against Iron Man and the Black Widow:

IRON MAN: The impact radius is getting bigger every second. We have to make a choice.

BLACK WIDOW: Cap, these people are going nowhere. Let's start to find a way to blow this rock.

CAPTAIN AMERICA: Not till everyone's safe.

BLACK WIDOW: Everyone up here vs. everyone down there? There is no math there!

CAPTAIN AMERICA: I am not leaving this rock with one civilian on it!

Shortly after this dialogue, S.H.I.E.L.D.'s giant helicarrier appears, and the Avengers evacuate all civilians before the final battle to defeat Ultron and the eventual explosion of the city in midair. In this case, too, fantasy rewrites history. While many cities have been subjected to battle during the war on terror, causing countless civilian casualties in the process, U.S. and allied forces have never insisted on the complete evacuation of civilians before taking military action. The complete destruction of Sokovia's capital city reminds the viewer of the destruction visited upon cities such as Homs, Aleppo, or Raqqa in Syria. In contrast to the fantasy tale of *Age of Ultron,* none of these cities were evacuated. What is more, toward the end of the Obama administration, "The Pentagon stopped releasing redacted investigations of major civilian casualty events, which are supposed to assign responsibility and lessen the probability of future civilian harm. Mr. Trump has so far accelerated this trend."[36] The Trump administration has not only continued the secrecy over civilian casualties caused by the war against ISIL but has also increased the number of bombings and with it the number of civilian casualties significantly: "In Iraq and Syria, at least 55 percent of all civilians killed by airstrikes since the air war began in August 2014 have died under Mr. Trump's watch."[37] The track record with regard to the concern for civilian casualties during the war on terror from the Bush administration to the present sharply contrasts with the priority that avoiding collateral damage takes in the MCU.

THE MORAL DILEMMA OVER COLLATERAL DAMAGE MOVES CENTER STAGE

With the seven-issue limited comic series *Civil War* (2006–2007) and the loose film adaptation *Captain America: Civil War,* the controversy about collateral damage and civilian casualties caused by superheroes finally becomes the central plot device itself. As Richard Stevens pointed out, the *Civil War* narrative is a particularly "effective allegory for contemporary America" as it demonstrates how during a post-9/11 atmosphere a "culture of fear encourages the reduction of disagreements into conflict frames that define opinion holders as 'good' or 'evil' depending on the popularity of their subscribed beliefs."[38] If read as allegory, the disagreement in *Civil War* is precisely about the question of the benevolence of America's military actions in response to terror. Ultimately, the conflict both in the Avengers' fictional world and in debates over the war on terror revolves around the question of whether collateral damage caused by overwhelming force against terrorism is justifiable in extreme situations–or not?

In the comic series *Civil War,* a group of superheroes called the New Warriors attempts to apprehend supervillain Nitro during a reality TV show. The arrest fails and Nitro destroys several city blocks in Stamford, Connecticut, causing the deaths of six hundred civilians. Although superheroes lead the rescue and relief operation, public sentiment turns against them, which leads to the implementation of the Superhuman Registration Act by the U.S. government. The law forces superheroes to reveal their secret identities and register as "living weapons of mass destruction." Under the act, superheroes become federal employees and are subject to government oversight. The proposed law leads to a schism among the superheroes, with Iron Man leading the pro- and Captain America leading the antiregistration factions.

Two spectacular panels show civilian deaths and collateral damage in the graphic narrative. The first example appears early in the series on the last page of the prelude to part 1, which depicts Nitro's explosion in Stamford, Connecticut (see figure 6.8). The third panel from the top of the page amplifies its effect by showing the silhouettes of playing schoolchildren at the moment of incineration and death. The contrast between the children's contours and the bright fire increases the image's effect. In addition, the fire in the preceding and succeeding panels visually traps the children. The sequence also alludes to a nuclear detonation, further amplifying the devastation brought about by the superheroes' irresponsibility to confront Nitro in the middle of a city and to gain added publicity by appearing on a reality TV show. The effect of their action is akin to that of a weapon of mass destruction.

The second example of collateral damage appears near the end of the narrative in part 7 and depicts the devastation in Manhattan caused by a battle between the two factions led by Iron Man and Captain America (see figure 6.9).

FIGURE 6.8. The panel sequence visually traps the schoolchildren and alludes to a nuclear detonation. © Marvel Comics.

The former friends and allies have become mortal enemies over the question of government control. In the top panel on the previous page, Captain America is about to deliver the final and deadly blow to Iron Man. He is stopped by a group of civilians, who force him to acknowledge the collateral damage. The next page is dominated by the top panel, which shows crumbling high-rises and fires in Manhattan. The smoke visually seems to tear the city into shreds. The next panel follows directly as a reaction to the scene of the top panel, depicting a close-up image of Captain America in which he concedes the damage. In the following two panels, he surrenders the fight as

FIGURE 6.9. Civilians force Captain America to realize the collateral damage. © Marvel Comics.

his shield is dropped, and his tears are shown. On the next page, Captain America orders his followers to stop fighting and submits to arrest by the government, holding up his red-gloved arms to be handcuffed in a striking image suggesting that his hands are drenched in blood.

Civil War complicates and elevates the discourse about civilian casualties. The issue has become central to a degree that it has replaced the conflict between superhero and supervillain. The dilemma of having to choose between sacrificing one group of civilians in order to save another pits the superheroes against each other. At the same time, the narrative alludes to the Patriot Act and the controversial issue of government surveillance. Captain America, as the ultimate defender of individual rights and freedoms, resists submission to government surveillance. This is consistent with his role in the

MCU films. He knows that civilians are his primary concern, and he does not need government oversight to protect them. However, the end of the comic series' narrative proves him wrong; he admits that the superheroes' fight has spiraled out of control, and the government succeeds with implementing a program in the name of controlling superheroes and protecting civilians.

The film adaptation of the *Civil War* comic series, *Captain America: Civil War,* was the third highest-grossing film in the U.S. market in 2016 after *Rogue One: A Star Wars Story* (2016) and *Finding Dory* (2016). However, like other superhero films before, it garnered a relatively higher percentage of its overall revenue in the international market (64.6 percent) and achieved the highest global box office revenue of any film in 2016 ($1.153 billion). Thus, the genre continues to be Hollywood's most successful export and by far the most popular genre in international markets and therefore remains, as of 2016, one of America's most universally distributed vehicles of soft power. Given the widespread unpopularity of U.S. foreign policy overseas, this is a paradox, which speaks to Hollywood's unmatched skill of staging visual spectacles.

Following the graphic narrative, *Captain America: Civil War* preserved collateral damage as a central plot element while including significant narrative changes. Those modifications were designed to relate the film more closely to the post-9/11 period and to downplay the negative effect of collateral damage. Instead, the film emphasizes the superheroes' benevolent intentions as well as their overall positive contribution in the global fight against evil, which continues to manifest as terrorism. First, by adding and emphasizing international locations, the story resonates with and alludes to the global war on terror. Second, the ideological implication of collateral damage in the film is inverted compared to the comics by adding plot elements that allow both adversaries of the "civil war," Captain America and Iron Man, to abandon the legal restrictions placed on the superheroes and once again join forces in the battle against the terrorist supervillain.

The collateral damage catastrophe that leads to the legislative restriction on the superheroes is no longer located in Connecticut but instead takes place in Lagos, where the Avengers are on a mission to prevent supervillain Brock Rumlow (Nitro) from stealing biological weapons. Rumlow wears an explosives vest in genuine terrorist suicide bomber fashion and attempts to kill Captain America by blowing himself up. In a desperate rescue effort, Wanda Maximoff (Scarlet Witch) catapults Rumlow upward via telekinesis.

The subsequent explosion damages a nearby office building, killing several Wakandan humanitarian aid workers, which recalls various U.S. bombings of civilian buildings and organizations during the wars since 9/11.[39]

The explosion is followed by a montage of four high-angle shots of first, Captain America saying "Oh, my god," and then of Maximoff, looking up in horror and covering her face in shock. The film then cuts to a medium shot of the wrecked building, followed by a close-up shot of Captain America initiating the search and rescue effort and finally, another close-up of a distraught-looking Maximoff. This scene mitigates the superheroes' responsibility for the civilian casualties in several ways. First, Maximoff saves Captain America and thereby acts in self-defense.[40] Second, the scene takes place in a busy street market, which is shown in several shots prior to the explosion. Hence, Maximoff prevents a possibly even larger catastrophe by removing Rumlow from this location. In sum, her motivations are well justified, and the execution achieves the goals of saving Captain America and the civilians on the street. The collateral damage is merely an unpredictable and tragic error, which also humanizes Maximoff and makes her more relatable to the viewer. Most important, however, is the melodrama in the reaction shots of her and Captain America. They highlight the devastating emotional impact of the civilian casualties on the superheroes and thus further amplify the purity of their motivations.

The narrative chain set in motion by the bombing further adds to the internationalization of the narrative and includes allusions to the actual war on terror. The limiting legislation on the superheroes is not enacted by the U.S. government, as in the graphic narrative, but by a special meeting of the United Nations (UN) with the participating superheroes in Vienna. The agreement is now called the Sokovia Accords, named after the nation where the controversial battle depicted in *Age of Ultron* took place. This narrative change echoes the general conflict between the United States and the United Nations with regard to the pursuit of the war on terror—for example, during the lead-up to the Iraq War, when the U.S. government and opposing countries such as China, Russia, Germany, and France were debating at various UN meetings.[41] The film presents the United Nations as dominated by nations that have frequently opposed U.S. policy, especially with regard to the Iraq War. For example, during a UN press conference led by the king of Wakanda, these languages are displayed behind the king in the following order: Spanish, Russian, Arabic, Chinese, and English, where Arabic is in the center of the frame and English is partially offscreen, providing the subtext that the United Nations is dominated by nations hostile to the United States, which is literally pushed aside. At the same time, the film presents the United Nations as weak and vulnerable. The very UN session in Vienna during which the accords are to be signed falls victim to a terrorist attack. The bombing kills the accords' chief proponent, the Wakandan king T'chaka, and questions the logic of restricting the superheroes' power to combat evil terrorists.

The most important and perfidious alteration of the comic series' narrative is that the main conflict is no longer among the superheroes, as the title would suggest, but between the superheroes and a victim of collateral damage turned supervillain. Thus, as A. O. Scott of the *New York Times* has pointed out, *Civil War* is a misnomer for the film, and *"Captain America: Collegial Misunderstanding"* would have been more fitting.[42] What sounds like a minor point is central indeed with regard to the representation of U.S. benevolence in the MCU.

The supervillain is a highly modified version of Helmut Zemo, played by German actor Daniel Brühl.[43] In the film, he is a former Sokovian colonel who became a terrorist after losing his entire family during the Battle of Sokovia. As Iron Man realizes Zemo's strategy of taking revenge by pitting the Avengers against each other, he retreats from the accords and joins Captain America in his attempt to stop Zemo. Thereby, the potential danger of civilian casualties is confirmed. Even if a battle is successful and evil is defeated, as happened in Sokovia, unintended consequences and especially collateral damage lead to new sources of terror and violence. However, the solution to this paradox, as the film suggests, is not to be found in restricting or controlling superhuman powers but in doubling down on the use of superhuman might. The more effective way to defeat the supervillain is through the united force of the superheroes. Sowing discord about the use of force is so much in the interest of the supervillain/terrorist that it is depicted as Zemo's very strategy. Unsurprisingly, after Zemo is apprehended and jailed, the film concludes with an offer of reconciliation by Captain America. He frees the superheroes who have been detained for breach of the accords and lays out his vision for the future in a letter to Iron Man:

> We all need family. The Avengers is yours. Maybe more so than mine. I have been on my own since I was 18. I never fit in anywhere, even in the army. My faith's in people, I guess. Individuals. And I am happy to say that, for the most part, they haven't let me down. Which is why I can't let them down either.... So no matter what ... I promise you ... if you need us ... if you need me ... I'll be there.

The film ends with Iron Man receiving a call from Secretary Ross, who reports a breach in the high-security Raft Prison where the renegade super-heroes are held. However, Iron Man puts him—that is, the U.S. govern-ment—on hold and does not interfere. The final shot shows Captain America arriving at the prison, presumably to liberate the superhero inmates. Thus, the film completes the striking reversal from the graphic narrative's conclu-sion. Instead of ending with the incarceration of Captain America and his allies, as in the comic series, the film concludes with a reaffirmation of Captain America's opposition to government control of superheroes' power. This fundamental change seems to anticipate the position that Donald Trump advocated during the 2016 presidential campaign. As Glenn Greenwald remembered after civilian casualties in Syria and Iraq increased during the first months of the Trump administration, candidate Trump did not lack clarity with regard to his plans for the war on terror: "Trump regu-larly boasted that he would free the U.S. military from rules of engagement that he regarded as unduly hobbling them. He vowed to bring back torture and even to murder the family members of suspected terrorists."[44] Throughout the campaign, Donald Trump argued during campaign speeches and in countless tweets that politicians in Washington should not restrict the power of the military. This attitude turned into policy after the inauguration and caused a near-instantaneous increase in civilian casualties caused by U.S. bombings in Syria.[45] At the same time, neither the war in Syria nor global war on terror near a successful conclusion, in stark contrast to the arrest of Zemo in *Captain America: Civil War.* Thanks to Captain America's defiance of government control, the unfettered power of the superheroes leads to the defeat of the supervillain.

CONCLUSION

When it comes to reading popular culture as an expression of its social, eco-nomic, and political contexts of production and reception, sooner or later the question arises: "How much of this is just a good old fashioned superhero story, and how much of it is meant as allegory and perhaps commentary on some of the political and social realities of the post-9/11 world?"[46] This ques-tion was directed at Mark Millar, who in addition to authoring the comic series *Civil War* was a script consultant for several superhero films, including *Iron Man.* Millar responded that the comics "should be read as a superhero story. The Golden Age Superman isn't about immigrants needing a hope figure in the middle of the Depression. It's about Superman fighting Luthor and mad robots."[47] However, he did not stop there and added: "The undercurrents are there with all these stories and it gives them a little depth. Children and adults will, even subconsciously, be able to identify this as the world they're living in and hopefully what's essentially a fanboy beat-em-up on some level will also have a little more resonance."[48] It is precisely superhero narratives' seeming distance from reality, their fantastic exaggeration, their reveling in the most unreal visual spectacle, that makes them one of the most effective tools in America's soft power arsenal. As Millar suggests, the relation of the superhero films to the world in which we are living is primarily subconscious and therefore potentially all the more effective as a medium to spread a specific ideology.

It appears that Karl Rove was an astute student of history and therefore knew exactly how the government's aim was best accomplished when he said at the aforementioned meeting with the Hollywood executives: "Contrary to the expectations that most people have, the government did not direct the movie industry during World War II. The industry sort of set its own course, and that is certainly what we would encourage at this point."[49] If General McChrystal is correct that civilian casualties might be more dangerous to the United States than the terrorists themselves, it appears that Mr. Rove could not be happier with Hollywood's contribution to the war effort—at least as far as the globally most popular genre is concerned. One wonders if Mr. Rove was also aware of another historical echo from World War II. As Eric Rentschler concluded in his study of Nazi cinema, "The era's many genre films maintained the appearance of escapist vehicles and innocent recreations while functioning within a larger program. Goebbels eschewed overt agitation [and] articulated a desire to create a cinema that could both satisfy the domestic market and function as a foreign emissary."[50] The superhero genre fulfills this dual function perfectly. As the globally most popular genre since September 11, superhero films reach a wider audience than any other narrative form, and because they are not explicit U.S. propaganda, they are more effective in transmitting their message. As this case study demonstrates for the MCU films, collateral damage is represented as a major dilemma that eventually becomes a primary concern of the American superheroes. The films discussed in this chapter at the least suggest that the solution to this problem is not accountability and government oversight of martial power and technology; this is not necessary because the superheroes naturally have the best interest of innocent civilians at heart. In contrast, the best way to save civilians is to return full authority back to the superheroes and let them defeat the enemy through force, which sounds exactly like Donald Trump's new strategy to loosen the rules of engagement, kill terrorists, and "let the commanders and the fighters in the field do what they think necessary."[51] This strategy shift has and will lead to more civilian casualties. At least the MCU films admit, by way of the character Zemo, that such a strategy might well backfire.

NOTES

1. Physicians for Social Responsibility, *Body Count: Casualty Figures after 10 Years of the "War on Terror,"* March 2015, Washington, DC, 5.

2. Rene Sanchez, "Hollywood's White House War Council," *Washington Post,* November 12, 2001.

3. Dana Calvo, "Hollywood Signs on to Assist War Effort," *Los Angeles Times,* November 12, 2001.

4. Sharon Waxman, "Hollywood's War Effort: A Script Still in Development," *Washington Post,* February 18, 2002.

5. Rick Lyman, "Hollywood Discusses Role in War Effort," *New York Times,* November 12, 2001.

6. Ibid.

7. Ibid.

8. Waxman, "Hollywood's War Effort."

9. Ibid.

10. Ibid.

11. The two main films of 1994 were the comedic Jim Carrey vehicle *The Mask* and the gothic cult film *The Crow,* featuring Brandon Lee. Interestingly, Marvel Comics' *The Fantastic Four,* a low-budget film, did not even get a theatrical release. After September 11, the same studio would eventually dominate the genre as well as the global box office.

12. Dave McNary, "'Captain America: Civil War' Box Office Opening Soars to $180 Million," *Variety,* May 7, 2016.

13. "Captain America: Civil War," Box Office Mojo, accessed January 30, 2017, www.boxofficemojo.com/movies/?id=marvel2016.htm.

14. *Avengers: Infinity War* was released in April of 2018. It cost $ 321 million to produce and became the most successful superhero film to date, grossing more than $ 1.8 billion during the first month. The sequel is scheduled for release in March of 2019.

15. African film markets are missing here because of their overall lower box office revenues. However, the superhero genre is also dominating many national markets in Africa. For example, *The Avengers* held the top spot in South Africa in 2012, *Age of Ultron* was number two in 2015, and the top four spots in 2016 were superhero films.

16. Philip Smith and Michael Goodrum, "We Have Experienced a Tragedy Which Words Cannot Properly Describe: Representations of Trauma in Post-9/11 Superhero Comics," *Literature Compass* 8, no. 8 (2011): 488.

17. Ibid., 490.

18. See Carl M. Cannon, "Collateral Damage," *National Journal* 35, no. 11 (2003): 801.

19. See Philip M. Taylor, *War and the Media: Propaganda and Persuasion in the Gulf War* (Manchester, UK: Manchester University Press, 1992), 31ff. Carnegie Mellon senior research scientist Beth Osborne Daponte estimated that 3,664 civilians were killed during the 1991 Gulf War. See "Appendix 2: Iraqi Combatant and Noncombatant Fatalities in the 1991 Gulf War," *Wages of War*, Project on Defense Alternatives, accessed March 1, 2017, www.comw.org/pda/0310rm8ap2.html.

20. Taylor, *War and the Media*, 33ff.

21. Debra Umberson and Kristin Henderson, "The Social Construction of Death in the Gulf War," *OMEGA—Journal of Death and Dying* 25, no. 1 (1992): 1. The edited volume *Inventing Collateral Damage* argues that civilian casualties played a crucial role in modern imperial warfare from the eighteenth to the twentieth centuries. Stephen J. Rockel and Rick Halpern, eds., *Inventing Collateral Damage: Civilian Casualties, War, and Empire* (Toronto: Between the Lines, 2009).

22. In addition to the civilian deaths directly caused by the war, Daponte estimated that "about 70,000 civilians died subsequently from war-related damage to medical facilities and supplies, the electric power grid, and the water system." Douglas Harbrecht, "Toting the Casualties of War," *Bloomberg*, February 6, 2003.

23. Henry A. Giroux, Colin Lankshear, Peter McLaren, and Michael Peters, *Counternarratives: Cultural Studies and Critical Pedagogies in Postmodern Spaces* (New York: Routledge, 1996), 127.

24. See Edward Epstein, "Success in Afghan War Hard to Gauge," *San Francisco Chronicle*, March 23, 2002. David Williams argued that this statement indicates that the U.S. military was still governed by the experience from the Vietnam War, which "acts as the natural embarkation point into the development of tensions and policy inside the Pentagon on the complex problem of civilian casualties." David Williams, "We Don't Do Body Counts: A Study of the Pentagon and the Controversy of Civilian Casualties in Modern Warfare," *CONCEPT* 29 (2005): 75–76. The policy of not conducting or not admitting to Iraqi casualty counts was also adopted by the British military. John M. Broder, "U.S. Military Has No Count of Iraqi Dead in Fighting," *New York Times*, April 2, 2003.

25. The Oxford Research Group, which was then led by Professor John Sloboda, played a crucial role in founding the initiative Iraq Body Count.

26. See Iraq Body Count, www.iraqbodycount.org/. Figures are as displayed on the website on August 29, 2017. The main source of IBC data is media reports. Secondary sources include nongovernmental organizations and official government figures. Please see iraqbodycount.org for a detailed discussion on the methods page.

27. "Get the Data: Drone Wars," Bureau of Investigative Journalism, accessed May 13, 2016, www.thebureauinvestigates.com/category/projects/drones/drones

-graphs/. Other organizations that compile casualty data from drone strikes include the *Long War Journal* and the New America Foundation. "Pakistan Strikes," *Long War Journal,* accessed May 13, 2016, www.longwarjournal.org/pakistan-strikes; "Drone Wars Pakistan: Analysis," New America, accessed May 13, 2016, http://securitydata.newamerica.net/drones/pakistan-analysis.html.

28. Jeremy Scahill, "The Assassination Complex," *Intercept,* October 15, 2015.

29. Ryan Devereaux, "Manhunting in the Hindu Kush," *Intercept,* October 15, 2015.

30. *Body Count: Casualty Figures after 10 Years of the "War on Terror,"* 15.

31. Ibid., 15. Again, the estimates vary widely. For example, a Johns Hopkins University study from 2006 estimates 655,000 deaths through June 2006, while a study by the British Opinion Research Business estimated that by 2008 more than one million Iraqis had died as a result of war and its direct and indirect consequences. Ibid., 16.

32. Lawrence Wright, "The Rebellion Within," *New Yorker,* June 2, 2008. See also Wright's Pulitzer Prize–winning history of al-Qaeda, *The Looming Tower: Al-Qaeda and the Road to 9/11* (New York: Knopf, 2006).

33. For example, George W. Bush famously visited the Islamic Center of Washington, DC, only six days after the September 11 attacks, where he said: "The face of terror is not the true faith of Islam. That's not what Islam is all about. Islam is peace. These terrorists don't represent peace. They represent evil and war." "'Islam Is Peace,' Says President," White House Office of the Press Secretary, September 17, 2001, accessed May 11, 2016, https://georgewbush-whitehouse.archives.gov/news/releases/2001/09/20010917-11.html. Barack Obama largely avoided the term *Islamic terrorism* when discussing, for example, ISIL, in an effort to delegitimize and isolate the group. Jon Greenberg, "War of Words: The Fight over 'Radical Islamic Terrorism,'" *PolitiFact,* December 11, 2015.

34. Those films were *Iron Man, The Incredible Hulk, Iron Man 2, Thor* (2011), and *Captain America: The First Avenger* (2011). Of those, the two Iron Man films were the most successful. As of May, 2018, nineteen films have been released as part of the MCU, with a combined box office of close to $17 billion, making it the highest-grossing film franchise of all time. "List of Highest-Grossing Films," *Wikipedia,* accessed May 11, 2016, https://en.wikipedia.org/wiki/List_of_highest-grossing _films#Highest-grossing_franchises_and_film_series.

35. Another aspect that has contributed to the promotion and popularity of the franchise has been the use of recurrent Hollywood stars. In part, they were created by being cast in the franchise, such as Chris Evans as Captain America and Chris Hemsworth as Thor. Others were already well known before playing superheroes, such as Robert Downey Jr. (Iron Man) and Mark Ruffalo (Hulk). Arguably, the two most prominent stars have been cast in supporting roles: Scarlett Johansson as the Black Widow and Samuel L. Jackson as Nick Fury.

36. Micah Zenko, "Bush and Obama Fought a Failed 'War on Terror.' It's Trump's Turn," *New York Times,* August 25, 2017.

37. Ibid.

38. Richard Stevens, *Captain America, Masculinity, and Violence* (Syracuse, NY: Syracuse University Press, 2015), 254.

39. One example would be the bombing of the Red Cross complex in Kabul during the invasion of Afghanistan in October of 2001. Another would be the shelling of the Palestine Hotel in Baghdad in 2003. Jon Schwarz, "A Short History of U.S. Bombing of Civilian Facilities," *Intercept,* October 7, 2015, accessed February 14, 2017, https://theintercept.com/2015/10/07/a-short-history-of-u-s-bombing-of-civilian-facilities/.

40. Captain America, via his name and ideology, represents traditional American ideals and values. In an allegorical sense, one could read Maximoff's intervention as saving America herself from terrorist destruction.

41. One of the most prominent and controversial UN meetings during the lead-up to the Iraq War was the presentation of then secretary of state Colin Powell to the UN Security Council about Iraq's failure to disarm in February of 2003. "Powell Presents U.S. Case to Security Council of Iraq's Failure to Disarm," *UN News Centre,* February 5, 2003, accessed February 15, 2017, www.un.org/apps/news/story .asp?NewsID=6079#.WKPlN7Fh22w.

42. A. O. Scott, "Review: In 'Captain America: Civil War,' Super-Bro against Super-Bro," review of *Captain America: Civil War,* directed by Joe and Anthony Russo, *New York Times,* May 5, 2016.

43. There are several other references to Germany in the film. Most importantly, the renegade Avengers are held in Berlin, and the climactic battle between Iron Man's and Captain America's faction takes place at Leipzig airport. This could be seen as an allusion to Germany's opposition to U.S. foreign policy, especially with regard to the Iraq War.

44. Glenn Greenwald, "Trump's War on Terror Has Quickly Become as Barbaric and Savage as He Promised," *Intercept,* March 26, 2017.

45. Ibid.

46. "Civil War and Peace of Mind with Mark Millar (Part 2)," Cinechew, accessed May 13, 2016, https://cinechew.com/civil-war-peace-mind-mark-millar -part-2/.

47. Ibid.

48. Ibid.

49. Lyman, "Hollywood Discusses Role in War Effort."

50. Eric Rentschler, *The Ministry of Illusion: Nazi Cinema and Its Afterlife* (Cambridge, MA: Harvard University Press, 1996), 16–17.

51. Fred Kaplan, "Trump Has No Plan for Afghanistan Other Than Killing More Terrorists," *Slate,* August 21, 2017. See also Helene Cooper, "Trump Gives Military New Freedom. But with That Comes Danger," *New York Times,* April 5, 2017.

SEVEN

Humanity's Greatest Hope

THE AMERICAN IDEAL IN MARVEL'S *THE AVENGERS*

Ross Griffin

THE SEEDS OF THIS CHAPTER BEGAN to ferment around May 2012. At the time, I had been struggling with a particularly obstinate chapter of a doctoral thesis on American exceptionalism and the nonfictional literature of the Vietnam War. Seeking respite from the never-ending debate relating to America's role in that conflict as relayed through the harsh realities portrayed by authors such as Tim O'Brien, Philip Caputo, and Neil Sheehan, I sought temporary shelter for a few hours, at least, in the Marvel Universe. Re-emerging back into the real world after a healthy dose of escapism, I could not help but overhear one other film-goer, a boy of about thirteen or fourteen years, say to his companion, "I'm glad *we* won." It might be pertinent at this point to highlight that this was a cinema in Ireland. Such a comment surprised me. Ireland is a country as far removed from geopolitical conflict as any you might find and one that has prided itself on its neutrality since its independence from Britain in the early 1920s. So how was it that an Irish teenager could so readily identify with characters so obviously steeped in the dominant discourse of American culture and myth? How was it that he now saw their enemies as his own? In a world of 9/11, al-Qaeda, and ISIS, it was this simple comment that got me thinking about the immense manipulative strength of American culture as a weapon to combat the aforementioned enemies or any that have previously arisen. Much more significantly, however, it struck me just how potent a tool the film industry was in transforming American aggression and repackaging it to a global audience as a uniquely benevolent brand of violence that was only ever used in order to protect the principles of democracy and freedom. The focus of this chapter is quite simple. Using *The Avengers* (2012) as a template, it examines how Hollywood allows the United States to represent itself as humanity's "last best hope" in any pending clash of civilizations with the Arab world and argues that super-hero films, such as *The Avengers,* are being used to elide U.S. imperialism in the Gulf and Middle East by portraying America and its agents as a global force for good, defending civilized society from a cultural Other intent on destroying it.

While the gaze of the Western media is nowadays firmly focused on the dangers posed by Arab terrorism, until the end of the Cold War, it was the ideological threat posed by the Soviet Union that prompted the aforemen-tioned media apparatus to portray American society as exceptional. This contrast, founded on insurmountable ideological differences between the respective nations, was one repetitiously reinforced by the West. The end of the Cold War in 1989 effectively neutralized this particular menace to the American way of life. Yet despite the subsequent shift in adversary from the godless communism of the Soviets to the religious extremism of Arab funda-mentalism, the methodologies used by the dominant hegemony to implicitly instill within the public psyche a fear of, and an alienation from, this ideo-logical Other remain the same. America's suitability to act as the global exemplar of political, moral, and economic behavior is still reiterated by the traditional cultural artifacts of newspaper, television, and literature. However, far surpassing these media outlets is the American film industry. Hollywood has become one of the most effective strategies used to imagine the benevolence of U.S. foreign intervention. In his comprehensive study of the representation of Arabs in mainstream cinema, Jack Shaheen rightfully claims that as "the world's leading exporter of screen images," the United States occupies an unparalleled position of cultural influence.[1] As such, the argument made by Melani McAlister in *Epic Encounters* that "culture is an active part of constructing the narratives that help [foreign] policy make sense in a given moment" becomes more credible.[2]

Although Hollywood's cultural products are outwardly often far removed from reality, since the end of World War II, their emergence into the public sphere frequently coincided with periods of national anxiety among the American people. Such events in living memory have included the Cuban Missile Crisis and the Soviet nuclear threat, the Vietnam War, and, in more recent times, the invasions of Iraq and Afghanistan. Richard Slotkin notes in *Regeneration through Violence* that American moviemakers throughout the second half of the twentieth century, heavily influenced by the idea that their nation was exceptional, had a tendency to "[use] the languages of their profession to represent the concerns of the moment."[3] Thus, suitably altered to adhere to the ideological outlook of the prevailing administrations, such anxieties were reposited to the general public in a manner that reinforced "the base assumptions of value and historical fact on which [their] culture's sense of its 'mission' [had] been based."[4]

A telling demonstration of this can be seen in the significant increase in the number of Westerns released throughout the mid-twentieth century as the Cold War between the United States and the Soviet Union escalated to an unprecedented level.[5] The genre was one frequently appropriated by the mythmakers of American culture to underline the superiority of their society's ideals in comparison with all other nations. It was also a golden age for films produced in the science fiction and spy genres. But regardless of whether the setting was the Rio Grande, an anonymous middle-American town in the 1950s, or the backstreets of Berlin, the plot of each film invariably involved a Caucasian state actor (while there have been variations of this trope in terms of number and gender, it has traditionally been a solitary male) posited as society's last, best hope in the Manichaean struggle against an irrational, uncompromising, and ruthless enemy intent on destroying civilization as we know it. Risking his own safety because no one else is prepared to do so, his methods may not be orthodox, or even completely acceptable, but they are represented as necessary to achieve victory over a great evil. Consequently, films such as *Shane* (1953) or *The Magnificent Seven* (1960) provided a form of state-sanctioned "interpretive grid" that enabled both the general public "to come to terms with contemporary political crises" and the governing authority "to manage the public's response to [these crises]."[6]

In the aftermath of 9/11, the U.S. government's "war on terror" has been yet another source of national anxiety, and Hollywood's response has been largely similar to what it was in the 1950s and 1960s. Since the September attacks on the Twin Towers, there have been over fifty superhero movies released by the two main studios—Marvel and DC Films—alone. Incorporating figures easily recognized by mainstream audiences (Superman, Spiderman, and Batman, for example), as well as including more diverse members of the superhero universe, such as Deadpool, the X-Men, and the Guardians of the Galaxy, the paradigm suggested by theorists such as Richard Slotkin and Donald Pease remains the same. Each of these films presents a situation to the American audience that encapsulates a contemporary concern—one that in the twenty-first century is derived from the idea that there exists a very existential threat to American, and thus by proxy all, civilized societies that must be dealt with, a diametric Other whose values and ideals are a danger to those espoused by the United States. Motivated solely by the desire to defend civilization from such catastrophe, personified by these superheroes, only America and its agents are suited to overcoming this threat. Throughout the era of Kennedy's New Frontier, Westerns such as *The Magnificent Seven* were frequently situated along that imaginary line that separated civilization and savagery in the American nation. These films frequently highlighted that, although it demanded a heavy price to be paid in terms of pioneering spirit and sacrifice, the "old frontier" also offered opportunity, reward, and a justification of the country's overlapping tenets of exceptionalism and Manifest Destiny.

Noticeably located in contemporary America, *The Avengers* can still be shown to inhabit the same metaphorical space as the prairies and "Injun" country portrayed to such stunning effect in the most American of film genres. Key to this process is what Pease calls the "mythological tropes . . . sedimented within the nation's master narrative."[7] Not only have these symbols and motifs provided "the transformational grammar" used by generations of Americans to comprehend the world around them, they also constitute an idiom that has been used with regularity by U.S. presidents and statesmen to frame American military endeavors overseas.[8] Foremost among these are what Pease describes as "virgin land narratives."[9] These portray a "movement of the national people across the continent in opposition to the savagery attributed to the wilderness."[10] Yet far from describing the American West in its historical entirety, these mythopoeic accounts have frequently exhibited a selective memory in retelling the realities of such events. Often overlooking the forced removal and subsequent genocide of America's original inhabitants, such narratives transform the unpalatable elements of the nation's past into a demonstration of American benevolence and fortitude in the face of danger. More clearly stated, events such as the Indian Wars or the Alamo, tragedies whose occurrence can be linked directly to a government policy of aggressive territorial expansion, are remembered and often cited as pivotal moments in U.S. history, where a commitment to American values such as democracy, individualism, and freedom of expression has allowed them to triumph over evil. Rather than presenting a narrative that reflected the perilous and often fatal reality of these situations for those unfortunate enough to be caught in their clutches and the often immoral and ethically dubious sociopolitical rationale for the occurrence of such events, virgin land narratives convert scenes of national tragedy into those that celebrate the altruism of American society. Instead of focusing on the past, such narratives perpetuate both the idea that the nation was "divinely ordained to serve as the only political, cultural, and economic model for the rest of the world" and its status as a global force for good.[11] Particularly prevalent in Westerns throughout the mid-twentieth century, a similar approach can be seen to unfold in *The Avengers* some fifty years later.

The first attack on home soil since Pearl Harbor, the terrible loss of civilian life and the indelible mark it left on the national psyche has meant that the terms *9/11* and *the Twin Towers* are now synonymous with one of the darkest days of U.S. history. By many Americans, they are uttered and received with the same mixture of anger, sadness, and pride that the mention of the Alamo or Custer's Last Stand would have elicited from previous generations. Yet in recent times, just as has been the case with many of the classic tropes of American mythology, these terms have also been transformed to suggest an American innocence—a people who became victims of their own benevolent nature and whose efforts to better a troubled world were rejected in the most brutal fashion by an irrational and uncompromising evil. This paradigm is quite evident in *The Avengers*.

Adhering to a formula that has become commonplace in many of the blockbusters released by Hollywood over the course of the twentieth and early twenty-first centuries, the film portrays the coming together of several of Earth's most powerful superheroes in order the save the world from the Norse demigod Loki and his alien army. *The Avengers*' decisive battle scene takes place above downtown New York, a sprawling metropolis whose blend of culture, creed, and race allows the city to be interpreted as a synecdoche for the United States and even the greater civilized world. Yet post 9/11, the city has become synonymous with a catastrophe caused in the most dramatic fashion by a fundamentalist breed of Arab terrorism. In *Arabs and Muslims in the Media: Race and Representation after 9/11*, Evelyn Alsultany notes how television dramas produced in the aftermath of the attack on the Twin Towers have in a variety of means "replayed the tragedy of 9/11 weekly to U.S. audiences, keeping the trauma fresh in the collective memory."[12] Extended also to the silver screen, this practice becomes quite apparent in the closing scene of *The Avengers*. An unprovoked assault on Manhattan by an alien Other intent on destroying the fabric of American society, images of airborne monoliths crashing into high-rise office buildings (see figure 7.1), and the desperate efforts of city police officers and firefighters to remove dust-clad civilians from the ensuing chaos ensures that this association is one that in *The Avengers* comes quickly to the fore.

FIGURE 7.1. The scene of an alien aircraft crashing into the Manhattan skyline harkened the 9/11 attacks on the World Trade Center. © Marvel Studios.

But what is the purpose of such a scene? It could be argued that it is an attempt to transform the sorrow and tragedy of the attack by altering the emotion surrounding the collective memory of that September day to one that underlines America's stance as a reluctant hegemon defending democracy and liberty from the barbarous hordes. Replete with many of the same visual cues, the final battle becomes an example of what Alsultany describes as "representations of reality— images, symbols, signs, media . . . [that] have come to stand in for the real to the extent that the representation becomes indistinguishable from the original."[13] The reception of *The Avengers* across both fan-based review websites, such as those archived on IMDb, and those found in the mainstream media has been largely positive. Writing for the *Los Angeles Times,* Kenneth Turan calls the film "the ultimate expression of today's Hollywood zeitgeist" while A. O. Scott of the *New York Times* describes it as "a snappy little dialogue comedy dressed up as something else."[14] However, the idea that *The Avengers* deliberately seeks to reshape the assault on the Twin Towers in the collective memory of the American people is not one that escapes the notice of critics. Fan reviews of the film describe its ability "to transform New York City into a place for heroes" while also allowing the viewer "to be thoroughly entertained while having your feeling [*sic*] played with at the same time."[15] Others have noted how it combines "personality and death-defying events and cultural themes somehow welded and soldered together in a kind of collage of imagination and experience and juvenile science fiction."[16] Similarly, when reviewing the film for the *New Yorker,* Richard Brody's view is that while at times "cartoonish," *The Avengers* is also adept at "addressing graver concerns—the construction of a post-9/11 revenge fantasy that takes place against the backdrop of unpopular wars."[17] Brody went on to highlight the filmmakers' use of mythopoeic triggers, which include the use of Manhattan as a setting for the decisive battle against Loki and the World War II references included in the introduction of Captain America. Most significantly, however, as we continue to live in a world where terrorist attacks fueled by all kinds of religious extremism have begun to occur with alarming frequency, Brody is aware of how *The Avengers* begins to mirror reality by delivering a narrative with the ability to satisfy the desire within many for "military solutions to potentially apocalyptic problems."[18]

As the superheroes combine not only to defeat Loki and his army on the ground but also to deliver a nuclear warhead successfully to the latter's place of origin, *The Avengers* delivers on this primordial desire within its audience. The most potent part of this process is thus the victory achieved. This not only enables a catharsis absent in the immediate aftermath of the actual event but, when combined with scenes of an enemy leader being led away in hand-cuffs and of ordinary men and women rejoicing, uses the conclusiveness of this victory to transform the uncertainty and anxiety surrounding the events of the real 9/11 attack into something that unmistakeably alters the tenor of the attack as Manhattan becomes a place of victory as opposed to one of sorrow and vulnerability. It is no longer a site that highlights the fragility and vulnerability of those who inhabit the West. Rather, the city can now be seen as a metonymic representation of America itself, one that can be understood as "a nexus of both energy and style, of both tenacity and groundedness" willing to do whatever is necessary to maintain the sanctity of civilized world order.[19] As buildings crumble and enemy soldiers lie dying in enormous num-bers at the feet of the various superheroes, it becomes clear that destruction has been wrought upon New York in equal measure by Captain America and his cohort. However, benefiting from what Alsultany calls "situational morality," the violence enacted by the Avengers is justifiable in that it is undertaken in order to save society rather than subjugate it.[20] Unlike previ-ous superpowers, the United States only resorts to such measures to protect the civilized world from those intent on destroying it. Referring once more to Brody's scathing review, "the super-group's climactic, heroic last stand takes the form of legitimate defence."²¹ As has occurred with the Alamo, the Battle of the Little Bighorn, and other events mired deep within the foundational narrative of the United States, with the aid of the silver screen, 9/11 is slowly being transformed into yet another crucial moment in American history that demonstrates how the values and beliefs that made the nation great are essential to protect the civilized world from the forces of evil.

This sense of transformation is continued and exponentially amplified in subsequent Marvel films, such as *Captain America: Winter Soldier* (2014), *Iron Man 3* (2013), and *Avengers: Age of Ultron* (2015). In each, the scenes of unprecedented violence described previously are mentioned in shorthand by numerous characters simply as "New York," a process whereby the real and the representations of the real become ever more blurred. Reduced to a single phrase, this moniker assumes the emotional load of the actual terms used outside the film's fictional universe. Crucially, however, a metamorphosis has taken place. The unsettling coincidence of motifs, images, and events that concludes *The Avengers* has begun the process whereby the frightening realities of 9/11 are transformed. Firmly embedded now in a state fantasy that encourages the portrayal of the United States in the dominant discourse as a force for good against evil, the closing scene can be seen as offering one of the lasting alterations to the narrative of 9/11. The film fades out to a New York skyline being rebuilt and essentially reborn, for the audience knows that the events of that tragic day were not the end but simply the first in a series of seismic battles against the barbarian hordes in which they, as the protectors of all that is civilized and good, will prevail. What is crucial to note here is that not only is the cultural memory of these events altered but so too is their status as a source of trauma. The dynamic at play here is one that Pease describes as the end result of the successful implementation of a state fantasy that "transposes these sites of trauma into the inaugural spaces within a newly configured order."²² In providing the viewer with a schematic by which to reinterpret 9/11 and the events thereafter, this transformation keys directly into the national fantasy that became predominant in the post-9/11 era. While the anxiety and uncertainty of that day will linger long within the mind of the American people, its symbolic replay depicting the defeat of an existential enemy offers a closure rarely enjoyed by victims of trauma in real life.

An essential part of this virgin land model suggested by Pease is the presence of a cultural Other that represented the contrapuntal values and beliefs of all that the New World settlers epitomized. Where the latter sought to build, the former sought to prevent such progress; while the latter represented enlightened society, the former represented a primitive world. Most importantly of all, the New World settlers were emissaries of a Christian God, one whose qualities were all the more enhanced when set alongside the pagan idols worshipped by Native Americans. Such binary comparisons would become an integral part of the dominant discourse as the nation encountered the totalitarian ideologies of fascism and communism throughout the course of the twentieth century. Since the Iranian hostage crisis of 1979, this rogue's gallery has been extended to include the Islamic extremist.

While little more than a caricature based on crass orientalism comprising many of the most inaccurate stereotypes of both Arab culture and Islam, this view of the Arab people was given fresh impetus in the aftermath of 9/11 and has been reinvigorated even further as ISIS-inspired attacks continue to spread across the West. Many depictions portray a people and a culture whose combination of ardent "medieval fanaticism and religiosity" is only matched by the strength of their alleged anti-Americanism.[23] In her excellent account of popular representations of the Arab Other over the latter half of the twentieth century, *Epic Encounters: Culture, Media, and U.S. Interests in the Middle East, 1945–2000*, Melani McAlister notes that since the late 1970s, the words and actions of those representing the second-largest religion in the world on the global stage have been interpreted by Western media most frequently using the trope of "Militant Islam." Citing the *Second International Conference on Terrorism* as a primary catalyst for this association between Islam and terrorism, McAlister describes how this conference concluded that Muslims as a people were "hostile to democracy," "ahistorical," and most significantly, the purveyors of a faith diametrically opposed to Christianity.[24] In short, as the twentieth century drew to a close, the term *Muslim* in Western culture was rapidly becoming synonymous with "terrorists ... and totalitarians," and the image of the Arab people as a viable threat to civilized society began to grow.[25]

The looming specter of Arab terrorism has also raised its head in the Marvel Universe. In his chapter "Superhero Films after 9/11," Tim Gruenewald highlights how the makers of the Marvel series of films have represented Islamic fundamentalism as a source of existential danger, citing both *Iron Man* (2008) and *Iron Man 3* as viable examples. However, it must be clearly stated that neither Islam nor the Arab people are directly impugned in any of *The Avengers* films to date (*The Avengers* and *Avengers: Age of Ultron*).

Yet despite this absence, a number of the motifs personified by Loki within the first film allude to the threat allegedly being presented to the West by Islamic extremism. In the broadest of strokes, Loki commands an alien army whose actions are shown in the closing battle scenes to be every bit as "violent, irrational, unappeasable [and] totally uncompromising" as Western media frequently portrays the Islamic Other to be.[26] While a deity in his own right, rather than acting as his own master Loki is shown throughout the film as representing a supreme being whose abilities far outstrip those of the Norse god. Using this crude yet effective framework, Loki now becomes a figure cognizant of the Prophet Mohammed, a deity who for Muslims the world over speaks the words of a higher power.

The analogy with the Prophet Mohammed continues to gain further traction when the character of Loki is analyzed alongside his brother Thor. In appearance and actions, the latter adheres to Western expectations of divinity. While the familial link between the gods should prevent any attempts to transform Loki into an Other, Thor's admission to his fellow Avengers that his brother is adopted allows the audience to view Loki in a different light. In doing so, *The Avengers* adheres to the model of same-but-different, which identifies the leading figures of both Christianity and Islam. It is within these scenes, however, that the allusion toward the possible threat presented by Islam becomes ever stronger and more sinister. In the eyes of a Western audience, the character of Loki is transformed into the symbolic representation of another culture, another belief system. This is one that does not seek to cohabit on peaceful terms with Western/American society. However, as the symbolic representation of an alien culture, Loki is not portrayed as someone who revels in wanton destruction for the sheer sake of it. He is not one "who simply wants to watch the world burn," as the Joker was famously described in *The Dark Knight* (2008).[27] Much more worrying for a Western audience is that the alien culture that Loki and his soldiers represent seeks to subjugate those they conquer. This is Loki's stated aim in the film as the resemblances between his actions and those of the "militant Islam" conjured by the West begin to solidify. As a consequence, the message to American and Western audiences becomes ever clearer. Should this Other ever be allowed to gain victory over the defenders of liberty and modern, progressive society, the resultant outcome would not be the wanton destruction of all mankind in the manner of the Cold War crises of the mid-twentieth century (where nuclear anxieties were often tempered by the paradoxically reassuring sense that the world as it was known would end should the Cold War ever get too "hot"). Rather, it would seek to impose upon the West the travails of a totalitarian belief system, replacing the lauded Western ideals of freedom, democracy, and basic human rights with what Western audiences have been encouraged to see as a culture characterized by religious extremism and medieval values.

Faced with such an existential crisis, these very values that made America great are utilized to save civilization from an alien entity intent on halting humanity's progression toward the utopian age promised by the Manifest Destiny of the United States. While these ideals were cited with regularity by cultural icons such as Henry Luce and John F. Kennedy throughout the mid-twentieth century, it was through the silver screen that these abstractions were given physical form. Beginning with John Wayne, the propensity to personify the American ideal has continued into the twenty-first century, most notably in the abundance of superhero films released after 9/11, and, one could argue, has reached its zenith in *The Avengers*. Reiterating this sense of uniqueness and preeminence, *The Avengers* casts the seven superheroes as a microcosm of an egalitarian, advanced, and ethnically diverse American society, in which each character can be interpreted as a metonymic representative of a specific cultural construct that stands alone among equals. This view that there can exist a deliberate corollary between film characters and the American public psyche is one suggested by Richard Slotkin. The composition of the superhero collective is strikingly similar to what Slotkin described as the "representation of the platoon" that was often seen as a "metaphorical America" in movies of the sixties and seventies in which the forces of good combat the forces of evil.[28] Therefore, just as each of *The Magnificent Seven* contributed to a cumulative image of the exceptional nation that the United States sought to portray as its own during the Cold War, *The Avengers* can also be seen to provide its audience with "a platoon of isolatoes whose . . . heroic motives and . . . ethnic possibilities" project the image of a progressive modern-day America, one that exists without peer in the contemporary geopolitical arena.[29] When combined to form one cohesive unit, the Avengers, and thus transitively the United States, present a societal model for the audience that reaffirms the nation's belief in its own uniqueness.

It is perhaps Nick Fury who allows the audience to make the easiest leap from fantasy to reality. The political leader of the Avengers is portrayed as spokesman for both the "metaphorical America" represented by the superheroes and for the actual American nation itself. Although depicted for decades in the comic-book series as a Caucasian male, the casting of Samuel L. Jackson in the role of Nick Fury not only presents a sense of ethnic diversity within a group dominated by white superheroes but also suggests to the viewer that America is a nation capable of transcending racial divides, particularly in times of crisis.[30] Fury presides over the Avengers, and while at times Machiavellian, his words and deeds are laced with a paradoxical combination of idealism and pragmatism that protects the American people in a manner that also protects the integrity of what are now portrayed as the American values of freedom and fairness. It is when Fury's words in relation to the Avengers are analyzed that they can be shown to present the superheroes as a synecdoche of the American people, a correlation that in turn permits the paradigm of the American nation defending the world to be perceived. Fury describes the Avengers as the end result of "the idea . . . to bring together a group of remarkable people and see if could they become something more," a concept that resonates strongly with the notion of the United States as the ultimate Enlightenment project. He goes on to state that the purpose of the Avengers is to "fight the battles that we never could." It is worth noting the distinction made by Fury—one that identifies the superheroes as a group carefully selected and uniquely capable of defeating any given enemy. What is important to realize here is that several of the heroes (Tony Stark, Natasha Romanoff, Bruce Banner, and Captain America) are chosen by Fury. In a manner similar to that when the United States forged a variety of alliances post-9/11 in order to combat George W. Bush's "axis of evil," Fury is the unifying force shown to be actively recruiting the various superheroes throughout the early stages of the film. The words "ask what you can do for your country" (John F. Kennedy) spring immediately to mind.[31]

The intention behind such recruitment appears to be the summoning of an arbitrary group of superheroes capable of defending not just the United States but also the Western world from any pending assault. Without too much of a cognitive leap, just as John Wayne came to epitomize the hypermasculinity and integrity of the Old Frontier, so too do each of these heroes represent a certain facet of contemporary American society. Crucially, however, when combined, this exceptional group of people demonstrates not only the outstanding qualities of the United States but also the selfless manner in which they use these abilities to defend the civilized world from malevolent forces intent on its destruction. Tony Stark, described in the film as a "genius, billionaire, playboy, philanthropist," demonstrates the altruism and potency of America's economic standing. He is a former weapons manufacturer whose time, fortune, and expertise are now dedicated to developing the ultimate sustainable energy source. U.S. dominance in the fields of technology and scientific development are reflected by Bruce Banner. Despite his alter ego being a volatile and indestructible entity capable of wreaking havoc indiscriminately, such knowledge is shown to be fundamental to defeating this alien Other. Working together in order to truly understand the properties of the Tesseract (the power source that Loki aims to steal), both Stark and Banner are shown to be men of extraordinary intelligence. Each in his own right represents the potentially limitless power of his respective fields—big business, technology, science, and weapons manufacturing. Particularly in relation to Stark's history with the latter and Banner's inability to control the raging behemoth that lies within, there is a subtle nod by the filmmakers as to potential negative effects of the developments being made in these fields.[32] However, what *The Avengers* is much more explicit in demonstrating is how when roused by a moral sense of purpose, such advances have the capability of nullifying any potential threat to the United States or any of her allies. Yet the insight provided by the film into the extent of both Stark's and Banner's respective abilities also has another purpose. Presented as sources of unparalleled technological or scientific expertise, the advances made by Stark and Banner not only help the Avengers to decipher Loki's ultimate intentions on Earth, they also provide the viewers with a panacea to diminish whatever doubts they may have regarding the role of technology as a threat in the twenty-first century. In a world where terms such as *cyberwarfare* and *drone strikes* are used with great frequency, the expertise of the Avengers indicates that regardless of the advances made in technology, the United States has the wherewithal to not only imitate but also emulate any of its rivals.

Conforming to Western stereotypes of a divinity, the Caucasian appearance of the Norse god Thor fighting alongside the other Avengers reinforces the view that the American people are endowed with specific purpose by a benevolent and, most significantly, Western-oriented deity. One of the most telling scenes occurs between the two brothers as the film draws to a conclusion, whereby Loki stabs Thor in a moment of deception. A minor wound, this action not only underlines the difference between the two demigods but also allows the film to demonstrate the New Testament qualities of forgiveness, patience, and mercy present in the "good" god that are lacking in his same-but-different stepbrother. The two master assassins, Hawkeye and Natasha Romanoff, are equally significant to the model of exceptionalism being constructed. Although technically not "super" heroes, both represent everyman (and -woman) characters whose skill sets locate them firmly among their fellow countrymen. While their abilities are comparable to the other superheroes in terms of their effectiveness, both Hawkeye and Romanoff are simply ordinary people with extraordinary talents whose presence allows the audience to view the Avengers on human terms.[33] More importantly, however, the inclusion of these two characters allows the Avengers as a collective to transcend the boundaries of history, nationality, and gender. Hawkeye is a famed agent whose name is synonymous with one of the legendary figures of the pioneers of the Old West (a trope amplified by his use of the bow and arrow). Brainwashed by Loki in the opening scenes of the movie, the character played by Jeremy Renner lives up to the frontier legacy of his moniker by temporarily crossing the figurative boundary between civilization and the savage Other, only to be brought back to civilization as the film progresses. Romanoff is the sole female actor within the group. Yet in addition to the gender diversity she brings to this patriarchal collective, Romanoff's explicit rejection of Old World/European values for a place in the Avengers, and thus transitively Slotkin's "metaphorical America," is in keeping with the often inaccurate view of the United States as a society that embraces all comers, regardless of origin or beliefs.

This demonstrated mixture of race, government, economy, science, religion, the mythic West, gender, and national equality can be easily seen to underline the image of itself that American exceptionalism seeks to portray of the nation. However, one vital attribute remains to be discussed in both *The Avengers* and real-world America that currently unites the individual tropes of its nation's exceptionalism and that is also synonymous with the United States and its current status as a "global policeman": its military. While Nick Fury is portrayed as the commander in chief responsible for the Avengers' actions on a geopolitical level, the leader on the ground is clearly shown to be Captain America. "Harking back to Second World War movies," he is introduced to the audience using a montage of him fighting "the Good War" against Nazi Germany.[34] Portrayed as being respectful of authority, Christian, and a willing, selfless patriot, he is described in the film as "the world's first superhero" and represents an old-fashioned value system of post-World War II America, a glory period for the country before doubt was cast on its uniqueness by the war in Vietnam. Significantly, however, the American military as a global force for good in times of emergency is a trope quite evident in *The Avengers*. Captain America is the orchestrating force in galvanizing the Avengers to come together to save the world before the conclusive battle against Loki. He is also the one who assumes the role of field general in leading the superheroes and both the New York Police Department (NYPD) and the firefighters against the alien Other seeking to destroy Manhattan. Significantly for the exceptionalist view of America's military power as one with a benevolent purpose, Captain America is the only character seen in the film saving the lives of normal American civilians.[35] The analogous link between Fury and Captain America is completed by the latter's declaration that "we won," matching and successfully concluding the declaration of war uttered by his commander in chief at the film's beginning. A critical part of the catharsis discussed earlier in this chapter, these words resonate as Loki is shown in handcuffs. Described as a "war criminal," the latter is led away by his stepbrother Thor to face the consequences of his actions. In his wake, the superheroes rejoice, having reasserted their place—and by transitive property America's standing—as the last best hope for humanity against any and all existential threats.

The message communicated to the viewer is thus quite clear. While each of the various aspects of American culture, viewed by proxy through the characteristics of the various heroes, allows it to assume the role of leader and protector during times of global crisis, to actually overcome these dangers requires a submission by ordinary society to the military. This idea is conveyed in several ways, as both recalcitrant superheroes as well as the NYPD and the New York firefighters eventually adhere to the direction of Captain America despite initial mistrust. *The Avengers'* endorsement of the military is not confined to the representation of character, however. Moving beyond the scope of the filmscript to the paratextual material surrounding it, the posters used to market the film to a public audience also demonstrate an unusual commonality.[36] Many of the posters depicting the heroes as a group more often than not have Captain America as the dominant figure. This in itself is not unusual until one considers the selection of Hollywood A-listers starring in the film. Among a cast that includes such luminaries as Robert Downey Jr., Samuel L. Jackson, and Scarlett Johansson, the prominence in the marketing material of the relatively unknown (and usually masked) Chris Evans does raise an eyebrow. Prior to his casting as *Captain America: The First Avenger* in 2011, his most prominent roles had been those of the Human Torch in *Fantastic Four: Rise of the Silver Surfer* (2007) and of Lucas Lee in *Scott Pilgrim vs. the World* (2010). Purely from a commercial perspective alone, it would surely have made more sense to have Johansson, Jackson, or Downey front and center in what was already becoming a marketplace saturated with superhero films. This is particularly the case with Robert Downey Jr., who with two highly successful outings as Iron Man in 2008 and 2011 had already gained both critical acclaim and a large cult following for his performances as the metal-suited superhero. However, in deliberately placing Evans/Captain America as the pivotal member of *The Avengers,* the posters combine with the themes, dialogue, and action of the movie in presenting military strength as the guiding principle of American ideology. While its corporate wealth, its advances in technology, and its diverse and classless society make the United States a formidable opponent for any would-be foe, without the guidance of a military to unify these aspects of American society as one cohesive force it would become an exponentially more difficult task.

From its humble beginnings to its current status as perhaps the world's only true superpower, one of the few constants in American culture is the exceptionalism that has persisted in the national psyche. A foundational narrative that describes the nation as an "instrument of Divine Providence for bringing liberty and democracy to all of humanity," this ideology has allowed the view of the United States as the primary defender of democracy and freedom to thrive.[37] Unthreatened by a significant cultural rival since the mid-twentieth century, the mythmakers of America have free reign to construct their model of an exceptional nation as they see fit. They are a force for good, both at home and abroad. While capable of violence, they employ it reluctantly and even then, only ever when confronted by an existential threat intent on destroying the civilized world. Viewed in hindsight, such a paradigm becomes more and more obvious in *The Avengers,* but it is a portrait of exceptionalism that cannot stand to bear too much scrutiny. It is all but impossible to identify who has done more damage to the city of New York— Captain America and his team or Loki and his minions. But echoing the muted public outcry when drone strikes are made in Afghanistan, Iraq, or Syria in response to terrorist attacks in London, New York, or Paris, the violence carried out by the superheroes is seen as legitimate. What is clearly being enacted here is a twenty-first-century version of what Richard Slotkin called "a pattern of reciprocal influence."[38] Endemic in Westerns throughout the Cold War, Slotkin saw such movies as demonstrations of how "the preoccupations of politics shape the concerns and imagery of movies, and in which movies in turn transmit their shapely formulations of those concerns back to political discourse, where they function as devices for clarifying values and imagining policy scenarios."[39]

Setting the Avengers against Loki as reluctant superpowers who selflessly defend humanity from an evil in a location steeped with meaning for both the people of the United States and indeed all the West, the film transcends the silver screen to impinge on the real world. In doing so, this spectacle of violence mediated through the comic-book-style fiction of the Marvel Universe recreates Slotkin's pattern, which highlights the underlying benevolence motivating all American foreign policy. But the final question that remains to be asked is why? Alluding to the events of the real world in such a deliberate fashion describes, to the American/Western mind, a permanent state of emergency. Reliving the trauma of 9/11 through the guise of *The Avengers*, only refashioning it to suit the mythopoeic structures of the American past, not only transforms the event into something less final and less terrifying but also provides a form of cultural catalyst that not only buffers the American government's war on terror from claims of imperialism but also transforms it into the actions of a reluctant superpower motivated by basic goodness. The American aim, then, in intervening in such far-flung locations as Syria, Iraq, and Afghanistan to combat ISIS and al-Qaeda becomes more justifiable. Despite claims to the contrary, America is not in these countries seeking oil or closer proximity to the borders of a potential enemy in the guise of Vladimir Putin's resurgent Russia. Rather, the United States is merely attempting to maintain world order. Reluctant to intervene until galled into action by an unprovoked attack, it is the superpower simply answering a call from the rest of humanity—a global leader that has decided to intervene by using its inherently exceptional abilities to defend human rights, law and order, and the basic tenets of freedom and democracy. "I'm glad we won" suddenly becomes a little clearer.

NOTES

1. Jack Shaheen, "Reel Bad Arabs: How Hollywood Vilifies a People," *Annals of the American Academy of Political and Social Science* 588, no. 1 (2003): 174.

2. Melani McAlister, *Epic Encounters: Culture, Media, and U.S. Interests in the Middle East, 1945–2000* (Berkeley: University of California Press, 2001), 6.

3. Richard Slotkin, *Gunfighter Nation: The Myth of the Frontier in Twentieth-Century America* (Norman: University of Oklahoma Press, 1998), 576.

4. Ibid., 577.

5. The link between the Western and the desire to forefront America's exceptionalism has been widely acknowledged. For further information, see, among

others, Slotkin, *Gunfighter Nation;* Slotkin, *Regeneration through Violence: The Mythology of the American Frontier, 1600–1860* (Middletown, CT: Wesleyan University Press, 1973); Ziauddin Sardar and Merryl Wyn Davies, *American Dream, Global Nightmare* (Thriplow, UK: Icon, 2004); Donald Pease, *The New American Exceptionalism* (Minneapolis: University of Minnesota Press, 2009); and John Hellmann, *American Myth and the Legacy of Vietnam* (New York: Columbia University Press, 1986).

6. Pease, *New American Exceptionalism,* 130.

7. Ibid., 157.

8. Ibid.

9. Ibid., 160.

10. Ibid.

11. Meghana V. Nayak and Christopher Malone, "American Orientalism and American Exceptionalism: A Critical Rethinking of US Hegemony," *International Studies Review* 11, no. 2 (2009): 260.

12. Evelyn Alsultany, *Arabs and Muslims in the Media: Race and Representation after 9/11* (New York: New York University Press, 2012), 45.

13. Ibid., 39.

14. Kenneth Turan, "'The Avengers,' a Marvel-ous Team," review of *The Avengers,* directed by Joss Whedon, *Los Angeles Times,* May 3, 2012; A.O. Scott, "Superheroes, Super Battles, Super Egos," review of *The Avengers,* directed by Joss Whedon, *New York Times,* May 3, 2012.

15. Lucyyy, review of *The Avengers,* directed by Joss Whedon, IMDb, 2012, www.imdb.com/user/ur54902861/.

16. higherall7, "Fanfare for the Merry Marvel Marching Society," review of *The Avengers,* directed by Joss Whedon, IMDb, 2012, www.imdb.com/user/ur25225705/comments?order=date&start=60.

17. Richard Brody, "'The Avengers': Not Unlike an F-16 Stunt Run," review of *The Avengers,* directed by Joss Whedon, *New Yorker,* May 4, 2012.

18. Ibid.

19. Murray Pomerance, "Prelude: To Wake Up in the City That Never Sleeps," in *City That Never Sleeps: New York and the Filmic Imagination,* ed. Murray Pomerance (New Brunswick, NJ: Rutgers University Press, 2007), 14.

20. Alsultany, *Arabs and Muslims in the Media,* 41.

21. Brody, "'Avengers.'"

22. Pease, *New American Exceptionalism,* 5.

23. Edward Said, *Orientalism: Western Conceptions of the Orient* (London: Penguin, 2003), iii.

24. McAlister, *Epic Encounters,* 220.

25. Ibid.

26. Said, *Orientalism,* xviii–xix. The practice of orientalizing Arab culture has been ongoing since the first interaction between the West and the Arab people and is much too complicated a topic to give due care and attention here. For further reading on the representation of the Arab world, particularly in the twentieth

century by Western media, see Edward Said, *Covering Islam: How the Media and the Experts Determine How We See the Rest of the World* (New York: Pantheon, 1981); Douglas Little, *American Orientalism: The United States and the Middle East since 1945* (Chapel Hill: University of North Carolina Press, 2002); Jack G. Shaheen, *Reel Bad Arabs: How Hollywood Vilifies a People* (New York: Olive Branch Press, 2001); and Alsultany, *Arabs and Muslims in the Media.* These offer some of the most acute and relevant analyses.

27. *The Dark Knight,* directed by Christopher Nolan (Warner Bros., 2008).

28. Slotkin, *Gunfighter Nation,* 359.

29. Ibid., 477.

30. This process of ethnic diversity has continued through the ever-expanding Marvel Universe film franchise. Samuel L. Jackson has reappeared on several occasions as Nick Fury while Anthony Mackie and Don Cheadle have had supporting roles in both *Iron Man 2* and *3* and *Captain America: The Winter Soldier,* respectively. However, it is in the most recent Marvel release, *Captain America: Civil War,* that racial parity begins to be restored as Jackson, Mackie, and Cheadle are all given prominent roles and are joined by Chadwick Boseman as Black Panther.

31. John F. Kennedy, "Inaugural Address," Washington, DC, January 20, 1961.

32. Having seen the damage his wares have caused with his own eyes, Tony Stark desires to move away from weapons manufacturing and into the field of renewable energy. Similarly, at the beginning of *The Avengers,* Banner is found hiding in India, seeking to cut himself off from potential triggers that would summon the Hulk. As *Avengers: Age of Ultron* closes, Banner is shown once more going into hiding in an effort to protect his fellow superheroes from his uncontrollable alter ego.

33. This trope becomes quite evident in *Avengers: Age of Ultron.* In the sequel, both Hawkeye and Romanoff are portrayed as characters with very human origins. As the heroes regroup to defeat Ultron, they take refuge in Hawkeye's home, which he shares with a wife and children. Removed from battle, the former is shown to be a character who engages with the ordinary aspects of domestic life, such as home renovation. Similarly, the audience is given an insight into Romanoff's experiences as an orphan in Soviet Russia who is subsequently trained as a highly skilled assassin.

34. Brody, "'The Avengers.'"

35. This paradigm expands in the later movies, with both Hawkeye and Pietro Maximoff/Quicksilver deliberately intervening to save the life of a young Sokovian boy. In order to maintain clarity of argument, this chapter focuses primarily on the first Avengers film. However, many of the tropes identified here, much like the Marvel Universe itself, become exponentially greater in appearance as the sequels and spin-offs reach the public sphere.

36. To be more concise, Gerard Genette, one of the canonical figures of genre theory, would define these posters as "epitexts." These are the literary constructs (interviews, reviews, media debate) that exist outside the cultural artifact that influence the reader. Epitexts, when combined with another type of extraneous literary construct, the peritext, constitute the broader category of paratexts. Gerard Genette,

Paratexts: Thresholds of Interpretation (Cambridge: Cambridge University Press, 1987), 264.

37. Hans Guggisberg, "American Exceptionalism as National History?," in *Bridging the Atlantic: The Question of American Exceptionalism in Perspective,* ed. Elisabeth Glaser and Hermann Wellenreuther (Cambridge: Cambridge University Press, 2002), 268.

38. Slotkin, *Gunfighter Nation,* 350.

39. Ibid., 350.

EIGHT

The Perfect Cold War Movie for Today?

SMOKE AND MIRRORS IN STEVEN SPIELBERG'S VISION OF THE COLD WAR

Tony Shaw

MUCH HAS BEEN WRITTEN ABOUT HOLLYWOOD'S ROLE in the so-called Age of Terror. Given the U.S. entertainment capital's worldwide influence, plus the fact that so many people thought the 9/11 attacks looked "just like a movie,"[1] this is hardly surprising. For some commentators, television shows like *24* and *Homeland* have performed an important role in powerfully underlining the very real threat that Islamic terrorism poses to each and every one of us. For others, features like Stephen Gaghan's *Syriana* (2005) and documentaries such as Alex Gibney's *Taxi to the Dark Side* (2007) have performed a more valuable service by forcing Americans to question the morality of U.S. foreign policy.[2] For others still, Hollywood products matter less and less in today's increasingly interactive and atomized media environment, where homemade online clips of ISIS beheadings compete with cell phone pictures of U.S. drone attacks in Pakistan.[3]

All the above views relate to explicit images about the Age of Terror and U.S. actions in the world since September 2001. But what about those Hollywood images that have spoken to these subjects indirectly, or even subconsciously? There are many examples of this, of course—so many, scholars like Tom Pollard argue, to justify the term "post-9/11 Hollywood movement."[4] Several scholars see links between "torture porn" film franchises like *Saw* and societal fears of torture following the release of the notorious Abu Ghraib photographs in 2004. The astonishing popularity over the past decade or so of movies in which superheroes defeat supervillains—the subject of the chapters by Ross Griffin and Tim Gruenewald in this volume—has inevitably been attributed partly to Americans' thirst for vengeance against terrorists whom the U.S. military seems incapable of beating. Meanwhile, post-9/11 sci-fi films have frequently depicted death and destruction on a massive scale, reflecting and projecting, some say, the alarm and paranoia induced by the seemingly endless number of shocking terrorist attacks on the West.[5]

This chapter takes Hollywood's indirect approach toward the Age of Terror in a different, more "realistic" direction by exploring how films have contributed to the contemporary debate about U.S. foreign policy by looking back at America's past wars. In particular, it examines how Hollywood has historicized the 1945–1991 Cold War against communism. Since September 2001, the U.S. government, news media, and think tanks have drawn many parallels between the Cold War and the global war on terrorism. Americans have been told that the war against Soviet communism was, like that against international terror today, the defining ideological conflict of its age; that the Cold War was, like that fought against al-Qaeda and ISIS, fought in the mind and in the media as much as on the battlefield; that many radical Islamist movements, like the Communist movements of the past, are fueled by nationalism; that the Cold War, like the war fought against Islamist "brainwashers" and suicide bombers, required vigilance at home as well as overseas; and, perhaps most importantly, that the struggle against Communist imperialism seemed a never-ending conflict—akin to the way President George W. Bush described the war on terror—only for it to conclude dramatically, with good vanquishing evil. Seen in this light, the Cold War would appear to be the go-to conflict for today's Americans concerned about their country's security and direction in the world. How Hollywood depicts the Cold War therefore deserves serious scrutiny, for cultural and political reasons.[6]

This chapter first gives a brief overview of Hollywood's on-screen treatment of the Cold War since 9/11 in order to show that, politically speaking, it has not been homogeneous. It then focuses just on one film, Steven Spielberg's 2015 Oscar-winning espionage drama, *Bridge of Spies*. The chapter argues that *Bridge of Spies* is probably Hollywood's most important, high-profile Cold War movie since the fall of the Berlin Wall and that the way it presents the United States as a liberal, combative protector of human rights is a near-perfect advertisement for American exceptionalism in a period characterized by doubts about the U.S. war on terror. Using a range of sources, including Central Intelligence Agency (CIA) papers and film production interviews, the chapter looks in detail at how and why *Bridge of Spies* came to be made. It then examines how and why the film put a politically positive spin on the events it recreated, thereby revealing Steven Spielberg's perspective on international politics and the politics of cultural production in Hollywood today. Finally, the chapter assesses the critical and public reception of *Bridge of Spies,* demonstrating how the film was appropriated for a variety of political ends even though most viewers seem to have read it as an inspiring, much-needed defense of U.S. foreign policy values in the early twenty-first century.

Let us begin by looking at an example of how the ultraconservative wing of Hollywood has historicized the Cold War since 9/11. *In the Face of Evil: Reagan's War in Word and Deed* is a two-hour-long documentary directed by Tim Watkins and Steve Bannon (who became White House chief strategist in the Trump administration in early 2017). Released in 2004, the film credits former U.S. president Ronald Reagan with winning the war against Soviet communism and saving the civilized world in the process. *In the Face of Evil* is based on journalist Peter Schweizer's best-selling triumphalist account of Reagan's period in the White House, *Reagan's War* (published in 2003), and blends stock footage, rousing music, and interviews with former Reagan aides to show—in rhapsodic fashion—how one man had the insight and determination to defeat America's greatest ideological foe. *In the Face of Evil* looks backward in time to portray Nazism and communism as totalitarian twins and forward to teach America vital lessons in, as the film puts it, "how we are to survive . . . as the 21st century's great conflict between freedom and Islamic Fascism takes shape."[7]

Why We Fight (2005) is also a documentary but comes from the opposite end of Hollywood's political spectrum to *In the Face of Evil.* Made by Eugene Jarecki, whose previous film accused former U.S. secretary of state Henry Kissinger of war crimes, *Why We Fight* explains how the Cold War gave birth to a "military-industrial complex" in the United States that distorted the nation's foreign policies for fifty years and led directly to present-day disasters like the war in Iraq. *Why We Fight* argues that the military-industrial complex is at the heart of American imperialism and—via harrowing stories about Vietnam veterans and disturbing images of American-made Saddam Hussein video games—asks its audience to consider the political, economic, and ideological forces that drive America's search for an ever-changing enemy.[8]

Both *In the Face of Evil* and *Why We Fight* were eulogized in certain quarters. Poland's famous Cold War dissident, Lech Walesa, and the prominent American conservative political commentator, Rush Limbaugh, enthusiastically supported *In the Face of Evil,* while the movie was ranked best documentary at the inaugural Liberty Film Festival in Los Angeles in 2004, an event tasked with promoting films that "celebrate freedom, democracy, and the dignity of the individual." *Why We Fight* won the prestigious Grand Jury Award at the 2005 Sundance Film Festival and other prizes in the United States and Germany. It also boasted support from the Eisenhower Project, an academic initiative named after the president who famously warned Americans about the dangers posed by the military-industrial project in his farewell address in 1961. However, the fact is that, being documentaries, neither *In the Face of Evil* nor *Why We Fight* was ever likely to make a significant public impact. Both films lacked major financial backing, had limited cinema releases, and probably preached to the converted.[9]

Over the past fifteen years or so, few other Hollywood movies' messages about the Cold War have been as overtly didactic as those in *In the Face of Evil* and *Why We Fight*. Broadly speaking, most movies instead fall into one of four categories. The first and largest category comprises those films that either celebrate American victories in Cold War hot spots—for example, *Miracle* (2004)[10]—or suggest that the Cold War continues in the form of terroristic fascists, Russian ultranationalists, or North Korean maniacs—for example, *The Sum of All Fears* (2002), *Salt* (2010), *Red Dawn* (2012), and *A Good Day to Die Hard* (2013).[11] The second category laments the human cost of the Cold War, particularly in the United States itself during the McCarthy era—for example, *Good Night, and Good Luck* (2005) and *Trumbo* (2015).[12] The third category suggests that U.S. mistakes during the Cold War have contributed to its present-day troubles, especially in the Middle East—for example, *Syriana* (2005) and *Charlie Wilson's War* (2007).[13] In the final category are those films that look back at the Cold War nostalgically, often in the form of atomic adventures or tales of superpower détente—for example, *Indiana Jones and the Kingdom of the Crystal Skull* (2008) and *Big Miracle* (2012).[14]

Like a number of the films above, Steven Spielberg's *Bridge of Spies* differs significantly from *In the Face of Evil* and *Why We Fight*. *Bridge of Spies* hails not from Hollywood's extreme fringes but from its political and artistic center. Indeed, *Bridge of Spies* is a quintessential mainstream Hollywood production. It is a period drama with a clear, linear narrative focused on a small number of characters. It has the pulling power of an A-list actor playing the lead and is set in familiar locations, the United States and Europe. It is produced and distributed by major studios and scripted and directed by some of the biggest names in the movie business. It is also conventional in Cold

War terms. It combines the two dominant cinematic paradigms of the Cold War—the nuclear and espionage dimensions. It is set, like many other films looking back at the Cold War, in the 1950s and the 1960s—the "golden era" of McCarthyism and the Cuban Missile Crisis. Finally, yet crucially, though it is a film about the Cold War, *Bridge of Spies* purports in many ways to be apolitical. Unlike *In the Face of Evil* and *Why We Fight,* few critics would (or did) describe Spielberg's movie as propaganda.[15]

Bridge of Spies centers on the first U.S.-Soviet spy swap of the Cold War, which saw KGB agent Rudolf Abel exchanged for CIA pilot Gary Powers on Berlin's Glienicke Bridge in February 1962. Abel had been arrested by the Federal Bureau of Investigation (FBI) in New York City in 1957 and charged with atomic espionage. At his trial, Abel was defended by James B. Donovan, a Brooklyn insurance lawyer who had worked as assistant to U.S. justice Robert H. Jackson at the Nuremberg war trials in 1945–1946. Abel was found guilty but controversially escaped execution in favor of a jail sentence after Donovan convinced the judge that the spy might be useful as a future bargaining chip in U.S.-Soviet relations. Powers had been shot down over the Soviet Union in May 1960 while carrying out a secret U2 reconnaissance flight. The U2 incident proved highly embarrassing to the U.S. government, not least because its initial claims that the U2 was a National Aeronautics and Space Administration (NASA) weather plane that had strayed off course were shown to be a lie. The U2 incident derailed impending superpower summit talks, and Powers, like Abel, was incarcerated. The two spies were exchanged in 1962 after complex negotiations between the Americans (aided by James Donovan), Soviets, and East Germans.[16]

Both the Abel and Powers cases caused a media sensation back in the 1950s and 1960s, as newspapers and television across the world feasted on a rare glimpse into the clandestine world of Cold War espionage. Capitalizing on this, James Donovan's own ghostwritten, CIA-cleared account of his role in the spy swap, *Strangers on a Bridge,* was published in 1964—much to the approval of former CIA chief Allen Dulles.[17] Donovan, who at the Nuremberg war trials had assisted U.S. film director John Ford with a documentary about Nazi atrocities, was very keen to see a Hollywood version of *Strangers on a Bridge,* and a draft filmscript (written by his son John) can be found in his private papers.[18] In 1965, Metro-Goldwyn-Mayer (MGM) tentatively agreed to finance a big-screen adaptation, written by television scriptwriter Stirling Silliphant and starring Gregory Peck as Donovan and Alec Guinness as Abel, but the studio then dropped out, apparently due to renewed Cold War tensions and a crowded market caused by an overabundance of James Bond-like movies.[19] This did not stop loose fictionalized takes on the Abel-Powers swap in films such as *Funeral in Berlin* (1966), nor Abel appearing in the 1968 Soviet espionage movie *Dead Season,* which featured an exchange of spies on the Glienicke Bridge. A decade later, Lee Majors, best known then as the star of American television's *Six Million Dollar Man,* played Powers in a television adaptation of the U2 incident. In 1999, the History Channel produced a drama-documentary titled *Mystery of the U2* that sought to tell the full story of the U2 incident. This followed the CIA's declassification of its U2 program materials amid a publicity campaign designed to celebrate the agency's fiftieth birthday.[20]

Unlike other recent movies such as *Zero Dark Thirty* (2012) and *Argo* (2012), both heavily influenced by CIA publicists,[21] apart from the logistical support provided by the U.S. Air Force,[22] there is no evidence linking the production of *Bridge of Spies* directly to any U.S. government body. The CIA, for one, privately charged the movie with committing a number of "egregious errors" in its depiction of the agency.[23] *Bridge of Spies* instead arose from the combination of a playwright's chance rediscovery of James Donovan's fifty-year-old book, the desire on the part of both the Donovan and Powers families to tell their fathers' heroic stories, the recent upsurge of Cold War nostalgia in Europe (for example, Trabant safaris in Berlin, Stalin's World theme park in Vilnius), and the renewed interest in the Cold War shown by authors, video game manufacturers, television producers, and filmmakers from across the world linked to the twenty-fifth anniversary of the fall of the Berlin Wall. Examples of this include British writer Ian McEwan's 2012 novel *Sweet Tooth,* whose main characters are spun around the British security service in the 1970s; the 2012 Chinese movie *Silent War,* set in the messy intrigues of 1949 Shanghai as the Chinese civil war comes to a climax; and the 2015 German television series *Deutschland 83,* which focuses on the adventures of a young, undercover Stasi agent in West Germany in the 1980s.[24]

In early 2013, the thirty-three-year-old award-winning British dramatist and self-confessed Cold War buff Matt Charman happened upon James Donovan's story in a footnote of historian Robert Dallek's best-selling biography of John F. Kennedy, *An Unfinished Life.* Charman learned from Dallek's book that as well as being involved in the Abel-Powers swap, Donovan had negotiated the release of a number of Cuban émigrés and CIA agents in the wake of the 1961 Bay of Pigs fiasco. Charman had worked for Britain's National Theatre for several years and initially thought of penning a two-handed play about the relationship between Donovan and Fidel Castro. After reading Donovan's *Strangers on a Bridge,* however, and meeting the lawyer's close relatives, Charman decided to use the book as the basis for what would be his first original screenplay. Charman believed that Donovan's story—half set in fifties New York, half in sixties Berlin—was full of Cold War iconography that was just perfect for cinema: "shadows, footsteps, snow, people emerging and disappearing." Visiting Hollywood on other business in November 2013, Charman took the opportunity to pitch his "James Donovan story" idea to a number of Hollywood film executives. One, Jonathan Eirich, vice president of DreamWorks Pictures, loved it, as did the company's cofounder and chief director, Steven Spielberg.[25]

Matt Charman's idea appealed to the world's most famous filmmaker—and prominent Hollywood liberal[26]—on a variety of levels. Critic Brian Tallerico has rightly called Steven Spielberg one of America's "most essential cinematic historians," referring both to Spielberg's knowledge of film history and to the director's landmark historical movies *Schindler's List* (1993), *Amistad* (1997), *Saving Private Ryan* (1998), *Munich* (2005), and *Lincoln* (2012).[27] Spielberg had already made one film set explicitly during the Cold War—the aforementioned *Indiana Jones and the Kingdom of the Crystal Skull*—but *Bridge of Spies* enabled him to say something more profound about a conflict that had helped define his early years. "I was a Cold War child, and the Cold War had a big impact on me, just as I presume the impact of 9/11 had on my older kids—as well as myself, of course," Spielberg told the press. "It's one of those benchmarks of history that become personal to all of us."[28] Spielberg drew inspiration for *Bridge of Spies* from 1960s spy movies such as *The Spy Who Came in from the Cold,* from his memories of being a fifteen-year-old frightened that the world was about to end during the Cuban Missile Crisis, and curiously, from his father's account of having been berated as an "American bandit" in front of a propaganda exhibit of Gary Powers's downed U2 in Red Square while making an engineering exchange visit to the Soviet Union in 1960.[29]

Based as they were on James Donovan's *Strangers on a Bridge,* Matt Charman's early scripts for what became *Bridge of Spies* were bound to take the lawyer's perspective on the Abel-Powers swap and therefore to view the Cold War episode through American rather than Soviet glasses. In following Donovan's book so closely, however, the scripts actually painted a more nuanced, politically balanced picture of events than the final film did. First, Charman portrays Donovan as much less of an Everyman than does *Bridge of Spies;* he is a big shot lawyer with a glamorous wife, a company man who frequents upper-class clubs (that have black servants) and happily uses his Harvard connections to land overpriced contracts. Second, Donovan is much more politically and ideologically motivated. Before agreeing to defend Abel, we see him supporting a client's complex insurance claim against the Soviet occupation of Poland. He wants to defend Abel not only for humanitarian reasons but also for propaganda purposes, to show that the American legal system is the best in the world. This relates to his strong connections with U.S. intelligence since the Second World War. Third, Charman's scripts faithfully detail both Donovan's and the CIA's (forlorn) efforts to turn Abel against his Soviet bosses, including the CIA's use of physical force and financial sweeteners. This conflicts with Donovan's insistence in *Bridge of Spies* that he works for the law, not the government, and suggests that Abel was subjected to some of the sorts of pressure the movie shows Gary Powers facing in the Soviet Union. Finally, Charman's scripts highlight the role played at Abel's trial by Soviet defector Reino Hayhanen, Abel's assistant in the United States and the prosecution's prime witness, who the defense counsel sensationally proved to be an alcoholic, embezzling bigamist. There is little doubt that Rudolf Abel was guilty as charged, but by airbrushing both Hayhanen and a U.S. embassy official in Moscow who was also working with Abel, *Bridge of Spies* misses an opportunity to add color and complexity to the case for and against the Russian spy's actions.[30]

Precisely who was responsible for the changes made to Charman's scripts is unclear, owing to the unavailability of documentation. What is known is that Spielberg himself had a hand in rewriting elements; for instance, the director claimed the scene showing Donovan's young son filling the family bath in readiness for the water shortage that would follow a Soviet nuclear attack on the United States mimicked his own actions during the Cuban Missile Crisis.[31] We also know that Spielberg loves to center his movies on ordinary people having to operate in extraordinary circumstances—hence, James Donovan's role in *Bridge of Spies,* "a non-spy at the heart of a spy story," as Charman later put it.[32] We know, too, that DreamWorks brought Joel and Ethan Coen on board at a relatively late stage to polish the scripts, to lighten the movie's tone with their trademark sardonic touches, and to punch up the dialogue. It was the Coens who were responsible for the scene in which we are introduced to Donovan, offering a master class in the deceitful defense of insurance companies in screwball-pattern style, and for Rudolf Abel's deadpan refrain, "would it help?" when Donovan asks the Russian why he displays no sense of anxiety.[33]

The involvement of the Coen brothers, Hollywood's best-known eccentrics,[34] might in some discerning viewers' eyes have weakened the Cold War history lesson that Spielberg and others were trying to deliver in *Bridge of Spies*. At the same time, their star billing undoubtedly helped underline the movie's high status. Having James Donovan played by Tom Hanks—an actor whose roles over the years had made him Hollywood's favorite Everyman and, as David Edelstein put it, "the standard-bearer for American decency"[35]—completed the "dream team" and further underlined the film's credibility. During production, Spielberg's crew and DreamWorks' marketing experts did all they could to emphasize *Bridge of Spies'* verisimilitude. The movie's $40 million budget and politically appropriate script facilitated access to real shots of U2 aircraft in action at a U.S. Air Force base in California and location shooting in Berlin. The German chancellor and one-time "Osti" Angela Merkel came to watch the film's denouement on the Glienicke Bridge itself, which the authorities agreed to close for three nights despite complaints from angry commuters. Cinematographer Janusz Kaminski, who had grown up in Cold War Poland, chose Wroclaw for the sequence showing the building of the Berlin Wall in August 1961, partly because most of the wall had been looted or touristified in Berlin itself and partly because present-day Wroclaw looked more like 1960s Berlin. Photographs of a wide-eyed Spielberg and Hanks on "research visits" to notorious Berlin sites such as the former Stasi remand prison (in which the American Frederic Pryor, a key real-life character in the second half of *Bridge of Spies,* was held) appeared in newspapers worldwide, serving to remind readers and viewers what the Cold War had really been about.[36] The Donovan and Powers families gave their own well-publicized stamps of approval to *Bridge of Spies* by either acting as consultants, playing cameo roles in the movie, or attending Q and A's at premieres.[37]

Bridge of Spies focuses on what historians now call the First Cold War, a tense period bracketed by Winston Churchill's famous Iron Curtain speech of early 1946 and the Cuban Missile Crisis of October 1962. The film leans heavily on stereotypical images of that era— showing a vividly colored, *Life Magazine*-version of 1950s New York in the first half juxtaposed with a paler-toned East Berlin in the second—and in some ways mimics a number of Hollywood Cold War movies that hail from that period. *Bridge of Spies* could neither be described as a recruiting sergeant for the U.S. military like the James Stewart vehicle *Strategic Air Command* (1955) nor as a virulent piece of anti-Communist "agit-prop" in the mold of Leo McCarey's *My Son*

John (1953).[38] But we must remember that U.S. filmmakers also produced positive Cold War propaganda in the 1950s and 1960s, showcasing the concrete benefits of capitalism and extolling the virtues of liberal democracy. William Wyler's romantic comedy starring Gregory Peck and Audrey Hepburn, *Roman Holiday* (1953), is just one well-known example.[39] *Bridge of Spies* is, in effect, a textbook amalgam of positive and negative propaganda, suitable for a post–Cold War age.

Bridge of Spies can best be thought of as a "character thriller"[40]—and a very Spielbergian one at that. The film's ideological lodestar is Jim Donovan, an ordinary man putting himself in danger to do the right thing, akin to Daniel Day-Lewis's sixteenth U.S. president in *Lincoln* and Harrison Ford's whip-snapping globetrotter in *Raiders of the Lost Ark* (1981). Donovan is a simple, reluctantly heroic family man who, like Atticus Finch in Harper Lee's classic novel *To Kill a Mockingbird*,[41] takes on the job of defending a man from the other side of the fence not for personal gain but because, in his view, it is the American way. Donovan is aware of the international publicity a free and fair trial for Rudolf Abel will give the United States in the context of the Cold War, but what is guiding him is a larger principle, adherence to the U.S. Constitution. This is his "rule book," he tells an interfering CIA agent in a key bar scene, one that cannot be manipulated for short-term political gain and that defines every American.

Fired by this zeal, Donovan does not just go through the motions in defending Abel. He treats the Russian spy with the respect any of his American clients would expect and builds as strong a case as possible. He finds a weakness in the prosecution's case pertaining to the dubious use of search warrants,[42] and when that is ruled invalid by a biased judge, he saves Abel from the electric chair. Even then, the lawyer is not done, and Donovan appeals Abel's case all the way to the U.S. Supreme Court, where he loses only by a whisker. Donovan's doggedness comes at great cost. He is ostracized by his colleagues and estranged from his wife, and bigots who believe he is a traitor shoot up his home, nearly killing one of his children.[43]

Having proven that America defends human rights, even of those who have sought to do the country harm, Donovan then takes us behind the Iron Curtain to a lawless land where humans are treated as mere cogs in a machine. The insurance lawyer takes even greater personal risks this time. Because he is not working officially for the U.S. government, Donovan has no diplomatic protection, not even from a group of East Berlin teenagers who steal his overcoat and still less from the Stasi who briefly imprison him.[44] In the face of this, Donovan uses his shrewd negotiating skills with the KGB to not only arrange the Abel-Powers exchange but also to get one over on the Communists by getting them to release an innocent American postgraduate student, Frederic Pryor (Will Rogers), who had found himself on the wrong side when the Berlin Wall was hastily constructed. Donovan thus gets a two-for-one deal, mainly by capitalizing on Soviet-East German infighting.

The fact that *Bridge of Spies* presents Donovan as a maverick, a man acting outside and sometimes even against the wishes of the U.S. security establishment, has the effect of significantly strengthening America's image. It shows that Americans have the freedom to challenge their government, even (or especially) in wartime. Spielberg was particularly keen to show that Donovan even has the temerity and liberty to ignore the CIA's angry order not to demand Pryor's release lest it jeopardize the all-important Abel-Powers deal.[45] In reality, Donovan and the CIA never had cross words during the Berlin operation and, with the help of East German lawyer Wolfgang Vogel, had worked in tandem to rescue Pryor, who the Stasi had arrested partly owing to his association with an East German woman dealing in false passports who had recently fled to the West. More generally, while not being a fully paid-up member of the U.S. national security bureaucracy, Donovan had strong links to it. Part of the reason why the New York Bar Association appointed him as Abel's lawyer in the first place was due to his having worked as a senior counsel and propagandist for U.S. intelligence during the Second World War. The CIA subsequently chose him as an interlocutor with the KGB in Berlin partly because of his ongoing connections with the agency, including with Allen Dulles himself, and ended up awarding Donovan the Distinguished Intelligence Medal for his work.[46]

After James Donovan, the second chief character in *Bridge of Spies* is Rudolf Abel. No Hollywood movie of the fifties or sixties—or, for that matter, any other period of the Cold War—presented a Soviet spy as positively as Spielberg does Abel. The director goes out of his way not to villainize Abel, and *Bridge of Spies* in some ways builds more sympathy and concern for the Russian than it does for his American counterpart, Gary Powers. Played by the slightly built British stage actor Mark Rylance (who won an Oscar for the role), Abel comes across as an honorable enemy combatant doing a job for his country. He is a gentle, cultured, good-humored family man who, as one critic put it, "displays all the menace of Eeyore, blinking innocently from behind thick glasses."[47] Importantly, Abel refuses to squeal or defect despite U.S. government blandishments and knowing that many Americans are baying for his blood. He remains dedicated to Mother Russia and becomes a firm friend to his defense lawyer, James Donovan.

As likeable a character as *Bridge of Spies* renders Rudolf Abel, however, the film in no way presents him as a poster boy for communism. There is no monologue where Abel explains his background and what formed and shaped his ideological goals. (Abel, whose real name was Willy Fisher, had worked for the Comintern in the aftermath of the Bolshevik Revolution and had trained radio operators for clandestine work behind German lines in World War II).[48] And, oddly perhaps given Donovan's international outlook, there are no scenes in which Abel and Donovan debate the relative merits of communism and capitalism. What we get instead is an emphasis on the master spy's loyalty and patriotism, as if the Cold War were a straightforward contest between Russia and America and not, as some people at the time and many historians now see it, either a battle between two imperial juggernauts or a conflict driven by ideas.[49] *Bridge of Spies* takes this narrow, some might say outmoded, approach toward the Cold War in many other places too, notably when Donovan justifies the recent execution (in 1953) of spies Julius and Ethel Rosenberg in New York State because, unlike Abel, they were American citizens and therefore traitors. Thus, on one level, *Bridge of Spies* is—as many people have pointed out[50]—unconventionally fairminded in its attitude toward America's Cold War enemy. On another level, the movie is highly conventional, and Spielberg's internationalism has strict limits.

Moreover, even if Rudolf Abel is a decent man and proves there are nice Russians, *Bridge of Spies* utterly dispels the notion that there is moral equivalence between the Soviet Union and the United States. The movie demonstrates that Abel's loyalty to Moscow is misguided, for it amounts to compliance with a fundamentally corrupt, capricious, and brutal "system" that devours rather than protects its citizens. When Donovan travels behind the Iron Curtain, Spielberg shows us he has passed into a different political universe. The sunny, squeaky-clean streets of New York and Washington, DC, are replaced by the washed-out blues and grays of a miserably wet East Berlin where the Cold War literally is cold (and, appropriately, Donovan quickly catches one). Communist apparatchiks like Vogel (Sebastian Koch) drink whiskey and drive sports cars, while the ordinary masses live in squalor and starve. People queue for everything, and crime is rampant. Further to the east, in the Soviet Union itself, we see the KGB interrogating and torturing Gary Powers (Austin Stowell) to secure U.S. intelligence secrets. The young pilot also suffers the indignity of a spectacular show trial, where he is forced to confess his guilt and beg forgiveness.

On occasions, likely due to the Coen brothers, *Bridge of Spies* depicts the peculiar or bizarre features of the Communist cosmos rather than its terrible side. Humorous touches help to lighten the film's mood and tone and, arguably, make it appear less propagandistic. At times, when Donovan is in East Berlin's netherworld of make-believe, lies, and distortion, it seems nothing or no one can be taken at face value or trusted. When on his first trip into East Berlin Donovan is semicomically relieved of his Saks coat, for instance, we do not know whether the teenage muggers are acting under KGB orders or simply envious of American tailoring. When the lawyer then meets with people claiming to be Abel's family, they act so outlandishly it is obvious they are KGB hirelings. One high-ranking East German official, the country's attorney general no less, seems plain crazy, having a temper tantrum one moment (and scaring the living daylights out of the office cleaners) and then farcically picking up the wrong telephone to answer a call the next.

It is the violence and fear characterizing everyday life under communism that stands out most in *Bridge of Spies,* however. Not surprisingly, the movie evokes this principally via scenes around the Berlin Wall—"that perfect symbol of the monstrosity of an ideology gone mad,"[51] as the British spy author John le Carré called it. First, Spielberg depicts the cruel arbitrariness of the wall's overnight construction, with panicked families rushing around, half-packed suitcases in hand, in an effort not to get caught on the wrong side as the giant breeze-blocks are lowered into place. The East German police arrest Frederic Pryor amid this frenzied chaos, thinking, incorrectly, that he is a spy or provocateur. Then later, in what many viewers thought was the most powerful scene in *Bridge of Spies* but was not part of Donovan's own experience in Berlin, we see Donovan riding an elevated train and watch through his eyes as a bunch of East Germans trying to climb over the wall into the West at night are gunned down from sentry towers. If this were a scene from a le Carré novel, it is likely we would subsequently learn that Western spies had been complicit in these murders. Not so in *Bridge of Spies*. At the very end of the movie, Donovan is taking another elevated train, this time on the way to work in New York. Outside, amid a poor Brooklyn neighborhood of tightly packed multistory buildings, he sees a gang of kids scrambling over a back fence from one yard to another, quite likely up to no good but coming to no harm. The message seems loud and clear—that the Cold War is at root a conflict between good and evil and that America stands and must fight for freedom.

Bridge of Spies was released amid great fanfare in October 2015. In Cold War terms, its marketing campaign bordered on triumphalist. "In the shadow of war, one man showed the world what we stand for," posters proclaimed, next to a giant portrait of Tom Hanks/James Donovan. At media junkets, Hanks, Spielberg, and Charman accentuated this point and, sometimes with the help of the Donovan and Powers families, emphasized the movie's truthfulness. Due in large part to the widely held belief that *Bridge of Spies* was an accurate account of the Abel-Powers case,[52] the movie was critically acclaimed and a major commercial hit. *Bridge of Spies* scored 81 out of 100 on metacritic and 7.6 out of 10 among IMDb users. The film received six Academy Award nominations, including Best Picture and Best Original Screenplay, and won one Oscar. Distributed by Walt Disney Studios and Twentieth Century Fox, *Bridge of Spies* grossed $165 million at the box office and $93 million overseas, making it the fourteenth best-selling political thriller since 1980.[53]

Viewers will almost always differ over the messages being carried by politically oriented movies, but what is striking in the *Bridge of Spies'* case, given that it is a film about events fifty years old, is the number of Americans who saw it as a comment on contemporary international politics and on the Age of Terror in particular. Many people clearly did see important links between the Cold War and the ongoing war on terror, whether in real life or on the cinema screen. Encouraged by *Bridge of Spies* perhaps, many seemed to look back at the Cold War nostalgically, as a conflict that united the nation against an easily identifiable and beatable enemy. This is in contrast to the war on terror, the tactics of which have divided many Americans and which has seemed unwinnable. Eight months before the release of *Bridge of Spies,* *Forbes* magazine reported that the war on terror had so far cost American taxpayers $1.7 trillion. In the month that *Bridge of Spies* hit the big screen, Barack Obama reversed course and announced that U.S. combat troops would stay in Afghanistan through the end of his presidency.[54]

After watching *Bridge of Spies,* several film critics, especially on the Left, argued erroneously that Spielberg was drawing comparisons between the United States' defense of international law during the Cold War and its illegal imprisonment of terrorist suspects at Guantánamo Bay. Thanks to men like James Donovan, in other words, America had stuck to its principles during the Cold War but since 9/11 had succumbed to paranoia, with grave consequences for civil liberties at home and the U.S. image overseas.[55] In a similar vein, other critics suggested *Bridge of Spies* was issuing a warning, akin to that in John le Carré's *The Spy Who Came in from the Cold* fifty years earlier, that the West risked losing its moral bearings if it continued to use nefarious methods to defeat its enemies.[56] Likely referring to U.S. presidential hopeful Donald Trump's comments about banning Muslims from entering the country, one ordinary American viewer said the movie's depiction of the fear of nuclear Armageddon during the Cold War reminded him of "our modern equivalent of being paranoid about anyone who comes from a Muslim country." In press conferences, Spielberg himself used *Bridge of Spies* to censure Trump. Given all the efforts Ronald Reagan and others had gone to in dismantling the Berlin Wall, the director said, it was scandalous that Donald Trump was calling for a wall to be built to protect the United States from Mexican immigrants.[57]

Another group of critics saw *Bridge of Spies* less as a liberal critique of America's war on terror and more as a call to arms against Vladimir Putin's Russia. For a brief period after 9/11, Moscow and Washington had been allies against Islamist terrorism, reflected in Russian movies like *Countdown* (2004), but U.S.-Russian relations had recently broken down over Ukraine and Syria in particular.[58] Several critics made links between Rudolf Abel's case in *Bridge of Spies* and the discovery in 2010 of a major Russian sleeper cell in the United States, as if Spielberg's film suggested that history was repeating itself or that the Russians had never stopped fighting their Cold War against the United States.[59] To these and other viewers, *Bridge of Spies* pointed above all to the deep mistrust exhibited not by the United States during the Cold War but by the Kremlin. "With a paranoid, desperate, and perhaps simply bored Russia re-starting the Cold War," critic Roger Moore wrote, "Spielberg & Co. do yeoman's service in reminding us of the stakes and the Russians of how ugly being on the wrong side of history looks, in retrospect."[60]

For all these noises off, however, a clear majority of critics and viewers in the United States thought of *Bridge of Spies* as Steven Spielberg did: as an inspiring, fact-based account of American heroism amid a historical conflict that had great relevance for present-day international affairs. Several critics emphasized how meticulous, how truthful, and consequently, how politically illuminating the movie was. *Bridge of Spies* was "a Technicolor newsreel," wrote *SFGate*'s Mick LaSalle, that "may be the most accurate depiction of cold war (or any era) espionage in recent cinema history." Every American and every citizen of a former Warsaw Pact country "MUST SEE this movie," one U.S. military veteran urged, emphasizing the threat posed by modern-day Russian imperialism. Rather than seeing *Bridge of Spies* as another example of Hollywood blaming Moscow for the Cold War (and international aggression, generally), numerous critics praised the movie for being extraordinarily evenhanded toward the Soviet Union. Encouraged by *Bridge of Spies,* perhaps, these and other critics appeared to give little or no thought to Russian actions being defensive or to the United States being in any way imperialistic, either during the Cold War or since.[61]

Some commentators felt *Bridge of Spies* delivered exactly the sort of positive, nation-loving message that the United States needed in 2015, as the country seemed rudderless, the world seemed to be growing ever more anarchic, and the war on terror dragged on. One of them thanked Spielberg explicitly for a "masterful" movie that could "summon patriotic feelings" in a period unfortunately so "devoid of true stand-up American figures of decency and dignity." Many critics gave *Bridge of Spies* the ultimate accolade by ranking it alongside the prodemocracy classics directed by Frank Capra in the World War II era. Like Capra's *Mr. Smith Goes to Washington* (1939) and *Why We Fight* (1942–1945) series, *Bridge of Spies* was, according to New Orleans journalist Mike Scott, "a reminder of what truth, justice, and the American way *really* means, and why it's something worth fighting to protect."[62]

No matter who thought what about it, Steven Spielberg's *Bridge of Spies* shows, despite the recent dramatic changes in the media landscape, that we disregard movies' power as instruments of entertainment and persuasion at our peril in the early twenty-first century. *Bridge of Spies* demonstrates that mainstream Hollywood—for a mixture of industrial, financial, cultural, and ideological reasons—prefers to present the United States as a global force for good rather than as an imperialist hegemon. It shows us that that message can be conveyed in a variety of forms, including the recycling of old wars, and it confirms the old maxim that propaganda is most effective when it is assured, simple, primarily positive, and entertaining. *Bridge of Spies* may not be the perfect Cold War movie for an America looking to reassert its moral authority on the world in the second decade of the twenty-first century, but it may be the closest we have to one to date.

NOTES

1. B. Ruby Rich, "After the Fall: Cinema Studies Post-9/11," *Cinema Journal* 43, no. 2 (2004): 109–115.

2. Steven Peacock, ed., *Reading 24: TV against the Clock* (London: I. B. Tauris, 2007); Anat Zanger, "Between *Homeland* and *Prisoners of War*: Remaking Terror," *Continuum: Journal of Media and Cultural Studies* 29, no. 5 (2015): 731–742; Douglas Kellner, *Cinema Wars: Hollywood Film and Politics in the Bush-Cheney Era* (London: Wiley-Blackwell, 2010), 169–170; Stephen Prince, *Firestorm: American Film in the Age of Terrorism* (New York: Columbia University Press, 2009), 213–214.

3. This is not how the U.S. government sees things, however, as evidenced by high-profile talks in 2016 between Secretary of State John Kerry and Hollywood's chief executives on how to combat ISIS. Ted Johnson, "John Kerry Meets with Hollywood Studio Chiefs to Discuss ISIS," *Variety,* February 16, 2016, http://variety.com/2016/biz/news/john-kerry-hollywood-studio-chiefs-isis-1201707652/.

4. Tom Pollard, *Hollywood's 9/11: Superheroes, Supervillains, and Super Disasters* (London: Paradigm, 2011), 149.

5. Andrew Ryan Rico, "Abu Ghraib and Torture Porn Cinema" (master's thesis, University of Texas, Austin, 2015); Kellner, *Cinema Wars,* 7–9; Prince, *Firestorm,* 282–286; Pollard, *Hollywood's 9/11.*

6. Zachary Keck, "America's War on Terror Mirrors Cold War," *Diplomat,* May 30, 2013, http://thediplomat.com/2013/05/americas-war-on-terror-mirrors-cold-war/; Anatol Lieven, "Fighting Terrorism: Lesson from the Cold War," Carnegie Endowment for International Peace Policy Brief, October 7, 2001, 1–8, https://www.ciaonet.org/attachments/3112/uploads; Philip H. Gordon, "Can the War on Terror Be Won? How to Fight the Right War," *Foreign Affairs,* November/December 2007, 53–66, www.brookings.edu/~/media/research/files/articles/2007/11/terrorism/11terrorism.pdf; James J. Carafano and Paul Rosenzweig, *Winning the Long War: Lessons from the Cold War for Defeating Terrorism and Preserving Freedom* (Washington, DC: Heritage, 2005); John Tirman, "The War on Terror and the Cold War: They're Not the Same," *Audit of the Conventional Wisdom,* April 2006, 06–06, 1–3, http://web.mit.edu/cis/pdf/Audit_04_06_Tirman.pdf; David Hoogland Noon, "Cold War Revival: Neoconservatives and Historical Memory in the War on Terror," *American Studies* 48, no. 3 (2007): 75–99.

7. Robert Koehler, "In the Face of Evil: Reagan's War in Word and Deed," *Variety,* October 11, 2004, 54.

8. Sony Classics, accessed March 1, 2016, www.sonyclassics.com/whywefight/; Gary Crowdus, "Why We Fight: An Interview with Eugene Jarecki," *Cineaste* 31, no. 2 (2006): 32–38.

9. Messenger Eagle Communications, https://store.messengereagle.com/merchandise/product/in-the-face-of-evil-reagans-war-in-word-and-deed-2004; Sony Classics, www.sonyclassics.com/whywefight/main.html; Box Office Mojo, accessed March 1, 2016, www.boxofficemojo.com/movies/?id=inthefaceofevil.htm; IMDb, accessed March 1, 2016, www.imdb.com/title/tt0436971/business?ref_=tt_dt_bus.

10. Michael Silk, Bryan Bracey, and Mark Falcous, "Performing America's Past: Cold War Fantasies in a Perpetual State of War," in *East Plays West: Sport and the*

Cold War, ed. Stephen Wagg and David L. Andrews (London: Routledge, 2007), 289–313; Michael Silk, Jaime Schultz, and Bryan Bracey, "From Mice to Men: Miracle, Mythology, and the Magic Kingdom," *Sport in Society* 11, no. 2–3 (2008): 279–297.

11. Robert Koehler, "The Sum of All Fears," *Variety*, May 28, 2002, 4; Anonymous, "A 'Salt' and Battery,'" *Variety*, July 19, 2010, 1; Joe Leydon, "Red Dawn," *Variety*, September 28, 2012, 2; Peter Debruge, "A Good Day to Die Hard," *Variety*, February 14, 2013, 12.

12. Thomas Doherty, "Good Night, and Good Luck," *Cineaste* 31, no. 1 (2005): 53–56; Larry Ceplair, "*Trumbo* (The Movie) versus Trumbo (The Life)," *Cineaste* 46, no. 2 (2016): 20–23.

13. Rahul Hamid, "Lord of War. Syriana," *Cineaste* 31, no. 2 (2006): 52–55; Todd McCarthy, "Charlie Wilson's War," *Variety*, November 29, 2007, 4.

14. Todd McCarthy, "Indiana Jones and the Kingdom of the Crystal Skull," *Variety*, May 19, 2008, 1; Justin Chang, "Big Miracle," *Variety*, February 2, 2012, 10.

15. My definition of propaganda goes far beyond those that focus on lies or government activities to include a whole range of mass media outputs that carry political and social messages. On the history and definition of propaganda, see Garth S. Jowett and Victoria J. O'Donnell, *Propaganda and Persuasion* (New York: Sage, 2011).

16. Michael R. Beschloss, *May-Day: Eisenhower, Khrushchev and the U-2 Incident* (New York: Harper and Row, 1986); Vin Arthey, *Abel: The True Story of the Spy They Traded for Gary Powers* (London: Biteback, 2015).

17. James B. Donovan, *Strangers on a Bridge* (New York: Atheneum, 1964); Allen Dulles to James Donovan, April 29, 1964, Allen W. Dulles Papers, box 17, fol. 16, Public Policy Papers, Department of Rare Books and Special Collections, Princeton University Library, http://diglib.princeton.edu/images/deliverable /MC019/c00263.pdf. On Dulles's efforts to bolster his own and the CIA's image during this period, including his friendship with the James Bond author Ian Fleming, see Christopher Moran, "Ian Fleming and the Public Profile of the CIA," *Journal of Cold War Studies* 15, no. 1 (2013): 119–146.

18. "The Defence of Colonel Abel, n.d. Teleplay Typescript," box 14, fol. 5, James B. Donovan Papers, Hoover Institution Archives, Stanford University, Stanford, CA; John Donovan and Beth Amorosi, James Donovan's son and granddaughter, correspondence with author, March 9, 2016.

19. Christopher Campbell, "Steven Spielberg Reveals the Original 1965 Casting Choice for 'Bridge of Spies,'" Movies.com, October 7, 2015; John Donovan and Beth Amorosi, correspondence with author, March 9, 2016.

20. IMBd, accessed March 1, 2016, www.imdb.com/title/tt0063332/, www .imdb.com/title/tt0060437/?ref_=fn_al_tt_1, www.imdb.com/title/tt0074545/; Turner Classic Movies, accessed March 1, 2016, www.tcm.com/tcmdb/title/472185 /Mystery-of-the-U2/. George W. Pedlow and Donald E. Welzenbach, "The CIA and the U2 Program 1954–1974," History Staff Center for the Study of Intelligence, CIA, 1998, www.cia.gov/library/center-for-the-study-of-intelligence/csi-publications

/books-and-mono graphs/the-cia-and-the-u-2-program-1954-1974/u2.pdf; George J. Tenet, "The U2 Program: The DCI's Perspective," *Studies in Intelligence,* Winter 1998–1999, 1–4.

21. Tony Shaw and Tricia Jenkins, "From Zero to Hero: The CIA at the Movies Today," *Cinema Journal* 56, no. 2 (2017): 91–113.

22. Develyn J. Watson, Deputy Director, Secretary of the Air Force Public Affairs Entertainment Liaison, e-mail correspondence with author, March 1, 2016; Gary Powers Jr., Skype interview with author, March 7, 2016.

23. David Robarge, CIA Chief Historian, e-mail correspondence with author, March 2, 2016. On the CIA's recent publicity surrounding the Abel-Powers case, perhaps inspired by *Bridge of Spies,* see www.cia.gov/news-information/featured -story-archive/2015-featured-story-archive/francis-gary-powers.html.

24. *Bridge of Spies* scriptwriter Matt Charman, telephone interview by author, April 4, 2016; David Lowe and Tony Joel, *Remembering the Cold War* (London: Routledge, 2013), 163, 167, 176–177, 213; Philip Olterman, "Deutschland 83 Has Wowed The World—Pity the Germans Don't Like It," *Guardian,* February 17, 2016, www.theguardian.com/commentisfree/2016/feb/17/deutschland-83-wowed-world -germans-dont-like-it. On video games and the Cold War, see the chapter by Penny Von Eschen in this volume.

25. Matt Charman, telephone interview by author; Benjamin Lindsay, "'Bridge of Spies' Screenwriter Matt Charman on the Virtue of Veracity," Backstage, October 15, 2015, www.backstage.com/interview/bridge-spies-screenwriter-matt-charman -virtue-veracity/.

26. Spielberg's staunch support for the Democratic Party and his socially liberal views are well known and may influence the way some people see his movies. See, for instance, Tom Kershaw, "The Religion and Political Views of Steven Spielberg," Hollowverse.com, March 27, 2012, http://hollowverse.com/steven-spielberg/; "How Liberal or Conservative Is Your Favorite Celebrity?," Crowdpac.com, n.d., www .crowdpac.com/games/lookup/celebrities?name=Steven+Spielberg.

27. Brian Tallerico, review of *Bridge of Spies,* directed by Steven Spielberg, RogerEbert.com, October 16, 2015, http://www.rogerebert.com/reviews/bridge-of -spies-2015.

28. Bill Zwecker, "Steven Spielberg's 'Bridge' Is about Family—Both Personal and Professional," *Chicago Sun-Times,* October 13, 2015, http://chicago.suntimes. com/entertainment/steven-spielbergs-bridge-is-about-family-both-personal -professional/.

29. Andy Lewis, "How Steven Spielberg's Childhood Inspired 'Bridge of Spies,'" *Hollywood Reporter,* November 20, 2015, www.hollywoodreporter.com/features /how-steven-spielbergs-cold-war-840896; Donovan, *Strangers,* 251.

30. Matt Charman, "Untitled James Donovan Project," first draft, January 20, 2014, in author's possession; Matt Charman and Ethan and Joel Coen, "Bridge of Spies," final shooting script, December 17, 2014, accessed March 1, 2016, http:// dreamworksawards.com/download/BOS_screenplay.pdf; Matt Charman, tele- phone interview by author.

31. Lewis, "How Steven Spielberg's Childhood Inspired 'Bridge of Spies.'"

32. Matt Charman, telephone interview by author.

33. David Crow, "Steven Spielberg and Tom Hanks Talk Bridge of Spies, Cohen Brothers, and Putin," Den of Geek, October 6, 2015, www.denofgeek.us/movies /bridge-of-spies/249612/steven-spielberg-tom-hanks-talk-bridge-of-spies-coen -brothers-putin; Andrew Blumenthal, "Bridge of Spies: Spielberg, the Cohens, and Tom Hanks," Creative Screenwriting, October 27, 2015, http://creativescreenwri ting.com/bridge-of-spies-spielberg-the-coens-and-tom-hanks/.

34. On the Cohens' *Hail, Caesar!* (2016), a comedy set during the McCarthy era, see "The Coen Brothers on Synchronised Swimming and Communism," *The Film Programme,* BBC Radio 4, March 6, 2016, www.bbc.co.uk/programmes/b071vlmv.

35. David Edelstein, "Bridge of Spies Is a Subtler Kind of Spielberg Movie," review of *Bridge of Spies,* directed by Steven Spielberg, *Vulture.com,* October 4, 2015, www.vulture.com/2015/10/movie-review-bridge-of-spies.html.

36. Develyn J. Watson, e-mail correspondence with author; Guy Martin, "Saving Pilot Powers; Tom Hanks and Steven Spielberg Film a Cold War-Thriller in Berlin," *Forbes,* December 16, 2014, www.forbes.com/sites/guymartin/2014/12/16/saving -pilot-powers-tom-hanks-and-steven-spielberg-film-a-cold-war-thriller-in-berlin /#61dd6eaf42e3.

37. Gary Powers Jr., interview by author; John Donovan and Beth Amorosi, cor- respondence with author.

38. Ron Briley, *The Baseball Film in Post-war America: A Critical Study, 1948– 1962* (Jefferson, NC: McFarland, 2011), 12–15, 131–141; Peter Biskind, *Seeing Is Believing: How Hollywood Taught Us to Stop Worrying and Love the Fifties* (London: Pluto, 1983), 64–69; and Glen M. Johnson, "Sharper Than an Irish Serpent's Tooth: Leo McCarey's *My Son John,*" *Journal of Popular Film and Television* 8, no. 1 (1980): 44–49.

39. Tony Shaw and Denise Youngblood, *Cinematic Cold War: The American and Soviet Struggle for Hearts and Minds* (Lawrence: University Press of Kansas, 2010), 98–112.

40. John Donovan and Beth Amorosi, James Donovan's son and granddaughter, correspondence with author, March 9, 2016.

41. Several critics made this comparison. See, for example, Neil Morris, "Tom Hanks Is a Cold War Atticus Finch in Spielberg's *Bridge of Spies,*" review of *Bridge of Spies,* directed by Steven Spielberg, IndyWeek.com, October 16, 2015, www.indy week.com/arts/archives/2015/10/16/movie-review-tom-hanks-is-a-cold-war-atticus -finch-in-spielbergs-bridge-of-spies; and Peter Debruge, review of *Bridge of Spies,* directed by Steven Spielberg, *Variety,* October 4, 2015, http://variety.com/2015 /film/reviews/bridge-of-spies-film-review-1201609677/.

42. On the bending of U.S. criminal justice rules during Abel's trial, see Jeffrey Kahn, "The Case of Colonel Abel," *Journal of National Security Law and Policy* 5 (2011): 263–301, http://jnslp.com/wp-content/uploads/2011/06/09_Kahn.pdf.

43. In real life, Donovan was indeed condemned as a Communist sympathizer by some Americans, but this shooting did not happen.

44. In real life, Donovan neither lost his coat nor was imprisoned. In an interesting case of fiction becoming fact, when promoting the film, scriptwriter Matt Charman treated the lawyer's imprisonment as fact. "Interview: Screenwriter Matt Charman Discusses Bridge of Spies," *DIY Magazine,* November 26, 2015, http://diymag.com/2015/11/26/screenwriter-matt-charman-discusses-bridge-of-spies.

45. Matt Charman, telephone interview by author.

46. Ryan Dougherty, "Economist Frederic Pryor Recounts Life as a 'Spy,'" *Swarthmore College News and Events,* October 21, 2015, www.swarthmore.edu/news-events/economist-frederic-pryor-recounts-life-a-spy; John Q. Barrett, "James B. Donovan, Before the 'Bridge of Spies,'" School of Law Legal Studies Research Paper Series, 15-0034, St. John's University, Queens, New York, 2015, 1–8; "The People of the CIA ... Milan Miskovsky: Fighting for Justice," *CIA News and Information,* April 30, 2013, www.cia.gov/news-information/featured-story-archive/milan-miskovsky.html; correspondence, Donovan-Dulles, Allen W. Dulles Papers, box 17, fol. 16, Public Policy Papers, Department of Rare Books and Special Collections, Princeton University Library, http://diglib.princeton.edu/images/deliverable/MC019/c00263.pdf; John Donovan and Beth Amorosi, correspondence with author, March 9, 2016.

47. Matthew Anderson, review of *Bridge of Spies,* directed by Steven Spielberg, *Cinevue.com,* accessed March 1, 2016, 2016, https://cine-vue.com/2015/11/film-review-bridge-of-spies.html.

48. Arthey, *Abel,* 76–81; Pavel Sudoplatov, Anatoli Sudoplatov, Jerrold L. Schecter, and Leona Schecter, *Special Tasks: The Memoirs of an Unwanted Witness, a Soviet Spymaster* (Toronto: Little, Brown, 1994), 168.

49. For a comprehensive overview, see Melvyn P. Leffler and Odd Arne Westad, eds., *The Cambridge History of the Cold War,* 3 vols. (Cambridge: Cambridge University Press, 2012).

50. Anderson, review of *Bridge of Spies;* Alex Perry, "Great Performances, Script Cross Spielberg's New 'Bridge of Spies,'" review of *Bridge of Spies,* directed by Steven Spielberg, https://thesunflower.com/4470/uncategorized/great-performances-script-cross-spielbergs-new-bridge-of-spies/.

51. Jon Wiener, *How We Forgot the Cold War: A Historical Journey across America* (Los Angeles: University of California Press, 2012), 16.

52. Crow, "Spielberg and Hanks Talk Bridge of Spies"; Mick LaSalle, "Spielberg's 'Bridge of Spies' Is Much More than a Solid Ride," review of *Bridge of Spies,* directed by Steven Spielberg, *sfgate.com,* October 15, 2015, www.sfgate.com/movies/article/Spielberg-s-Bridge-of-Spies-is-much-more-6566815.php.

53. Review of *Bridge of Spies,* directed by Steven Spielberg, metacritic, accessed March 1, 2016, www.metacritic.com/movie/bridge-of-spies; IMDb, www.imdb.com/title/tt3682448/; Box Office Mojo, www.boxofficemojo.com/genres/chart/?id=politicalthriller.htm.

54. Niall McCarthy, "The War on Terror Has Cost Taxpayers $1.7," *Forbes,* February 3, 2015, www.forbes.com/sites/niallmccarthy/2015/02/03/the-war-on-terror-has-cost-taxpayers-1-7-trillion-infographic/#644db3654154; "Statement by

the President on Afghanistan," October 15, 2015, https://obamawhitehouse.archives
.gov/the-press-office/2015/10/15/statement-president-afghanistan.

55. Amy Nicholson, "Cold War on Terror: Spielberg's 'Bridge of Spies' Finds Murk in Everyone's Moral Certainty," review of *Bridge of Spies,* directed by Steven Spielberg, *Village Voice,* October 13, 2015, www.villagevoice.com/film/cold-war -on-terror-spielberg-s-bridge-of-spies-finds-murk-in-everyone-s-moral-certainty -7769477.

56. Manohla Dargis, "Review: In 'Bridge of Spies' Spielberg Considers the Cold War," review of *Bridge of Spies,* directed by Steven Spielberg, *New York Times,* October 14, 2015, www.nytimes.com/2015/10/16/movies/review-in-bridge-of-spies -spielberg-considers-the-cold-war.html?_r=0.

57. Trangia55, "Did You Spot the Oopsy?," IMDb, January 21, 2016, www.imdb .com/user/ur34652841/; Steven Rea, review of *Bridge of Spies,* directed by Steven Spielberg, *philly.com,* October 11, 2015, http://articles.philly.com/2015-10-11 /news/67288311_1_steven-spielberg-the-spy-james-donovan.

58. Tony Shaw, *Cinematic Terror: A Global History of Terrorism on Film* (New York: Bloomsbury, 2015), 224–243.

59. Crow, "Steven Spielberg and Tom Hanks."

60. Roger Moore, review of *Bridge of Spies,* directed by Steven Spielberg, October 13, 2015, https://rogersmovienation.com/2015/10/13/movie-review-bridge -of-spies/. On *The Americans,* the U.S. television series that focuses on Soviet spies living in plain sight during the Reagan era and which premiered in 2013, see Brian Lowry, *Variety,* January 30, 2013, 14.

61. LaSalle, "Spielberg's 'Bridge of Spies' Is Much More Than a Solid Ride"; zephyrnewyork, "A Must-See for Cold War and Post-Cold War Generations Alike," review of *Bridge of Spies,* directed by Steven Spielberg, IMDb, February 20, 2016, www.imdb.com/user/ur48709100/.

62. Pete Hammond, "'Bridge of Spies' Review: Spielberg, Hanks, and the Coen Brothers Team for Landmark Cold War Thriller," review of *Bridge of Spies,* directed by Steven Spielberg, *Deadline.com,* October 6, 2015, http://deadline.com/2015/10 /bridge-of-spies-review-steven-spielberg-tom-hanks-coen-brothers-cold-war -thriller-1201568373/; Mike Scott, "'Bridge of Spies' Movie Review: Steven Spielberg, Tom Hanks Reteam for Cold war Drama," review of *Bridge of Spies,* directed by Steven Spielberg, *Times-Picayune,* October 13, 2015, www.nola.com/movies/index .ssf/2015/10/bridge_of_spies_movie_review_s_1.html.

NINE

Disfiguring the Americas

REPRESENTING DRUGS, VIOLENCE, AND IMMIGRATION IN THE AGE OF TRUMP

Patrick William Kelly

"THE WORLD WE LIVE IN has come into its own as an integrated globe, yet it lacks narration and has no history." That statement is no less true today than it was when historians Michael Geyer and Charles Bright wrote it in 1995. They were ahead of their time. The idea of the West once had a unity of purpose. That unity of purpose was called anti-communism. But the end of the Cold War did not bring the "end of history." It brought its converse: the alarming end of liberalism itself. Indeed, pessimism is now the prevailing mood in our age of human rights. Pessimism is the prevailing mood in our age of human rights that is also, paradoxically, the Age of Trump. Pessimism is the prevailing mood, indeed, but we are right to be pessimistic: Donald Trump is president, a man who was voted into office based on his denial of the equal status of women, his denial of the humanity of Mexicans and migrants, his denial of the dignity of the disabled, and his denial—or rather, his inability to grasp—the irony that he rose to power through a cynical manipulation of populism while simultaneously embodying the avarice and the elitism that fuels the anger of his populist base.

What is the West in the Age of Trump? Trump is less an embodiment than a synecdoche of the fracturing of the West, the disintegration of the very notion of liberalism itself. The signs are everywhere, and they are so disturbingly pervasive that we need only mention a few: the meaning of Brexit, the rise and replication of little Marine le Pens and the revanchist nationalism that capitalized on the horror of the present, the destruction of democracy in Brazil—no, it was not a coincidence that Dilma Rousseff, the country's first *female* president, was deposed—and the rise of ethno- and nuclear violence from *antifas* and white nationalists in the United States to North Korea. What is the West in our moment of despair? For those of us with any interest in making the world a better place, we do not know where we are, and we do not know where we are going. As George Smiley remarks in John le Carré's *A Legacy of Spies,* we are, today, nothing more and nothing less than "citizens of nowhere." The future is a fearful Occam's razor.

In our contemporary Age of Trump, which is also now part of the Age of Terror, where in the world is Latin America? Since the 1959 Cuban Revolution through the end of the 1980s, Latin America occupied the pride of place that the Middle East holds today. The Cold War, especially as it turned notably hot in numerous proxy wars throughout the global South in and beyond the 1970s, saw the front pages of American dailies carry story after story about Latin America. It was there that dictators and paramilitaries, covertly funded and tacitly approved by the United States, tortured and disappeared thousands of their citizens.[1] It was there, too, that President Ronald Reagan and his acolytes kicked the so-called Vietnam Syndrome that to many neoconservatives and their partisans had turned America into a feckless and sleepy superpower. His administration's claim that Latin America was the "most important place in the world" culminated in genocidal civil wars in Central America.[2]

But in the post–Cold War era, it became harder to place Latin America in the American imaginary. Even as most Latin American countries overcame a dark period of dictatorial rule and adopted democratic governments, signed onto the market-friendly ethos of the Washington Consensus, and endorsed the American fight against the scourge of drugs in the region, Americans still wondered: Is Latin America a friend, a foe, or something in between? In the absence of the Cold War's organizing binary—communism versus anti-communism—Latin Americans are now fractured into a scattering of disparate images, caricatures, and commodities. The "bad" stereotypes—drugs, violence, rape, civil wars, corruption, cartels, disease, Cuba, and the Castros—remain uncontested alongside the fleeting "good" stereotypes—beautiful women, beaches, rain forests, tequila, Cancún with its *girls gone wild,* and Argentine wine.

Since 9/11, these stereotypes persist as they were drawn under a new geopolitical and cultural penumbra: the global war on terrorism (GWOT). The literal landscapes of these battle lines in the GWOT are now clear, if at first they were shrouded in mystery, as to the nature of Central Intelligence Agency (CIA) "black sites," the illegal and global reach of U.S. drone warfare, and the extent of American intelligence spying on leaders across the world.[3] The figurative landscape of the GWOT reduced the world's complexities to a seductively simple dichotomy of good Americans fighting evil terrorists.[4] In the realm of U.S. popular culture, this has manifested most clearly in the year-in and year-out pummeling of superhero and fantasy epics, which have offered escapist antidotes to a sickened and exhausted American public during America's great "unwinding" of the last few decades.[5] Here I ask: In this reordered worldview, how have cultural representations of Latin America changed since 9/11? How have they changed since the end of the Cold War itself? To what extent do they challenge or confirm the broader effort to depict U.S. power in the world as one divinely bestowed upon a wanting sea of non-American masses? And what is the future of American exceptionalism in the Age of Trump?[6]

Through an analysis of film, television, music, and video games, I examine how U.S. popular culture creates a U.S. "imperialist discourse" and what it means for contemporary conceptions of the Americas. This discourse, I suggest, warps the complexities of Latin America in the service of a national narrative that justifies the past, present, and future of U.S. interventionist policies.[7] The most prominent examples are depictions of the drug wars, where television shows like Netflix's *Narcos* (2015–) apply the template of the GWOT to anoint Americans as the good agents of "imperial benevolence" who wage battle against culturally corrupt and violent Latin Americans. Culture, in this sense, maps onto history: a provision of the 2006 Patriot Act created a new crime of narco-terrorism, linking the newly coined struggle against terrorism to the long-standing transnational battle against drugs in the Americas.[8]

In other areas, video games such as *Grand Theft Auto* and *Call of Duty* celebrate gun violence as they allow players to relive and "win" old Cold War battles. To assuage the concerns of white Americans who fell on hard times, especially after the 2008 Great Recession, television shows like *Ugly Betty* (2006–2010) and *Modern Family* (2009–) stereotyped and scapegoated *Latino* immigrants. Only in rare instances, such as in, for example, Shakira's music, were critiques of American imperialism leveled. As a result, U.S. popular culture largely leaves unexamined the entangled histories of U.S. policies on free trade, immigration, and the war on drugs that have underpinned the increase in political violence and economic dislocation throughout the Americas. In these ways, I suggest that the projection of U.S. imperial benevolence in popular culture today sustains itself through a willful and often deliberate disfiguring of both the history of U.S. foreign policy in Latin America and the transnational ties that bind the Americas—even as the American president desires to construct impenetrable walls.

Of all the representations of Latin America in U.S. popular culture since 9/11, perhaps the most damaging is the frequent refusal to recognize U.S. complicity in the origins and structural maintenance of drug violence. For there is no disputing the facts: Americans are doubly responsible for the intensification of repressive state and nonstate regimes throughout the hemisphere. Americans are the primary consumers of illicit drugs, and the leaders of the United States have for decades militarized the U.S.-Mexico border and funneled billions of dollars to the Colombian and Mexican governments, which in turn have funded the questionable practices of paramilitary organizations.[9] Moreover, free trade policies, such as the North American and Central America Free Trade Agreements (NAFTA and CAFTA), pushed many desperate peasants into the drug industry when they lost their jobs to more competitive American corporations. While U.S. popular culture has long sensationalized the violence of the drug wars, the latest examples, with a few exceptions, elide this nuanced history. And more perniciously, as in the broader GWOT, shows such as *24* (2001–2010) and *Homeland* (2011–) sanction the increased militarization of the drug wars, including illegal tactics like torture, as necessary for "civilizing" Americans to fight the endemic corruption and the culture of malevolence south of the border.[10]

Consider Netflix's *Narcos,* released in 2015 and billed as an in-depth treatment of the rise of Pablo Escobar's transnational cocaine empire. In an effort to convey the show's authenticity, the viewer is told at the outset that "this television series is inspired by real events." Characters speak in drug-war jargon to establish credibility, casually referencing "paste-processing plants" and "transshipments." Yet *Narcos* displays a very loose attachment to Latin American history, geography, and culture. The show's action follows protagonist Drug Enforcement Administration (DEA) agent Stephen Murphy as he hunts Escobar and his Medellín Cartel in the 1980s, although the "real" Murphy did not arrive in Colombia until the eve of Escobar's arrest in 1991.[11] Murphy flies over the Amazon—a symbol of an unruly, untamed South America—even though such a flight from Miami to Bogotá would not need to traverse the jungle. The show also creates the perception of historical accuracy with a surplus of spoken Spanish accompanied by subtitles, yet many of the actors are not Colombians or native Spanish speakers. Similarly, Pablo Escobar, portrayed by a Brazilian, Wagner Moura, speaks in an accent heavily inflected by his native Portuguese. With only a few mentions of international and domestic antidrug policies, the show elevates Escobar as solely responsible for the rise in the transnational trade of cocaine and treats other Colombian cartels as bit players. Most all Colombians in *Narcos* are drug criminals, thieves, or sexually aggressive women.[12] Make no mistake: this show is intended for American audiences.

As a result, the exoticism of Colombia is translated through the repeated voice-overs of the show's agent of imperial benevolence, Stephen Murphy. He functions as Colombia's "cultural and historical mediator" to an American public—one who never deems it appropriate to learn Spanish. Murphy explains in the first episode his rationale for fighting the good fight: "My dad volunteered to fight in World War II because of Pearl Harbor.... He was a West Virginia farm boy, but these fuckers stepped on our soil, so he laced up his army boots and went to fight. It was his duty. Cocaine in Miami, kilos from Colombia. This was my war. This was my duty. And I was ready to fight it, and my wife was ready to fight it with me too." In other words, Murphy links his "duty" to liberate the streets of Miami from the grip of cocaine to his father's effort to fight the "fuckers" who bombed Pearl Harbor in World War II, the quintessentially "good" war in the popular American imagination. As Colombian literature scholar Juliana Martinez explains, this framing upholds "the Reagan Era's teleology on the war on drugs ... [as] the inevitable and just—albeit undesirable—consequence of a foreign attack on the social fabric of the United States."[13]

The show traces Murphy's civilizing mission in the "Amazonian" Colombia, rendered as a quaint and feckless country crying out for American assistance. Murphy is the "hero" Colombia needs, often swooping in to save innocent Colombian women and children as they are in the clutches of narco violence. Murphy is also the kind of "hero" that America needs: as in productions such as *24* and the film *Zero Dark Thirty* (2012), Murphy's use of torture in interrogations is justified as a necessary evil in the fight against terror.[14] In that sense, the need to root out malevolent forces in Colombia functions as a justification for the projection of U.S. imperial benevolence. As one Colombian observer of the show protested, the show "[robs us] of our own history, which becomes a mere plot device, cut down to fine, shredded pieces for American audiences to digest without having to gnaw on the bones."[15]

While it glorifies U.S. interventionism in the drug wars in Ciudad Juárez, the 2015 film *Sicario* presents a somewhat more complicated picture. The

movie follows well-intentioned Federal Bureau of Investigation (FBI) agent
Kate Macer as she joins a powerful if nebulous special operations force tasked
with stemming the drug wars in Ciudad Juárez along the U.S.-Mexico border. On the one hand, in presenting an aggrandized version of U.S. power
that brazenly conducts operations in Mexico during the cold light of day, the
movie has a tendency to glorify drug violence as a means to create suspense
for the viewer. On the other hand, as Macer is drawn deeper and deeper into
the dark underbelly of border warfare, she begins to question its fundamental
ethics. In the show's dramatic reveal, she raises objections about questionable
tactics to her superior, only to have him admit that the drug war has no
foreseeable end; because of U.S. consumer demand, their best outcome is to
establish a balance of power among the warring cartel factions. Still, the
movie offers too simplistic of a conclusion in the notion of a forever war along
the border that is driven solely by the American consumer appetite for drugs.
Most obviously, in endorsing the U.S. government's militarization of the
border as seemingly inexorable, it lets American policy makers off the hook
for their blind devotion to the war on drugs over a half century without
considering alternative paths.[16]

Other representations examine the drug wars from the perspective of
enterprising Americans. Vince Gilligan's highly popular series *Breaking Bad*
(2008–2013) connects the drug wars to white male disempowerment after the
2008 financial crisis (*Weeds* [2005–2012] accomplished a similar feat,
although with a female lead). The show features the wildly unlikely story of
its antihero Walter White, a former high school chemistry teacher turned
vigilante expert alchemist of "blue sky"—the highest-quality crystal meth-
amphetamine (99.1 percent pure!) ever seen by the cartels. While some have
suggested that *Breaking Bad* actually broke stereotypes of Latin Americans,
I am less convinced.[17] The viewer's first sustained encounter with a drug lord
is with meth-head Tuco Salamanca—whose name alone is discomforting and
disturbing. Tuco is a sociopath par excellence who extinguishes a cigarette on
his tongue, threatens to rob White, and brutally murders his lackey in the
cold light of day just because she spoke out of turn. Few Latino characters on
the show break this mold. The Salamanca cousins are more patient; they
barely utter a complete sentence, slithering like snakes through a handful of
episodes.

Later in the series, White's primary adversary becomes Gustavo Fring,
who, in contrast to Tuco, is methodical, cunning, and, shockingly, not a
meth-head. He is, rather, a stealth drug dealer who launders money through

his fast-food chain, the brilliantly conceived Los Pollos Hermanos. But Fring, in my estimation, is less about breaking Latino stereotypes than defying logic. While his character is ostensibly of Chilean descent—a smart twist given the connections between Chilean drug lords and the rise of Pablo Escobar, a fact nicely described in *Narcos*—his accent is decidedly not Chilean. Fring is portrayed by Giancarlo Esposito, a man born in Denmark and the son of African American and Italian parents. Even more, although the show gestures to American complicity in the drug trade—Walter White is the main producer, after all—it only occasionally considers the root cause of American consumer demand. While a few episodes shine a light on the meth crisis that is afflicting rural towns across America, the viewer is left with a general impression of a show that sidesteps the thorny politics of the drug wars in order to perpetuate a discourse of white economic resentment.[18]

In that sense, Walter White becomes the antihero of the post-2008 crash. Adopting the pseudonym of German physicist Heisenberg, he puts his expertise in high school chemistry to work to construct a vastly improbable drug empire in order to make millions. The show reached a phenomenal level of critical and popular success: numerous publications and critics have hailed it as one of the best television shows ever made, and by the end of its five-season story arc, it had become one of the most widely watched television shows.[19] And yet that same success seemed to prevent much nuanced discussion of the problematics of its cultural representation of the war on drugs.

The white discourse of resentment animating *Breaking Bad* also propels part of the narrative in Matthew Heineman's 2015 documentary *Cartel Land,* which follows vigilante groups on both sides of the U.S.-Mexico border in their violent struggles against Mexican cartels. On the American side, we meet Tim Foley of the Arizona Border Recon, who vacillates between denouncing the "illegals" who took his construction jobs after 2008—"I see this as an invasion," he states—and the Cartel "fuckers" who are "terrorizing their own country, and now they're starting to do it here." Foley represents the tradition of the American vigilante of what he calls the "Wild, Wild West," willing to pick up the banner of the good fight in the absence of the American government. And while he's utterly convinced of the sanctity of his fight, describing in biblical terms, "We're David, they're Goliath," his conflation of undocumented immigration with the drug wars reflects the documentary's broader flattening of these issues, which are at once distinct and interconnected. On the Mexican side of the border, we meet Dr. José Manuel Mireles, who organizes a series of *autodefensa* groups in the state of

Michoacán. The *autodefensas* form a citizen revolt against both the violence of the Mexican cartels, who terrorize and extort citizens, and the corruption and inefficacy of the Mexican government, which is either complicit in the perpetuation of cartel violence or ill-equipped to stop it.

Even as it offers a refreshing on-the-ground take on the drug wars, *Cartel Land* fails to provide any editorial perspective, much less an explanatory framework that might help the viewer untangle the issues of undocumented immigration and drug violence. Par for the course in these representations, it obsesses over gratuitous cartel violence: we hear heart-wrenching stories of murdered babies, decapitated heads, and bodies dismembered or burned alive. The documentary alternates between these graphic images, conveyed in moving interviews with the victims of cartel violence, and shoot-outs between vigilantes on both sides of the border, leaving the viewer with few options other than to sympathize with the vigilante response. Director Heineman explained in interviews that he "did not want to do a policy film"—ostensibly a defensible position—but in this instance, more context is needed given the complicated web of issues at stake, of which the viewer likely knows very little. And while the film purports to be apolitical, it establishes a false parity: the Mexican government comes off as wildly corrupt, while the U.S. government is left relatively unscathed. It does not, moreover, question the "war on drugs" paradigm nor does it mention American consumption. And in treating Foley of the Arizona Border Recon as a vigilante agent of "imperial benevolence," the film sustains an argument for the interventionism inherent in the GWOT. It is no surprise, then, that Kathryn Bigelow, the director of the jingoistic American films *Zero Dark Thirty* and *The Hurt Locker* (2008), was *Cartel Land*'s executive producer.[20]

What is most missing from these cultural artifacts is that they rarely indict Americans or American policies in the drug wars; the drug wars are simply the raw ingredients to whet the appetite of the American viewer. A standout exception is Don Winslow's 2015 novel *The Cartel,* which is a masterful and closely drawn narrative on the drug wars' rapidly shifting terrain from 2004 to 2014; it is a sequel to his 2005 thriller *The Power of the Dog,* which surveys the drug wars' first thirty years. Winslow confessed in an interview about his motivation for writing the book: "We stand here on the northern side of the border and point the finger south. And talk about Mexican corruption. Of course, there is corruption in Mexico, no one is going to argue that." He continued: "But I ask a different question: What kind of corruption of our collective soul does it require to be the largest drug market in the world?" Aside from Winslow and a few films (for example, *Kill the Messenger* [2014]), U.S. popular culture largely tells a comforting narrative that the war on drugs, like the broader war on terror, is a good, if sordid, American fight. For in the end, there is no profit motive in pointing to the hypocrisy that, in Winslow's words, "We are all the cartel."[21]

Video games also provide Americans with feel-good versions of the history of American intervention in the Americas. Have you ever wished you could virtually kill Fidel Castro? Millions of people did just that in the opening scene of the video game *Call of Duty: Black Ops*. When it was released in 2010, it had one of the most commercially successful launches of any video game in history, earning $360 million from 5.6 million consumers *in one day*. Six weeks later, it had grossed $1 billion.[22] In the opening scene's climactic moment, the player approaches a set of wooden doors outside Castro's lair, which is darkly romantic, a fireplace still burning. The player's avatar asks rhetorically to his fellow soldier but indirectly to the gamer herself, too: "Are you ready to make history?" The doors open to reveal a youthful, slim Castro with a freshly groomed beard. Castro quickly shields his body with that of his Latina mistress, who is partially covered in a revealing white dress. In charge of assassinating Castro, you as the player have one chance to aim accurately and kill him. When you pull the trigger, the scene slows down, *Matrix*-style, as the camera hovers behind the bullet approaching Castro's skull. A celestial choir begins to sing and, if you are lucky, you shoot him directly in the forehead, fulfilling the dream of American intelligence operatives for decades.

Gamers can not only take out Castro but they can also relive Reagan-era adventurism and capture Panamanian leader Manuel Noriega or overthrow Venezuela's former socialist president Hugo Chávez. In simulation games such as 2001's *Tropico,* where the player assumes a godlike role as the creator and controller of a civilization, users construct a fictional island and play under the avatar of an infamous Latin American leader, all of whom are dictators or fascist populists: Anastasio Somoza, François Duvalier (called by his *apodo* Papa Doc in the game), Manuel Noriega, Fidel Castro, Che Guevara, Juan Perón, António Salazar, Anastasio Somoza García, Alfredo Stroessner, Rafael Trujillo, Eva Perón, or Augusto Pinochet. (Violeta Chamorro from Nicaragua is the only exception and an odd if welcome choice; she was the first democratically elected female head of state in the Americas and president of Nicaragua from 1990–1997.) Such games, as cultural studies scholar Phillip Penix-Tadsen notes, are both "colonialist and demeaning," and moreover, they adopt a "veiled essentialism [that] contributes to the hegemony of imperialist discourse."[23]

Long neglected in studies of popular culture, scholars have started to engage in earnest with the study of video games, or *ludology*. A look at the representation of Latin America in video games is called for, then, given the growing importance of this field and the increasing presence of video games in the cultural domain. Some fear the coming singularity, the moment when technology recursively betters itself in a manner that surpasses human intellectual comprehension (think Skynet from the *Terminator* series). Video games, we are told, "commodify our cyborg desires" and attest to our "will to merge with and become technology."[24] Yet this dystopic perspective, especially when written in 2003, strikes me as a bit overblown. Still, video games are widely used: almost 70 percent of households in the United States play them; the average gamer is thirty-eight years old; and, against popular presumption, more adult women are gamers than males under the age of seventeen (30 vs. 23 percent, respectively).[25]

If we agree that video games are worthy of close cultural analysis, how might we analyze video games? Scholar and programmer Alexander R. Galloway explains in lucid terms one prevailing approach: if photographs are images and film connects the parts of images into a moving whole, then "video games are actions" that assume an "alternative semiotical structure known as simulation."[26] Given their dominance of the cultural terrain and their efficacy in mirroring the world and one's interactions in it, it is prudent to consider how this new cultural realm shapes perceptions of Latin America.

For instance, Phillip Penix-Tadsen observes the myriad ways, both innocuous and damaging, that games distort Latin America. He injects vital theoretical energy into the largely unstudied field of video game studies as he makes a persuasive case that we must take seriously Latin American ludology because "it represents an attempt to understand who we are as a field [Latin American cultural studies], how our area of research functions, and what we want it to become as the future unfolds and our lived and virtual experiences overlap and become one." These take the form of omnipotent control a la *Tropico* or games that foreground the militaries and paramilitaries of the Americas, often with drug narratives at their center (for example, *Contra, Tom Clancy's Rainbow Six* and *Ghost Recon: Advanced Warfighter, Call of Duty: Modern Warfare 2, Code Name: Viper, Shoot to Kill: Colombia Crackdown, Call of Juarez: The Cartel*), historical dramatizations (*Tropico,*

Call of Duty: Black Ops), and contemporary fictionalizations *(Mercenaries 2, Tom Clancy's Ghost Recon: Island Thunder).*[27]

Towering over all video games, however, is the *Grand Theft Auto (GTA)* series, first released in 1997 and now in its fifth installment. Over the course of the various releases, *GTA* imagines a number of thinly disguised American cities: Liberty City (NYC), Vice City (Miami), and Los Santos (Los Angeles). Each contains a number of Latinos and Latin Americans who weave in and out of the plot as members of drug cartels and drug gangs. To hammer the point home, Vice City is connected to the world by [Pablo] Escobar International Airport.

GTA reached the peak of its cultural saturation following criticism of its promotion of wanton violence. The latest incarnation, *Grand Theft Auto V* in 2013, sold a billion copies even faster than 2010's *Call of Duty.* As the Columbine theory asserts: the game's gory nature, not the lobbying power of the National Rifle Association or the fanciful reinterpretation of the Second Amendment, engenders such rampant societal violence in America. Two scholars mocked such a conflation—only the press could suggest that *GTA* could be ridiculed as "Video Game Allows Kids to Solicit Prostitutes, Run Them Over, Get Their Money Back."[28] Defenders of the game pushed back against this characterization. *GTA* permits players to *choose* their own adventure, as it were. One is ostensibly as violent as one wants to be while playing. "You can learn a lot about a person by watching how they play *GTA,*" one defender argues.[29]

Still, even if one accepts the argument of individual choice, one cannot escape its gratuitous depiction of violence against women. *GTA V* encourages its players, quite literally, to purchase women (or are they underage girls?), who in turn sexually gratify their male avatars (and they are only male). More points are earned in the game if one kills the woman/underage girl after the fact. Clearly, the series could *only* have been made by men. As one women's rights activist lamented, *GTA V* "comfortably exists in our rape culture, and reifies the distinct ways in which women and girls are properties, humiliated, and abused."[30]

Perhaps the joke is on us as Americans: the Scottish creators of the *GTA* series forthrightly admit their intentionality. "We wanted to poke fun at U.S. culture and could do pretty much whatever we wanted, since from day one the plan was for it to be 18-rated. Sometimes we went too far. In one mission idea, which was later cut, you had to go around burning churches. You'd probably be arrested for putting that in a game now, even though it was all very tongue in cheek."[31] For all the fun, satire has its limits: by rewarding violent behavior, the game validates a culture of violence in the Americas and reifies stereotypes of Latino culture as intricately intertwined with the transnational drug trade.

Stereotypes of Latino culture and Latino immigrants took on a new valence in the years after the 2008 Great Recession. The "mancession"—the notion that the loss of manufacturing and construction jobs hurt men more than women—reflected the need to tell soothing tales to relieve the anxieties of hegemonic white males, even as minorities felt more economic pain.[32] Dislocated by the ramifications of a global neoliberal economy, torn asunder by the predations of greedy capitalists inventing complex financial instruments that they themselves barely understand, U.S. popular culture since 2008 has reflected a newly invigorated anxiety and aggression that is displaced on Latinos and the "problem" of "illegal" immigration.

Latinos, as the displaced culprits of the mancession, worked against the dreams of marketing executives to unite the Americas in one free-flowing zone of consumption. The changing nature of U.S. demographics, particularly the increased prevalence and cultural and economic capital of Latino populations in the United States, led to the growth of the Spanish channels Univisión and Fusion.[33] Executives began to globalize the melodramatic, uniquely Latin American *telenovela* format.[34] This led to the global diffusion of one Colombian *telenovela* in particular, *Yo Soy Betty, La Fea* (1999–2001).

Copied by various countries throughout the Americas, Disney-ABC elevated it to a new global status when it turned its ugly duckling fable into *Ugly Betty,* the latest incarnation of what one scholar calls the "foundational myth of a U.S. meritocracy," the American Dream. Featuring Honduran actress America Ferrera, Betty is a second-generation Mexican who lives in New York City. Those facts alone are hard to swallow: it is strange to see a Honduran actress sold as a Mexican who lives in a city, indeed the American city, most defined by its non-Mexican Latino population. Betty, even more, does not speak Spanish and knows little of her history or the plight of U.S. Latinos. *Ugly Betty* was released in 2006, at the very moment that Republicans sought to impose a draconian immigration law—a callous provision in a bill in the House of Representatives would have made it a felony for an undocumented person *to reside* in the country, as well as for someone to help the person—that alienated and enraged wide swaths of the undocumented and documented Latino immigrants throughout the country, resulting in widespread protests.[35] Betty is shorn of any complicated politics in order to be palatable to the hegemonic white majority. Like *The Cosby Show* (1984–1992), which allowed white Americans to empathize with a black family to "absolve themselves of social responsibility for ongoing racial prejudices and discrimination," the facile Horatio Alger version of Betty did much the same for the issue of undocumented immigrants in the United States. A testament to the enduring portrait of Latino culture, Ferrera became the first Latina to win the Emmy for best actress in a comedy series.[36]

In a similar manner, *Modern Family* debuted in 2009 at the same cultural moment as Sonia Sotomayor's contentious nomination to the Supreme Court; as a Puerto Rican, she would be the first Latina justice to ascend to the nation's highest juridical body. Sotomayor was hounded by conservative media and pundits for suggesting that a judge's ethnicity and gender "may and will make a difference in our judging." Her widely maligned line modestly expressed hope that a "wise Latina woman with the richness of her experiences would more often than not reach a better conclusion than a white male who hasn't lived that life."[37] To many observers, it was an obvious, even banal, point. We judge the world too often through our own personal experience, and a diversified judiciary, it follows, would more accurately and empathetically reflect the diversity of the American experience.

Enter Gloria from *Modern Family* in the wake of the Great Recession of 2008, when anxiety and anger manifested in what some have called the "white discourse of resentment."[38] Once an undocumented immigrant herself, Gloria is portrayed by actress Sofía Vergara, a physically stunning and curvaceous Colombian who marries Jay, played by Al Bundy (Ed O'Neill) reliving his *Married with Children* (1987–1997) days in the most unlikely of never-explained romantic couplings in the history of television. Gloria is a rethinking of the traditional trope of the Latina spitfire. "The ideological role of the spitfire archetype," media studies scholar Isabel Molina-Guzmán writes, "was to make foreign Latin America less threatening through humor while celebrating the potential for intercultural exchange and heterosexual romance."[39] And thus we have Gloria's first dialogue sequence in the show's debut:

GLORIA: We're very different. Jay's from the city, he has a big business. I come from a small village—very poor, but very, very beautiful. It's the number one village in all Colombia for all the . . . what's the word?

JAY: Murders.

GLORIA: Yes, the murders.

The English word for *murder (asesinato)* is not a difficult word for a Spanish-to-English speaker; it even has a cognate in *assassinate (asesinar)*. That Gloria would not know it as a flawed, if still coherent, English speaker, especially if it is so foundational to her life story, is nothing short of preposterous. It marks her as inept, even willfully ignorant ("the" murders, in injecting the direct article, renders her even more clueless). And the content of her history is perhaps the most offensive, recapitulating stereotypes of Colombia as little more than a poverty-stricken wasteland of killing.

Similar examples abound. Later in the first season, Jay's ex-wife Deedee comments at their wedding that Gloria is Charo—the iconic 1970s Latina spitfire. Deedee continues, "Seriously, I knew they were perfect for each other when I saw his wallet and her boobs." The relationship between Jay and Gloria is indeed jarring: Jay feasibly could be Gloria's father. But that is the point. The relationship and the jokes about the disconnect between her physical beauty and his lack thereof serve to palliate white economic disloca-tion. Gloria hails from an epicenter of Latin American violence, where, she admits in one episode: "In Colombia, when we got pulled out of class, it was, you know, to identify a body." Jay is the white male savior: he provides literal shelter for her and her son, Manny, his marriage a throwback to the days of the *feme covert*, granting Gloria's documented status as an American citi-zen.[40] We are led to believe that Gloria is little more than the embodiment of the Latina spitfire, with only fleeting moments that transcend her physicality, such as her empathy in relationships, her insight into parenting, and the importance she places on cultural tradition.

It seems fitting to close with one final example, that of the "wise Latina" voice of Shakira, in order to reflect on the rise of Latina music in the global age of terror. The twenty-first century has seen a surge in interest in Latin American music in the United States. A surfeit of stars have made it big: from Jennifer Lopez to Ricky Martin, Enrique Iglesias, Paulina Rubio, Carlos Santana, and Marc Antony. But while these artists have achieved a degree of recognition in the political culture, Shakira is the only one from Latin America who has done so while launching a blistering critique of the very notion of U.S. "imperial benevolence."

On the surface, Shakira's background seems ill-suited for stardom in the post-9/11 environment. Her first name is Arabic for "full of grace." But it is in *Arabic,* her full name being Shakira Mebarak Ripoll and therefore suspicious (recall how conservatives wielded Barack *Hussein* Obama?). But Shakira's breakthrough decade after 9/11 offers an exception to the more general rule of the flattening of Latin America in U.S. popular culture. In large part, this was because Shakira defied nationalism: born in Colombia of Lebanese descent, Shakira has been called the "embodiment of globalization."[41] And while her crossover appeal as a performer who has gradually incorporated English into her bilingual repertoire has been controversial, Shakira, especially in the early part of her career, took overt political actions in defiance of U.S. foreign policy.

Her politics were at times mocked as discordant with the awkward trinity of pop stars in which she was placed alongside Madonna and Britney Spears. One journalist assured her readers in late 2002 that Shakira was "far more than just a pretty face . . . there may actually be a *real person* struggling to emerge from the perfect pop package presented to the world as Shakira."[42] Similarly, in response to a question from a reporter, Shakira offered a valuable history lesson so often missing from representations of the drug wars: "Colombia is a beautiful country. There are 40 million people there and only a small number are dedicated to the business of drugs. . . . And remember, Colombia and the United States are involved in the same business, because who's the biggest importer of drugs? The United States, of course."[43]

Building on the success of her first crossover album, *Laundry Service,* released less than two months after 9/11, Shakira launched the Tour of the Mongoose on the eve of the invasion of Iraq.[44] The Mongoose was chosen because, Shakira explained, it could stop a poisonous snake with only one bite. To supplement her song "Octavo Día," the tour featured a video of President George W. Bush and Iraqi leader Saddam Hussein playing chess. As the video zooms back on the chess game, the viewer is surprised to see the grim reaper as the puppeteer controlling Bush and Hussein. For such a "pretty face," some may have thought, it was a defiantly bold act. Shakira explained its significance in that "Octavo Día" takes place in the aftermath of God creating the world. On the eighth day, "He went for a walk to outer space and when he came back he found our world in an infernal mess. And he found that we were being controlled and manipulated by just a few leaders and that we were like pieces of a chess game." She elaborated that her experiences growing up in war-torn Colombia, where she felt the "whip of violence" and saw "the consequences of war" and the "psychological damage it does to a society," gave her insight into the problematics of war.[45]

Americans, we are too rarely reminded, accept the nature of their forever war because they do not have to face the facts of it. It does not, as in Colombia, stalk the realities of our daily lives. Shakira saw this. And curiously, unlike the Dixie Chicks, who similarly castigated the Bush administration's jingoism only to be treated to death threats, Shakira faced no backlash. Perhaps her exotic foreign status shielded her? Perhaps few were paying attention at all.[46]

Coming to terms with the long reach of U.S. foreign policy in the Americas—the legacy and lived reality of political, cultural, and economic imperialism—would force a reckoning among Americans on a variety of fronts. We might reconsider the fervent American belief in the sanctity of free trade and its bestowal on a hungry world. We might rethink the rationale for a decades-long global drug war that has killed so many not where "illegal" drugs are primarily consumed—in the United States—but in Latin America. It is the U.S. popular imagination that renders Latin America as a primordial culture of violence; it is an imagination that reflects the "deviant" forms of globalization that are fostered by the neoliberal disruptions of the post-NAFTA Americas.[47] Consider, for instance, the rise of *maquiladora* factories along the border and the recurrent rape of women in Ciudad Juaréz.[48] Consider, too, the desperate journeys of poor Central American migrants, whose dislocation might be seen as caused by those neoliberal disruptions; they might, they should, be seen as American problems too.

What if it were different? What if the U.S. role in destabilizing the Middle East to promote "democracy" could be viewed against its legacy in the U.S. "workshop" of Latin America: most recently, in Venezuela and Honduras, where the United States supported coups against democratic leaders in 2002 and 2009, respectively; and in Colombia and Mexico, where millions of U.S. dollars in the form of the Plan Colombia and the Mérida Initiative have fueled the fight against drugs—one that has brought little more than devastation and death to millions.[49] But what is the future of American exceptionalism, the ideology that underpins the projection of "imperial benevolence" around the world, in the Age of Trump?[50]

The point of this ink spilled is not that the United States is responsible for all the ills of Latin America; that would be absurd. But, rather, the systematic distortion of Latin America in U.S. popular culture allows for a purified version of U.S. foreign policy—one that reflects the capillary nature of U.S.

power in an age of global terror. This power operates, indeed it disguises itself, by projecting a particular and particularly maligned vision of the Americas, its people, its history—and the place of the United States and its citizens within it.

NOTES

1. Alan McPherson, ed., *Encyclopedia of U.S. Military Interventions in Latin America,* 2 vols. (Santa Barbara, California: ABC-CLIO, 2013).

2. Van Gosse, "Unpacking the Vietnam Syndrome: The Coup in Chile and the Rise of Popular Anti-Interventionism," in *The World the Sixties Made: Politics and Culture in Recent America,* ed. Van Gosse and Richard R. Moser (Philadelphia: Temple University Press, 2008), 100–113; Greg Grandin, *Empire's Workshop: Latin America, the United States, and the Rise of the New Imperialism* (New York: Holt, 2007).

3. Dana Priest, "CIA Holds Terror Suspects in Secret Prisons," *Washington Post,* November 2, 2005; "U.S. Military Drone Network in the Middle East and Africa," *Washington Post,* July 19, 2013.

4. Andrew McKevitt, "'Watching War Made Us Immune': The Popular Culture of the Wars," in *Understanding the U.S. Wars in Iraq and Afghanistan,* ed. Beth Bailey and Richard H. Immerman (New York: New York University Press, 2015), 240–241.

5. George Packer, *The Unwinding: An Inner History of the New America* (New York: Farrar, Straus and Giroux, 2013).

6. Stephen Wertheim, "Trump and American Exceptionalism," *Foreign Affairs,* January 3, 2017.

7. Phillip Penix-Tadsen, *Cultural Code: Video Games and Latin America* (Boston: MIT Press, 2016), 207, 223.

8. Ginger Thompson, "Trafficking in Terror," *New Yorker,* December 14, 2015.

9. Winifred Tate, *Drugs, Thugs, and Diplomats: U.S. Policymaking in Colombia* (Palo Alto, CA: Stanford University Press, 2015); Christy Thornton, "Pressure Mexico to Respect Human Rights," *New York Times,* December 2, 2014.

10. For a critique of *24* and torture, see Jane Mayer, "Whatever It Takes," *New Yorker,* February 19, 2007.

11. See the trenchant critique in Jon Lee Anderson, "The Afterlife of Pablo Escobar," *New Yorker,* March 5, 2018; Steven Cohen, "Narcos: Life after Escobar?," *NACLA,* September 22, 2017; Christopher Looft, "The New Drug War Cinema: On Netflix's 'Narcos,'" *LA Review of Books,* September 16, 2015.

12. Juliana Martinez, "Netfix 'Narcos': 'Cultural Weight' or Cultural Maquila," InSight Crime, November 27, 2015, www.insightcrime.org/news-analysis /netflix-narcos-cultural-weight-or-cultural-maquila.

13. Ibid.

14. Steve Coll, "Disturbing and Misleading," *New York Review of Books,* February 7, 2013.

15. Pablo Medina Uribe, "Netflix's Narcos Cheapens Colombia and Its History," *Fusion,* September 29, 2015, http://fusion.net/story/205405/netflixs-narcos -cheapens-colombia-and-its-history/.

16. Michael Lohmuller, "'Sicario' Presents Dramatized Yet Refreshing Drug Critique," InSight Crime, November 26, 2015, www.insightcrime.org/news-analysis /sicario-presents-dramatized-yet-refreshing-drug-critique-review.

17. Andrew Howe, "Not Your Average Mexican: *Breaking Bad* and the Destruction of Latino Stereotypes," in *Breaking Bad: Critical Essays on the Contexts, Politics, Style, and Reception of the Television Series,* ed. David P. Pierson (Lanham, MD: Lexington, 2014), 87–102.

18. For a more complicated treatment, see Nick Reding, *Methland: The Death and Life of an American Small Town* (New York: Bloomsbury, 2009).

19. See, for example, Rob Sheffield, "100 Greatest TV Shows of All Time," *Rolling Stone,* September 21, 2016; James Hibberd, "'Breaking Bad' Series Finale Ratings Smash All Records," *Entertainment Weekly,* September 30, 2013.

20. Kenneth Maffitt, "Visualizing the War on Drugs in 'Sicario' and 'Cartel Land,'" *LA Review of Books,* December 31, 2015.

21. Robert Anglen, "'The Cartel' Author Don Winslow Says America Is Addicted to the Drug War," *AZCentral,* July 1, 2015, www.azcentral.com/story /entertainment/arts/2015/06/19/america-addicted-drug-war-author-don-winslow -says-yes/28956175/.

22. Phillip Penix-Tadsen, "Latin American Ludology: Why We Should Take Video Games Seriously (and When We Shouldn't)," *Latin American Research Review* 48, no. 1 (2013): 74.

23. Penix-Tadsen, *Cultural Code,* 223–224. Manuel Noriega filed a lawsuit against Activision, the publisher of *Call of Duty: Black Ops II,* for "us[ing] his image and likeness in a defamatory manner." Ibid., 73.

24. Martti Lahti, "As We Become Machines: Corporealized Pleasures in Video Games," in *The Video Game Reader,* ed. Mark J. P. Wolf and Bernard Perron (New York: Routledge, 2003), 166.

25. Penix-Tadsen, *Cultural Code,* 176.

26. Alexander R. Galloway, *Gaming: Essays on Algorithmic Culture* (Minneapolis: University of Minnesota Press, 2006), 2.

27. Penix-Tadsen, "Latin American Ludology," 181, 185. For a breakdown of a "chronological taxonomy" of games, split by *Tomb Raiders, Contras,* and *Luchadores* from 1982–2012, see 186–187.

28. Penix-Tadsen, *Cultural Code,* 64.

29. "Even the torture scene in *GTA 5* can be short or long depending on what the player decides," writes Malcolm Aquino in "A Defense of Violence: The Cultural Impact of the Grand Theft Auto Series," *Huffington Post,* January 23, 2014, www .huffingtonpost.com/uloop/a-defense-of-violence-the_b_4173854.html.

30. Malika Saada Saar, "Grand Theft Auto V and the Culture of Violence against Women," *Huffington Post,* December 9, 2014, www.huffingtonpost.com/malika -saada-saar/grand-theft-auto-v-and-the-culture-of-violence-against-women_b _6288528.html.

31. Keith Stuart, "How We Made . . . Grand Theft Auto," *Guardian,* May 18, 2015, www.theguardian.com/technology/2015/may/18/how-we-made-grand-theft-auto.

32. Derek Thompson, "It's Not Just a Recession. It's a Mancession!" *Atlantic,* July 9, 2009; Rob Wile, "The 'Mancession' Is Over—But Not for Black Men," *Fusion,* June 24, 2015.

33. Arlene Dávila, *Latinos, Inc.: The Marketing and Making of a People* (Berkeley: University of California Press, 2001).

34. Ana M. López, "Our Welcomed Guests: Telenovelas in Latin America," in *To Be Continued . . . Soap Operas around the World,* ed. Robert Clyde Allende (New York: Routledge, 1995), 256–275.

35. Randal C. Archibold, "Immigrants Take to U.S. Streets in Show of Strength," *New York, Times,* May 2, 2006.

36. Isabel Molina-Guzmán, *Dangerous Curves: Latina Bodies in the Media* (New York: New York University Press, 2010), 120–140. See also Michelle Martinez, "Keeping Betty Ugly: Manufacturing Diversity for Network TV" (PhD diss., Arizona State University, 2015).

37. Quoted in Charles Savage, "A Judge's View of Judging Is on the Record," *New York Times,* May 14, 2009.

38. Cameron McCarthy and Greg Dimitriadis, "Governmentality and the Sociology of Education: Media, Educational Policy, and the Politics of Resentment," in *Race, Identity, and Representation in Education,* ed. Cameron McCarthy, Warren Crichlow, Greg Dimitradis, and Nadine Dolby (New York: Routledge, 2005), 321–336.

39. Molina-Guzmán, *Dangerous Curves,* 67.

40. Quoted in Molina-Guzmán, *Dangerous Curves,* 70.

41. Frank Tannenbaum, "Who Does Shakira Think She Is?," *Blender,* December– January 2001/2002; Tannenbaum, "Miss Universe," *Blender,* July 2005, 72–80.

42. Siobhan Grogan, "Don't Be Fooled by the Pictures," *Guardian,* December 2, 2002 (emphasis added).

43. Paul Young, "Shakira Rocks," *Maxim,* July 2002, 90–96.

44. This and my broader analysis draws from Cynthia Fuchs, "'There's My Territory': Shakira Crossing Over," in *From Bananas to Buttocks: The Latina Body in Popular Film and Culture,* ed. Myra Mendible (Austin: University of Texas Press, 2007), 167–182.

45. Corey Moss, "Shakira Calls for Peace, Explains Mongoose Mystery," MTV News, February 4, 2003. For more, see Hillary Frey, "Shakira's Pop," *Washington Post,* April 26, 2003; Hisham Aidi, *Rebel Music: Race, Empire, and the New Muslim Youth Culture* (New York: Vintage, 2014); Alona Wartofsky, "Pop's Fluent Asset," *Washington Post,* March 10, 2002.

46. Fuchs, "'There's My Territory'"; McKevitt, "'Watching War Made Us Immune.'"

47. David Bacon, "How U.S. Policies Fueled Mexico's Great Migration," *Nation,* January 23, 2012; Nils Gilman, Jesse Goldhammer, and Steven Weber, eds., *Deviant Globalization: Black Market Economy in the 21st Century* (New York: Continuum, 2011).

48. Sergio González Rodríguez, *The Femicide Machine* (Los Angeles: Semiotext(e), 2012).

49. Greg Grandin, "Democracy Derailed in Honduras," *Nation,* July 13, 2009.

50. Wertheim, "Trump and American Exceptionalism."

TEN

Black Ops Diplomacy and the Foreign Policy of Popular Culture

Penny M. Von Eschen

IN NOVEMBER 2010, TELEVISION VIEWERS encountered an action-packed commercial featuring heavily armed young people and adult civilians (including NBA star Kobe Bryant in Nike sportswear) engaged in fierce urban combat, with the rapid-fire of automatic weaponry and explosions punctuating the strains of "Gimme Shelter" by the Rolling Stones ("War, children, is just a shot away") and a declaration at the end that "There's a Soldier in All of Us." If the tagline evokes U.S. military recruitment ads, the commercial in fact promoted *Call of Duty: Black Ops,* an Activision video game in the wildly successful franchise that has been hailed as a "state of the art" first-person shooter game. Upon release, the game broke first-day sales records and sold 9.4 million copies in the first week. Described in the *New York Times* as "exciting, intense, and engrossing," the game reviewer explained that *Black Ops* "has become the definitive first-person shooter game."[1]

In the commercial's offer of personal pleasure and empowerment through an equal-opportunity, multicultural orgy of decontextualized warfare, an adorable little plump girl, a hotel concierge, a cab driver, and a short-order cook strike cinematic poses as they do battle alongside Bryant and television late-night host Jimmy Kimmel. Activision, the leading company in the multibillion-dollar video game market, an industry that has now eclipsed Hollywood, beckons to the gaming community and beyond—to the "Soldier in All of Us." One may wonder what response actual combat veterans might have to the ad's realistic, albeit low-risk, portrayal of military combat heroism as a matter of recreational choice available to ordinary civilians. Be that as it may, the ad's corporate, multicultural, and neoliberal scenario of decontextualized and sanitized war (children, just a shot away) is celebrated as cathartic and patriotic—only a game.

If the ad's scenes of armed civilians waging war against an unspecified enemy seek to enlist a community of gamers, the game itself invites consumers to replay the Cold War, to stage reenacted victories, and to participate in imagined future wars with Russia. Such Russia bashing is hardly unique to video games. Just steps from the U.S. Capitol, a toppled decapitated statue of Lenin imported from Tevriz, Russia, lies near the entrance of the Newseum in Washington, DC. Visitors encounter the statue in a corner, displayed near a photograph depicting the removal of another Lenin statue. On the adjacent wall, visitors can glimpse another photograph of yet another statue of the Bolshevik leader from Bucharest, this one with a noose around the neck. In Las Vegas, Nevada, diners stroll past a gargantuan statue of Lenin, also headless, to dine in Russian imperial splendor at the Red Square Restaurant and Vodka Lounge. For $14, a triumphalist tippler can order such cocktails as the "Chernobyl" or "Rude Cosmo-not" martini. Those seeking a more rarified experience can enter the "exclusive" Vodka Vault, where they can "do shots off Vladimir Lenin's head" with a choice of two hundred varieties of top-shelf vodka, starting at $200 per shot. Vulgar displays and commodifications of what Mikhail Gorbachev termed America's "winner's complex" have proliferated in the post-9/11 years—despite the fact that Russia was a stalwart ally of the United States in the war on terror.

This essay considers contemporary machinations of benevolent empire through the prism of the "new Cold War" with Russia, from the mid-2000s onward, with a particular focus on the relationship between claims about the Cold War and the war on terror. On the one hand, like Joseph Nye's idea of "soft power," the notion of benevolent empire—the idea that the United States has led through example and has appealed to the outside world by spreading its culture, values, and economic system rather than traditional modes of imperial control and coercion—falls apart when held to actual historical examples or practices. Even the most seemingly benign exercise of U.S. power, such as humanitarian aid or cultural circulation, has depended on a level of resources that in turn has depended on military intervention as an integral part of U.S. policy.[2]

On the other hand, the wielding of "soft power" in economic, cultural, and political arenas is critical to understanding post-Soviet United States-Russia relations from the "new" Cold War in the 2000s to the unprecedented and seemingly paradoxical Russian alliances of the Trump administration. In a global order shaped by neoliberalism—dedicated to diminishing or destroying regulatory and redistributive state capacities even as its architects fundamentally rely on state violence to enforce its policies—foreign policy making increasingly becomes the province of unconventional actors, at once powerful and unaccountable to nation states.[3] Foreign policy, like the conception of empire advanced by Michel Hardt and Antonio Negri in *Empire*, is both ubiquitous and decentered, enacted by a congeries of nongovernmental organizations (NGOs), popular culture, corporations, and social media sites rivaling and often exceeding the influence of nation states.[4] First visible in crises involving failed states but echoing throughout the developed world, private actors and NGOs increasingly do the things states used to do. Much of this work involves providing relief and social services that states are no longer able or willing to undertake. But at the same time, as Jan Eckel has argued, what many NGO and human rights activists consider an "ethical imperative of intervention" often entails working for "profound changes in the political systems and even social practices of foreign countries."[5]

Benevolent empire has historically worked through the projection of soft power, with a revolving door between corporations, NGOs, and human rights groups on the one hand and the State Department on the other. The neoliberal post-Soviet order, however, has allowed new tools for U.S. soft power intervention, enabling robust involvement in elections in the post-Soviet sphere by U.S. politicians, NGOs, and human rights groups. More recently, the U.S. state has become vulnerable to external destabilization as Russians have stepped up their own soft power efforts, as well as internal capture by authoritarian figures such as Donald Trump. Building on GOP voter suppression since 2000 and the gerrymandering of congressional districts, Trump hacked American democracy by manipulating corporate media and capitalizing on a weak and fragmented party and electoral system.[6]

In the deterioration of U.S.-Russian relations, a host of nonstate actors from lobbyists to NGOs and popular culture products, including video games, reshaped public discourse and power relations by calling into being a new public eager for geopolitical intervention based not on facts but a socially constructed "tabloid geopolitical imaginary."[7] Fighting back, Russians used many of these seemingly privatized structures, from banks to NGOs—and drew on an old Cold War playbook—to fashion an effective public diplomacy that went over the head of the U.S government and "straight to the people." Effectively courting an alliance of National Rifle Association (NRA) members, antigay activists, and right-wing Christians drawn to Putin's advocacy of traditional Christian values, Putin generated not just sympathy but admiration in Trump's base, a key factor in the apparent lack of concern about Russian interference in the 2016 U.S. presidential election.[8]

Highlighting the interactions of multiple agents in U.S.-Russian relations, I focus on the imagined political landscape of *Call of Duty* games as they move between war on terror and Cold War scenarios and the construction of truth and subjectivity in the failed 2008 John McCain and Sarah Palin campaign. Both were potent and productive sites of meaning making, producing a synergy between the corporate narratives purveyed by Activision's *Call of Duty* Cold War gaming scenarios on the one hand and the political sphere on the other.

I focus on Senator John McCain's role in the Georgia crisis; McCain's interactions with Georgian politicians exceeded the scope of his office as he challenged President Bush through his aggressive promotion of anti-Russian policies. While the later Ukraine crisis and the 2016 presidential campaign are beyond the scope of this essay, I argue that in its spectacle of populist authoritarianism and disregard for facts, expertise, and the very idea of the truth, the 2008 campaign was a precursor to the Trump campaign and election victory in 2016. The apparent reversal of hostility toward Russia evident in Trump's campaign is a twist in a broader drama involving new techniques of intelligence and information warfare in an era of weakened states and fragmented publics.

Trump's campaign and governance represented a rupture in U.S. political norms, but not a sudden rupture. The ascendancy of authoritarian populism depended on a white nationalist vision of the United States besieged from without by nonwhite immigrants and Muslims and from within by racialized minorities viewed as undeserving beneficiaries of government largesse. This recasting of Cold War binaries of infiltration and subversion by Soviets and their agents shows Trump's effective strategy of mobilizing white resentment among his supporters and sowing fear among targeted populations. The utter demonization of Hillary Clinton, his wanton lying, and the authoritarian spectacle witnessed at Trump's campaign rallies built on a global process long underway, in which weakened Western industrial democracies, unable and often unwilling to protect citizen/workers from the destructive effects of "globalization," have turned to right-wing authoritarian leaders. I put *globalization* in quotes to emphasize that the process was not inevitable, driven by supposedly inexorable market forces. Rather, the ways that global economic integration occurred, accelerating in the 1970s and then taking new forms after the collapse of the Soviet bloc, was the result of the deliberate decisions and deregulatory policies of U.S. and Western politicians, bankers, and financiers whose highly profitable actions deepened economic inequality within their societies and globally. In the U.S. context, with an external Cold War enemy purportedly vanquished, U.S. norms of political compromise and acceptance of the legitimacy of the opposition party quickly eroded. Republican Party politics embraced partisan antigovernment warfare predicated on scapegoating enemies within. The litany of post-Cold War attacks on internal enemies includes Dan Quayle's targeting of poor African Americans and single women in his family values and law-and-order speech of May 1992. That same year, Pat Buchanan declared that the "culture wars" had replaced the Cold War. Following the 1993 hysteria over the Clinton health-care proposal, likening it to "cradle to grave slavery," the scorched-earth partisanship of Newt Gingrich's Contract with America culminated in his 1995 and 1996 shutdown of the government over Republican attempts to slash government spending, an agenda facilitated by antiblack racial stereotypes of crime and welfare.

From the early 1990s conception of outlaw, rogue states to the post-9/11 "Axis of Evil," Republican rhetoric resorted to a similar Manichaeanism, a rearticulation of external enemies that questioned the legitimacy of diplomacy toward those deemed hostile to U.S. interests. In part, the rejection of diplomacy drew on the triumphalist story of the United States supposedly having won the Cold War through the assertion of military might.

My title, "Black Ops Diplomacy," employs an oxymoron to highlight a popular geopolitical imaginary that not only views military operations, particularly special forces covert operations, as the default mode of international relations but also exudes contempt for diplomacy. John McCain voiced such disdain for diplomacy during the 2008 presidential campaign. The senator claimed that his rival, Barack Obama, would "condone the positions of our enemies" and "legitimize illegal behavior by sitting down for negotiations without preconditions." McCain lamented that Obama "thinks that he can negotiate with Iran and get anything he wants."[9]

The 2008 campaign unveils the renunciation of political expertise and procedures in yet another way. In putting forward an inexperienced, charismatic vice-presidential candidate in Alaskan governor Sarah Palin, the campaign seemed to reject knowledge, facts, and logic as basic qualifications for a "leader of the free world." With her "authentic" demeanor and syntax, Palin's evident weaknesses, combined with her dominionist fervor, only enhanced her appeal to many Republicans. To the astonishment of political observers, Palin's deficiencies resonated with a broad swath of the Republican base. There would be more astonishment to come, as Palin was in important ways a precursor to Donald Trump.

Emphasizing the production of meaning in the interwoven realms of cultural production, media, and politics, this essay proceeds in three sections.[10] The first section historicizes the relationship between claims about the Cold War and the war on terror and examines the synergetic production of meaning across and between seemingly unrelated cultural and political spheres. It ends by considering the institutional relationship between the U.S. military and the *Call of Duty* franchise. The second section outlines the breakdown of U.S.-Russian relations, with the Activision games coinciding with the new Cold War with Russia and the 2008 presidential campaign. In the third and longest section, while highlighting political and epistemological resonances between the games and the 2008 presidential campaign, I turn to a focus on the games themselves, noting two critically important but distinct elements: first, the subjectivity encouraged and produced in first-person shooter and zombie modes and in online social sites and second, the production of a realm of people-to-people undiplomacy. The foreign policy controversies produced by the games themselves offer a glimpse into the power dynamics and new modes of warfare unleashed by neoliberalism.

CULTURE, POWER, AND DISSING DIPLOMACY

The delegitimation of diplomacy in foreign affairs governance against a background of escalating U.S.-Russian tensions did not simply gain a larger following through popular culture. Cultural production was critical in producing an alternate geopolitical reality where political compromise, diplomacy, and conceptions of human rights had no place. The sentiments produced by popular culture enabled elites to mobilize consent for an interventionist foreign policy by neoconservative Republicans. Yet there are certainly no direct correlations between the production of meaning in popular culture and any particular political position. Indeed, describing the "monster power" of "rootless white males," Steve Bannon intuited that a digital world of "intense young men" who "disappeared for days and even weeks into alternative realities" could be transformed for his political purposes.[11] In this case, rather than interventionist instincts directed at Russians, Bannon nurtured pro-gun, antigay, white nationalist alliances with Russians who were all too happy to cooperate as they built dialogues with the NRA and the National Organization for Marriage, whose president, Brian Brown, visited Russia four times in four years and testified in 2013 before the Russian Duma (Parliament) "as Russia adopted a series of anti-gay laws."[12]

My analysis posits a dialectic between the constitution of power though a social reshaping of reality—for example, politicians calling into being a constituency that recognizes their claims as aligning with their own—and individual participation or recalcitrance in this recasting of social reality. I reject any notion of passive reception in this process. Whether thinking about the dynamics of a Palin rally or displays of triumphalism in popular cultural stagings of the Cold War, people actively see, hear, smell, and engage the sites. Encounters with representations of the past or active engagements in reenactments in museums or video games may subtly, perhaps dramatically, reinforce, challenge, or alter prior assumptions and beliefs. As museum visitors, consumers of post-Soviet kitsch, and gamers participate and react, popular culture becomes a field for the production of knowledge and subjectivity in ways that may or may not have been intended by the cultural producers and entrepreneurs. Hence, a gaming public, like the voting public, is unstable, and the *Call of Duty* franchise cannot be said to represent hegemonic American values or interests. Yet at stake in these contested visions of the Cold War is the power to reshape political knowledge and points of reference, the power to open or foreclose possibilities to imagine the future. Or as Edward Said put it, "The power to narrate, or to block other narratives from forming and emerging, is very important to culture and imperialism, and constitutes one of the main connections between them."[13]

Popular culture was critical in developing a narrative about the relationship between the Cold War and the war on terror in which Americans were at once victors and victims. The *Call of Duty* franchise mediated contradictions between Cold War triumphalist claims that "we won" the Cold War through an assertion of military might, on the one hand, and fear, on the other hand, promoting American innocence and victimhood through conflating Russia and terrorism in a supposed past as well as a supposed future. Paralleling the escalation of U.S.-Russian tensions over the expansion of the North Atlantic Treaty Organization (NATO) but also marking the period when Russia was a critical ally of the United States in the war on terror, the *Call of Duty* franchise released four games between 2007 and 2012 premised on Russia as a major U.S. adversary. *Call of Duty 4: Modern Warfare,* released in 2007 and set in 2011, and its sequel, *Call of Duty Modern Warfare 2,* both envision terrorism—attacks in Europe and an attack on the United States—as emanating from an unholy alliance of ultranationalist Russians and separatists in an unnamed but small and oil-rich country in the Middle East. The game's fictitious dictator, Khaled Al-Asad, signals not simply Bashar al-Assad, president of Syria, for the more geopolitically informed. More importantly, the Middle Eastern dictator hails an indiscriminate Islamophobia, conflating richly diverse cultures and forms of Islam into what is posited as a single and inherently violent whole.

Writer Moustafa Bayoumi and the legal historian Aziz Rana have called our attention to the relationship between anticommunism and Islamophobia. Islamophobia operates within a different logic than forms of racism that mark perceived difference and inferiority on or within the body. Islamophobia, as recently illustrated in the rhetoric of Donald Trump, Steve Bannon, and Michael Flynn, views Muslim people not as having a religion or a culture but rather as having made an ideological choice to align themselves with an ideology that is inherently violent. In February of 2016, Flynn tweeted, "Islam is not necessarily a religion but a political system that has a religious doctrine behind it."[14] Like communism, Islam is viewed as a political ideology, and Islamophobia resuscitates the language and logic of the 1950 National Security Document 68, which names the Soviet Union as a slave society to which its adherents have willingly submitted. Steve Bannon, who was a top strategic adviser to President Donald Trump, described Islam as submissive, arguing on his Breitbart News radio program that "Islam is not a religion of peace—Islam is a religion of submission" on the rise as Christianity is dying out.[15]

Calling gamers to duty in the war on terror through the activation of Cold War tropes, *Call of Duty: Black Ops* (2010) reenacted such events as U.S. attempts to assassinate Fidel Castro and U.S. missions in Vietnam, only to end with the thwarting of an imagined 1968 toxic chemical weapon attack by the Soviets on the United States. *Modern Warfare 3* (2011) imagined a 2016 surprise Russian invasion of the United States in which the player engages in firefights with Russian troops in the streets of Washington, DC, and an armed conflict with China in 2025. Like *Metal Gear Solid 2* (2001), also imagining Russian instigators of terror attacks against the United States, and the 2005 Cold War-themed *Metal Gear Solid 3* (set in 1964), all four *Call of Duty* games were wildly successful and broke industry sales records.[16]

By 2011, Activision, the makers of the *Call of Duty* franchise, had garnered enough cultural cachet that *Time* magazine was willing to lend its logo and cover design to advertise the release of *Modern Warfare 3*. The faux cover

FIGURE 10.1. Image of a mock-up of an Activision promotional poster with artist filter and imposed flipped title of *Time-Life* cofounder and editor Henry Luce's 1941 essay "The American Century." Created by Maceo Gaines.

showed a world "on the brink" with New York City under attack by Russia in the year 2016 (see figure 10.1). Indeed, exposing an inversion of cultural capital— and likely turning *Time-Life* founder and editor Henry Luce over in his grave—*Time* hoped to boost its brand recognition and credibility with a younger audience by associating the logo with *Call of Duty*.[17]

In the context of NATO expansion and repeated warnings about outlaw states, battling Russian enemies in the virtual streets of the nation's capital imagines a world weary of the ideal of international cooperation. These cultural representations and fantasies not only mitigate against historical and political understandings of war, in setting up Russia as a purveyor of terrorism, they efface Russia's actual support of the United States after 9/11 and project onto Russia U.S. attempts to control Caspian oil supplies.[18]

Along with the promotion of a hawkish foreign policy over right-wing cable television and talk radio, a long-standing collaboration between the military and the video game industry produced claims about the war on terror in what journalist Simon Parkin has aptly termed the "military-entertainment complex." The scholar Roger Stahl has documented the extensive military employment of video games in the training of soldiers.[19] In the 1980s, the U.S. Defense Advanced Research Projects Agency (DARPA) approached video game developers with "the idea of writing video games that could be used to train soldiers."[20] Current and former government and military officials who have consulted for the industry include members of the Navy SEALSs and other special operations units.[21] The U.S. Army has its own consultation bureau to service the high-demand soliciting of military officials by Hollywood filmmakers and the video game industry for expert advice.[22]

The close collaboration between the *Call of Duty* franchise and the U.S. military included the consultation and promotion of *Black Ops 2* by none other than Oliver North. In addition, Hank Keirsey, a "retired Army Lieutenant Colonel and decorated combat veteran who had served during the Cold War and the first Gulf War," had been assigned through the military consultation bureau to advise initial game development. Initially suspicious of game developers, Keirsey quickly embraced what he viewed as a shared energy and commitment between soldiers and game developers. Impressed by the imaginative scope of the *Call of Duty* franchise and its implications for envisioning future warfare, the military hired *Call of Duty* writer and producer Dave Anthony.[23] Anthony's appeal stemmed from his "out of the box thinking on future threats" and intrigue about his ability to "propose proactive solutions."[24] Reporting on the cooperation between the military and the Treyarch group (an umbrella parent of Activision) producing *Black Ops 3*, MSN reported that the military—through DARPA, the section of the Department of Defense formed in 1958 in response to the 1957 Soviet launching of *Sputnik* and responsible for emerging military technologies—was interested in "bio-augmentation or human enhancement" involving the use of "various neurotechnologies, including neural implants to improve the performance of the human mind and body." *Black Ops 3* features augmented special ops soldiers; players can customize their soldiers with new cyber systems, programming them not only to run faster and jump higher but to process information faster and more efficiently. Indeed, the collaboration was facilitated by the Obama administration's "Brain Research Advancing Innovative Neurotechnologies (BRAIN) initiative, backed by $300 million in funding" and aimed at developing "reliable neural interface technology."[25]

THE NEW COLD WAR WITH RUSSIA AND ITS DIPLOMATIC ALTERNATIVES

As live military research imitated the imaginary world of gaming, the growth of a tabloid geopolitical imaginary and the deterioration of U.S.-Russian relations took place against the backdrop of sharply divided opinion in the United States and internationally about the potential for diplomatic solutions to the vexing problems facing the international community.

In the 2008 campaign, GOP nominee McCain took up the cause of Georgia to promote the isolation of Russia and the expansion of NATO. The deterioration of U.S.-Russian relations accelerated in tandem with NATO expansion and U.S. oil pipeline projects in the former Soviet bloc, which were pushed aggressively by the U.S. oil industry from at least 1995 onward. The Republicans' 1994 Contract with America made expanding NATO a central tenet of the party's foreign policy demands, along with its goal of limiting U.S. involvement in actions by the United Nations (UN). A *New York Times* 1995 editorial discussed the "Cold War Nostalgia" of Republican legislators, who "press[ed] ahead with a mischievous piece of legislation that would undo the Clinton Administration's modest efforts to adjust U.S. national policy to post-cold war realities." The legislation, the *Times* continued, "would increase pressure for higher defense spending, revive efforts to develop star wars missile defense systems, encourage reckless expansion of NATO defense guarantees to Eastern Europe, and hobble U.S. participation in United Nations peacekeeping."[26]

In 1999, the Czech Republic, Hungary, and Poland became the first former Soviet bloc states to join NATO. Leaders of these countries had pursued membership in NATO. After first questioning the relevance of NATO and the Warsaw Pact as irrelevant Cold War creations, Václav Havel came to see NATO's expansion as an important form of cooperation that would stabilize Europe—perhaps a consolation for the loss of his original dream of demilitarized multilateralism. Yet NATO's expansion led to the 2002 invitation to seven countries to join— Lithuania, Estonia, Latvia, Bulgaria, Romania, Slovakia, and Slovenia—setting off what was to be the first "new Cold War with Russia."[27]

By 2005, scholars such as Stephen F. Cohen, as well as former Soviet leader Mikhail Gorbachev, criticized U.S. triumphalism and the wasted opportunities for improved U.S.-Russian relations, warning of a new Cold War.[28] In 2006, Gorbachev mused that "Americans have a severe disease—worse than AIDS. It's called the winner's complex."[29] Amid mounting tensions, Gorbachev declared in 2008: "We had 10 years after the Cold War to build a new world order and yet we squandered them." Gorbachev, like James Baker, secretary of state under President George H. W. Bush, believed at the time of the Malta Summit on December 3, 1989, that NATO would not expand, and certainly not to Russia's borders. For Gorbachev, promises to Georgia and Ukraine about future NATO membership in 2002 signaled an attempt to extend the U.S. sphere of influence into Russia's backyard.[30]

Later, as tensions over Ukraine led to the effective collapse of the Obama administration's 2009 "reset" with Russia, former U.S. ambassador to the Soviet Union Jack Matlock Jr. argued that the "U.S. and Europe brought on this whole mess in the first place by trying to place military bases outside of Russia." Comparing active American influence in Ukraine politics to the prospect of foreigners leading Occupy Wall Street movements, Matlock argued that American policy had provoked Russia by telling Ukrainians and Georgians, "You can join NATO, and that will solve your problems for you."[31] For these critics, the problem was that the United States was taking sides in internal disputes and actively fomenting dissent rather than leaving countries to work out their own paths and choices about political and economic reform.

The spectacle of NGOs and aspiring politicians making foreign policy surfaced in the "going rogue" foreign policy celebrated by Palin and advanced by Republican candidates and McCain during the 2008 presidential campaign. As Palin declared her willingness to attack Russia if she were in the Oval Office, McCain's involvement in the 2008 Georgia crisis prompted questions of propriety from the media, the Obama campaign, and even President George W. Bush.

The Georgia crisis erupted into war on August 7, 2008, when the Georgian government launched an attack on a rebel group based in the city of Tskhinvali, South Ossetia, a province that had been part of Georgia within the Soviet Union. South Ossetia had declared its independence from the Soviet Union in 1991. Georgia attempted to reestablish control, leading to the 1991–1992 war, which ended in the de facto secession of South Ossetia as well as Abkhazia.

To this day, U.S. press accounts of the 2008 conflict routinely omit the fact that Georgia attacked before Russia did, portraying the war as a simple act of Russian aggression. And indeed, Russians remember the Georgia crisis as the time they lost the information war—with international media showing invading Georgian tanks but attributing them to Russia—a lesson that Russians would not forget as they vowed to step up their efforts at information wars.[32] In response to the Georgian attack, Russian troops repulsed the Georgian military in Tskhinvali and occupied part of Georgia until August 23. A European Union (EU) commission ruled a year later that Georgia had initiated the conflict by invading South Ossetia in violation of international law. Finding fault with all three parties, the EU report rejected the claim by Georgian president Mikheil Saakashvili that Russia had initiated the conflict. At the same time, the report branded the secession of South Ossetia and Abkhazia from Georgia to have been "illegal and Russian recognition of the two 'states' in violation of international law."[33]

Inserting himself into the conflict, McCain told Saakashvili, "I know I speak for every American when I say . . . today we are all Georgians."[34] As one journalist remarked, "Spare me. You couldn't find one American in a thousand who could find Georgia on a map." McCain added that "the thoughts and prayers and support of the American people are with that brave little nation as they struggle for their freedom and independence."[35] As McCain ridiculed Obama's call for diplomacy, the Arizona senator emphasized his past trips and experience in the region. Saakashvili reported speaking with McCain several times a day. The crisis provided background for McCain's relentless criticism of Obama's inexperience and naiveté. Further inquiry into McCain's Georgia policy reveals the stakes that shaped his bellicose stance and the nonstate actors involved.[36]

Randy (Randall James) Scheunemann, McCain's principal foreign policy advisor during his campaign, was a board member of the neoconservative Project for the New American Century (PNAC) and president of PNAC's

Committee for the Liberation of Iraq. In the months he worked for the McCain campaign, earning $70,000, his two-man lobbying firm Orion Strategies received $270,000 from the Georgian regime of Saakashvili, with marching orders to get Georgia a NATO war guarantee.[37] In fact, Scheunemann's firm had received $800,000 since 2004 to bring Georgia into the NATO alliance and was paid by Romania and Latvia to do the same."[38]

McCain's hawkishness—his inability to imagine diplomatic solutions—mirrored the campaign's assault on facts. In the 2008 election, the experiences of candidate John McCain as a prisoner of war (POW) in North Vietnam rose to unimpeachable knowledge about the realities of war and foreign policy. Prior to 2000, McCain had invoked his experiences of torture as a POW to defend his right to use the epithet "gook" to refer to his Vietnamese prison guards.[39] Candidate McCain asserted that the American war in Vietnam had been winnable and that the war in Iraq was winnable. He charged that Obama "would rather lose a war in order to win a political campaign" than commit to a U.S. victory in Iraq. McCain repeatedly stated that the United States could win any war if only the will to do so existed.[40] Evidence to the contrary, in his view, was simply appeasement.

This elevation of the authority of the willful individual as the final arbiter of truth is antipolitical. In this world of "knowledge," there is no room for politics, for negotiation, or for considering the possibility that any interests of one's opponent might be legitimate. The substitution of bluster for facts was dramatically evident in the 2008 U.S. presidential election and in the fierce partisan battles that followed. "Woman warrior" politicians, such as Palin and Minnesota congresswoman Michele Bachmann, can simply make things up, such as the claim that Barack Obama was not a U.S. citizen, or that Obama was a Muslim, with no accountability. After the campaign, Palin used her celebrity to trumpet her status as a climate change denier. Confusing climate with weather, she posted on Facebook, "Global warming my gluteus maximus," pointing to a picture of her daughter Piper in the snow after her May graduation.[41] In a world of unhinged referents where social knowledge is replaced by the subjective, through their unrestrained assault on facts, expertise, and decency, such politicians as Palin, Bachmann, and Trump (from his persistent "birtherism" charges that Obama was not born in the United States through the 2016 campaign and into the Trump administration) wage war on the very idea of truth and subjectivity.

GAMING NEOLIBERALISM: SUBJECTIVITY IN
FIRST-PERSON SHOOTER AND ZOMBIE MODE

Black Ops and its *Modern Warfare* predecessors are part of a synergistic field of cultural practices, performances, and enactments that taken together reboot the Cold War conflict, efface the actual history of the Cold War, and produce a powerful commonsense narrative about the relationship between the Cold War and the war on terror. Playing through *Black Ops,* I ask what kind of knowledge and subjectivities are created in these enactments. Arguing that the structure of the games undermines participant senses of historical/political reality, the games' refusal of social knowledge is further implicated in the paralyzing polarization and dysfunction in contemporary U.S. politics. Finally, I consider the games in the context of online sociality within a community of gamers as well as in the production of what I call a people-to-people undiplomacy.

To play is to immerse one's self. Subject position and narrative are fundamentally interwoven; form and function unite. As demonstrated by the gaming industry's reliance on military consultants, designers put great stock in authenticity. Some gamers dispute the importance of narrative, noting that after beating the game in first-person shooter mode, most players play in online multiplayer modes. Yet with an eye to manufacturing a realistic experience, game designers emphasize the narrative plot along with the visual and aural prompts that move the shooter through the game. Like *Black Ops,* *Modern Warfare,* the immediate predecessor to *Black Ops,* and its successor *Modern Warfare 2* both set sales records and were acclaimed for their story lines as well as their technical advancements. (And it bears repeating that both games imagine Russian attacks on the United States.) In *Modern Warfare,* ultranationalist Russians start a civil war in Russia and plot a coup in the Middle East in order to draw the United States in. Played from the perspective of U.S. Marines or NATO allies, the player battles across the Middle East, Azerbaijan, Russia, and Ukraine, and most of the thirty thousand U.S. marines are killed when Russian terrorists detonate a nuclear device. (And then things get worse.) *Modern Warfare 2* jumps to 2016. The ultranationalists have taken over Russia, and the terrorist Vladimir Makarov stages a civilian massacre there, framing a Central Intelligence Agency (CIA) agent and convincing people that the United States is responsible. Russia launches a surprise invasion of the United States, and the player is now fighting Russia in the streets of Washington, DC, and on top of the Capitol build-

FIGURE 10.2. *Call of Duty*'s faux Fidel. © Activision.

ing. The November 2012 release, *Black Ops 2*, revisits the Cold War with branching story lines set in the late 1980s in southern Africa, Afghanistan, and Latin America, then jumps to 2025, where a new Cold War with China has been set off by a cyberattack on China followed by the Chinese banning the export of all rare minerals.

In the first-person mode, *Black Ops* is an entirely scripted narrative with no moral decisions or alternative narratives available to the player. Combining real historical settings mirroring the foreign policy objectives of the United States, the game's scripted narrative produces strong claims to authenticity. Opening with a reenactment of the 1961 U.S. invasion of the Bay of Pigs (including the player's virtual attempt to assassinate Fidel Castro, punctuating the CIA's myriad real-world assassination attempts—see figure 10.2), the player's missions from 1961–1968 include imprisonment and escape from a Soviet gulag and a journey through Vietnam's Mekong Delta. The game features historical figures, events, and settings. Players of *Black Ops* encounter Fidel Castro, John F. Kennedy, and Secretary of Defense Robert McNamara. These reenactments promise to rewrite failed policies and objectives, indulging in the visceral fantasy of toppling Castro "this time."

As the *New York Times* reviewer enthused, "I couldn't wait to go back and try to assassinate Castro and kill Russians." The game reinforces a bipolar

Cold War in which Third World Asians, Africans, and Latin Americans are mere backdrops to the "real" fight against the Soviets. In other words, Cuba and Vietnam serve as background proxies to the main fight with the Russians. The game's celebration of counterinsurgency and combat violence constitutes a fantasy do-over, this time with more firepower.

At the same time, the game doesn't simply replay the Cold War; it provides riveting twists experienced through 1968 flashbacks that unpack a 1961–1968 U.S. Cold War narrative. As the game opens, I/Mason am under interrogation (with torture) by someone desperate to decipher the meaning of numbers that are going through my/Mason's brain. The game moves in time between the 1968 interrogation and flashbacks, including meetings with President Kennedy and Secretary of Defense McNamara. As mysterious numbers flash through my/Mason's head, the interrogators force Mason to relive a series of missions ("Bay of Pigs—you were there"). First, I/Mason am in Cuba at the Bay of Pigs, thinking I have assassinated Fidel Castro only to find out I killed a double. I/Mason am captured and taken to a gulag camp in the Soviet Union, where I am befriended by Reznev, a Soviet defector. Reznev and I escape—so I think—with the ultimate goal of capturing a Nazi scientist now working on a chemical weapon for the Soviets, along with the Russian general Nikita Dragovitch. The pursuit takes me/Mason to Vietnam. With a vague reference to "Tet" placing me in 1968, there are no Vietnamese whatsoever. I/Mason am captured for interrogation. I/Mason flash back to Dallas, seeing myself with a gun pointed at Kennedy. "Oswald has been compromised." I/Mason killed Kennedy? I/Mason recover my history (or do I?) through the interrogators. Back at the gulag, I/Mason had initially been brainwashed by General Dragovitch and programmed to kill Kennedy. Interrogators tell me/Mason that Reznev, who I believe I have been working with for the past five years, has actually been dead the entire time. I/Mason had been rebrainwashed by Reznev to stop Friedrich Steiner, a former Nazi scientist who had defected to the Soviet Union. Why did I go off mission and kill the Nazi scientist? I am asked. I was supposed to capture him. I was trying to stop them—but from what? The numbers—what do the numbers mean? The interrogators are still desperate for the numbers.

In an obscene displacement of the fact that in 1968 the United States was poisoning Vietnam and its people with Agent Orange, in the game I/Mason am the only one able to stop the activation of Soviet sleeper cells in the United States ready to stage a chemical warfare attack. Since I/Mason killed the Nazi scientist, I am the only remaining key. I/Mason successfully break the code and give my interrogators the location of the Soviet base on a ship, preventing the attack. But if I/Mason think that the series of brainwashings and actions have been unpacked, in the final scene, Reznev speaks to me/ Mason, undermining any resolution and any sense of objective reality.

Filled with double agents, brainwashing, and defectors, the game produces a story and experience evocative of the Manchurian candidate and John le Carré. I/Mason/you not only is undergoing interrogation and attack but is enduring a disintegration of the self through brainwashing. Coupled with the experience of the breakdown of the real and the fabricated in the experience of the first-person player, this goes well beyond undermining the historical record, raising an epistemological quandary that blurs the line between lies and truth, what can be known, and what cannot.[42] Unlike the Jason Bourne character in the Bourne trilogy, who achieves an implausible reintegration of the self through sheer strength of will as the superior agent, Mason's remaining doubt about his own actions and the role of his major Russian nemesis (the certainty of his death has also been undermined) reinforces the idea of the inaccessibility of stable truth in the Cold War. The reinforcement of the "truth" that nothing is what it seems, in tandem with the powerful subjective experience offered through the technical brilliance of the game with its innovative creation of first-person shooter subjectivity, ultimately leaves the fragmented agent/individual as the sole arbiter of truth.

NEOLIBERAL ZOMBIES

Directed by zombie-horror director George A. Romero, *Black Ops'* over the top "zombie mode" presents an alternate but, I would argue, reinforcing experience of a fragmented subject navigating a world without stable social or objective moorings. In a campy counter-post-1945 history spanning WWII to the 1960s, the discovery of element 115 in a meteorite in Japan has led to the creation of zombies. Romero explained that his idea for the game emerged from research he had done for a World War II movie. He had come upon Nazi documents with discussions of element 115 and crazy discussions of raising the dead.[43]

The alternate post–World War II reality revolves around four soldiers representing imperial Japan and Germany as well as the United States and the Soviet Union. At one point the zombies breach the Pentagon with John F. Kennedy, McNamara, Nixon, and Castro trapped inside and attempting to fight their way out. At another point, in a self-referential film within a game, the soldiers are trapped in a room and have to rely on four actors who are in a film directed by George A. Romero, but Romero has been infected and is transitioning to the undead. A later special *Black Ops* map game extension release included *Call of the Dead,* mapping locations from Romero's movies.[44] In hilarious trailers for the map version, Romero tells a zombie, "Get back to hair and make-up, you don't look dead enough." As the trailer closes, a zombified Romero emerges from the water.

Romero's 1968 *Night of the Living Dead* depicts, as he put it, the "monster within, the zombie being us," taking a stab as it were at the dark underside of Cold War/Vietnam War–era America, where the real horror is that Ben, the black hero, survives the zombies only to be perceived as a threat and killed by white law enforcement.[45] Romero's 2011 zombies take on a different valence. In zombie mode, the player experiences a relentless impersonal—and inhuman—assault, mirroring the assault on the self in neoliberal workplace and political environments. Just as neoliberalism cannot abide history—wiping out past practices, organic knowledge, and norms of every state or private organization it mows through (restructures)—it cannot tolerate a coherent modern subject. Neoliberal practices demand, instead, an infinitely malleable subject, zombified and commanded to respond to discrete tasks without questioning the logic, purpose, or outcome. If it is cathartic to kill a bunch of zombies, bringing a temporary relief from the onslaught, the exhausted and spent subject learns that the social contract is broken. They are coming to get you, and there is no one out there (no state) to come to the rescue when your town's water is poisoned (as in Flint, Michigan), your homes are flooded, or your child is sick and you do not have health care.

In an interview about the trailer for *Call of the Dead,* Romero calls his zombies "blue-collar monsters." In a totalizing trap, zombies are at once the impersonal force of chaos and the helpless and murderous rage of those infected by its poisons. And as the logic of the zombie is to bring chaos and human apocalypse, at the end of *Black Ops* zombie mode, the earth is destroyed. Destruction is the only solution.

The intertwining of desire and violence in the *Call of Duty* franchise is elaborated in multiple play modes. Undergirding Activision's claims to Cold War authenticity, the much-anticipated Berlin Wall extension of *Call of Duty: Black Ops* used actual maps of the city, recreating landmarks and streets. The Berlin Wall extension television advertisement begins with desire. To the soundtrack of the German-based band the Scorpions' international hit "Wind of Change," two men—one on each side of the wall—reach out to one another.

The commercial evolves from a classic Cold War trope—not based on the idea of an absolute other, but desire, how East and West become objects of mystery and longing for each other—but then evolves into an individual expression of violence. But if the Berlin Wall ad begins with desire, with guns turning into guitars and a peace dove flying in, with no foreshadowing and in complete dissonance with the song's history, in the *Call of Duty* ad, the peace dove explodes, and the guitars turn back into guns (spewing flames in a simultaneous ejaculation). The climactic resolution of desire in violence is fully borne out by the game.

Ironies abound when the song "Wind of Change" is contextualized. Later remembered as a song about the fall of the Berlin Wall, it was actually inspired by the August 1989 Moscow Music Peace Festival, a two-day hard rock festival in the one-hundred-thousand-seat Lenin Stadium, where Western heavy metal acts, including Ozzy Osbourne, Mötley Crüe, Cinderella, and Skid Row joined local bands such as Gorky Park and Brigada S. The festival inspired Scorpions vocalist Klaus Meine, who had grown up in the shadow of the Iron Curtain (but not in Berlin), to write the song, as it turned out, three months before the Berlin Wall came down. With its sentiments of hope and peace ("the world is closing in/and did you ever think/that we could be so close/like brothers") and, after the wall came down, a Wayne Isham-directed music video featuring the construction and then tearing down of the Berlin Wall, the song became a soundtrack for political and cultural revolution.[46] But employed in an advertising video for the Berlin Wall extension of *Call of Duty,* the video's effacement of Russia erases not only the song's genesis in solidarity with Soviet reform and antinuclear demilitarization, it suggests that history is consonant with libidinal, violent, right-wing populism.

The game's glorification of violence takes place in the particular sociality of online communities forged through multiplayer games and online discussion groups. There is a now vast genre of videos produced by gamers for other gamers that track real-time playing through games that are then voiced over with commentary, instructions, and advice on how to get through the game. In early 2010, "Goldglove" had over ninety-four thousand hits for his video showing gamers how to play through the Berlin Wall extension of *Black Ops.* Addressing "My people of the youtubes," Goldglove exemplifies this genre. I will return to this in a moment, but I want to underscore the casual effacement of historical and political reality. Calling out for online help in clarifying whether Berlin was divided by North/South or East/West, Goldglove both signals that this matters—because this is the Berlin Wall dressed up in historically authentic maps and references—and simultaneously that it doesn't matter because violence is the context and the story of the game.

Here, it is not simply that viewers lack historical context; the problem is that for the players, *Black Ops* provides *the* content as well as the context for knowledge and memory. Here, "my people of the youtubes" addresses a world in which speech and practice are untethered from the referent.

Goldglove's genuine solidarity with other gamers—"my people of the youtubes"—and his concern for the PlayStation 3 gamers and other gamers who had been denied his X-Boxer first access to the Berlin Wall game extension—"not fair that you have to wait a month"—sits juxtaposed with his casual embrace of violence and reveling in the aesthetic and sensual delights of blood: "Just can't get over that blood sticking snow—when I was playing I didn't really notice but now it is gorgeous—it's just a sexy time."

The sociality of the games is also seen in this commentary on the "There's a Soldier in All of Us" *Black Ops* commercial: "I nearly choked on my beverage when I saw this on the TV the other day. I love the fact that they have basketball star Kobe Bryant and late night talk-show host Jimmy Kimmel running around with people from all walks of life. Of course, you already know that there are all sorts of people playing with you online, but seeing it represented visually in this way really brings the point home and makes me smile."[47]

This online commentator, "Les," reads a highly controversial commercial – deplored by many for its casual glorification of war—as a warm shout-out to an intimately connected community of gamers. That makes him smile. What happens when friendship is forged and experienced in the context of violence, and what happens when violence is learned in the context of love? And what happens when that dynamic—arguably present in the military and a myriad of institutions—extends its reach to the virtual world? Can diplomacy/politics exist in this community of warmth, solidarity, guns, and unhinged referents?

Meanwhile, in the vacuum created by the exit of diplomacy, warfare morphs into ever-new forms. As *Call of Duty* military collaborations imagine new neurotechnologies facilitating communication with and enhancement of the individual soldier, in the merging virtual-physical worlds, a hollowed-out subject plugged into a Borg has new potential for maneuvering through a world of gutted out state-to-state relations.

GAMING INTERVENTIONS

The practice of gaming allows popular participation through first-person shooter enactments of a rebooted, darker Cold War. Paralleling increasing spats among U.S. politicians over policies toward Russia, fictional full-on warfare with Russia escalated in the virtual world, touching off real-world international incidents. In tandem with a bipartisan, aggressively anti-Russian foreign policy, the *Call of Duty* franchise enacted with gamers a shadow foreign policy through the subjectivities and worldview promoted in the games, as well as from the international controversies they provoked. Despite the open-ended engagements of gamers, the virtual Russia created by game designers arguably led an alarming number of Americans to imagine going to war with Russia over Ukraine by 2014 because they had already been fighting Russians in a campaign across Crimea and Ukraine and in hand-to-hand combat in the streets of DC and its suburbs for years in the *Call of Duty* and *Modern Warfare* games.

The lucrative *Call of Duty* franchise touched off multiple international controversies, prompting censorship bans by Germany and Cuba on certain games and Russian complaints of its potentially destabilizing effect on counterterrorism and foreign policy. The day after the January 24, 2011, terrorist bombing at the Domodedovo Airport in Moscow, *Russian Times* (RT) television noted a troubling similarity between the details of the bombing and the 2009 video game *Modern Warfare 2*'s "No Russian" story line. It is critical to note that the entire game, set in 2016, involves U.S. war with Russia. Ultranationalists have taken over Russia, and the terrorist Vladimir Makarov stages a civilian massacre in a fictitious Moscow airport. The Russian ultranationalists who have planned the bombing convince the public that the United States is responsible. Russia then launches a surprise invasion of the United States, and in these scenarios, the player is now fighting Russian forces in the streets of Washington, DC, and on top of the Capitol building.

The *Russian Times* coverage, as the *New York Times* reported, disclosed that counterterrorism experts from Russia, Europe, and the United States weighed a causal connection between the gaming segment and the terrorist bombing. In the "No Russian" segment, the gamer plays in character as a CIA agent who needs to establish credibility with the ultranationalists in his ultimate mission as a double agent. Hence, the character engages in terror attacks, gunning down civilians at the airport. In first-shooter mode, the game player has no choice and must mow down the civilians. RT broadcaster Lauren Lister reported that the November 2009 release surpassed $1 billion in sales in its first two months. Indeed, without buying the game, the "No Russian" segment could be viewed on YouTube. The segment had 870,000 YouTube views by the time of the bombing. Counterterrorist experts cautioned against drawing causal links between the game and the bombing, but the similarities raised questions about whether the perpetrators of the attack "might have trained using the game or others like it." Others argued that "those already radicalized," such as jihadists or al-Qaeda, could be influenced by the game.[48]

The fact that the segment required the gamer in first-person mode to commit an act of terrorism raised hackles, and the game was banned in Germany. Fearing for its profits, the franchise rushed out a toned-down version that allowed players to opt out of slaughtering innocents. Russians objected to other U.S. productions, including the film *Indiana Jones and the Crystal Skull*, released in 2008. Set in 1957, Harrison Ford returns as the anthropologist adventurer, this time matching wits with an evil KGB agent (Cate Blanchett). The predictable Cold War plot incensed Saint Petersburg Communist Party member Victor Perov: "What galls is how together with Americans we defeated Hitler; and how we sympathized when Bin Laden hit them. But they go ahead and scare kids with Communists. These people have no shame."[49]

Allowing that responses to video games may be as varied as the people who have played them, I still suggest that in the context of the 2007–2008 "new" Cold War with Russia and now the "new new" Cold War with Russia, the *Call of Duty* franchise introduces audiences to an open disregard for diplomacy and statecraft—a people-to-people *un*diplomacy, as it were. In an informal Bishkek, Kyrgyzstan, focus group in 2013 with a group of successful professional architects in their early thirties who were gamers, the participants admitted that the *Black Ops* story line was very stupid. But rather than interpreting it as "just a game," they thought *Black Ops* "definitely" represented the way Americans perceived the Cold War and that the game's portrayal of Cuba, the Soviet Union, and the Vietnam War was how the producers wanted people to perceive it. The players described the game as poorly translated into Russian. In the words of one of the participants, the "characters talk too much and the interrogations take too long and irritate the people who play the game as the 'illogical story line' unfolds through the perspective of flashbacks and many interrogation scenes where it is gradually revealed that the Russians had recoded his memory."[50]

The players further described the World War II predecessors of *Call of Duty* as creating a very crude version of Germans and Japanese; they are treacherous, they cheat, and they shoot you when you turn away. Russians are heroic, Germans are evil, and Japanese are inhuman, simply like animals. In the WWII games, Russians are strong and heroic, but other games portray Russians as helpless. Russians are portrayed as weak, unable to cope with problems of terrorism, or duped by terrorism such that Americans must fight Russian terrorists in cahoots with vaguely defined Middle Eastern terrorists. At the very least, the games confirm for these players that Americans are stupid and know nothing about Russia or the post-Soviet sphere.

This realm of cultural undiplomacy has worked in tandem with the expansion of NATO to produce an anti-American "fever" in Russia that observers contend goes beyond that of the Soviet era. Anger toward the United States, reported the *Washington Post* in 2015, is "at its worst since opinion polls began tracking it," with more than 80 percent of Russians holding negative views of the country.[51] Russian journalists have documented a widespread perception in Russia that after 1989, Russians modeled themselves after the West but "experienced humiliation and hardship in return." Evgeny Tarlo, a member of Russia's upper house of parliament, argued that after Russia had completely reoriented toward the West, Russia expected that "they would finally hug and kiss us and we would emerge in ecstasy." Instead, he argued, the West has been trying to destroy Russia.[52]

CONCLUSION

This sense of betrayal caused by what many Russians view as U.S. attempts to isolate Russia diplomatically and economically led intelligence services to strike back. In the 2016 U.S. election, Russian intelligence officials hacked Democratic Party e-mails and conducted information warfare against the U.S. electorate with a deluge of fake news stories. There was no shortage of "useful idiots" susceptible to Russian meddling in the election. Hyperpartisan GOP congressional scrutiny of Hillary Clinton's use of a private e-mail server as secretary of state now pales in comparison to confirmed contacts between the Trump campaign and Russian intelligence officials. Those contacts, flatly denied from the start by Trump and his associates, have been unearthed by investigative journalism. Such effective reporting was all too rare during the campaign, as credulous U.S. corporate media organizations reported the steady drip of negative stories about the Clinton campaign obtained from Wikileaks. Capitalizing on its reputation on the left as a whistle-blower, Wikileaks, by releasing hacked e-mails of the Democratic National Committee (DNC), convinced many progressive Democrats that the primary was rigged for Clinton against her rival, Vermont senator Bernie Sanders. And Federal Bureau of Investigation (FBI) director James Comey's unprecedented intrusions, whether motivated by bias or poor judgment, played no small part in Russia's hack of the election. Rebooting the Cold War in cyberspace, Russian intelligence and its legion of hackers left the U.S. flat-footed in a manner reminiscent of the *Sputnik* satellite launch in 1957, showing that they too can play at cyberwar and the projection of alternate realities.

It is impossible to determine the extent of the damage done to Hillary Clinton's campaign by Russian hacking and active attempts to influence U.S. politics or by Director Comey's interference just eleven days before the election. However bizarre the circumstances leading to Trump's election, a precondition for the candidate's success was the ongoing undermining of norms of diplomacy and political compromise at home, as Trump prevailed despite his vitriolic attacks against the intelligence community and atrocious personal conduct. Throughout his campaign and in the first months of his presidency, Trump wielded executive power, bypassing legislative and governing processes altogether—the state is him. Contemptuous of precedent or procedure, Trump willfully sowed chaos and contemplated dismantling government regulatory agencies. And in predictable Orwellian fashion, the administration and its allies accused the bureaucrats and government employees, who do the unsung and essential work of keeping the wheels of government turning, of functioning as a hostile "deep state," a concept mostly invoked by left-wing critics of U.S. foreign policy to criticize the activities of a covert, unaccountable alliance of military contractors and intelligence operatives without the oversight of elected officials.[53] If during the Cold War the U.S. government claimed legitimacy by offering citizens the benefits of consumerism and the social safety net and the NATO alliance abroad, the Trump administration now demands payment from allies and assures the abandoned citizens/subjects that they will be taken care of by an authority figure, only to engage in constant kleptocratic dealmaking at his luxury offices and estates, subsidized by taxpayers.

NOTES

1. Seth Schiesel, "Suddenly the Cold War Is a Cool Event," *New York Times,* November 12, 2010, www.nytimes.com/2010/11/13/arts/television/13duty.html?ref =video-games.

2. In other words, historically, the United States has dominated in a global economy through access to and control over resources that have often been secured through interventions such as in Iraq in 1991 and 2003, covert operations in Iran in 1953, and the Congo in 1960 and beyond.

3. From its first mass implementation in Chile and Bolivia, to the shock therapy and structural adjustment policies enforced throughout the global South and former Soviet sphere, neoliberal privatization ushered in not the disappearance of the state but a lopsided shift in state capacity to the punitive. I stress this here to emphasize that the fact of NGOs and private actors doing many of the things that states used to do is in no way incompatible with an often concurrent militarization of the state.

4. Michael Hardt and Antonio Negri, *Empire* (Cambridge, MA: Harvard University Press, 2001).

5. Jan Eckel, "The Rebirth of Politics from the Spirit of Morality," in *The Breakthrough: Human Rights in the 1970s,* ed. Jan Eckel and Samuel Moyn (Philadelphia: University of Pennsylvania Press, 2014), 257.

6. Both a set of economic ideas and an ideology of managerial governance, neo-liberalism was disputed at every turn, and it is critical to keep an eye on roads not taken—what neoliberalism was displacing.

7. Frédérick Gagnon, "Invading Your Hearts and Minds: *Call of Duty* and the (Re)Writing of Militarism in U.S. Digital Games and Popular Culture," *European Journal of American Studies* 5 (Summer 2010): 1–20.

8. Rosalind S. Helderman and Tom Hamburger, "Guns and Religion: How American Conservatives Grew Closer to Putin's Russia," *Washington Post,* April 30, 2017, www.washingtonpost.com/politics/how-the-republican-right-found-allies -in-russia/2017/04/30/.

9. "Transcript of First Presidential Debate," CNN, October 14, 2008, www.cnn .com/2008/POLITICS/09/26/debate.mississippi.transcript/.

10. My model for thinking about the production of meaning remains Melani McAlister's brilliant "Benevolent Supremacy," in *Epic Encounters: Culture, Media, and U.S. Interests in the Middle East since 1945* (Berkeley: University of California Press, 2001), 43–83.

11. Esme Cribb, "Bannon's 2016: 'Rootless White Males,' 'Pure Evil,' and 'F*cking Hammerhead,'" July 18, 2017, http://talkingpointsmemo.com/dc/joshua -green-steve-bannon-trump-campaign; Bret Stephens, "How Steve Bannon Rode

the Honey Badger into the White House," *New York Times,* July 18, 2017, www
.nytimes.com/2017/07/18/books/review/devils-bargain-steve-bannon-donald
-trump-joshua-green.html.

12. Helderman and Hamburger, "Guns and Religion."

13. Edward W. Said, *Culture and Imperialism* (New York: Alfred A. Knopf,
1993), xiii.

14. Scott Shane, Matthew Rosenberg, and Eric Lipton, "Trump Pushes Dark
View of Islam to Center of U.S. Foreign Policy-Making," *New York Times,* February
1, 2017, www.nytimes.com/2017/02/01/us/politics/donald-trump-islam.html.

15. Ibid.

16. Schiesel, "Suddenly the Cold War is a Cool Event."

17. Jeremy W. Peters, "Time Lends Cover for Apocalyptic Image," *New York
Times,* June 12, 2011. While my essay is concerned with interweaving gaming with
the development of specific foreign policy developments, see Frédérick Gagnon's
parallel work on *Call of Duty.* The game, Gagnon argues, "invites gamers and
Americans to conceive war and the preparation for war as the chief instruments of
foreign policy." Gagnon, "'Invading Your Hearts and Minds,'" 5.

18. Ahmed Rashid, *Taliban: Militant Islam, Oil, and Fundamentalism in
Central Asia* (New Haven, CT: Yale University Press, 2000); Timothy Mitchell,
Carbon Democracy: Political Power in the Age of Oil (London: Verso, 2013); Marjorie
Cohn, "Cheney's Black Gold: Oil Interests May Drive U.S. Foreign Policy," *Chicago
Tribune,* August 10, 2000, http://articles.chicagotribune.com/2000-08-10/news
/0008100507_1_caspian-oil-caspian-sea-gas-journal.

19. Roger Stahl, *Militainment: War, Media, and Popular Culture* (New York:
Routledge, 2009); see, in addition, Nick Dyer Witheford and Greig de Pueter,
Games of Empire: Global Capitalism and Video Games (Minneapolis: University of
Minnesota Press, 2009).

20. Simon Parkin, "Call of Duty: Gaming's Role in the Military-Entertainment
Complex," *Guardian,* October 22, 2014, www.theguardian.com/technology/2014
/oct/22/call-of-duty-gaming-role-military-entertainment-complex.

21. Dave Thier, "Oliver North Is Selling Call of Duty Black Ops 2," *Forbes,* May
2, 2012; Davis Itzkoff, "Oliver North, Now in the Service of TV's K.G.B.," *New York
Times,* April 15, 2014, www.nytimes.com/2014/04/16/arts/television/oliver-north
-now-in-the-service-of-tvs-kgb.html?mcubz=3; Stephen Totilo, *"Call of Duty*
Creators Say Oliver North Helped Make Their Game More Authentic," *Kotaku,*
May 24, 2012, kotaku.com/5913092/call-of-duty-makers-say-controversial-oliver
-north-helped-make-theoir-game-more-authentic; Robert Burns, "AP Source: Navy
SEALs Punished for Secrets Breach," *USA Today,* November 9, 2012, www.usatoday
.com/story/news/nation/2012/11/08/navy-seals-punished/1693453/.

22. See Army Public Affairs, www.army.mil/info/institution/publicAffairs/;
Derek Caelin, "More Than a Game: The Defense Department and the First-Person
Shooter," *Take Five,* October 9, 2012, https://takefiveblog.org/2012/10/09/.

23. Parkin, "Call of Duty."

24. Ibid.

25. Keith Stuart, "Does Call of Duty: Black Ops 3 Predict the Terrifying Future of Warfare?," *Guardian,* May 21, 2015, www.theguardian.com/technology/2015/may/21/call-of-duty-black-ops-3-terrifying-future-warfare.

26. "Cold War Nostalgia," *New York Times,* February 3, 1995.

27. Uwe Klußmann, Matthias Schepp, and Klaus Wiegrefe, "NATO's Eastern Expansion: Did the West Break Its Promise to Moscow?" *Der Spiegel International,* November 26, 2009, www.spiegel.de/international/world/nato-s-eastward-expansion-did-the-west-break-its-promise-to-moscow-a-663315.html. See also the BBC timeline on NATO: http://news.bbc.co.uk/2/hi/europe/country_profiles/1543000.stm.

28. Stephen F. Cohen, "The New American Cold War with Russia," *Nation,* July 10, 2006, with a new introduction by Cohen, June 8, 2007; Stephen F. Cohen, *Soviet Fates and Lost Alternatives: From Stalinism to the New Cold War* (New York: Columbia University Press, 2011).

29. Claire Shipman, "Gorbachev: 'Americans Have a Severe Disease,'" ABC News, July 12, 2016, http://abcnews.go.com/GMA/story?id=2182020&page=1; "Gorbachev: Americans Have 'Winner's' Disease," *Truthdig,* July 13, 2006, www.truthdig.com/eartotheground/item/20060712_gorbachev_americans_severe_disease.

30. Adrian Blomfield and Mike Smith, "Gorbachev: U.S. Could Start a New Cold War," *Telegraph,* May 6, 2008, www.telegraph.co.uk/news/worldnews/europe/russia/1933223/Gorbachev-US-could-start-new-Cold-War.html.

31. "Former US Ambassador to Russia: Ukraine Situation Result of US and EU Aggression toward Russia," *Democracy Now!,* March 20, 2014; Jack F. Matlock Jr., "Who Is the Bully? The U.S. Has Treated Russia Like a Loser since the End of the Cold War," *Washington Post,* March 14, 2014, www.washingtonpost.com/opinions/who-is-the-bully-the-united-states-has-treated-russia-like-a-loser-since-the-cold-war/2014/03/14/b0868882-aa06-11e3-8599-ce7295b6851c_story.html; Klußmann, Schepp, and Wiegrefe, "NATO's Eastern Expansion."

32. On Russian lessons from Georgia, see Evan Osnos and David Remnick, "Trump, Putin, and the New Cold War," *New Yorker,* March 6, 2017, *www.newyorker.com/magazine/2017/03/06/trump-putin-and-the-new-cold-war.*

33. Ian Traynor, "International: Georgia Blamed for Starting Russia War," *Guardian,* October 1, 2009, 23.

34. Adam Aigner-Treworgy, "McCain: 'We Are All Georgians,'" NBC News, August 12, 2008, http://firstread.nbcnews.com/_news/2008/08/12/4431528-mccain-we-are-all-georgians.

35. Rod Dreher, "We Are Not All Georgians Now," *Real Clear Politics,* August 26, 2008, www.realclearpolitics.com/articles/2008/08/we_are_not_all_georgians_now.html; Aigner-Treworgy, "McCain."

36. Dan Eggen and Robert Barnes, "McCain's Focus on Georgia Raises Question of Propriety," *Washington Post,* August 15, 2008, www.washingtonpost.com/wp-dyn/content/article/2008/08/14/AR2008081403332.html; Dreher, "We Are Not All Georgians Now."

37. Pat Buchanan, "Georgia's Man in the McCain Camp," *Toronto Star,* September 2, 2008, AA06.

38. Matthew Mosk and Jeffrey H. Birnbaum, "While Aide Advised McCain, His Firm Lobbied for Georgia," *Washington Post,* August 13, 2008, www.washington post.com/wp-dyn/content/article/2008/08/12/AR2008081202932.html; Buchanan, "Georgia's Man in the McCain Camp."

39. Bob Collins, "The 'G' Word," NewsCut (blog), July 23, 2008, http://blogs .mprnews.org/newscut/2008/07/the_g_word.

40. Jeffrey Goldberg, "The Wars of John McCain," October 2008, www.theat lantic.com/magazine/archive/2008/10/the-wars-of-john-mccain/306991/.

41. Nick Wing, "Sarah Palin: It Snowed in Alaska in May, So There Is No Global Warming," *Huffington Post,* May 20, 2013, www.huffingtonpost.com/2013 /05/20/sarah-palin-global-warming_n_3306867.html.

42. Another mode of play within *Black Ops,* completely unrelated to the plot but linked in the assault on the subject, is Zombies.

43. Brian Crecente, "George Romero Explains the Story behind *Call of the Dead* . . . Then Gets Zombified," *Kotaku,* May 3, 2011, http://kotaku.com/5798024 /george-romero-explains-the-story-behind-call-of-the-dead-then-gets-zombified.

44. YouTube video, www.youtube.com/watch?v=fZmoY3JfUig; Crecente, "George Romero Explains the Story."

45. A. O. Scott and Jason Zinoman, "In George Romero's Zombie Films, the Living Were a Horror Show, Too," *New York Times,* July 17, 2017, www.nytimes .com/2017/07/17/movies/in-george-romeros-zombie-films-the-living-were-a-horror -show-too.html.

46. Richard Beinstock, "Scorpions' 'Wind of Change': The Oral History of 1990's Epic Power Ballad," *Rolling Stone,* September 2, 2015, www.rollingstone.com /music/features/scorpions-wind-of-change-the-oral-history-of-1990s-epic-power -ballad-20150902.

47. Les, "CoD: Black Ops Commercial 'There's a Soldier in All of Us,'" *Stupid Evil Bastard,* November 10, 2010, http://stupidevilbastard.com/2010/11/cod-black -ops-commercial-theres-a-soldier-in-all-of-us/.

48. *Modern Warfare 2,* YouTube video, November 7, 2009, www.youtube.com /watch?v=BvHvYZNtbQQ.

49. Denis Pinchuk, "Indiana Jones Makes Russian Communists See Red," Reuters, May 23, 2008.

50. Focus group with the author, Bishkek, May 2013.

51. Michael Birnbaum, "Russia's Anti-American Fever Goes beyond the Soviet Era's," *Washington Post,* March 8, 2015.

52. Ibid.

53. Julie Hirschfeld Davis, "Rumblings of a 'Deep State' Undermining Trump? It Was Once a Foreign Concept," *New York Times,* March 6, 2017, www.nytimes .com/2017/03/06/us/politics/deep-state-trump.html?mcubz=1.

ABOUT THE CONTRIBUTORS

REBECCA A. ADELMAN is associate professor of media and communication studies at the University of Maryland, Baltimore County (UMBC). Her research focuses on the intersections of visual culture and militarized violence, with a particular interest in ethics, affect, and imagination. Her first book, *Beyond the Checkpoint: Visual Practices in America's Global War on Terror* (University of Massachusetts Press, 2014), maps the visual circuits linking the terrorized American nation-state, its citizens, and its enemies. Her next, *Figuring Violence: Affect, Imagination, and Contemporary American Militarism* (Fordham University Press, forthcoming), queries the politics of sentiment, visibility, and subjectivity in the ongoing war.

ROSS GRIFFIN is an early-career academic who teaches American literature and post-colonialism at Qatar University. His research interests include cultural studies, particularly Western portrayals of the Arab world; Vietnam War writing; and American studies.

TIM GRUENEWALD is assistant professor and director of American Studies at the University of Hong Kong. He has published on U.S. popular culture and is currently completing a monograph on the remembrance of difficult pasts and the U.S. national imagination. His documentary film, *Sacred Ground* (2015), explores the remembrance of Native American history by contrasting Wounded Knee and Mount Rushmore.

PATRICK WILLIAM KELLY received his doctorate in history from the University of Chicago and is a postdoctoral fellow at the Buffett Institute for Global Studies at Northwestern University. He was previously a Mellon fellow at the University of Wisconsin-Madison, where he completed his first book, *Sovereign Emergencies: Latin America and the Making of Global Human Rights Politics* (Cambridge University Press, 2018). A recipient of grants from the Kluge Foundation, SSRC, and Fulbright-Hays, he has published in the *Journal of Global History* and *Humanity*. Kelly is currently researching and writing a book on the global history of AIDS.

DAVID KIERAN is assistant professor of history at Washington & Jefferson College in Washington, Pennsylvania. He is the author of *Forever Vietnam: How a Divisive*

War Changed American Public Memory (University of Massachusetts Press, 2014), the editor of *The War of My Generation: Youth Culture and the War on Terror* (Rutgers University Press, 2015), and the coeditor of *At War: The Military and American Culture in the Twentieth Century and Beyond* (Rutgers University Press, 2018). He is completing a book about the army's and the VA's efforts to address mental health issues during the Iraq and Afghanistan wars.

SCOTT LADERMAN is professor of history at the University of Minnesota, Duluth. He is the author of *Tours of Vietnam: War, Travel Guides, and Memory* (Duke University Press, 2009) and *Empire in Waves: A Political History of Surfing* (University of California Press, 2014), as well as the coeditor, with Edwin Martini, of *Four Decades On: Vietnam, the United States, and the Legacies of the Second Indochina War* (Duke University Press, 2013). He and Martini coedit the Culture and Politics in the Cold War and Beyond series of the University of Massachusetts Press.

EDWIN A. MARTINI is professor of history at Western Michigan University, where he currently serves as associate dean of Extended University Programs. He is the author and editor of several books, including *Agent Orange: History, Science and the Politics of Uncertainty* (University of Massachusetts Press, 2012) and, with David Kieran, *At War: The Military and American Culture in the Twentieth Century and Beyond* (Rutgers University Press, 2018).

TONY SHAW is professor of contemporary history at the University of Hertfordshire in the United Kingdom. He specializes in the modern history of international propaganda. He is the author of five books, including *Cinematic Cold War: The American and Soviet Struggle for Hearts and Minds* (with Denise J. Youngblood, University Press of Kansas, 2010) and *Cinematic Terror: A Global History of Terrorism on Film* (Bloomsbury, 2015). He is currently cowriting a history of the relationship between Hollywood and Israel.

STACY TAKACS is professor and director of American Studies at Oklahoma State University and an associate member of the faculty in screen studies. She is the author of two books—*Terrorism TV: Popular Entertainment in Post-9/11 America* (University Press of Kansas, 2012) and *Interrogating Popular Culture* (Routledge, 2014)—and coeditor of *American Militarism on the Small Screen* (with Anna Froula, Routledge, 2016). Her work on the mediation of American foreign policy has appeared in a variety of scholarly journals. She is currently at work on a cultural history of the American Forces Network, specifically its television service.

PENNY M. VON ESCHEN is L. Sanford and Jo Mills Reis Professor of Humanities, Department of History, Cornell University. She received her PhD from the Department of History at Columbia University in 1994. Her books and essays include *Satchmo Blows Up the World: Jazz Ambassadors Play the Cold War* (Harvard University Press, 2004) and *Race against Empire: Black Americans and Anticolonialism, 1937–1957* (Cornell University Press, 1997). She is currently finishing a book tentatively titled *Rebooting the Cold War: Nostalgia, Triumphalism, and Global Disorder since 1989* (Harvard University Press, forthcoming 2018).

MIN KYUNG (MIA) YOO is a lecturer in the Department of Sociology at the John F. Kennedy Institute of North American Studies in Berlin, Germany. She recently received a PhD from the Graduate School of North American Studies at Freie Universität Berlin, with a dissertation titled "Performing and Narrating Identity: South Korean Kuk-min TV Series and 'America.'" She is continuing her research in transnational North American studies, media, and national identity within the frame of the U.S.-South Korean relationship.

INDEX

Abel, Rudolf, 192, 195, 197–199, 202

Activision, 230, 239

Adelman, Rebecca, 12

Afghanistan War, 27, 35, 73, 107, 146

Agamben, Giorgio, 119

Age of Terror, 188–189. *See also* global war on terrorism (GWOT); terrorism

Age of Trump, 210–212. *See also* Trump, Donald

Ahmed, Sara, 45n10

Albright, Madeleine, 7

Allison, Tanine, 97

Alsultany, Evelyn, 172–174

America: as benevolent, 17, 58, 109, 150, 156, 168, 172, 178, 203; drug war and, 212–213; exceptionalism and, 10, 31, 44, 46n19, 109–112, 168–172, 180–183, 184n5; foreign policy and, 5, 10, 91, 98, 167n43, 225; freedom and, 7, 104, 158, 178; human rights discourses and, 5, 10, 16, 119, 124, 178, 184, 189, 197, 210, 235; ideology and, 5, 118, 179, 181, 201, 203; imperialism and, 4–8, 25, 28, 58, 66, 169, 190; just war theory and, 14, 36–39, 43, 51, 118–126, 131, 133–134; military and, 34, 67, 86, 188; mythos of, 103, 170–172, 174, 176; national security discourses and, 107, 112; popular culture and, 15, 212, 250; Russia and, 190, 194, 202, 231–233, 235–236, 253–254; surveillance and, 158–159, 162; values of, 87, 104, 167n40, 171–172, 176–179, 182–184, 190, 195–197, 232. *See also* democracy; global

war on terrorism (GWOT); imperialism

American-Arab Anti-Discrimination Committee, 61

American Odyssey (TV), 110

American Sniper, 12, 50–68, 74, 85–86

America's Army: Making the All-Volunteer Force (Bailey), 113n8

America's Heroes Enjoying Recreation Outdoors, 82

Amistad (movie), 194

Andrejevic, Mark, 42

The Angry Birds Movie, 17

Anker, Elisabeth, 29, 43, 97

Ansara, Michael, 101

Anthony, Dave, 239

Antigone's Claim (Butler), 26

Antony, Marc, 223

Aquino, Malcolm, 227n29

Arabs and Muslims in the Media: Race and Representation after 9/11 (Alsultany), 172

Argo (movie), 193

Arkin, Alan, 18n3

Army Wives (TV), 74

Al-Asad, Khaled, 237

Asaro, Peter, 35, 48n57

The A-Team (TV), 13, 100, 103–104

The Avengers (movie), 15, 143–144, 150–154, 164n15, 168–174, 176–184

The Avengers: Age of Ultron (movie), 142–144, 150, 153–155, 160–161, 164nn14–15, 175–176, 186n33

85–87, 90, 111, 138n54, 163–164, 212; privatized military and security corporations (PMSCs), 98, 103–105; Russian, 202–203; terrorism and, 169, 184. *See also* colonialism; Latin America; propaganda; *specific conflicts*
The Incredible Hulk (movie), 144
Indiana Jones and the Kingdom of the Crystal Skull (movie), 15, 191, 194, 252
Indian Wars, 171
In the Face of Evil: Reagan's War in Word and Deed (movie), 190–192
In the Valley of Elah (movie), 10, 22n44
Inventing Collateral Damage (Rockel and Halpern), 165n21
Iraq War, 5, 10, 27, 35, 51–56, 62–63, 73–75, 107
Iron Man (movie), 142, 147, 149–150, 162, 176, 183
Iron Man 2 (movie), 148, 150, 186n30
Iron Man 3 (movie), 144, 150, 175–176, 186n30
Islam and Muslims, 10, 55, 106, 141, 202, 233, 237; Arab Americans and, 61, 64–66, 176; extremism and, 166n33, 176–177; Islamophobia and, 9, 15, 51, 55, 61–64, 237, 243; media representations of, 55, 61–64, 127, 141–148, 172–176, 183n26, 233, 237; Muslim ban, 202. *See also* media; religion
Islamic Center of Washington, DC, 166n33
Islamic State of Iraq and Syria (ISIS), 128, 168, 176, 184, 188–189. *See also* terrorism
Islamic State of Iraq and the Levant (ISIL), 107, 148, 155, 162. *See also* terrorism

Jackson, Robert H., 192
JAG (TV), 108
Jarecki, Eugene, 190
Jennings and Rall (J&R), 109
Jericho (TV), 108–109
Johnson, Lyndon, 6
Johnson, Ted, 204n3
Johnston, Eric, 6
Jones, Karen R., 77–78
Jordan, Gregor, 1, 4–5
Justified (TV), 74

just war theory, 14, 36–39, 43, 51, 118–126, 131, 133–134

Kaminski, Janusz, 196
Kaplan, Amy, 6, 73
Karpinski, Janis, 30
Kelly, Patrick William, 16–17, 31
Kennedy, John F., 102, 114n17, 178–179
Kerry, John, 204n3
Khalaf, Samer, 61
Khalili, Laleh, 29
Kieran, David, 13, 45n6, 53, 63
"Killing Ragheads for Jesus" (Hedges), 60
Kill the Messenger (movie), 218
Kinder, John, 75–76, 81
Kissinger, Henry, 190
Koch, Sebastian, 199
Kyle, Chris, 12, 50–55, 57–58, 60–65, 67–68, 86
Kyle, Taya, 52–54, 56, 62

Lansing, Sherry, 141
Lara Croft: The Cradle of Life (video game), 17
Lara Croft: Tomb Raider (video game), 17
La Salle, Mick, 202
Laundry Service (movie), 224
Lee, Harper, 197
A Legacy of Spies (Le Carré), 211
Lenin, Vladimir, 231
le Pen, Marine, 201
Letters from Iwo Jima (movie), 60
Libya, 27, 104
Lifton, Robert Jay, 84
Lim, Dennis, 4
Limbaugh, Rush, 190
Lincoln (movie), 194, 197
Lippmann, Walter, 97, 112
Lister, Lauren, 252
Littlefield, Chad, 53
Los Angeles Times, 57, 141
Luce, Henry, 178, 238
Lutz, Tom, 28, 30, 45n11
Lynch, Jessica, 35, 47n35
lynching, 109–110

The Magnificent Seven (movie), 170–171, 178

Modern Warfare 2 (video game), 244, 251–252
Modern Warfare 3 (video game), 237
Moore, Michael, 19n24, 22n44, 61
Morales, Esai, 109
morality: good *vs.* evil, 2, 108, 119, 121, 131–132, 134, 159, 180–181, 200; just war theory and, 14, 36–39, 43, 51, 53–55, 63, 104, 111, 118–126, 131–134
Morris, Edmund, 78
Morris, Errol, 30–31
Mötley Crüe, 249
Moura, Wagner, 214
movies: collateral damage and, 143, 145, 150–151, 153, 156, 160, 163, 191; earnings and, 143–144, 159, 164n14, 166n34, 201; superheroes and, 142–146, 148–156, 160, 163. *See also* media; *specific movies*
Mr. Smith Goes to Washington (movie), 203
Munich (movie), 194
Murphy, Stephen, 213–214
Muslims. *See* Islam and Muslims
Muslim Student Association (MSA) at University of Maryland, 66
My Lai Massacre, 56
My Son John (movie), 196
Mystery of the U2 (movie), 193

Narcos (TV), 16, 213–214
National Organization for Marriage, 236
National Public Radio (NPR), 61, 104
National Review, 60
National Rifle Association (NRA), 232, 236
NATO, 8, 236, 239–241, 243, 254. *See also* Cold War
Nazaryan, Alexander, 61
Negri, Antonio, 232
neoliberalism, 10, 221, 231, 235, 244
New Cold War, 231, 240–241
New York (magazine), 60
New York Times, 4, 8–9, 12, 230, 245, 251
Ngai, Sianne, 44
Niebuhr, Reinhold, 118, 121, 135n16
Nisour Square, 13
Nixon, Richard, 6
nongovernmental organizations (NGOs), 232, 241

Noriega, Manuel, 218
North American Free Trade Agreement (NAFTA), 213
North Korea, 10, 201
Nye, Joseph, 114n15
Nyman, Matt, 79–80

Obama, Barack, 7, 27–32, 40–41, 59, 117–121, 127–134, 136n18, 146, 242–243
O'Brien Tim, 168
Occupy Wall Street, 241
Oliver, Kelly, 41
O'Neill, Ed, 222
Operation Anaconda, 146
Operation Condor, 16
Operation Enduring Freedom (OEF), 74
Operation Iraqi Freedom (OIF), 74
Orientalism (Said), 185n26
Orion Strategies, 243
Orwell, George, 254
Osbourne, Ozzy, 249
Outward Bound, 88

Paddington (movie), 65
Pakistan, 73, 147, 188
Pak Nung Wong, 137n32
Palin, Sarah, 61, 234–236, 243
Parkin, Simon, 239
Parten, Lona, 80–81
Patriot Act (2006), 158, 212
Pease, Donald, 46n19, 175
Penix-Tadsen, Philip, 219
Physicians for Social Responsibility, 147
The Pianist (movie), 2
Platoon (movie), 7, 56
PMSCs (privatized military and security corporations), 98–99, 105, 108, 110–112
police forces, 125–131
Post-Traumatic Stress Disorder (PTSD), 13, 22n44, 53–54, 63, 74–77, 83–84
Powell, Colin, 167n40
The Power of the Dog (Winslow), 217
Powers, Gary, 192–195, 198
Prince of Persia: The Sands of Time (video game), 17
Prisoners of War (TV), 40

Veterans Eagle Pass Parks Act, 71
video games. *See* media; *specific games*
Vietnam Syndrome, 211
Vietnam War, 2–5, 53, 56, 101, 103, 105,
165n24, 168
Vigil, Ariana E., 86
Vogel, Wolfgang, 198
Von Eschen, Penny, 16
Vosloo, Arnold, 107

Walesa, Lech, 190
The Walking Dead (TV), 119–120, 122–127,
133
Walzer, Michael, 118
war: collateral damage and, 145–147, 150–151,
155–156, 158, 160, 163; counter-insurgents
and, 29–30; death and, 13–14, 57, 146–
147, 166n31; gender and, 26, 30–33, 35–36,
40–42, 47n35, 103, 112, 225; ideology and,
44, 124–127; just peace and, 133–134; just
war and, 14, 36–39, 43, 51, 104, 117–126,
131, 133–134; media and, 19n24, 30, 36,
95n58, 98; morality and, 29, 39, 63, 119–
121, 131–132, 135n14; in popular culture,
64, 75, 90; propaganda and, 3, 51, 57–58;
PTSD and, 13, 22n44, 53–54, 63, 74–77,
83–84; soldiers and, 13, 40, 51, 63–64,
98–99; violence and, 28–29, 75, 104;
weapons of, 8–9, 145–146. *See also* mercenaries; military; privatized military and
security corporations (PMSCs); soldiers;
veterans; *specific wars*
War on Terror. *See* global war on terrorism
(GWOT); terrorism
Washington Post, 9, 142, 253

Washington Times, 57, 60
Watchmen (movie), 144
Watkins, Tim, 190
Weeds (TV), 215
Weiss, Eric, 5
Why We Fight (movie), 22n44, 191
Wikileaks, 254
wilderness, 77–78, 87–88, 171. *See also*
veterans
Williams, David, 165n24
Williams, Linda, 97
"Wind of Change" (Scorpions), 248–249
Winfrey, Oprah, 42
Winslow, Don, 217–218
Wool, Zoe H., 75
World War II, 6, 163, 169, 181, 195, 203
Wounded Veterans Recreation Act, 71, 77
Wounded Warriors in Action Foundation,
83
Wounded Warriors Project, 74. *See also*
bodies; soldiers; veterans
Wyden, Ron, 71

xenophobia, 103. *See also* Islam and Muslims; race and racism; refugees

Yoo, Min Kyung (Mia), 14
Yo Soy Betty, La Fea (TV), 221. *See also*
Ugly Betty (TV)

Zabel, Bryce, 142
Zanger, Anat, 41
Zero Dark Thirty (movie), 12, 25, 27, 29,
32–34, 42, 193, 214, 217
zombies, 137n33, 247–248, 250–251